Y0-BVQ-236

Introduction

Life can be such a struggle with all the obstacles we must navigate through day by day. Perhaps the hardest challenge is simply staying true to God and remaining on the path He has set out for us in His Word. It wasn't easy for the Jews to stay on the path after the Exodus, after all, and they had the advantage of an ever-present guiding light in the form of a pillar of fire.

We don't have that kind of advantage—yet we do have an advantage. The Bible speaks of God's creative wonders *and* has so much practical advice on how to best live our lives. It's our own pillar of fire, to be sure. But as it was with the Jewish people, with work, family, friends, and the busyness of life, we are so easily distracted from taking the time to listen to His voice and follow His directions ... and, as a result, we miss the opportunity to move mountains.

Jesus said, "If you have faith as a mustard seed, you will say to this mountain, 'Move from here to there,' and it will move; and nothing will be impossible for you" (Matthew 17:20). That's a wonderful promise, right? Imagine what God will do for you when you are faithful to Him!

He doesn't ask a lot: just the faith of a mustard seed. But to have even that small amount of faith, you need to keep looking at His guiding light. That's why this devotional is about getting back to the Bible and enabling you to listen better to His voice—to get the answers to life's biggest questions and to overcome the obstacles in your way. Taking time each day to reconnect with our heavenly Father is the surest way to build your faith.

You're going to have fun exploring this book and expanding your faith. It's filled with hundreds of amazing facts and faith-building spiritual insights—each written by a team of young, energetic Christian writers who want to help make a difference in your life. Many of these facts reveal God's awesome power throughout the universe and will give you faith in His ability to help you here on Earth. Others show what mankind can do with the wisdom God has granted us. Sometimes we don't always use this wisdom the right way, but God offers the assurance that if we keep seeking Him even when we stumble, we will find Him and reconnect with Him—and moving mountains will be only the beginning of the wonders you will be able to do with Him.

–Amazing Facts

"So Jesus answered and said to them, 'Have faith in God. For assuredly, I say to you, whoever says to this mountain, "Be removed and be cast into the sea," and does not doubt in his heart, but believes that those things he says will be done, he will have whatever he says. Therefore I say to you, whatever things you ask when you pray, believe that you receive them, and you will have them.'"

Mark 11:22–24

DAY 1 Trust, Faith, and Belief Begins Here

An Amazing Fact: *According to recent polls, over the past 50 years, Americans have been rather consistent in their belief of the six-day Creation as found in the book of Genesis. A little less than 50 percent still believe the Bible's account happened as written. Others believe that microevolution is the sole cause of all life on earth—while an increasing number of people, including many Christians, now believe in theistic evolution, i.e., Intelligent Design.*

The Bible says that in the beginning, God created the heavens and the earth (Genesis 1:1).

With all the evidence mounting against it, the theory of evolution (or Darwinism) is coming under increasing scrutiny. Indeed, despite pressure and persecution from their peers, more scientists are boldly suggesting that the complexity of even the smallest cell points to a powerful designer.

Even though that seems like a good thing, and in some ways it is, the theory of Intelligent Design still falls woefully short, because it still puts forth that it took millions of years of death and trial and error for a man to evolve from an ape-like ancestor. It is still a de facto rejection of God's written Word.

Why? Because it suggests that even before Adam and Eve sinned, death was a natural part of life and was not a curse as a result of rebellion against God. This contradicts not only the Creation account, but it also undermines the need for salvation through Christ's atoning death and resurrection—and even the Seventh-day Sabbath.

A clear and complete understanding of God and our place in the great controversy begins with Genesis. Remember, if you believe in Jesus, God in human flesh, then like Him you should believe that Adam and Eve, Noah's Flood, and Sodom and Gomorrah were real events that speak to our faith experience in ways that no simple-minded myth can.

You can and should trust God's Word. Not only is it the true key to the past, it is the only key to discovering true salvation.

That's a great foundation to have when you are beginning a new year!

KEY BIBLE TEXTS: "Thy word is true from the beginning" (Psalm 119:160). "All Scripture is given by inspiration of God" (2 Timothy 3:16).

Jesus Is Coming Back the Same Way He Left

DAY 2

An Amazing Fact: *The ancient Aztec empire had a prophecy about a feathered god-king with light skin and a beard who would return in the clouds from across the sea. In 1519, Spanish conquistadors, led by Hernando Cortez, arrived on the scene. When the Aztecs saw the Spanish ships, they thought the billowing sails looked like clouds. Cortez was able to use the prophecy to his advantage, assuming the mantle of deity. Before a bv Aztec capital. By the time the people realized that Cortez was not the savior they were expecting, it was too late.*

The conquistadors proceeded to plunder, enslave, and kill the Aztec people. A once-powerful nation was deceived and destroyed, in part because the prophecies of their god's return were so ambiguous that almost anyone could have served as a counterfeit. The same will happen to God's people if they are not careful to accept the Bible's teaching, which leaves no doubt about the manner of His return.

Believers cannot afford to make the same mistake. Yet in keeping with the mistakes of God's people throughout history, deception has made its way into many interpretations of Bible prophecy, including the preeminently popular but utterly false "secret rapture" theory.

In the near future, Satan will attempt to impersonate Jesus and counterfeit His return to earth. But God's people need not be deceived. When the disciples asked Jesus for the signs of His coming and the end of the world, the very first thing He told them was to be on guard against impostors. "Take heed that no man deceive you. For many shall come in my name, saying, I am Christ; and shall deceive many" (Matthew 24:4, 5).

Christ then proceeded to give His followers a wealth of information about His second coming so there would be no doubt as to how He would return. Jesus not only wants us to know that He is coming and that He's coming soon, He wants us to understand the manner of His coming.

KEY BIBLE TEXTS: "This same Jesus, who was taken up from you into heaven, will so come in like manner as you saw Him go into heaven" (Acts 1:11). "For as the lightning comes from the east and flashes to the west, so also will the coming of the Son of Man be" (Matthew 24:27).

DAY 3 Small Places, Big Faces

An Amazing Fact: *Based on National Climatic Data Center records, New York state is home to the snowiest cities in the United States: Syracuse averages 115 inches of snow per year, and Rochester averages 93 inches per year. However, when it comes to the highest average snowfall, small towns win hands down. For instance, Mount Washington, New Hampshire, has an average annual snowfall of 260 inches, and Valdez, Alaska, averages 326 inches annually.*

Did you grow up in a small town or village? Sometimes the big cities can make the little-known places seem insignificant. But don't be fooled. Here's a short list of famous people who lived in smaller towns and attended community colleges at one time: Nolan Ryan, John Walsh, Sarah Palin, George Lucas, and Ross Perot.

Bethlehem of Judah was the small town where Jesus was born. It was so insignificant that even the Scribes and Pharisees seemed to forget about it when Herod asked them where the Messiah would be born. When Matthew quotes Micah 5:2 to show prophecy fulfilled, he describes this small town as being "the least among the rulers of Judah."

God doesn't need big places to make big things happen. The Lord is interested in using the insignificant. It takes the glory away from man and points us heavenward. It teaches us that no matter who we are or where we come from, Jesus can shine through our lives in a powerful way. Someone once said, "A snowflake is a powerful thing. Just look at what they can do when they stick together!"

Today, ask God to use you—as small as you might feel—to do big things that point people to the Child of Bethlehem.

KEY BIBLE TEXT: "But you, Bethlehem, in the land of Judah, Are not the least among the rulers of Judah; For out of you shall come a Ruler Who will shepherd My people Israel" (Matthew 2:6).

Breakdown in Communication

An Amazing Fact: *Nearly 7,000 languages are spoken around the world today, but about 2,000 of those languages have fewer than 1,000 speakers.*

Until after the global flood, everyone on earth spoke the same language. In order to stick together, some of Noah's descendants conspired to build a great city with a sky-high tower. But God made it so the people couldn't understand each other, so they had to abandon the tower. This is how the Bible explains the origin of the many languages spoken today.

Even communication in the same language can be tricky. With the many different life experiences that form the backdrop of our every interaction, the hurts and disappointment, the egos and preconceptions, it's amazing we get through to each other at all!

Enter the digital age. According to the United Nations International Telecommunication Union, nearly 200,000 text messages were sent *every second* in 2010, in addition to 107 trillion e-mails throughout the year. Auto-correct can make things even more confusing. When one retired couple headed to Nepal for a month-long trek, their daughter asked the older couple to e-mail from Internet cafés along the way. The very first message their daughter received said, "Help. Visa bad. Can you send money to the water? Autopsy not working."

It took $150 and 16 hours over numerous calls to the U.S. Embassy for the concerned daughter to discover that her parents' credit card wasn't letting them pay their water bill automatically. Auto-correct had changed "auto pay" to "autopsy." They laughed about it afterwards, but not all miscommunications have a good ending.

When it comes to communicating with God, Paul says we don't even know what to pray for. Thankfully, "The Spirit Himself makes intercession for us with groanings which cannot be uttered" (Romans 8:26). And God promises to hear your prayer—regardless of the language you speak or the eloquence (or lack thereof!) with which you speak it.

KEY BIBLE TEXT: "Then you will call upon Me and go and pray to Me, and I will listen to you" (Jeremiah 29:12).

DAY 5 Rescuers

An Amazing Fact: *In January 2010, as Wesley Autrey waited for a subway train in New York, a fellow traveler fell to the floor in convulsions. With help he was able to get up, but he stumbled and fell between the tracks. Then the train's headlights appeared. Mr. Autrey made an instant decision, leaping onto the helpless man and pressing him down as the train thundered inches above them. Both men survived. Mr. Autrey insisted he wasn't a hero; he simply saw someone that needed help and did what he felt was right.*

"Choose which land you would like," Abraham offered. You can imagine the dollar signs popping up on Lot's eyes as he gazed over the green, fertile valley. "I'll take this area," he told his uncle. Soon Lot had moved his livestock, servants, and family onto the preferred land.

Abraham and Lot had their differences. But when Abraham heard that Lot had been captured by heathen kings, he didn't hesitate. Never mind that he had only 318 servants to fight with him against potentially huge armies. He bravely armed his men, tracked down his nephew's abductors, and freed Lot and his family.

Although Lot had been selfish, had distanced himself from his uncle, and had probably moved close enough to heathen cities to be influenced by them, Abraham still loved him. He was family; nothing would keep him from rescuing Lot.

Isn't that what God does for us? Even when we're selfish, distant, or straying in the wrong direction, He still loves us. He comes to our rescue when we least deserve it. What grace! What a Rescuer!

KEY BIBLE TEXT: "Now when Abram heard that his brother was taken captive, he armed his three hundred and eighteen trained servants who were born in his own house, and went in pursuit as far as Dan. ... So he brought back all the goods, and also brought back his brother Lot and his goods, as well as the women and the people" (Genesis 14:14, 16).

An Involuntary Reaction

An Amazing Fact: *The human brain is responsible for a number of involuntary actions within our bodies, such as breathing and the blinking of our eyes. According to TSA.gov, some airports are even training security officers to recognize involuntary physical and physiological reactions that people exhibit in response to a fear of being discovered.*

Have you ever experienced an exciting event that left you full of the anticipation of sharing it with others? Perhaps you made a breakthrough on a difficult project. Or maybe you watched a new milestone in your child's development, like his or her first steps. When a young daughter makes her mother laugh by trying a new word or skill, the mom always wants to share that moment with her husband. Our natural response is often a desire to share our news with the world. Instinctively, we want to share the joy! It's an involuntary reaction.

As the followers of Jesus learned of His resurrection and began to develop a deeper understanding of the gospel, they couldn't resist sharing it with the world either. When Peter and John were called before the Sanhedrin and were reprimanded for sharing the good news, they responded, "We cannot but speak the things which we have seen and heard." The knowledge was too great to keep to themselves. It had to be shared!

Today, ponder how the gospel has been meaningful in your life recently. How has God touched your heart? And with whom can you share it?

KEY BIBLE TEXT: "So they called them and commanded them not to speak at all nor teach in the name of Jesus. But Peter and John answered and said to them, 'Whether it is right in the sight of God to listen to you more than to God, you judge. For we cannot but speak the things which we have seen and heard'" (Acts 4:18–20).

DAY 7 God Never Gets Lost

An Amazing Fact: *Scientists are still mystified by how animals know when it's time to migrate. And how do they unerringly find their way back to the same beach, stream, or feeding ground they've not seen since birth? Consider the green turtles that swim from their feeding grounds off the coast of Brazil to tiny Ascension Island about 3,000 miles away, which they might not have visited since they were hatched. After depositing their eggs, they swim back to Brazil!*

The Arctic tern has the longest migration of any animal, winging each year from their nesting grounds in the Arctic North to the Antarctic and back, a roundtrip journey of nearly 25,000 miles!

These migratory habits of animals baffle scientists. Do they chart their courses by the sun, moon, or stars? Does the earth's magnetic field direct them? What inner sense did God plant within every species (birds, mammals, fish, reptiles, amphibians, insects, and even crustaceans) to move such long distances on a seasonal basis? Especially amazing is their return is not just to a general locale, but to a very specific spot!

The God who created all the animals of the earth and placed within them a homing instinct is the God who said to Sarah, "I will return to you" (Genesis 18:14). God doesn't get lost. The Lord doesn't need a GPS to find us. God doesn't need us to wear an ankle bracelet to track our movements. Our Creator always knows where we are. God promised Sarah that she would have a child of promise. She laughed. "I am old!" she chuckled. Yet the Lord guaranteed she would have a baby.

At the appointed time the Lord returned and blessed Abraham and Sarah with a child. Just as God sets appointed times within the creatures of the earth to migrate, so the Lord sets special times for us. Are you tuned in to the God who comes to you?

KEY BIBLE TEXT: "Is anything too hard for the Lord? At the appointed time I will return to you, according to the time of life, and Sarah shall have a son" (Genesis 18:14).

Pioneers

An Amazing Fact: *Only half of all Americans live within 50 miles of their birthplace.*

Perhaps it's bred into them by their pioneering ancestors who first moved to the New World to seek adventure and freedom, but Americans are by and large a mobile people. When God told him to venture out into the unknown, Abraham too left the place of his birth to find a new life in the land God promised him. "By faith," the author of Hebrews says, "He went out, not knowing where he was going... For he waited for the city which has foundations, whose builder and maker is God" (Hebrews 11:8–10).

Likewise today, we live as if in the foyer, waiting to enter the place God has promised. "I go to prepare a place for you. And if I go and prepare a place for you, I will come again and receive you to Myself; that where I am, there you may be also" (John 14:2, 3). As the old gospel song says, "This world is not my home." That's why Jesus instructed His followers to "lay up for yourselves treasures in heaven, where neither moth nor rust destroys and where thieves do not break in and steal. For where your treasure is there your heart will be also" (Matthew 6:20, 21).

We don't know the day or the hour that we'll be taken to our home in the clouds. Live like you're ready!

KEY BIBLE TEXTS: "From that time Jesus began to preach and to say, 'Repent, for the kingdom of heaven is at hand'" (Matthew 4:17). "For you yourselves know perfectly that the day of the Lord so comes as a thief in the night" (1 Thessalonians 5:2).

DAY 9 Bold Fishermen

An Amazing Fact: *While deep-sea fishing, professional angler Stewart Campbell was jerked over the side of his boat and into the ocean by a giant marlin. Fortunately, the line that was connected to his fishing harness snapped within seconds and he survived. Others have not come out so well. A number of people have drowned in similar circumstances as the line held and the fish dragged them deep into the sea.*

It's doubtful that the fisherman Peter ever had to deal with a fish that rambunctious. However, after he changed his career and began fishing for people, he certainly encountered more dangerous game.

When Peter kept his eyes on people and situations rather than on Jesus, he was dragged down and nearly drowned spiritually. But the lesson he learned in the courtyard at Jesus' trial changed his focus. From then on, he was centered on Christ.

After Pentecost, Peter and the other apostles were determined to preach in Jerusalem in the name of Jesus, whatever the cost. When threatened by the angry priests and rulers, they responded with boldness, "We ought to obey God rather than men. The God of our fathers raised up Jesus whom you murdered by hanging on a tree. Him God has exalted to His right hand to be Prince and Savior, to give repentance to Israel and forgiveness of sins. And we are His witnesses to these things, and so also is the Holy Spirit whom God has given to those who obey Him" (Acts 5:29–32).

KEY BIBLE TEXTS: "Then He said to them, 'Follow Me, and I will make you fishers of men'" (Matthew 4:19). "But Peter and the other apostles answered and said: 'We ought to obey God rather than men'" (Acts 5:29).

No More Oppression

An Amazing Fact: *One in every four women will experience domestic violence in her lifetime, and more than three million reports of child abuse are made every year in the United States. It is also estimated there are between 143 million and 210 million orphans worldwide.*

Reading drastic statistics about oppression in our world can feel staggering. And when it hits closer to home, the knowledge of how sin impacts people's lives becomes more real. If you've watched a family member suffer in an abusive relationship or seen a family lose a parent or child, the weight of pain and loss is overwhelming. How can God let this happen? Why?

After feeling this weight and seeing the suffering of his own family, David recognized God's awareness of sin and His heart of justice. In Psalms 10, he writes, "You will ... do justice to the fatherless and the oppressed, that the man of the earth may oppress no more."

God sees the oppressed. His heart breaks for their suffering, and He promises that, someday, oppression will cease. As Christians sharing that heartbreak, we have the opportunity to make a difference and end oppression in small ways. Perhaps He has called you to foster a child. Or maybe He's leading you to volunteer at your local domestic violence shelter. Ask God for His awareness of oppression to become active in your heart and life.

KEY BIBLE TEXT: "Lord, You have heard the desire of the humble; You will prepare their heart; You will cause Your ear to hear; to do justice to the fatherless and the oppressed, that the man of the earth may oppress no more" (Psalm 10: 17, 18).

DAY 11 The Power of a Seed

An Amazing Fact: *The oldest known viable seeds were found in 1954 in a lemming burrow in Canada's frigid Yukon. The frozen burrow, buried in silt and sediment, was 4,200 years old. When the arctic tundra lupine seeds were placed in favorable conditions, several seeds sprouted within 48 hours. One of the plants later bloomed.*

There is power hidden deep within a seed. It is the power of a promise that, given the right conditions, a plant should sprout and grow. Today's amazing fact illustrates that even ancient seeds can retain this power. Bean seeds have even been found in the 3,400-year-old tomb of Egyptian King Tutankhamen. After planting them in rich soil and providing proper water and sunshine, the seeds sprouted and grew into healthy plants.

God promised a seed of blessing to Abraham and his descendents that a Savior would come from his lineage. This birthright was to be passed from generation to generation through the eldest son. In Genesis 27 we discover that through trickery, Isaac blessed Jacob. Even though Jacob deceived his father, he still received the power of this blessing. The words spoken by the aging father to his second son came true. Esau later came and begged for his father to pray over him, but it was not with the same richness as Jacob's blessing.

The Savior of the world did come through the lineage of Jacob. The seed of Abraham did sprout and bear fruit. Jesus Christ came as a son of Abraham, Isaac, and Jacob. This birthright is available to us today. We may receive a promise of eternal life if we do not despise God's hand, which reaches out to bless us. Let the seed of faith be planted in our hearts. Let us water and nourish our hope every day. Then we will watch with amazement as the tiny seed, no matter how old it might seem, sprouts and grows into a life that will last for eternity.

KEY BIBLE TEXT: "In your seed all the nations of the earth shall be blessed, because you have obeyed my voice" (Genesis 22:18).

Patience and Fortitude

An Amazing Fact: *The two stone lions in front of the New York Public Library were named Patience and Fortitude in the 1930s by then-mayor Fiorello LaGuardia for the qualities he felt New Yorkers would need to survive the Great Depression.*

The two lions in front of the public library in Manhattan have enchanted New York residents and tourists since the library's dedication on May 23, 1911. The lions received several affectionate monikers over the years, but the names that finally stuck were Mayor LaGuardia's.

When Jacob met the woman of his dreams at the well in Haran, little did he know how much patience and fortitude their love story would demand of him! First, he had to serve his father-in-law for seven years to acquire his bride. Then Laban tricked Jacob into marrying Rachel's sister. When Jacob finally got to marry his dream girl, they were struck with the painful reality of infertility. Then the poor man had to endure his wives' sibling rivalry and Rachel's obsession with becoming a mother. In Jacob's culture, a woman's value stemmed from childbearing, and Rachel was keenly aware of this societal pressure. When she was finally able to conceive, she died while giving birth to their second son.

No matter how "perfect" a potential mate seems at first sight, time reveals all faults. Not only are our loved one's faults magnified under the microscope of intimacy, but our own faults show up as well. Christian music artist Stephen Curtis Chapman says, "Without my marriage I may have actually been able to get through life under the illusion that I'm a pretty decent guy." Paul says that love is patient, kind, and longsuffering. Marriage offers the opportunity to learn—and demonstrate!—the unconditional love shown to us by our great God.

KEY BIBLE TEXTS: "So Jacob served seven years for Rachel, and they seemed only a few days to him because of the love he had for her" (Genesis 29:20). "Love is patient, love is kind" (1 Corinthians 13:4 NIV).

DAY 13 The Sheep Incident

An Amazing Fact: *During World War I, President and Mrs. Woodrow Wilson kept a flock of sheep on the White House lawn. The woolies, including Old Ike—a ram that enjoyed chewing tobacco—kept the lawn in beautiful condition. This saved money that would have been spent on grounds keeping. Each year the sheep were sheared and their wool auctioned, which raised more than $100,000 for the Red Cross.*

Sheep were central to the conflict between Jacob and his often-underhanded father-in-law, Laban. While Jacob labored for him with all of his might, Laban changed Jacob's wages ten times and tried to cheat him.

But God was watching out for Jacob. As Jacob explained to his wives, if Laban said, "'The speckled shall be your wages,' then all the flocks bore speckled. And if he said thus: 'The streaked shall be your wages,' then all the flocks bore streaked" (Genesis 31:8).

As God commanded him, Jacob took all of his possessions and secretly left Laban's property. Laban, unhappy with the manner of Jacob's leaving, pursued him for an entire week and finally caught up with him.

Bitter words poured out, but eventually they made a covenant between them. Laban, a heathen man, said in parting, "May the LORD watch between you and me when we are absent one from another." He asked Jacob to be good to his daughters, and the two men agreed never to harm each other.

As God had been merciful and forgiving toward him, Jacob forgave Laban, who had spitefully used him.

KEY BIBLE TEXTS: "But I have trusted in Your mercy; my heart shall rejoice in Your salvation. I will sing to the LORD, because He has dealt bountifully with me" (Psalm 13:5, 6). "But I say to you, love your enemies, bless those who curse you, do good to those who hate you, and pray for those who spitefully use you and persecute you, that you may be sons of your Father in heaven" (Matthew 5:44).

Secret Giving

An Amazing Fact: *According to Business Week, the United States' richest one percent—who own two-fifths of the country's wealth—donate only two percent of their incomes each year to charity. In contrast, families in the bottom income bracket donate an average of six percent. At least 20 percent of the wealthiest estates leave not even a penny to charity.*

The top philanthropists in our society donate millions to charity each year. On the list are names such as Oprah Winfrey and Bill and Melinda Gates, names familiar to most of us. In comparison to such massive amounts, it is easy to see our own contributions as tiny drops in a bucket of water. But surprisingly, while the numeric amount of these rich donations is quite high, the percentages tell a different story. Families in the bottom income bracket actually donate a higher percentage of their income to charity than the wealthiest in the nation.

Jesus' words to His disciples remind us of the importance of our small gifts. "When you do a charitable deed, do not let your left hand know what your right hand is doing, that your charitable deed may be in secret; and your Father who sees in secret will Himself reward you openly." A spot on the top philanthropy list and millions given to charity might bring worldly attention and acclaim, but God sees the significance of the small, unnoticed gifts. In His eyes, they are even more valuable.

KEY BIBLE TEXT: "When you do a charitable deed, do not let your left hand know what your right hand is doing, that your charitable deed may be in secret; and your Father who sees in secret will Himself reward you openly" (Matthew 6: 3, 4).

DAY 15 Your Holy Hill

An Amazing Fact: *At 29,035 feet, Mt. Everest is the highest mountain in the world. It was named after Sir George Everest, a British surveyor, in 1865. The mountain has actually had many different names, including Sagarmatha (Nepalese for 'goddess of the sky'), Chomolungma (Tibetan for 'mother goddess of the universe'), and the simple designation, 'Peak 15.'*

If you decide to make the trip to Nepal to climb one of the highest mountains in the world, you'd better plan ahead. Reaching the tallest summits on our planet is not for the faint of heart. Many have died making little mistakes while trying to make it to the top. Oxygen levels are one-third of that of sea level amounts, so without supplemental air, you easily get foggy in your thinking. Energy levels plummet above the death zone—8,000 meters—where the amount of oxygen is not enough to sustain life.

Good mountain climbers respect the mountain. They know their limits. Perhaps the greatest tragedy on Mt. Everest took place in 1996, when several groups pushed beyond the turn-around time. It takes humility to admit defeat, turn around, and go back down.

David asks God in Psalm 15:1, "Lord, who may abide in Your tabernacle? Who may dwell in Your holy hill?" The Lord answers, "He who walks uprightly, and works righteousness, and speaks the truth in his heart" (v. 2). To walk uprightly is to walk in humility. Philippians 2:3 explains it like this: "Let nothing be done through selfish ambition or conceit, but in lowliness of mind let each esteem others better than himself."

The highest place we can climb is through bowing low in humility at the foot of Mt. Calvary where Jesus died for us. Christ lowered Himself to our earth that we might be lifted up with Him to heavenly places—mountains higher than even Mt. Everest.

KEY BIBLE TEXT: "For this is what the high and lofty One says—he who lives forever, whose name is holy: I live in a high and holy place, but also with him who is contrite and lowly in spirit, to revive the spirit of the lowly and to revive the heart of the contrite" (Isaiah 57:15).

Seek Him First

An Amazing Fact: *During the California Gold Rush, people often sent their clothes all the way to China to be laundered. It took three months to receive the clean clothes back ... and longer if the ships encountered a typhoon.*

In 1848, James Marshall found gold in the American River northeast of present-day Sacramento. Newspapers reported the discovery, but no one believed it until Sam Brannan flaunted a bottle of gold dust around San Francisco two months later. Then San Franciscans dashed inland. That summer, New York newspapers reported the find and the gold rush began.

Miners flooding into California envisioned wealth untold, but in reality, hard work, diminishing gold, and stiff competition awaited them. One wrote, "Mining is the hardest work imaginable. ... A weakly man might as well dig his grave as dig for gold."

Mining camps' inflated prices required a miner to find a half-ounce of gold a day just to get by. A thousand dollars worth might emerge from a single pan, but few miners ever found that much. About 400,000 men from around the world thronged to California in the 1850s, but most of them returned home with less than what they'd arrived with. Despite finding the first nugget, Marshall died broke.

Chinese immigrants took over the minefields that white miners abandoned. Laundry was women's work, so at first dirty clothes were sent to China. But the immigrants saw opportunity, and Chinese laundries popped up everywhere. Miners in Weaverville, California, ridiculed John for washing their clothing for free. But a year later, the immigrant sported a fancy wardrobe; he'd found his fortune in the miners' pants cuffs!

The 49ers sought material wealth. Today, in the scramble to acquire our needs and wants, it's easy to neglect what's really important. But God promises that when we put Him first, our needs will be taken care of —and more!

KEY BIBLE TEXT: "But seek first the kingdom of God and his righteousness, and all these things shall be added to you" (Matthew 6:30, 31).

DAY 17 Treasure Hunting

An Amazing Fact: *In July 2009, Terry Herbert was combing the rural Staffordshire, England, countryside with a cheap metal detector when he stumbled across the biggest hoard of Anglo-Saxon gold ever discovered. He found more than 500 artifacts or pieces thereof before he called in experts, who found another 800 pieces. All were located near the surface. The treasure trove consisted mainly of war implements and included 11 pounds of gold and over five pounds of silver.*

Practically everyone has, at one time or another, dreamed of finding rare coins or a buried treasure. It's an exciting thought! But we have something priceless right in our own homes that should be much more exciting—the Holy Bible.

No matter how much you have or haven't read them, the Scriptures contain awesome treasures yet to be discovered—wise guidance, encouraging promises, the truth about our Savior, and how to find eternal life.

Gaining a benefit from any search of the Scriptures requires the guidance of the Holy Spirit. God wants to give us good things. Some of the treasures lie near the surface and are easy to find. Others require deep digging. Yet all are worth looking for! Are you ready to go treasure hunting?

KEY BIBLE TEXTS: "Ask, and it will be given to you; seek, and you will find; knock, and it will be opened to you. For everyone who asks receives, and he who seeks finds, and to him who knocks it will be opened" (Matthew 7:7, 8). "If you then, being evil, know how to give good gifts to your children, how much more will your Father who is in heaven give good things to those who ask Him!" (Matthew 7:11, 12).

Far From Home

An Amazing Fact: *Most of us are familiar with the enslavement of Africans in the United States, but the enslavement of Native Americans is a little known part of history. For many years the Southern colonies carried out slave trade among Native American tribes, shipping tens of thousands of people far from home, many to the "sugar islands" of the Caribbean.*

Like the Native Americans of the United States, Joseph was taken as a slave and sent far from his home to a foreign land. Used to a comfortable life with a loving father, he was suddenly isolated from everything and everyone he knew. The shock of the strange language and culture of Egypt must have been great, but despite this, Joseph held fast to his faith. His walk with God gave him the strength to live each day in captivity, and even those around him could see that God was with him. Even in the face of great temptation and trials, he did not waver. He faced imprisonment rather than compromising obedience to God.

As you go through the day, how does your walk with God affect you? Can others around you see that God influences the way you live? Sometimes our greatest witness isn't telling others about our faith, but living it as an example. The words we say and the attitude in our hearts speak volumes about the God we serve. Sometimes it might be a small thing, like treating others with patience in a stressful work environment. Other times it could be the choice to stand up for what is right even when the consequences are difficult. Like Joseph, our example can show others how following God changes lives. Does being a Christian mean merely going to church each week and keeping a Bible on your bookshelf? Or has your walk with God truly made a difference in the way you live throughout your entire week?

KEY BIBLE TEXT: "Now Joseph had been taken down to Egypt ... and his master saw that the Lord was with him and that the Lord made all he did to prosper in his hand" (Genesis 39: 1, 3).

DAY 19 Which Way Is Up?

An Amazing Fact: *Shrimp lay near the bottom of the marine food chain. But these little creatures have a strange habit that can teach us some important lessons. As shrimp mature, they outgrow their skins and need to molt. But every time a shrimp molts, it does something bizarre. It places a tiny piece of sand on its own head. This grain of sand is called a "statoscyst stone." Without it, the shrimp has a difficult time knowing which way is up. The small tug of gravity from the sand particle helps the shrimp to know if it is right side up or upside down. The sand grain is crucial for the shrimp to maintain its equilibrium when tossed by the surging seas.*

A marine biologist learned about this when he replaced the sand with metal filings in an aquarium. When the shrimp began to molt, they stuck a tiny piece of steel on their heads instead of the usual grain of sand. The biologist then placed a magnet at the top of the tank, and the shrimp flipped upside down. The pull of the magnet was stronger than the tug of gravity.

The scientist then took another shrimp and put it into the aquarium with a grain of sand on its head. This shrimp was the only one who swam right side up! The other inverted shrimp were probably thinking, "Look at that fanatic swimming upside down!"

Pharaoh of Egypt once had a dream. His wise men could not interpret the dream. He heard of Joseph and asked him to explain the dream. "So Joseph answered Pharaoh, saying, 'It is not in me; God will give Pharaoh an answer of peace.'" Joseph knew which direction to turn. When you find yourself needing to know which direction to swim, turn to the Lord in prayer. Study your Bible. These will be your "statoscyst stones" to lead you in the right way.

KEY BIBLE TEXT: "Then Pharaoh said to Joseph, 'Inasmuch as God has shown you all this, there is no one as discerning and wise as you. You shall be over my house, and all my people shall be ruled according to your word; only in regard to the throne will I be greater than you'" (Genesis 41:39, 40).

The Lord Is My Rocket Booster

An Amazing Fact: *The now retired NASA Space Shuttle burned most of its fuel within the first two minutes of flight.*

The Space Shuttle used two rockets, known as Solid Rocket Boosters, or SRBs, for launch. Located on either side of the shuttle's fuel tank, the SRBs constituted about 83 percent of the shuttle's liftoff thrust, propelling the spacecraft 28 miles into the air.

The SRBs burned more than half of their propellant—about 41 percent of the shuttle's total fuel—in the first minute after liftoff, and thrust was reduced by approximately one-third. Two minutes after launch, the SRBs separated from the shuttle. Parachutes then deployed to slow their descent back to earth. NASA then recovered the SRBs from the ocean and reused them.

Life is often like that. Between planning and preparation, it seems to take the most effort to get something going—a project, a business, a life-change. But once you're off and running, so to speak, it gets easier.

So often when we make a decision based on the Holy Spirit's prompting, we encounter resistance that feels as though we are under attack by forces unknown. It takes physical and emotional energy to push through that resistance. Peter says that Satan roams around like a lion searching for its prey (1 Peter 5:8). The devil seeks to thwart our plans to follow God. But God promises us strength to keep going. He is not only our Rock, but also our rocket booster!

KEY BIBLE TEXTS: "The Lord is my rock and my fortress and my deliverer" (Psalm 18:2). "But those who wait on the Lord shall renew their strength; ... they shall run and not be weary" (Isaiah 40:31).

DAY 21 Holding the Universe

An Amazing Fact: *Though scientists can't see all the galaxies in the universe, there are an estimated 100,000 galaxies in the observable universe. Full-size galaxies (as opposed to "small" galaxies) generally contain at least 100,000 stars, as well as planets, moons, asteroids, comets, and dust-and-gas-composed nebulae. There are three major types of galaxies—spiral, elliptical, and irregular. The Milky Way is a spiral galaxy.*

All you need to do is look up on a dark, starlit night to be awed and perhaps a bit overwhelmed by the beauty of the heavens. How does it all mesh together into one perfect and exciting universe? The simple answer is: God holds it together.

The physical laws He has ordained all work together to control the power and movements of the planets, stars, and galaxies. He keeps them all synchronized. Without the precise physical laws God created, the universe would crumble into chaos.

The law of God prevents chaos in the spiritual realm as well; it holds everything together. In Psalm 19, the Scripture says that God's perfect spiritual law converts our souls, makes us wise and happy, and opens our eyes to truth.

The same God who magnificently coordinates every sun, moon, and star in the entire universe is eager and willing to bring peaceful coordination and meaning to your life, to hold it together by His power and love.

KEY BIBLE TEXT: "The heavens declare the glory of God; and the firmament shows His handiwork. Day unto day utters speech, and night unto night reveals knowledge. There is no speech nor language where their voice is not heard. ... The law of the LORD is perfect" (Psalm 19:1–3, 7).

Who Is the Strongest?

DAY 22

An Amazing Fact: *If asked what the world's strongest animal might be, you would probably imagine a large animal like an elephant or whale. Surprisingly, the title actually goes to the Onthophagus Taurus dung beetle. This little creature can pull 1,140 times its own body weight!*

A recent study from Queen Mary University of London reveals that the dung beetle uses its great strength to battle other male beetles during mating season. Imagine pulling 100 tons of weight—an impossible feat for any human. Yet a dung beetle can do the equivalent.

The strength of God's creatures might cause us to pause in wonder, but the power of our Creator is even greater. The psalmist praised, "Be exalted, O Lord, in Your own strength! We will sing and praise Your power." David recognized with awe the strength of our God as something to be praised. In the world around him and the events of his life, he could see God's might at work.

The same God who created an astonishingly strong insect has the strength to orchestrate the powers that control our world, yet at the same time He knows and cares about the small details of our lives. The trials on your heart are close to His heart too, and His strength is always ready to carry us through each day. Like David, many of us face difficult trials; it can be easy to let fear overwhelm us. But if we pause to step back and recognize that our lives are not in *our* hands, we can rest easy. Our lives are in the hands of an incredibly strong and caring Creator.

KEY BIBLE TEXT: "Be exalted, O LORD, in Your own strength! We will sing and praise Your power" (Psalm 21: 13).

DAY 23 Horses, Chariots, and Battleships

An Amazing Fact: *A floating city awash in elegance, the Queen Mary is one of the most famous ships in history. Launched in 1934 by Her Majesty Queen Mary, it was a wonder of modern times. The ship was considerably bigger than the infamous Titanic—with a 1,019-foot length and 12 decks reaching 181 feet high. The engines produced 160,000 horsepower to move the 81,000 tons! On August 30, 1934, the Queen Mary shattered a speed record by crossing the Atlantic in just under four days, averaging over 30 knots.*

Militaries the world over have always looked for bigger, better, stronger, and more powerful instruments of war. Today's vehicles include tanks, fighter jets, helicopters, armored cars, and battleships. However, sometimes vehicles are modified for use in war. During World War II, the commercial ocean liner *Queen Mary* was converted into a troop ship and transported more than 700,000 military personnel a total of 569,000 miles. Many allied troops looked fondly on this powerful mother of the sea, especially when carried home.

People in Bible times also looked to vehicles for warfare. At the time of King David, chariots began to appear in Israel, and his son Solomon greatly increased their usage. Yet David gives this warning in Psalm 20:7: "Some trust in chariots, and some in horses; but we will remember the name of the Lord our God." It is not in the strength of man that victory is found. The greatest war to be fought and won is the battle over the self. Horses or battleships will not bring triumph over sin in the heart.

In 1967, the city of Long Beach bought the Queen Mary. Since then, $63 million has been spent on its conversion into a tourist spot with a museum, shops, restaurants, and hotel. With no possibility of sailing the seas, the Queen Mary is filled with activity but never leaves port. Likewise, the greatest military strength will never bring us home to heaven. Only in God's name can we find victory over our battle with sin.

KEY BIBLE TEXT: "No king is saved by the multitude of an army; A mighty man is not delivered by great strength. A horse is a vain hope for safety; neither shall it deliver any by its great strength" (Psalm 33:16, 17).

Lifting the Burden

An Amazing Fact: *Roman emperor Justinian once ordered a compilation of all the laws governing ancient Rome. A lawyer named Tribonian directed the five-year-long project, which resulted in nearly 300 volumes of laws!*

From its founding in 753 BC, Rome began accumulating laws. Any leader—local or national—could introduce new laws to govern his subjects. When Justinian came to power in AD 527, Roman law was a confusing mass of contradiction and redundancy. Justinian appointed Tribonian to thoroughly examine the laws, determining what to keep and what to discard. Seven years later, in 534, the Justinian Code was finally finished.

Today, most European nations owe the structure of their legal systems to Roman law. Even in the United States, many legal concepts that we take for granted originated in Rome.

Like their hated captors, the Jews amassed an enormous set of confusing and burdensome laws. Regarding the Sabbath alone, Pharisees created 39 categories of activities that might be considered work and were therefore taboo on Sabbath.

Enter Jesus and His no-nonsense spirituality. A lawyer once asked Jesus which law was most important. Jesus summarized the Ten Commandments into two simple ideas: "Love Me, and love your neighbor."

We serve a God who keeps it simple! Christians still gravitate toward black and white lists of dos and don'ts; with lists, thinking and communing with God over life's unique situations becomes unnecessary. But God promises that when we ask Him for guidance, He will direct us—to actions that demonstrate our love for Him and for our neighbor.

KEY BIBLE TEXTS: "Jesus said to him, '"You shall love the Lord your God with all your heart, with all your soul, and with all your mind." This is the first and great commandment. And the second is like it: "You shall love your neighbor as yourself." On these two commandments hang all the Law and the Prophets'" (Matthew 22:37–40). "Trust in the Lord with all your heart, and lean not on your own understanding. In all your ways acknowledge Him, and He shall direct your paths" (Proverbs 3:5, 6).

DAY 25 God Clears the Way

An Amazing Fact: *The mythological birthplace of the Greek goddess of love and beauty, Aphrodite, the town of Paphos was steeped in idolatry. For a while, it served as the island's capital. Today, the modern town of Paphos is considered an "open museum" featuring Paphos Castle—a Byzantine fort on the harbor—and many historical ruins. Some ruins contain large and beautiful mosaics, including some that were buried for 16 centuries.*

When they reached the city of Paphos on Cyprus, Paul and Barnabas ran into big trouble. Sergius Paulus, the Roman proconsul for the region, had called for the apostles to come to teach him about God. The Scripture says he wanted to hear the Word of God. Here was a seeker after truth, and the apostles were happy to share it with him.

But a man with the proconsul, a false prophet called Bar-Jesus (the name fits, doesn't it?), tried to stop them from preaching and attempted to prevent the proconsul from believing in Christ.

Finally, Paul rebuked the sorcerer and told him he would be blind for a time. The prediction immediately came true. Amazed by what had happened, and "astonished at the teaching of the Lord," the proconsul believed.

Jesus is the "Light which gives light to every man." If a person is sincerely seeking truth, God will clear the way. He will let no circumstance, thing, or person stand in the way of a searching heart.

KEY BIBLE TEXT: "Now when they had gone through the island to Paphos, they found a certain sorcerer, a false prophet, a Jew whose name was Bar-Jesus, who was with the proconsul, Sergius Paulus, an intelligent man. This man called for Barnabas and Saul and sought to hear the word of God. ... Then the proconsul believed, when he saw what had been done, being astonished at the teaching of the Lord" (Acts 13:6, 7, 12).

An Amazing Fact: *The act of fasting is an ancient one, carried out for several reasons. In pre-Christian Ireland, for example, a person might have fasted on the doorstep of someone against whom he had a grudge. According to some historians, the culture's strong emphasis on hospitality made it an insult for a person to starve on the doorstep of your home.*

Sometimes a person fasts to make a political statement, i.e., a hunger strike. Other times it is meant to show mourning or a lack of attachment to earthly needs. It might be exercised for a limited amount of time or on a regular basis or even as an ultimatum with the possibility of starvation.

The Pharisees of Jesus' day fasted as a mark of piety, to show humility before God. They fasted on certain days throughout the year; fasting was often associated with prayer. Attention was given to God, rather than earthly needs or desires. In Matthew 9, Jesus' disciples wondered about this common custom. Why didn't Jesus require His followers to fast? Jesus reminded them that there was no need mourn while He was with them.

Our bridegroom has been taken away from us for now. Sometimes we might feel that sense of mourning, when the world feels like a dark and lonely place and our Savior is far away. But the time for mourning is only temporary and soon the bridegroom will return. It won't be long until the darkness vanishes forever and the bridegroom arrives to receive His bride. The day of rejoicing is near! Our Savior, the bridegroom, will be with us forever.

KEY BIBLE TEXT: "Then the disciples of John came to Him, saying, 'Why do we and the Pharisees fast often, but Your disciples do not fast?' And Jesus said to them, 'Can the friends of the bridegroom mourn as long as the bridegroom is with them? But the days will come when the bridegroom will be taken away from them, and then they will fast'" (Matthew 9: 14, 15).

DAY 27 From the Womb

An Amazing Fact: *The most children ever born to one mother took place in the 18th century in Shuya, Russia, near Moscow. In a total of 27 pregnancies, the wife of a peasant named Feodor Vassilyev gave birth to 69 children. The litters were comprised of 16 pairs of twins, seven sets of triplets, and four sets of quadruplets! The case was reported to Moscow by the Monastery of Nikolskiy on February 27, 1782. Only two of the children born died in infancy. Among all their children, there were no single births.*

In Psalm 22 David not only describes his own suffering, but his words move beyond his own experience to describe the coming Messiah. Though he felt forsaken, David remembers the trust he learned at birth. "But you are He who took Me out of the womb; You made Me trust while on My mother's breast" (Psalm 22:9). The first lesson of life that babies learn is trust. Mothers play a significant role in teaching their little ones to have a sense of security in this often cold and difficult world.

Some mothers have a bigger job because they have more children. Currently, the world's most prolific mother is Leontina Albina nee Espinosa, of San Antonio, Chile, who in 1981 produced her 55th and last child. Her husband, Gerardo Seconda Albina, states that they were married in Argentina in 1943 and have had five sets of triplets (all boys) before arriving in Chile.

Like David, we can find our source of trust in God. "Our fathers trusted in You; They trusted, and You delivered them" (Psalm 22:5). Though Jesus cried out on the cross, "My God, My God, why have you forsaken Me?" He still trusted His life in the Father's hands. "Father, into Your hands I commit My spirit" (Luke 23:46).

The Lord has many children. We can trust the heavenly Father to never forget one of us. Put your trust in God today.

KEY BIBLE TEXT: "I was cast upon You from birth. From My mother's womb You have been My God" (Psalm 22:10).

The Cattle on a Thousand Playing Fields

An Amazing Fact: *It takes about 35,000 cows to make a year's supply of regulation NFL footballs.*

Despite the nickname "pigskin," today footballs are actually made of leather. Wilson Sporting Goods, official supplier of NFL footballs, says one cowhide produces 15 to 25 footballs. Wilson makes about 700,000 regulation NFL footballs every year.

David Gassko and Ian Stanczyk decided to ask one day, "What are the odds that any given cow will make it into the Super Bowl, via a football?"

Of those 700,000 regulation balls, the NFL uses just 12,000 per year. Meanwhile, one in two adult cattle are slaughtered every year. Of those, the hides of one in 952 will become NFL footballs, of which one in 58 will be used in an NFL game, and about one in 158 of those will be used in the Super Bowl. So what are the odds that a random cow will be in the Super Bowl? About 1-in-17,420,000, or so say Gassko and Stanczyk.

The Psalm says God owns "the cattle on a thousand hills." In fact, God claims every beast of the forest as well. Not even a sparrow falls to the ground without Him noticing. "Of how much more value are you?" Jesus asked. "Even the hairs on your head are numbered."

With a God who loves you this much, do you know the odds that you'll go to heaven and live with Him forever? Accept Him as your personal Savior, and they're one in one.

KEY BIBLE TEXTS: "For every beast of the forest is Mine, and the cattle on a thousand hills. I know all the birds of the mountains and the wild beasts are Mine" (Psalm 50:10, 11). "Are not two sparrows sold for a copper coin? And not one of them falls to the ground apart from your Father's will. But the very hairs of your head are all numbered. Do not fear therefore; you are of more value than many sparrows" (Matthew 10:29–31). "For God so loved the world that He gave His only begotten Son, that whoever believes in Him should not perish but have everlasting life" (John 3:16).

DAY 29 An End to Affliction

An Amazing Fact: *Erik Weihenmeyer became the first blind man to climb to the highest peak in the world. He and his sighted friend, Eric Alexander, along with other members of their climbing team, reached the summit of Mount Everest on May 25, 2001. Mark Inglis, who lost both of his legs below the knee, conquered Everest in 2006. He is the first person to successfully scale the mountain with two false legs.*

Since almost 20 percent of Americans are disabled in some way, chances are you have a friend or family member with a disability of some kind, or perhaps you are disabled yourself. Perhaps you have an illness or have had an accident that causes suffering. The Bible assures us that when an afflicted person cries out to God, He hears. And He cares.

When God healed the crippled man in Lystra, through Paul, the Bible says the man "leaped and walked." Can't you just see him jumping high into the air, again and again, landing on his new, healthy feet? Don't you think he was laughing in delight?

This is what it will be like when Jesus returns. For those who belong to Him, all disabilities, deformities, diseases—afflictions of any kind—will vanish in that glorious instant. Freed from the effects of sin, we will be completely healthy, happy, and restored to the likeness of God. It's what He has always wanted for us. As we praise Him, we will almost certainly leap for joy!

KEY BIBLE TEXT: "And in Lystra a certain man without strength in his feet was sitting, a cripple from his mother's womb, who had never walked. This man heard Paul speaking. Paul, observing him intently and seeing that he had faith to be healed, said with a loud voice, 'Stand up straight on your feet!' And he leaped and walked" (Acts 14:8–10).

The Dove

An Amazing Fact: *According to the Cornell Lab of Ornithology, the oldest known mourning dove to ever live was 31 years and four months old!*

The mourning dove is a common bird in North America and the most widespread game bird in the United States. Its diet consists mostly of seeds and occasionally berries. Unlike humans, doves are able to survive in the desert due to their ability to drink brackish (salty) water from springs without becoming dehydrated. And while the oldest known mourning dove lived for the incredible length of 31 years, the average lifespan of the dove is only four to five years.

These doves are particularly known for their recognizable call. Their soft cooing is a beautiful sound and, perhaps, it was this call that Jesus was thinking of when He encouraged His followers to be "shrewd as serpents and innocent as doves." The bird's call is a gentle, innocent sound and reminds us of a calm country morning, sunshine in the trees, and dew sparkling on the grass. The sight of a snake will immediately put you on guard and make your muscles tense, but the call of a mourning dove is a restful sound. It gives you a sense of peace.

As Christians living in a sinful world, interacting daily with temptation and seeking to live our lives as a witness to others, we need the shrewdness of a snake. We need to be watchful and wise. But Jesus also reminds us to be innocent and gentle. Our hearts should be soft toward others and washed clean and pure by His blood. Our presence shouldn't put others on guard with impatient words or an argumentative attitude, but should reflect the call of the mourning dove, peaceful and innocent.

KEY BIBLE TEXT: "I am sending you out like sheep among wolves. Therefore be as shrewd as snakes and as innocent as doves" (Matthew 10:16 NIV).

DAY 31 Greyfriars Bobby

An Amazing Fact: *Near Greyfriars Churchyard in Edinburgh, Scotland, stands a memorial fountain and statue to a little Skye Terrier named Greyfriars Bobby. According to legend, in the 1850s, a shepherd named John Gray made his way in from the meadows with Bobby to the local inn each day at one o'clock. At the café, John would eat lunch as Bobby lay at his feet chewing a bone tucked under his paw. The daily tradition went on for many years, but ended when old John collapsed and died. When he was buried in the Greyfriars Churchyard cemetery, his faithful little dog mournfully watched and marked the spot where his old master was buried.*

The Lord is described as a faithful shepherd by David in Psalm 23. He provides for all our needs. When we need rest, we may "lie down in green pastures." When we are thirsty, He leads us "beside still waters." The Lord leads us in the right pathways when we need direction. Even in the face of death, God does not forsake us. Greyfriars Bobby illustrates such faithfulness.

A few days after John's funeral, the proprietor of the inn was surprised when the little terrier showed up at one o'clock begging for a bone. The kind man gave him a roll and a bone, but the same thing happened the following day, and the next, and the next. On the fourth day, when Bobby finished his afternoon bun and bone, the owner followed the little shepherd dog through town—to the Greyfriars Churchyard. There, Bobby lay down at his master's tombstone.

For the next 14 years, day and night, rain or shine, until his own death in 1872, the loyal little canine virtually lived on top of his master's grave. The little terrier left the site for only an hour at a time to visit his two friends, the restaurateur who fed him and the sexton who built a shelter for him at the cemetery.

A little dog teaches us about God's loyalty and faithfulness. Greyfriars Bobby followed his master wherever he went, even after the old shepherd died. Do we have a loyalty to follow our Shepherd, even to the end of our lives?

KEY BIBLE TEXT: "Yea, though I walk through the valley of the shadow of death, I will fear no evil" (Psalm 23:4).

I AM

An Amazing Fact: *The shortest complete sentence in the English language is "I am."*

While Moses tended his father-in-law's flocks in the desert at the base of Mount Horeb, he stumbled upon a burning bush. The bush caught his attention because, although it burned, it did not burn up. Suddenly God's voice came out of the bush and told Moses to return to Egypt and lead the Israelites out of slavery. Moses challenged the voice, saying, "Who shall I tell them sent me?" God replied, "I AM WHO I AM."

God needs no definition, no justification, no explanation. He simply is.

"Why do we define ourselves by our circumstances or by what we do for a living?" asks life coach Judy Kelly. I am a housewife, we say. I am a student. I am a father. I am an engineer. I am a doctor. "As Christians, our identity is Child of God," Kelly says. "All children of God are given gifts, or talents, which can be used to fulfill different roles." Paul describes these roles as parts of the body of Christ. We are placed in certain roles—son, daughter, brother, sister—and we choose others—student, wife, mother, business owner, church secretary, etc. "Our roles are to be used simply to express our talents, not define who we are," Kelly says. When we use them to define who we are, we inevitably set unreachable standards that we think we have to achieve in order to be valuable.

But the I AM says you are valuable not for what you do, but simply because YOU ARE—just because He made you.

KEY BIBLE TEXTS: "For as we have many members in one body, but all the members do not have the same function, so we, being many, are one body in Christ, and individually members of one another. Having then gifts differing according to the grace that is given to us, let us use them" (Romans 12:4–6). "But you shall be called Hephzibah; ... for the Lord delights in you" (Isaiah 62:4).

DAY 33 Cure for the Shadow

An Amazing Fact: *Hundreds of years ago in parts of Europe, people watched hedgehogs on February 2, observing their shadows or lack thereof to predict the end of winter. German settlers in America adopted groundhogs to continue the tradition. Originally called Candlemas or "Candle Mass"—an ancient feast that celebrated the presentation of Christ at the temple 40 days after His birth—the tradition became known in America as Groundhog Day.*

From Candlemas to Groundhog Day ... that's quite a switch. This is not to suggest that Groundhog Day should be any type of religious holiday. However, this does seem to be a small example of secularization—the act of changing something so it's no longer influenced by religion.

Secularization usually involves a movement away from God, and humans have become very good at it. Just glance at our major holidays (which were once "holy days") to see if this isn't true in the lives of most holiday observers. And there are so many other ways we distance ourselves.

The natural heart is proud and habitually turns away from its Creator. Confronted by its own wrongdoing, it tries to cut God out of the picture to alleviate its guilt.

Consider this: If we turn away from Jesus, our only source of Light, we will definitely see a shadow. But face the Sun of Righteousness, seek His forgiveness, and all shadows disappear. The promise of true spring!

KEY BIBLE TEXTS: "And blessed is he who is not offended because of Me" (Matthew 11:6). "Good and upright is the LORD; therefore He teaches sinners in the way. The humble He guides in justice, and the humble He teaches His way. All the paths of the LORD are mercy and truth, to such as keep His covenant and His testimonies. For Your name's sake, O LORD, pardon my iniquity, for it is great" (Psalm 25:8–11).

Earthquakes

DAY 34

An Amazing Fact: *Alaska has the most earthquakes of any state, with a magnitude seven earthquake nearly every year. The state also experienced the United States' most violent recorded earthquake in March of 1964.*

Earthquakes are a natural disaster that occurs as a result of the shifting of the earth's places. Although we often think of California when we consider earthquakes within the United States, Alaska actually has more earthquakes than any other state. The state's most violent earthquake occurred on Good Friday in 1964, lasting four minutes and measuring a magnitude of 9.2. Many homes and communities were devastated by the quake, and an underwater landslide caused a massive tsunami. About 131 people were killed, most as a result of the tsunami.

In Acts 16, Paul and Silas were prisoners in a Roman jail in the city of Philippi. Having been beaten and chained, they spent the night singing and praising God in the dark cell. In the middle of their singing, a massive earthquake shook the prison. Their chains were broken, and the prison gate opened. Yet rather than flee, the men took this opportunity to reach out to the keeper of the prison ... and their words led him to follow Christ!

This fast-paced story moves from a beating and imprisonment to freedom, witnessing, and finally baptism. In a twist of irony, God used hard circumstances to bring about positive results. Paul' and Silas's mistreatment led to the baptism of several new believers. A natural disaster led to freedom. And throughout each moment, both men refused to let circumstances around them take away from their purpose. They kept their focus on one thing: following their Master.

KEY BIBLE TEXT: "Suddenly there was a great earthquake, so that the foundations of the prison were shaken; and immediately all the doors were opened and everyone's chains were loosed" (Acts 16:26).

DAY 35 Blinding Light

An Amazing Fact: *The popularity of sunglasses is a 20th century phenomenon. In the 1930s, the Army Air Corps commissioned the optical firm Bausch & Lomb to produce a highly effective spectacle that would protect pilots from the dangers of glare when flying above clouds. The company opticians perfected a special dark-green tint that absorbed light in the spectrum's yellow band. They also designed a frame size to maximize the shielding of an aviator's eyes. Fliers were issued the "ray-banning" glasses at no charge, but soon the public was able to purchase the "Ray-Ban aviator sunglasses." A chic and clever 1960s advertising campaign by Foster Grant made sunglasses a must have.*

Light permits us to see. But too much light can be hard on the eyes. David writes, "The Lord is my light and my salvation; Whom shall I fear? The Lord is the strength of my life; Of whom shall I be afraid?" (Psalm 27:1). With God as his light and salvation, David had nothing to fear. Even when his enemies attacked him, "They stumbled and fell" (v. 2).

Light can help you to see, but some light can blind you. Certain ultraviolet rays are harmful to vision. This spectrum is actually invisible to the naked eye. That is why pilots need to wear sunglasses in the brilliant light of the sun. David found God's light to bring him salvation. But his enemies stumbled. The light had not changed. The difference is found in the person viewing the light. David trusted in the Lord for strength. His eyes looked to the light for hope.

Much like the pilots who wear sunglasses in the brilliant sunshine when flying high, we too can enjoy the light of God's salvation when our eyes have been shielded from harmful rays. Such protection comes from Jesus Christ, who filters out sin so we can behold more clearly the heavenly Father.

KEY BIBLE TEXT: "He who has seen Me has seen the Father" (John 14:9).

All Other Ground

DAY 36

An Amazing Fact: *The University of Nebraska at Omaha Library is sinking.*

Legend has it that the Indiana University Library sinks an inch per year because its engineers failed to account for the weight of its books. But this legend is older than the IU library itself—built in 1969—and has also been falsely attributed to several other libraries, including the University of Waterloo Library, Calgary's McKimmie Library, and the University of Nottingham's Jubilee Library.

However, the University of Nebraska at Omaha Library is actually sinking. In the mid-1980s, cracks developed in the library's first floor—but not because its books were too heavy. Rather, engineers discovered cracks in the air ducts running under the floor slab. The cracks allowed warm air to circulate, drying and shrinking the soil and creating voids under the slab.

But five feet below the Indiana University library, explains Robert Meadows, an IU architect, "is a 94-foot-thick layer of limestone. When the library was constructed, the upper layer of this rock was harder than expected. Rather than blast, we raised the lowest level of the building a number of feet."

Jesus compares His followers to the one who built upon a rock. Despite rain, floods, and wind, the wise man's house stood strong. On the other hand, those who do not heed Christ's words are like he who built on the sand: When rain and floods beat down on this man's house, "Great was its fall," Jesus said.

The old hymn declares, "On Christ, the solid Rock I stand; all other ground is sinking sand." Hear and do what Jesus says; build your life on the Foundation that won't fail!

KEY BIBLE TEXT: "Therefore whoever hears these sayings of Mine, and does them, I will liken him to a wise man who built his house on the rock: and the rain descended, the floods came, and the winds blew and beat on that house; and it did not fall, for it was founded on the rock" (Matthew 7:24, 25).

DAY 37 Thunderstorm Blessings

An Amazing Fact: *We know thunder as the sonic shockwave created by lightning. Though scientists are still exploring the exact cause of the shockwave, one theory considers as a factor the extreme heat generated by lightning. The average temperature inside a bolt of lightning has been estimated at 36,300 degrees Fahrenheit, though it can spike as high as 54,000 degrees. Worldwide, there are about eight million lightning strikes per day—or 100 times every second.*

Thunder is mentioned in the Bible 42 times, and reference to lightning is made 28 times. This should come as no surprise since thunder and lightning are such riveting displays of God's awesome power.

Although the potentially devastating effects of lightning are well known, people are less aware of its beneficial side. Lightning helps to dissolve the atmosphere's nitrogen, enabling it to combine with raindrops, which makes a great fertilizer for plants. Lightning also helps to balance Earth's electrical field, and it contributes to the ozone layer, which helps shield the Earth from the harmful rays of the sun. Lightning storms also clean and revitalize the air.

Our planet is dependant on thunderstorms, and so are we. We couldn't survive for long without them. Next time you see a flash of lightning and hear the rumble of thunder, why not whisper a prayer of thanks to our almighty God, who gives us blessings through the storms?

KEY BIBLE TEXT: "The voice of the LORD is over the waters; the God of glory thunders; the LORD is over many waters. The voice of the LORD is powerful; the voice of the LORD is full of majesty ... The LORD will give strength to His people; the LORD will bless His people with peace" (Psalm 29:3, 4, 11).

God's Commandments

An Amazing Fact: *The question of whether the Ten Commandments should be posted on public property is a passionate one, but many are unaware of another related conflict. The Ten Commandments are actually numbered differently by Protestants, Roman Catholics, and Jews, creating yet another controversy!*

The discussion over the posting of the Ten Commandments on public property has lasted for a long time, but most of the controversy has settled on *whether* they should be posted. Conflict also exists over *how* they ought to be posted. Protestants split the commandment regarding no other gods and making no graven images into two commandments, while Roman Catholics keep those commandments together and split the commandment regarding covetousness. In addition, Jewish tradition recognizes "I am the Lord Your God" as part of the first commandment, unlike the others.

The original Hebrew does not number the commandments, but whatever you believe about the numbering of the Ten Commandments and where they are posted, there is a more important question. Are God's commandments posted on your heart? God's laws reflect His heart for His people. Rather than arbitrary rules, they are created with the ultimate law of God as their basis: love for God and love for others.

A person with God's commandments posted on his or her heart will reflect that love in the way they live their lives. We choose to worship God alone out of love and respect for Him. We refuse to commit adultery or covet because we care about those we love. We don't steal because we respect the property of those around us. God's laws are perfectly in tune with His character of love. When our hearts are in tune with Him, that love shines through us.

KEY BIBLE TEXT: "And God spoke all these words, saying ..." (Exodus 20: 1).

DAY 39 Like a Turnip Seed

An Amazing Fact: *A turnip seed under good conditions can increase its weight 15 times a minute—and in rich soil, after sprouting, it can increase its weight up to 15,000 times a day! Still, there is no seed force more powerful than a growing squash seed. An 18-day-old squash was harnessed on a lever and lifted 50 pounds as it grew! Nineteen days later, it raised 5,000 pounds!*

In Matthew 13:24–34, Jesus compares the kingdom of heaven to a mustard seed. For people in Palestine, this was probably the smallest seed used by farmers. Under good conditions, it could grow to a plant 10 feet tall. Though it has humble beginnings, this mighty little seed can do great things! Jesus later said, "If you have faith as a mustard seed, you can move mountains" (Matthew 17:20).

Your faith is like an insignificant seed. It might appear plain, brown, and even dead on the outside. But underneath are all the elements needed to grow a mighty plan. When you die to self, bury your life in Christ, and allow the Holy Spirit to water your faith, it will grow. Day by day the seed will become stronger as it is connected to the elements that God provides.

Is your faith weak? Does it seem that your willpower falls at the slightest temptation? Come to Christ. Confess your sins. Cast yourself at His feet. Cling to the promises of the Bible. Pray, "Dear Lord, though my faith is weak, when I come to You, I believe through Your power that my faith will grow stronger every day. I give you my small faith. Make it grow mighty and strong! Amen!"

KEY BIBLE TEXT: "But grow in grace and knowledge of our Lord and Savior Jesus Christ" (2 Peter 3:18).

Neither Height Nor Depth

An Amazing Fact: *It would take more than nine Empire State Buildings stacked one on top of the other to measure the Gulf of Mexico at its deepest point.*

Bordered by the United States, Mexico, and Cuba, the Gulf of Mexico measures about 550 miles north to south and nearly 1,000 miles east to west—a surface area of more than 930,000 square miles. The Gulf has about 3,700 miles of shoreline and contains 643 quadrillion gallons of water! The Mediterranean-like sea resembles a deep basin with a wide, shallow rim; about a third is comprised of shallow intertidal areas. The Sigsbee Deep, located in the southwestern quadrant, is the deepest part of the Gulf, measuring from 12,303 to 14,383 feet—experts can't agree on its exact depth.

The Empire State Building, meanwhile, stands 1,454 feet tall from the ground to the tip of its lightning rod. Construction on the tower began in 1930 and took more than a year to complete. With 102 floors, the building was the world's tallest until completion of the World Trade Center's North Tower in 1972. On September 11, 2001, the Empire State Building reclaimed its status as New York City's tallest building.

Regardless of where you travel, to the top of the tallest building on earth, or to the depths of the deepest sea, God the Omnipresent goes with you. Paul puts it this way: "Neither height nor depth ... can separate us from the love of God."

KEY BIBLE TEXTS: "If I take the wings of the morning, and dwell in the uttermost parts of the sea, even there Your hand shall lead me, and Your right hand shall hold me" (Psalm 139:9, 10). "For I am persuaded that neither death nor life, nor angels nor principalities nor powers, nor things present nor things to come, nor height nor depth, nor any other crated thing, shall be able to separate us from the love of God which is in Christ Jesus our Lord" (Romans 8:38, 39).

DAY 41 Ocean Treasures

An Amazing Fact: *Our oceans contain 97 percent of the water on Earth and 99 percent of our planet's living space. Less than 10 percent of this space has been explored by humans. In 2010, the world's first "Ocean Census" was released. After 10 years of research, scientists discovered at least 20,000 new species of ocean animals. Some of these were found in areas that had already been well explored. Researchers believe there might be millions of ocean species that have yet to be identified.*

The oceans of the world contain strange, mysterious, and sometimes alien-looking creatures of every imaginable shape and size: fish like living gems; corals in hundreds of forms and colors; immense, intelligent mammals that follow the pathways of the sea. What treasures are hidden in those storehouses of the deep!

The incredible diversity we find in the ocean shows us that our Creator is a God who enjoys endless variety and stunning beauty ... and wants to share it with us.

The Bible encourages us to study the world God made in all its intricacy. It assures us that wisdom comes from studying nature. Spending time in God's "other book" gives us a chance to draw closer to the Creator and to be amazed by the splendor and harmonization of the living things He has made.

The majesty of the ocean and its myriad of creatures is just one reason we should stand in awe of the One who spoke it into existence.

KEY BIBLE TEXT: "He gathers the waters of the sea together as a heap; He lays up the deep in storehouses. Let all the earth fear the LORD; Let all the inhabitants of the world stand in awe of Him. For He spoke, and it was done; He commanded, and it stood fast" (Psalm 33:7–9).

Liquid Mountaineering

An Amazing Fact: *A video clip spread around on the Internet revealed a new sport called liquid mountaineering—aka, walking on water! The video showed several young men appearing to walk on water and described their techniques in such a convincing, scientific manner that many viewers believed the hoax was true ... and one news station even reported it as true.*

You might have seen this "Liquid Mountaineering" video posted on a friend's Facebook page or in an email forward. A group of European pranksters created a video cleverly describing and displaying their new sport. The video was made in documentary style, full of "facts" explaining how the sport was made possible, such as gaining speed and entering the water at a slight curve. Flashing video clips of runners taking "steps" on the water and intense music led many viewers to believe this might be a new extreme sport!

It is easy to laugh at people's gullibility and the pranksters' creativity. But they weren't the first to come up with this idea. In Matthew 14, the disciples were on their boat at sea when Jesus walked out to meet them. Peter responded incredulously, calling, "Lord, if it is You, command me to come to You on the water!" Jesus did and for a few moments, Peter walked on water. But his faith faltered as he saw the waves around him and he began to sink, until Jesus reached out to grasp his hand.

Walking on water didn't require clever techniques or practice. It was a simple matter of faith. When we think of God's power in our lives, it can be easy to think of His help as something that we earn through our actions. Eventually, we imagine, we might become practiced enough to gain His blessing more often. But God's work in our lives is not the result of our own behavior. He only wants us to ask and believe, like Peter, so He can work in our hearts.

KEY BIBLE TEXT: "And immediately Jesus stretched out His hand and caught him, and said to him, 'O you of little faith, why did you doubt?' And when they got into the boat, the wind ceased" (Matthew 14:31, 32).

DAY 43 The Little-Big Muscle

An Amazing Fact: *Like the heart, the tongue is almost all muscle. But unlike the repetitive cardiac contractions, it is capable of very precise, complicated, and elaborate movements. It has many important responsibilities that we usually take for granted. For instance, without a tongue there would be no talking, no singing, and no whistling.*

The tongue is capable of much more than speech. This fascinating muscle is indispensable in eating our food. The upper surface is covered with small projections called papilla, which give it a rough texture. This design helps the tongue move food around in the mouth and direct it to your throat. Without your tongue, you would have to lay back to eat.

Another important function of the tongue is the sense of taste! It is covered with approximately 10,000 taste buds, grouped in different areas sensitive to sweet, sour, salty, and bitter flavors. The sense of smell adds information, providing a wide range of taste. Imagine food with no taste; that's what it would be without your tongue! Chemicals from the food we eat stimulate receptors in each of these areas, and nerves transmit this input to the brain.

In Psalm 35, David calls to God to avenge him. "Vindicate me, O Lord my God, according to Your righteousness" (v. 24). He concludes, "And my tongue shall speak of Your righteousness and of Your praise all the day long." Take time today to praise the Lord with your tongue.

KEY BIBLE TEXT: "At the name of Jesus every knee should bow ... and that every tongue should confess that Jesus Christ is Lord, to the glory of God the Father" (Philippians 2:10, 11).

Happily Ever After

DAY 44

An Amazing Fact: *A poem written to celebrate a wedding is called an epithalamium.*

In ancient Greece, to celebrate a wedding, a poem filled with blessings and predictions of happiness was written in honor of the bride and groom. Boys and girls sang the song for the happy couple at the door of the nuptial chamber. The custom spread to the Romans, and eventually the classical poets developed the epithalamium into a special literary form, which then spread to the French, Italians, and English. Even Tennyson wrote an epithalamium, in honor of his sister's wedding. Eventually the term evolved to cover musical works—like Wagner's Bridal March in *Lohengrin*—and Italian Renaissance paintings depicting Venus and Cupid, gifted to newlyweds to wish them happiness and fertility.

More than once the Bible compares God's love for His people to that of a bridegroom and the coming of the kingdom of heaven to a wedding celebration. In American culture, Disney-like dreams of a carefree "happily ever after" fill the typical blissful wedding day. But unfortunately, with more than half of all marriages ending in divorce, "happily ever after" remains a fairytale just out of reach.

Praise God for the hope of a real Happily Ever After. John received a vision of Christ's coming, in which an angel said, "Come, I will show you the bride, the Lamb's wife," and showed John the New Jerusalem (Revelation 21:9). On the day Christ comes to take us to that bright city, we will celebrate a marriage like no other, and there really *will* be no more sorry, nor crying, nor pain.

KEY BIBLE TEXTS: "As the bridegroom rejoices over the bride, so shall your God rejoice over you" (Isaiah 62:5). "Then I, John, saw the holy city, New Jerusalem, coming down out of heaven from God, prepared as a bride adorned for her husband. ... And God will wipe away every tear from their eyes; there shall be no more death, nor sorrow, nor crying" (Revelation 21:2, 4).

DAY 45 The Greatest Love

An Amazing Fact: *Valentine's Day originated centuries ago, likely from the celebration of at least two different Christian martyrs named "Valentine," or from Eros in Greek mythology (or a combination of these). The holiday enjoyed an explosion of popularity beginning in the early 19th century and is celebrated in different ways around the world. In parts of Asia, for example, women give chocolate candy to men on February 14. Usually, the men return the favor at a later date.*

Whatever the holiday's origin, people love to be remembered on Valentine's Day. We all enjoy receiving gifts on the day commemorating "love"—even a simple card or a handwritten note—because it shows that someone cares about us.

Of course, love—genuine love—involves much more than giving and receiving material gifts. It involves a constant flow of kind deeds, encouraging words, and selfless acts.

Love should be celebrated and practiced every day. The Scriptures tell us to "Love one another fervently with a pure heart" (1 Peter 1:22). And Jesus said, "This is My commandment, that you love one another as I have loved you" (John 15:12).

The most impressive instance of love is not found in the mythical exploits of Eros or even in the sacrifices of the Valentine martyrs. The greatest example of love, by far, is found in Christ who sacrificed Himself for the ungrateful and ungodly, giving everyone an opportunity to be saved. And that is the priceless gift He offers especially to you every day.

KEY BIBLE TEXT: "Trust in the LORD, and do good; dwell in the land, and feed on His faithfulness. Delight yourself also in the LORD, and He shall give you the desires of your heart. Commit your way to the LORD, trust also in Him, and He shall bring it to pass. He shall bring forth your righteousness as the light, and your justice as the noonday" (Psalm 37:3–6).

The Righteous

An Amazing Fact: *During the dark years of the Holocaust, hundreds of non-Jews throughout Europe risked torture and death rescuing their Jewish neighbors and protecting them from the Nazis. The state of Israel has honored these courageous individuals with the title "righteous among nations."*

As the dark wave of Nazi Germany spread across Europe, a few courageous people chose to risk their lives to protect others. Defying the Nazis' efforts to exterminate the Jewish population, some families hid Jews in their barns or basements. Others assisted Jews in fleeing to safer countries. In Denmark, the Danish underground movement worked to save the Jewish citizens of their country. In France, where the memory of the Huguenot Protestants' suffering under Catholic rule remained fresh, the entire village of Chambon-sur-Lignon saved an estimated 3,000 Jews, many of them young children.

Decades have passed since World War II, but the courage of these individuals has not been forgotten. The state of Israel honored these rescuers with the title "righteous among nations." An organization known as The Jewish Foundation for the Righteous was founded to financially support and provide for the aged and needy among these people. It is a touching reminder of the words of David in the book of Psalms. "I have been young and now am old; yet I have not seen the righteous forsaken, nor his descendents begging bread."

God honors those who choose to follow Him. The actions of "the righteous" truly reflect God's character and survive as an example to us all. Will we choose to stand up for what is right when evil surrounds us? Will we refuse to passively sit back but rather follow our Savior at any cost? When we make that choice, He will not forsake us.

KEY BIBLE TEXT: "I have been young, and now am old; yet I have not seen the righteous forsaken, nor his descendants begging bread. He is ever merciful, and lends; and his descendants are blessed" (Psalm 37:25, 26).

DAY 47 Broken Bones

An Amazing Fact: *Did you know that you are born with 300 bones but only have 206 when you die? Of these many bones, the thighbone is stronger than concrete. And the only bone fully grown at birth is located in the ear.*

Broken bones require a mending process. The bone needs to be set properly in a cast. If this is not done correctly, you will experience a lot of pain, discomfort, and even disability. But if your doctor does the job well and you care for your injury during the healing process, your bone can eventually return to near-normal functioning.

Our emotions might impact the health of our bones. Guilt is like a broken bone. Grief over sin has been shown to weaken our skeletal structure. King David understood bone health. In Psalm 38 he expresses grief over wrongdoing. He writes, "There is no soundness in my flesh because of Your anger, nor any health in my bones because of my sin" (Psalm 38:3).

How do you heal bones broken because of guilt and sin? Confession. David writes, "For I will declare my iniquity; I will be in anguish over my sin" (v. 18). Deep, heartfelt repentance over sin brings healing to our minds and bodies. Withholding confession destroys our bodies. "When I kept silent, my bones grew old through my groaning all day long" (Psalm 32:3). But then, "I acknowledged my sin to You, and my iniquity I have not hidden. I said, 'I will confess my transgressions to the Lord,' and you forgave the iniquity of my sin" (v. 5).

Do you have broken bones that need mending?

KEY BIBLE TEXT: "A merry heart does good, like medicine. But a broken spirit dries the bones" (Proverbs 17:22).

He Who Laughs Lasts

DAY 48

An Amazing Fact: *Women laugh more than men do.*

A hearty laugh spreads faster than the flu and quickly involves your whole body. First, your epiglottis begins to vibrate, half-closing over your larynx and making breathing difficult. When strong enough, the struggle for air activates your tear ducts. Laughter engages muscles all over your body—15 in your face alone.

It's unclear why women laugh more than men, but research shows women's brains are generally more responsive to emotional stimuli and suggests gender helps determine how our brains respond to humor. Regardless of who's doing it, the average adult laughs 15 times a day.

Children are attributed 400 laughs per day. This figure is unsubstantiated, but a study at one nursery school revealed 18.4 to 45 incidents of "glee" per child per hour. Perhaps their teacher was a comedian, but these kids have the right idea!

Science confirms the merry heart's benefits. Laughter lowers blood pressure and enhances immune function. The physiological opposite of stress, laughter stimulates the circulatory and digestive systems that stress suppresses. Bringing you into the present moment, laughter precludes worry about the past or future. It releases endorphins, diminishing pain and heightening feelings of well-being. A good laugh relaxes muscles for up to 45 minutes. By toning and firming facial muscles, laughter can fight aging. It has been called "internal jogging," increasing the heart rate in one minute as much as 10 minutes on an exercise machine. Laughter also boosts energy, inspires hope, and fosters intimacy.

So go have a good laugh ... and enjoy the abundant life Jesus promised!

KEY BIBLE TEXT: "A merry heart makes a cheerful countenance. ... He who is of a merry heart has a continual feast" (Proverbs 15:13, 15).

DAY 49 In Spite of Intelligence

An Amazing Fact: *Researchers at the University of Cambridge discovered that sheep are much smarter than previously thought. In one study, the woolies passed an intelligence test that most monkeys flunk. During the test, sheep learned to recognize patterns in colors and to change their behavior when the patterns changed. They also learned to respond to shapes of objects instead of the color, something most large animals find very difficult.*

In spite of their apparent intelligence, however, sheep seem to have a knack for getting themselves into trouble. They tend to follow the leader, even if that leader goes the wrong way. They sometimes wander, or flee in fright, and become separated from the flock. Lacking agility, they easily become trapped. Without much to defend themselves, they're an easy target for predators.

We're more like sheep than we want to admit. In spite of our apparent intelligence, we seem to have the same knack. We tend to follow the crowd. We wander off the right path. We frighten easily. We trap ourselves by our own foolish choices. We have no defense, in ourselves, against the enemy.

Thankfully, when we get ourselves into trouble, Jesus comes searching for us. If we let Him, He will carry us back and set us on the right path. "For the Son of Man has come to save that which was lost" (Matthew 18:11).

Aren't you glad we have a Good Shepherd who watches out for us continuously?

KEY BIBLE TEXT: "What do you think? If a man has a hundred sheep, and one of them goes astray, does he not leave the ninety-nine and go to the mountains to seek the one that is straying? And if he should find it, assuredly, I say to you, he rejoices more over that sheep than over the ninety-nine that did not go astray. Even so it is not the will of your Father who in is heaven that one of these little ones should perish" (Matthew 18:12–14).

Forgiveness

An Amazing Fact: *In 1961, 21-year-old civil rights activist John Lewis got off a bus in Rock Hill, South Carolina. Upon entering a "whites only" waiting room, he was attacked and beaten bloody by a young white man named Elwin Wilson. Years later, the two met in person and Wilson apologized for his actions. Lewis responded, "I forgive you. I don't have any ill feelings, any bitterness, any malice."*

The atmosphere in the southern United States during the Civil Rights movement was full of explosive tension. As the movement for racial equality gained momentum, non-violent demonstrations were often met with violence and even death. Young John Lewis, who would later become a senator, survived more than one brutal attack. But this situation ended differently, with resolution and forgiveness. Wilson apologized, reporting that he had found the Lord and recognized his wrong; Lewis described it as a moment of grace and forgiveness, representing what the struggle was about.

In Matthew, Jesus shares a story with His disciples about an ungrateful servant who, after having been forgiven of his debts, went after a fellow servant who owed him a small sum and threw him in prison. The angry master sent the first servant back to prison. Jesus told the disciples, "So My heavenly Father also will do to you if each of you, from his heart, does not forgive his brother his trespasses."

John Lewis made that difficult choice. Rather than harboring anger for how unjustly he had been treated, he chose to forgive from his heart. We might not have experienced a violent physical attack, but most of us have been wronged in some way. Will we choose to forgive?

So go have a good laugh ... and enjoy the abundant life Jesus promised!

KEY BIBLE TEXT: "So My heavenly Father also will do to you if each of you, from his heart, does not forgive his brother his trespasses" (Matthew 18: 32–35).

DAY 51 Tears Communicate

An Amazing Fact: *There are three different types of tears. Basal tears keep the cornea wet and nourished. Reflex tears wash out foreign particles or irritable substances (onion vapors). Crying tears are due to strong emotional stress, anger, suffering, mourning, or physical pain. Each type has a different chemical make-up and can relay messages to others.*

Did you ever get a piece of sawdust in your eye? You blinked and blinked as tears spontaneously came and helped wash out the irritant. Tears not only lubricate your eyes so you can see more clearly, they help keep the surface of your cornea clean every time you blink. During the fight-or-flight response of an intense situation, you produce more tears. Tears come to people under deep emotional distress such as anger or grief.

The chemical make-up of tears differs. Emotional tears actually contain more of the protein-based hormones. Some of these contain natural painkillers. But not all emotional tears are genuine. We refer to an insincere display of grief or dishonest remorse as "crocodile tears." An ancient Greek anecdote stated that crocodiles would pretend to weep while luring their prey. Societies generally accept the public display of tears in women and children, but only a few cultures find it socially acceptable for men to cry in public.

David writes Psalm 42 out of deep distress. He yearns for God's presence. He feels alone and forgotten by God. Enemies surround him. David longs to be in the temple where he can worship God. Out of this pain he cries, "My tears have been my food day and night, while they continually say to me, 'Where is your God'?" (Psalm 42:3).

David did not withhold his tears. His genuine display of grief spilled out as he wept in prayer. We too may come before the Lord with our emotions and pain. We can also know that God sees our hurt and feels our sorrow. Like David, we can find hope in God as we bow in anguish and shed tears.

KEY BIBLE TEXT: "Why are you cast down, O my soul? And why are you disquieted within me? Hope in God; for I shall yet praise Him, the help of my countenance and my God" (Psalm 42:11).

Highland Praise

An Amazing Fact: *Although identified with Scotland, bagpipes are actually a very ancient instrument, introduced into the British Isles by the Romans.*

We associate bagpipes with kilts, funerals, and Amazing Grace. But the first bagpipe actually came from the Middle East. *The Oxford History of Music* describes the first sculptured bagpipe found on a Hittite slab, dated to 1,000 B.C. Historians from the first and second centuries A.D. depict Nero playing an instrument whose description fits that of a bagpipe. Roman armies carried pipes into Europe, and beginning in the second millennium, European art features bagpipes with increasing frequency. Their first certain connection with the British Isles appears in *The Canterbury Tales,* written around 1380.

Bagpipes became most popular in Scotland and Ireland, where their distinctive sound brightened an otherwise drab existence. During the expansion of the British Empire, a large number of pipers trained for military service and carried the Scottish Great Highland Bagpipe worldwide. But as Western classical music developed into a sophisticated art that used technology to improve its instruments, the bagpipe, with its limited range and function, couldn't keep up.

Nevertheless, a number of countries modeled their militaries after the British Army and adopted the bagpipe, as have police and fire forces. The pipes are commonly used today in military and police funerals.

God endowed humanity with a bit of His creativity. Music is one way we express that creativity. David instructs us to praise God with all manner of instruments. Whatever you use, praise God today for His surpassing greatness!

KEY BIBLE TEXT: "Praise the LORD. Praise God in his sanctuary; praise him in his mighty heavens. Praise him for his acts of power; praise him for his surpassing greatness. Praise him with the sounding of the trumpet, praise him with the harp and the lyre, praise him with timbrel and dancing, praise him with the strings and pipe, praise him with the clash of cymbals, praise him with resounding cymbals. Let everything that has breath praise the LORD. Praise the LORD." (Psalm 150 NIV).

DAY 53 Free to All

An Amazing Fact: *The earliest denarius coins showed up in 269 B.C., but the Romans began producing a standardized silver denarius of 4.5 grams in 211 B.C. The name "denarius" stems from a Latin word meaning "containing ten." The denarius was the equivalent of 10 "assarius," which was made of bronze or copper.*

In Jesus' parable of the vineyard laborers, all the workers were paid equally at the end of the day. This created a problem in the minds of the men who had been sweating long hours in the sun. They thought the men who worked fewer hours didn't deserve as much pay.

By human standards, the long-day workers had a point. But the kingdom of God doesn't work that way. No one can really "earn" anything. No one is given salvation because he or she has done something to deserve it. It's a free gift, and it's offered equally to all. A person who has just come to Christ has eternal life as completely as someone who's been in the church all his life.

God doesn't treat any of us as our sins deserve. If He did, there would be no one left to save. Instead, He lovingly washes us in Christ's blood, covers us with His righteousness, and gives us the eternal gift none of us deserve. That's something for which we can all be thankful.

KEY BIBLE TEXT: "For the kingdom of heaven is like a landowner who went out early in the morning to hire laborers for his vineyard. ... And when those came who were hired about the eleventh hour, they each received a denarius. But when the first came, they supposed that they would receive more; and they likewise received each a denarius. And when they had received it, they complained against the landowner, saying, 'These last men have worked only one hour, and you made them equal to us who have borne the burden and the heat of the day'" (Matthew 20:1, 9–12).

Thirst

An Amazing Fact: *What animal can run faster than a horse, see behind itself without turning its head, and go without drinking water for longer than a camel? The giraffe!*

The giraffe is the world's tallest mammal. It lives in parts of Africa on the savannah or grassland, avoiding thick woods that might conceal predators. A giraffe's diet consists of insects and plants, primarily leaves from tall trees. Their long black tongues can be up to 45 centimeters long, helping the animal reach and grab food. It is the water content of these leaves that enables the giraffe to go for weeks without drinking water.

Thirst is the body's natural response to a need for water. As our bodies use up water, the sensation of thirst drives us to seek out and consume more. Some creatures can go longer than others without water. As humans, we can only go a few days, depending on factors such as temperature and age. Some animals can last more than two weeks, depending on available food sources.

King David recognized another kind of thirst in Psalm 42. He observed how animals thirst and seek out water and compared it to his own thirst for God. "My soul thirsts for God, the living God. When shall I come and appear before God?" David had walked with God and knew what it was like to have close communion with Him. When he didn't have that time with God, he missed it. He realized his need. He remembered the times of joy and praise when he had a close connection with God, and he wanted those times to return. Sometimes it is this thirst that can help us turn back to our Savior. When we look back on our walk with God and remember what He has done in our lives, we want that relationship to stay strong. We know what a difference He makes in our lives!

KEY BIBLE TEXT: "As the deer pants for the water brooks, so pants my soul for You, O God. My soul thirsts for God, for the living God. When shall I come and appear before God?" (Psalm 42:1, 2).

DAY 55 Boat Boasting

An Amazing Fact: *The most famous shipwreck in history is the RMS Titanic, which sank on April 15, 1912, on her maiden voyage. No pains were spared to supply this luxurious first-class ocean liner, including fewer lifeboats in order to provide more deck room for passengers to lounge and play. Out of 2,228 passengers only 705 survived.*

The world was captured by the construction of the massive and unsinkable Titanic. The White Star Line publicized the amazing engineering of this "invincible ship." As she first headed out to sea, her massive propellers created a wake that pulled a smaller ship into a near-deadly collision. Four days later as she approached a massive iceberg and attempted to divert, a giant rip was torn parallel across the ship's bulk. Some believe the crew was warned of coming icebergs but ignored the warnings.

Most passengers were unaware of the tragedy when it first happened. Some reported feeling a strange quivering in the ship but didn't think anything of it. Others saw icebergs through their portholes but were assured there would only be a slight delay. But passengers located at critical points knew the truth. The Titanic was sinking fast. An SOS was sent out to nearby ships. By the time the Carpathia arrived to help there were only a handful of lifeboats full of shocked survivors.

The apostle Paul was once in a shipwreck. In fact, he said, "Men, I perceive that this voyage will end with disaster and much loss, not only of the cargo and ship, but also of our lives" (Acts 27:10). Unfortunately, these men (like so many of us) trusted in their own inventions and met with near disaster. David wrote, "For I will not trust in my bow, nor shall my sword save me" (Psalm 44:6).

Where do you put your trust? What do you boast about? Where is your hope?

KEY BIBLE TEXT: "In God we boast all day long" (Psalm 44:8).

The King Lives

DAY 56

An Amazing Fact: *There have been as many as a quarter of a million Elvis sightings since his death.*

With his daring music, his clothing, and his dance moves, Elvis Presley embodied the rock and roll movement and sent music and pop culture in an all-new direction. From the moment he hit the public stage, Elvis became a cultural phenomenon. Today, his popularity has hardly waned. Thirty-four years after his death on August 16, 1977, the decades-long debate continues: Is Elvis still alive?

Elvis sightings began almost the day he died, but it wasn't until Louise Welling of Vicksburg, Michigan, said she saw Elvis in the grocery store on a Sunday morning in 1987 that tabloids picked up the stories. Since then, the King of Rock and Roll has allegedly been seen around the country. Some sightings are even accompanied by fuzzy pictures, like those of Bigfoot or UFOs.

Another "celebrity" was once reported alive after His very public death. Mary Magdalene went with some other women to His tomb the Sunday morning after His death, intending to anoint His body. Instead, the women were met by an angel who reminded them that Jesus had predicted His resurrection. The women returned to the disciples and reported the empty tomb, but the disciples didn't believe them. Then Peter and John ran to the tomb and saw the lonely grave clothes for themselves.

When news of the first Jesus sighting circulated, the Pharisees accused the disciples of stealing Jesus' body. But for 40 days Jesus appeared repeatedly to His people, "presenting Himself alive ... by many infallible proofs" (Acts 1:3), and preaching about the kingdom of God. Then one day, with a promise to send the Holy Spirit, Jesus ascended into the clouds and out of sight.

Thus 2,000 years later we await His return; for assuredly, the King lives!

KEY BIBLE TEXTS: "Why do you seek the living among the dead? He is not here, but is risen!" (Luke 24:5, 6). "But now Christ is risen from the dead" (1 Corinthians 15:20).

DAY 57 Symbol of Victory

An Amazing Fact: *During the mid-1960s, archeologists found Judean date palm seeds in the ruins of Herod the Great's palace. They had been stored in a jar in a dry area. After 40 more years in storage, a few seeds were planted in the desert in southern Israel. One of the seeds sprouted, setting a record for the oldest known tree seed to successfully germinate. By 2010 it was about seven feet tall. The palm tree is named "Methuselah" after the longest-living human. Judean date palm trees had been extinct for 1,800 years.*

Since ancient times, palm branches have been a symbol of victory and triumph. In Roman times, game champions were awarded palm branches and armies used them to celebrate successful battles. The Jews often carried palm branches during festive times.

When the crowd saw Jesus riding on the young donkey, they got excited and began breaking off palm fronds to wave in celebration. They believed He was about to take the throne as king. Wouldn't it have been thrilling to be part of that throng, to shout the 'Hosannas' and the blessings?

Yet Jesus' kingdom was not earthly but spiritual. Although the peop didn't fully comprehend that, their response was appropriate. There we good reasons for shouting and praise. Jesus was the Messiah. He had alread lived a victorious, sinless life. And He would very soon attain the ultimate triumph with His sacrifice on the cross—the crowning achievement in His mission to save us.

KEY BIBLE TEXT: "And a very great multitude spread their clothes on the road; others cut down branches from the trees and spread them on the road. Then the multitudes who went before and those who followed cried out, saying: 'Hosanna to the Son of David! Blessed is He who comes in the name of the LORD! Hosanna in the highest!'" (Matthew 21:8, 9).

Shipwrecked

An Amazing Fact: *Scuba diving and exploring shipwrecks off the coast of Bermuda is a popular tourist attraction. There are about 20 ships that wrecked on the island itself and nearly 300 wrecked ships in the area surrounding the island!*

The island of Bermuda is a common tourist destination, with tropical weather and beautiful coral reefs. It is these coral reefs that have been responsible for the wrecks of nearly 300 ships in years past. One ship wrecked and brought Bermuda's first settlers to the island. Other sunken ships included luxury liners, military ships, and merchant freighters. More recently, a smuggling ship known as the Xing Da sank in 1997 there after a pirating career that went back to smuggling contraband weapons during the Vietnam War.

The apostle Paul also experienced a shipwreck on his journey to Rome. His ship wrecked as a result of a violent storm rather than coral; still, God's watchful care brought Paul and the other passengers safely to the island of Malta. There he was able to pray, heal, and share the news of Jesus with the island's inhabitants.

As you read the story, it is hard not to notice Paul's persevering attitude. Rather than bemoaning his circumstances, he told the ship's crew not to fear, commanded the officers not to kill the prisoners, and helped the passengers swim to shore. He gathered wood for a fire to warm the wet survivors, survived a snake's bite, and went to heal and pray with the people of Malta. As sinful humans, facing difficult circumstances often leads us to complain. We feel we deserve better and wish to make ourselves feel better. But what a difference it makes when we choose to move forward with God's work, even when the way is hard. God will bless those who press forward into the storm!

KEY BIBLE TEXT: "Now when they had escaped, they then found out that the island was called Malta" (Acts 28:1).

DAY 59 Let It Pour

An Amazing Fact: *Rain is recycled water that evaporated from the world's oceans, lakes, and rivers. Rain actually starts off as ice or snow crystals at the cloud level.*

Life would be pretty difficult without rain. A lack of precipitation has dramatic effects on agriculture. All plants need some water to survive, so regular rain patterns are necessary. Even too much rain can harm crops. Drought not only can destroy plants but can also increase erosion. Some plants, like cactus, need very little water, whereas some tropical plants require up to 100 inches per year.

God promised rain to the Israelites as a blessing for obedience. "If you walk in My statutes and keep My commandments, and perform them, then I will give you rain in its season, the land shall yield its produce, and the trees of the field shall yield their fruit" (Leviticus 26:3, 4). But if they were disobedient, there would be curses. "I will make your heavens like iron and your earth like bronze" (v. 19). In other words, there would be no rain. During the time of Elijah, King Ahab's disobedience brought this covenant curse on Israel. Elijah spoke to Ahab and said, "As the Lord God of Israel lives, before whom I stand, there shall not be dew nor rain these years, except at my word" (1 Kings 17:1).

Rain also represents our spiritual need of Jesus, the water of life (John 4:10), and the Holy Spirit (Zechariah 10:1). Ask the Lord for rain to pour on your heart. Seek to walk in obedience and receive this blessing today.

KEY BIBLE TEXT: "And whatever you ask in prayer, believing, you will receive" (Matthew 21:22).

Direct Line

An Amazing Fact: *President Grover Cleveland personally answered the White House telephone.*

In one of the United States' most controversial presidential campaigns ever, Grover Cleveland narrowly won the 1884 election and became the first Democratic president after the Civil War.

Cleveland disliked showing special favor to any group. When a bill was passed granting aid to drought-stricken farmers in Texas, Cleveland vetoed it because he thought such aid fostered an expectation of "paternal care" by the government and "weakened our national character." To criticism that his tough policies would work against his reelection, Cleveland retorted, "What is the use of being elected or re-elected unless you stand for something?" Sure enough, he lost in 1888, but won again in 1892, still the only president to serve two non-consecutive terms.

Despite his controversial campaign and tough reputation, New Jersey-born Cleveland was an ordinary man. A bachelor when he first entered office, Cleveland is one of only three presidents to marry while in office—and the only one to do so in the White House. His five children kept pet canaries, a mockingbird, and a dog. And Cleveland liked to answer the White House telephone himself.

President Cleveland had discovered a cancerous growth on the roof of his mouth. But in case the illness might cause the public to panic, Cleveland snuck aboard a boat over the Fourth of July holiday with several doctors, who surgically removed the cancer. For five days virtually no one knew where the President really was; the truth wasn't revealed until nine years after his death.

Like President Cleveland, God answers anytime we call. In fact, He promises to hear and listen. (Jeremiah 29:12). And unlike President Cleveland could be, the Psalms promise that God is always on the job.

KEY BIBLE TEXTS: "He shall call upon Me, and I will answer him; I will be with him in trouble" (Psalms 91:15). "He that keeps you will not slumber. Behold, He who keeps Israel shall neither slumber nor sleep" (Psalm 121:3, 4).

DAY 61 Saved to Serve

An Amazing Fact: *The Bible contains almost 900 references to the word 'servant,' 65 references to 'slave,' and 18 references to 'bondservant.' In ancient Israel, if a freed bondservant chose to remain with the family for the rest of his life, his ear was pierced as a sign that he had freely chosen to serve.*

A bondservant is one obligated to service without wages. Paul proclaimed himself to be a bondservant of Jesus Christ. It was both his duty and joy to share the gospel with people in many parts of the world. He met with plenty of opposition and suffered greatly for the cause of Christ, but he never regretted working for his Master.

Jesus said, "Therefore if the Son makes you free, you shall be free indeed" (John 8:36). But how can a person be both free and a bondservant?

The Scripture says, "Whoever commits sin is a slave of sin" (John 8:34). But when God sets us free from sin, we become "slaves of righteousness" (Romans 6:18).

Jesus set the example for serving others. "For even the Son of Man did not come to be served, but to serve, and to give His life a ransom for many" (Mark 10:45). Christ put aside His own interests and feelings and committed Himself completely to His mission of rescue.

We have been set free from slavery to sin by His sacrifice and grace. Love for our Redeemer obligates us. We have been saved to serve.

KEY BIBLE TEXT: "Paul, a bondservant of Jesus Christ, called to be an apostle, separated to the gospel of God which He promised before through His prophets in the Holy Scriptures, concerning His Son Jesus Christ our Lord, who was born of the seed of David according to the flesh, and declared to be the Son of God with power according to the Spirit of holiness, by the resurrection from the dead" (Romans 1:1–4).

Mansions

An Amazing Fact: *In July 2011, America's most expensive home went on the market for $175 million, surpassing previous sales of $100 million and $150 million. This home and estate in Wyoming includes a house, equestrian center, and massive acreage. Only the wealthiest in the nation could consider real estate like this!*

For the time, news regarding real estate typically focused on how poorly the housing market was doing, but this piece of news was different. The cost of this estate surpassed two large mansions purchased in California, one by a billionaire investor and another by a billionaire heiress. The Wyoming property would ultimately require a special buyer. The property's home is actually fairly modest, but the property covers more 1,750 acres and includes a large 52-stall equestrian center with an indoor and outdoor riding rink.

Since most people are more concerned with making the mortgage payment than finding the perfect mansion to fulfill our dreams, a piece of property like this is mind-boggling. We're focused on making ends meet, not buying a million-dollar estate. But King David reminds us in one of his psalms that earthly wealth of this sort is only temporary. "Do not be overawed when others grow rich...for they will take nothing with them when they die." Money and property are only here for a season before they vanish, but our heavenly treasure will last forever. Keep your focus on what is eternal. Sharing the love of God with our family, friends, and those around us will have more lasting consequences than storing up earthly wealth.

KEY BIBLE TEXT: "Do not be overawed when others grow rich, when the splendor of their houses increases; for they will take nothing with them when they die, their splendor will not descend with them" (Psalm 49:17).

DAY 63 The Greatest Banquet

An Amazing Fact: *The largest single dish served in the world is roasted camel. To celebrate a wedding or honor a visiting dignitary, Mohammedan tribes in the Arabian, Syrian, and North African deserts usually give a feast where the main dish is without equal. This is how the stuffed camel is put together: Eggs are stuffed inside fish; fish are, in turn, stuffed into chickens; the chickens are then stuffed into sheep, which are roasted. Then the entire cooked sheep are stuffed into a camel. This colossal culinary concoction is the main course at these special feasts. Would you like fries with that?*

Jesus tells the story of a wedding feast in which a king prepares a banquet for his son and daughter-in-law. Social gatherings in Bible times often involved large quantities of food. Unfortunately, the guests in Christ's parable are not willing to come. The king sends out servants again, "Tell those who are invited, 'See, I have prepared my dinner; my oxen and fatted cattle are killed, and all things are ready. Come to the wedding'" (Matthew 22:4). Once more the guests spurn the invitation. The king destroys them.

"Then he said to his servants, 'The wedding is ready, but those who were invited were not worthy. Therefore go into the highways, and as many as you find, invite to the wedding'" (vs. 8, 9). The Pharisees listening to Jesus viewed the Jews as sitting down to eat a great meal while the Gentiles looked on with jealousy. Jesus showed that the very ones first called turned away from the invitation. Everyone is invited to the marriage banquet.

Christ calls us to come to a wedding banquet prepared for those who love Him. "Blessed are those who are called to the marriage supper of the Lamb!" (Revelation 19:9). What excuses do we make? Are we so preoccupied that we miss the greatest feast ever made? Or do we feel that we have an exclusive right to this banquet but are not truly ready? Unless we have on Christ's robe of righteousness (the wedding garment), we will be cast out (v. 12). God wants all to come to the great supper.

KEY BIBLE TEXT: "For many are called, but few are chosen" (Matthew 22:14).

The Beginning of Wisdom

An Amazing Fact: *Abdul Kassem Ismael, Grand Vizier of Persia in the 10th century, traveled with his entire library, carried on the backs of 400 camels.*

During the Middle Ages, an Arab invasion into Iran resulted in sweeping changes to Persian life and culture. But some Iranian groups resisted Arabic influence and eventually regained their independence, launching a revival of Iranian national identity and culture that peaked during the 9th and 10th centuries.

Part of this cultural movement was the development of Persian literature, keeping the Persian language alive and securing its place as an important Indo-European language. Persian remains Iran's official language today. After the 10th century, Persian literature played a formative role in Muslim civilization.

Around this time, Abdul Kassem Ismael (A.D. 938 to 995) became Grand Vizier of Persia. Legend has it that the avid reader was so enthralled with literature and learning that he never left home without his personal library. The 400-camel caravan carried 117,000 books and must have been more than a mile long! Nevertheless, Ismael's camel-drivers were also librarians, each responsible for the books on his camel, and could locate any book almost immediately because the animals were trained to walk in alphabetical order.

The Bible says that "the fear of the Lord is the beginning of wisdom" (Psalm 111:10; Proverbs 1:7; Proverbs 9:10) and "knowledge of the Holy One is understanding" (Proverbs 9:10). We may, like Ismael, pursue all the knowledge of the Lord. But Paul says that if we don't have love, we are nothing. (1 Corinthians 13:2). John says that when we know God, we love. (1 John 4:7, 8) True wisdom—a knowledge of God—will result in His love being embodied in us. Until then, our knowledge means nothing.

KEY BIBLE TEXTS: "The fear of the Lord is the beginning of wisdom, and the knowledge of the Holy One is understanding" (Proverbs 9:10). "And though I understand all mysteries and all knowledge, ...but I have not love, I am nothing" (1 Corinthians 13:2).

DAY 65 The Second Great Commandment

An Amazing Fact: *In 2010, almost 200,000 people in 153 countries were surveyed about helping others during the previous month. The survey found that about 20 percent had done volunteer work, almost a third had given money to charity, and about 45 percent had helped a stranger. Surprisingly, half of the top 20 most charitable countries are developing countries, and the happiest countries—not necessarily the most wealthy ones—tended to give the most (maybe that's why they are the happiest).*

Julie's husband had been laid off work, and they had been forced to accept government assistance for the first time. It was difficult, especially since they had a small child and one on the way.

One afternoon a knock sounded at the door, and Julie answered it. There stood a stranger holding bags brimming with groceries.

"I hope you don't mind," the lady said, an apologetic look on her face. "I heard there were some financial difficulties, and I just wanted to help."

Julie stood there and cried over the kindness. She offered to pay for the food, but the lady would not accept money. Instead she suggested, "When you get back on your feet, you can do the same for someone else."

Julie has been blessed in following the stranger's advice. There is always a blessing in doing good for others.

KEY BIBLE TEXT: "Then one of them, a lawyer, asked Him a question, testing Him, and saying, 'Teacher, which is the great commandment in the law?' Jesus said to him, '"You shall love the LORD your God with all your heart, with all your soul, and with all your mind." This is the first and great commandment. And the second is like it: "You shall love your neighbor as yourself." On these two commandments hang all the Law and the Prophets'" (Matthew 22:35–40).

Hypocrisy

An Amazing Fact: *A police chief in the Seattle area was arrested and sentenced to several years in prison for swindling disabled citizens of their social security money, the very people he was paid to protect!*

Police chief Charles Allen of Granite Falls, Washington, was sentenced to five years in prison for embezzling money from disabled citizens. The chief used the label of a non-profit agency, allegedly helping manage finances for citizens in need. But rather than assisting his clients in making the best use of their funds, Allen admitted to unlawfully taking up to $14,000 for himself on a monthly basis, for a total of more than $600,000 over several years.

A special assistant attorney called Allen's deed an "act of extreme hypocrisy." As a police chief, his duty was to protect the citizens of his city, but instead the city had to step in and protect citizens from him. The chief knew that his clients were mentally and physically unable to manage their funds for themselves, yet he did not hesitate to steal from their small monthly checks.

It is easy to recognize the abhorrence of Allen's actions. Jesus clearly taught His followers not to follow in the paths of hypocrites who "say, and do not do," and Allen's crime is a clear example of such hypocrisy. But we might find ourselves sliding into hypocrisy on a smaller level. A Christian life is more than becoming a part of Christian subculture and living under a Christian label. Do our lives reflect the Savior we profess to follow? Do our words and attitudes to others speak of God's love?

KEY BIBLE TEXT: "Then Jesus spoke to the multitudes and to His disciples, saying: 'The scribes and the Pharisees sit in Moses' seat. Therefore whatever they tell you to observe, that observe and do, but do not do according to their works; for they say, and do not do'" (Matthew 23:1–3).

DAY 67 God's Positioning System

An Amazing Fact: *Ancient explorers knew their exact location based on the sun, moon, and stars. Between 1768 and 1775, the British explorer James Cook made two voyages around the world, charting much of the South Pacific, using nothing more than a sextant, a simple compass, and the heavens above for navigation. For years, submarine navigation was a big problem. These secret vessels had to frequently surface to get their basic bearings, exposing themselves to enemy fire. But eventually, the U.S. Navy developed the internal marine gyro-navigation system. This sophisticated apparatus enabled subs to get a precise fix on their location even while isolated deep beneath the surface of a dark ocean.*

If you don't know where you are, you can put yourself at greater risk of getting hurt. Have you ever taken the wrong exit and ended up in a risky part of a city? GPS (global positioning system) units are becoming standard in most vehicles. Using satellite technology, they help you know your exact location. James Cook's GPS unit was the sun, moon, and stars.

If you are going to avoid enemy fire, you need to know where you are. The U.S. Navy's gyro-navigation system was fully proven in 1958 when the USS Nautilus accomplished the impossible. With 116 men on board, the nuclear-powered vessel became the first submarine to traverse the Arctic Ocean under the polar ice. It traveled from the Bering Strait to Iceland via the North Pole in four days. Unable to surface, had the system failed, the crew would have been doomed.

David called on God to save him from his enemies. "For strangers have risen up against me, and oppressors have sought after my life; they have not set God before them" (Psalm 54:3). David's navigation system was turning to the Lord. He set God before him and could praise the Lord. "He has delivered me out of all trouble" (v. 7).

KEY BIBLE TEXT: "Trust in the Lord with all your heart, and lean not on your own understanding; in all your ways acknowledge Him, and He shall direct your paths" (Proverbs 3:5, 6).

Not Merely Outward

An Amazing Fact: *Before the 1930s, diamonds were rarely given as engagement rings.*

Egyptians worshiped the circle as a symbol of eternity. They plaited rings out of reeds and gifted them to symbolize everlasting love. They wore them on the third finger of their left hands because they believed the vein of that finger traveled directly from the heart. The Greeks learned this tradition from Egypt, passing it to Rome and beyond. But it wasn't until a diamond cartel coined the best advertising slogan of the 20th century for the hardest substance in nature, convincing us that "a diamond is forever."

In the Bible, a king's ring symbolized his authority. Rings were given to trusted servants (Genesis 41:41, 42), to potential mates (Genesis 24:22), and in celebration (Luke 15:22). Like today, jewelry and fine clothing were also used simply for beauty (Ezekiel 16:11–14). Of what purpose are the gems and bright colors God created except to lend beauty? We express ourselves through our wardrobes, homes, and landscapes. But self-expression goes awry when we rely on clothing, hairdos, houses, cars, gardens, and gadgets for our value (Ezekiel 16:15).

Swinging the pendulum in the other direction, Puritanism shunned the use of superfluities like jewels, color, and modern technology. But Peter's balanced approach, "Do not let your adornment be merely outward" (1 Peter 3:3), ensures that the beauty of your character matches—or exceeds!—that of your person or possessions.

In Haggai, God promises His people a ring as a sign of being chosen (Haggai 2:23). But even better, God adorns us with the "garments of salvation" and the "robe of righteousness" (Isaiah 61:10). It's okay to surround yourself with beauty, but don't let it replace the beauty of salvation.

KEY BIBLE TEXT: "Where can wisdom be found?... It cannot be purchased for gold, nor can silver be weighed for its price. ... Neither gold nor crystal can equal it, nor can it be exchanged for jewelry of fine gold. ... For the price of wisdom is above rubies" (Job 28:12–18).

DAY 69 Whose Slave Are You?

An Amazing Fact: *It is estimated that there are more people in slavery today than at any previous time in history, with estimates as high as 27 million. The majority of these are debt slaves living in southern Asia.*

In a sense, we are all slaves. We serve either righteousness or unrighteousness—God or sin. There is no neutral ground; we serve either one or the other.

Sin is a deceptive and brutal taskmaster. There is no real or lasting benefit in it. It does not easily release its subjects. And in the end it pays out death to its slaves.

But the Scripture says that being a slave of obedience gives hope. It leads to righteousness and, ultimately, eternal life.

How can a slave to sin change masters? If sin has a grip, how can one be freed? The only way to be rescued from this hopeless situation is to accept God's gift. To anyone who asks, He will give freedom, forgiveness from sin, and everlasting life in Christ Jesus. That is the grace He offers to everyone.

KEY BIBLE TEXT: "What then? Shall we sin because we are not under law but under grace? Certainly not! Do you not know that to whom you present yourselves slaves to obey, you are that one's slaves whom you obey, whether of sin leading to death, or of obedience leading to righteousness? ... What fruit did you have then in the things of which you are now ashamed? For the end of those things is death. But now having been set free from sin, and having become slaves of God, you have your fruit to holiness, and the end, everlasting life. For the wages of sin is death, but the gift of God is eternal life in Christ Jesus our Lord" (Romans 6:15, 16, 21–23).

The Fig Tree

DAY 70

An Amazing Fact: *Figs are a tasty fruit common to the Middle East, but one fact about their pollination might cause some consumers to squirm with distaste. All figs must be pollinated by a fig wasp, after which the wasp dies and decomposes inside the fruit!*

Throughout nature, God created mutual relationships necessary to sustain life. Pollination is one such relationship. In the case of the fig plant, pollination must occur with the help of a small wasp. Female fig wasps implant themselves inside of either the male or female (edible) fig, both of which grow on the same plant. In either case, the wasp will pollinate the fig. Inside the male fig, the wasp lays her eggs. But if she lands in a female fig, she will be unable to lay her eggs and eventually dies.

Does this mean there is a female wasp inside that fig you bought at your local grocery store? No! Figs contain an enzyme called ficin, which breaks down and essentially digests the wasp, making it a part of the fruit. While this might cause you to shiver a little as you bite into a fresh fig and feel a crunch, the crunching is only from the fig seeds, not from a dead wasp!

Jesus had another lesson for us to learn from figs in the book of Matthew. He described to His followers a familiar sight to their eyes: "Now learn this lesson from the fig tree: as soon as its twigs get tender and its leaves come out, you know that summer is near." Jesus reminded His listeners that, similarly, they had knowledge of what the world would be like before His return. "Watch," He warned them. "Be ready!" Jesus calls us to be watchful, ever ready for His soon return!

KEY BIBLE TEXT: "Now learn this lesson from the fig tree: As soon as its twigs get tender and its leaves come out, you know that summer is near. Even so, when you see all these things, you know that it is near, right at the door" (Matthew 24:32, 33).

DAY 71 Wicked and Deadly

An Amazing Fact: *Cobra venom is not the strongest in the world, but cobras can inject so much venom in a single bite that they can kill an elephant. Moreover, cobras are the only snake in the world that can spit their venom. Still, cobras are not poisonous; they are venomous. That means they have deadly venom, yes, but the rest of the snake is edible to predators if they dare to try!*

The King Cobra is not a snake you would want to run into when going for an afternoon stroll. Most cobras are shy and will run when people are around. Not the King Cobra. It is aggressive and will rear up and stand its ground when confronted. There are actually hundreds of different types of cobra snakes. The King is the longest venomous snake in the world and grows to 18 feet long. Some have measured at 20 feet long!

In Psalm 58 David describes the judgment of the wicked. He says, "The wicked are estranged from the womb; they go astray as soon as they are born, speaking lies. Their poison is like the poison of a serpent" (v. 3). It is interesting that the baby cobra has full strength venom and can defend itself just like the parent. Sin is deadly! We should avoid it at all costs.

David continues, "They are like the deaf cobra that stops its ear, which will not heed the voice of charmers, charming ever so skillfully" (vs. 4, 5). A cobra's best hearing comes not from it ears but through sensations through the ground. Most charmers will remove the fangs and venom sacs from cobras because they are so dangerous.

Living a wicked life makes our words deadly. We become stubborn and will not listen. In the end God will judge the wicked and they will be destroyed. Let us strive to live a pure and righteous life. Let our words bring life, not death.

KEY BIBLE TEXT: "Now the serpent was more cunning than any beast of the field which the Lord God had made. And he said to the woman, 'Has God indeed said, "You shall not eat of every tree of the garden?"'" (Genesis 3:1).

Embryo Adoption

An Amazing Fact: *While the concept of adoption is fairly common in today's world, a new type of adoption is lesser known: embryo adoption. Embryo adoption allows an infertile couple to adopt a life beginning with pregnancy!*

Today's technology has created a number of ethical questions. One such question is what to do with frozen embryos, created as a result of infertile couples attempting in vitro fertilization. When a couple has successfully achieved pregnancy, there might be embryos left over and stored. If a couple is finished having children, they are forced to decide what to do with these embryos. Should they allow these lives to be destroyed? Or continue to pay to have them stored for an unknown length of time?

Some families have chosen a third alternative. Giving up their embryos for adoption opens the door for other infertile couples to raise these children as their own. This incredible opportunity allows the adoptive parents the chance to experience pregnancy and childbirth with their adopted child. While the child is not biologically their own and does not share their DNA, [illegible]re able to look back on their journey as a family from an earlier point [illegible]er before.

[illegible]mans, Paul describes a similar analogy. He points out that "it is [illegible]ildren by physical descent who are God's children, but it is the [illegible]the promise who are regarded as Abraham's offspring." God's [illegible]de not only the physical children of Israel, but also all who [illegible] the promise of Messiah. We don't need the literal physical [illegible] DNA as it were, to be part of God's family. When we accept [illegible]lvation, we are adopted into His family!

KEY BIBLE TEXT: "In other words, it is not the children by physical descent who are God's children, but it is the children of the promise who are regarded as Abraham's offspring" (Romans 9:8).

DAY 75 Singing Sand

An Amazing Fact: *Did you know that sand can sing? Often referred to as singing or booming sand, this rare sand produces a tone when walked on or blown around by the wind. Some sands will even create sparks of light at night when walked or driven across. This sand creates sound waves by the friction caused between the grains of this sand's unique crystalline structure.*

God promised Abraham that, because of his faith, his descendants would multiply as the "sand which is on the seashore" (Genesis 22:17). That's a lot of sand! There are other interesting properties of sand that can teach us about being a true son of Abraham. Not all sand is sand. Carbonate sand will completely dissolve in vinegar. Paul quotes Isaiah 10 when he writes, "Though the number of the children of Israel be as the sand of the sea, the remnant will be saved" (Romans 9:27). That is, not all "sand" will be saved.

Some sand is magnetic. If you happen to notice black particles in sand, run a magnet across the sand. There might be particles of iron or magnetite mixed in. It is interesting that sand that contains magnetite often is sa
that contains gold. We often look at other people and judge them
but God can see deep inside humans and knows who His true follo

As mentioned in the amazing fact, some sand sings! But it
harder to find such sand, as modern pollution tends to coat the san
and destroy its ability to produce sound. At the time of this wri
it still exists on every continent of the world. That describes
who come from every nation, tribe, kindred, tongue, and p
harder and harder to find because sin pollutes people. But
will gather before God's throne and sing.

KEY BIBLE TEXT: "They sing the song of Moses, the servant of God, and the song of the Lamb, saying: 'Great and marvelous are Your works, Lord God Almighty! Just and true are Your ways, O King of the saints!'" (Revelation 15:3).

Opening the Way

An Amazing Fact: *A 60-year-old man of genius, Pierre-Paul de Riquet began the grandest project of his life when most his age are thinking retirement. In the 17th century, the intrepid French engineer conceived the idea of constructing a canal across France from the Mediterranean to the Atlantic. Since the government refused to share the cost of the gigantic enterprise, he assumed the enormous project himself.*

Riquet's design called for a canal that traveled uphill to a point and then downhill the other way, like crossing a bridge, whereas most canals of the day simply descended. This design would serve to save time and help ships avoid pirates lurking along the straits of Gibraltar. It would also join the economies of the Mediterranean to the Atlantic. With shovels and primitive tools, 12,000 laborers worked 14 years from 1666 to 1681 to create the incredibly long trench.

During its construction, Pierre-Paul Riquet oversaw the entire project. The 79-foot-wide passageway with its 8-foot depth, 228 bridges, and 114 locks, gradually lifted water 621 feet and then back down to the level of the Atlantic. This feat beckoned the amazement and the admiration of all Europe. King Louis XIV referred to it as the greatest achievement of his entire 72-year reign.

This purely civil project was paid for by the money of one man—158 miles costing $68 million. It came from his fortune earned as the salt-tax collector. He sacrificed everything to ensure the canal's completion—even using his wife's fortune and his daughters' dowries for the cause. Six months before its completion, Riquet, exhausted and sick, retired at home and died without ever seeing his life's masterpiece achieved.

The Bible describes the Lord's power with these words: "By awesome deeds in righteousness You will answer us, O God of our salvation, You who are the confidence of all the ends of the earth, And of the far-off seas" (Psalm 65:5). Just as Riquet gave his life to open a waterway that brought strength to France through his famous canal, so Jesus performed an awesome deed when He gave His life to bridge the gap between heaven and earth.

KEY BIBLE TEXT: "Thomas said to Him, 'Lord ... how can we know the way?' Jesus said to him, 'I am the way'" (John 14:5, 6).

DAY 79 Fit for a Temple

An Amazing Fact: *Metamorphic rocks are created when other types of rocks are transformed due to great pressure and heat within the earth. The meaning of the term "metamorphic," in fact, is "changed." When igneous rocks, sedimentary rocks, or even metamorphic rocks get buried very deep under the earth's surface, they get changed into something else by the enormous pressure and heat inside the earth.*

Metamorphosis is a word we often associate with caterpillars and butterflies or tadpoles and frogs. But rocks can change too. For instance, limestone can be changed into marble and shale can turn into slate. The process requires an intense amount of pressure.

Marble is a beautiful stone that can be polished. That's why it is often used in elaborate buildings for bathtubs, floors, and countertops. Marble is also a popular stone used for carvings to make statutes. There are many different types of marble because of various elements present during formation. It also has different sizes of crystals, which make for a wonderful variety of this rock. And it all comes from sandstone, which is a soft stone that easily crumbles.

Paul urges the Christians in Rome, "And do not be conformed to this world, but be transformed by the renewing of your mind, that you may prove what is that good and acceptable and perfect will of God" (Romans 12:2). God wants you to be changed into something beautiful for the Lord's temple, a pillar or a vessel that serves others. How does this happen? Often under pressure. Some of the hardest lessons in life come from difficulties. But as we persevere our hearts are changed. We become more like Christ, fit to be in a heavenly temple.

KEY BIBLE TEXT: "I beseech you therefore, brethren, by the mercies of God, that you present your bodies a living sacrifice, holy, acceptable to God, which is your reasonable service" (Romans 12:1).

Whom Will You Choose?

An Amazing Fact: *According to early Greek manuscripts, the full name of Barabbas, the prisoner who was released instead of Jesus, was actually Jesus Barabbas.*

The story of Barabbas is an interesting one. The Gospel accounts explain how Pontius Pilate gave the Jewish people the choice of releasing Jesus or Barabbas. Sadly, the people called for Barabbas to be released and for Jesus to be crucified.

Barabbas was a notorious prisoner who had caused insurrection in Jerusalem, ultimately committing murder. He was a hardened criminal. Yet what is perhaps most interesting about him is his name. According to the early Greek manuscripts of Matthew 27:16, his first name was also "Jesus," which, in Hebrew, means "the Lord saves." Furthermore, the name "Barabbas" means "son of the father" in Aramaic.

So the Jewish people were faced with a choice between two saviors. They could choose Jesus Christ or Jesus "son of the father." The first Jesus came to give eternal salvation, achieved by grace through faith. The second Jesus came pursuing earthly salvation, achieved by violence.

At the heart of the choice between the two was an understanding of what the character of the heavenly Father really is. Either He is a God of vengeance who takes life, or He is a God of love that gives life. And so the Jewish people chose to reflect their understanding of Him and took life.

Yet in their act of taking life, Christ was able to give life.

Of course, it wasn't them alone who chose to take Christ's life. All who have sinned have ultimately chosen Jesus Barabbas. But we can start afresh today and choose the life of Christ over the life of Barabbas.

KEY BIBLE TEXT: "Choose for yourselves this day whom you will serve. ... But as for me and my house, we will serve the Lord" (Joshua 24:16).

DAY 81 Ultimate Peace Prize

An Amazing Fact: *The youngest person to receive the Nobel Peace Prize was Mairead Corrigan, co-founder of the Northern Ireland Peace Movement. She received the prestigious award in 1976 at the age of 32. The oldest recipient was Joseph Rotblat, who received the prize in 1995 at the age of 87. He, along with his organization, worked to diminish nuclear arms in the world.*

Do you know any peacemakers? Some people seem to be born peacemakers. They devote their lives to it. They truly deserve rewards. Others might think they deserve some kind of a peace prize, considering whom they have to contend with on a daily basis!

Since the Scripture says we should "live peaceably with all men" as much as possible, and since it's not in our human nature to do so, we need to find the source of true peace.

The Bible mentions peace 384 times. Here is a sampling of peace verses: "Grace, mercy, and peace will be with you from God the Father and from the Lord Jesus Christ" (2 John 1:3). "Now may the Lord of peace Himself give you peace always in every way" (2 Thessalonians 3:16). "And let the peace of God rule in your hearts" (Colossians 3:15). Only God can give us peace, for He is the Source.

Jesus deserves the ultimate peace prize, for He has "made peace through the blood of His cross" (Colossians 1:20). The "Prince of Peace" has reconciled us to God. And being at peace with God is an excellent starting point for being at peace with one another.

KEY BIBLE TEXT: "Repay no one evil for evil. Have regard for good things in the sight of all men. If it is possible, as much as depends on you, live peaceably with all men. Do not be overcome by evil, but overcome evil with good" (Romans 12:17, 18, 21).

Scarlet Red

DAY 82

An Amazing Fact: *Scarlet is a bright red color with a hue that leans toward orange. It is sometimes used as the color of a flame but is often used to describe the color of blood from a living person. The earliest use of the word in the English language to describe a color dates to 1250.*

Scarlet is a popular color. It is used in academic dress in the United Kingdom for people awarded doctorates and the undergraduate gowns in the ancient universities of Scotland. In the United States, scarlet is used for the hood borders and other parts to denote a degree in some form of branch of theology. Scarlet is also used in military uniforms. The colors of the United States Marine Corps are scarlet and gold. It is an official school color for many educational institutions and the official color for dozens of sports teams.

It's also been used in literature. We've all heard of The Scarlett Letter and Scarlett O'Hara in the novel Gone With the Wind. Scarlet is a women's magazine in the UK, a vocal duo, an American music band, a telecommunications company, a Welsh rugby team, and the name of a camera. It's even the name of a type of streptococcal infection called "Scarlet Fever."

The Bible talks about the color scarlet (also called crimson). "Then the soldiers of the governor took Jesus in to the Praetorium, and gathered the whole garrison around Him. And they stripped Him and put a scarlet robe on Him. When they had twisted a crown of thorns, they put it on His head, and a reed in His right hand. And they bowed the knee before Him and mocked Him, saying, 'Hail, King of the Jews!'" (Matthew 27:27–29).

Why did Christ wear a robe of scarlet? Isaiah gives us the answer when Israel's sins are described as "scarlet" and "crimson." Jesus took upon Himself our sins. He carried our iniquities on His shoulders. Scarlet is a popular color—too popular and common—because it describes our sinful condition. We should be glad Christ wore scarlet that we may be clean. "Wash me, and I shall be whiter than snow" (Psalms 51:7).

KEY BIBLE TEXT: "'Come now, and let us reason together,' says the Lord, 'Though your sins are like scarlet, They shall be as white as snow'" (Isaiah 1:18).

DAY 83 Clothed in Christ

An Amazing Fact: *Levis Straus made working pants out of denim for people during the California gold rush. The Levis company is now the world's largest maker of jeans. The YKK on the zipper of your Levis stands for Yoshida Kogyo Kabushibibaisha, the world's largest zipper manufacturer.*

What is one of the most popular pieces of casual clothing worn in the world? Denim jeans. Blue jeans are especially connected to American culture. Originally created for the working class, jeans became a favorite of teenagers in the 1950s. They now come in many styles such as skinny, straight, tapered, boot cut, maternity, and flare. In 1850 the cost for a pair of jeans was about $1.50, which is approximately $95 in today's money value. Americans spent about $15 billion for jeans in 2005.

You've heard the phrase, "You are what you wear." Clothing styles are important to most people. They want to be viewed in a certain way. It is interesting to apply adjectives used for jeans to moral values: casual, loose, or flared. We certainly can be impacted by our clothing.

Perhaps that is why the apostle Paul encouraged us to "put on Christ." The terminology in Romans 13 is the same used for putting on clothing. He writes, "But put on the Lord Jesus Christ, and make no provision for the flesh, to fulfill its lusts" (Romans 13:14). To "put on" Christ means to wear the mindset of Jesus and to walk in the ways of the Lord. It is much more than wearing a certain type of clothing. It means to behave so much like Jesus that we are mistaken for Christ by others.

The oldest pair of Levi's jeans still around was made around the 1890s and is on display at Strauss & Co. Archives in San Francisco. But what Christ offers is a garment that will never wear out. One bale of cotton can make 215 jeans. Jesus has a supply that will never fail. Put on Christ today.

KEY BIBLE TEXT: "For as many of you as were baptized into Christ have put on Christ" (Galatians 3:27).

A Sign From Above

An Amazing Fact: *The world's largest sign was set up in Gloucestershire, England. Standing at 50 feet high, the sign stretched for 270 feet!*

The sign was actually raised as a humorous stunt at one of England's premier horse racing tracks. Paddy Power, Ireland's largest bookmaker, where people can place bets, decided to pre-empt the horse track's primary sponsor for its marquee race in March 2010. They concocted the plan to raise the gigantic Hollywood-style sign on Cleeve Hill, overlooking the racetrack. It took planners three years to design the white-lettered sign, and then it required a 60-man crew working a total of 1,000 hours to raise it.

One would think that everyone would be excited about the record-setting sign. But just the opposite was the case. Officials from the racetrack and town were not enthused at all about the eyesore, ultimately threatening legal action if the company did not take it down. Paddy Power's hand was forced, and they took it down after the race was over.

In Deuteronomy 27, we read about instructions Moses gave the children of Israel for when they crossed over the Jordan River. They were to set up large stones, whitewash them with lime, and then write God's law upon them. The large stones, with the writing upon them, was to keep a reminder before the people of God's law, His leading, and His claims on their lives.

God wishes to raise signs in our lives as well, reminding us of His leading in our lives. More than this, though, He longs to write His law upon our hearts (see Jeremiah 31:31–34), so that we, like David, will say that we "delight" to do God's will (Psalms 40:8).

KEY BIBLE TEXT: "And these words which I command you today shall be in your heart. You shall teach them diligently to your children, and shall talk of them when you sit in your house, when you walk by the way, when you lie down, and when you rise up" (Deuteronomy 6:6, 7).

DAY 85 Don't Sink!

An Amazing Fact: *Not all types of quicksand are created equal. Most quicksand is slow and relatively easy to escape from. But if a fast-flowing water source lies beneath it, the quicksand is called "super-quick." It can appear as solid as concrete, but a human being who steps on it will sink instantly. If you're hiking in an area known for quicksand, it's a good idea to carry a pole as an escape tool.*

The scary thing about quicksand is that you can never see below the surface. You don't know how deep it goes or how fast you might sink into it. Farm animals, humans, and machinery have been engulfed by quicksand. According to historical records, in 1875 a train that derailed from a bridge in Colorado sank so deep in quicksand that it was never found.

The Bible mentions several instances when someone or something was sinking. When David was sinking into the "deep mire" of trials and discouragement, he called to God for help. When Peter was sinking in the waves of the sea, he cried out, "Lord, save me!" When their boat was sinking, the disciples turned to Jesus for help. They obviously looked to the right Deliverer, because He rescued them all.

If you find yourself sinking in the spiritual quicksand of sin, trouble, or discouragement, no matter how deep, God is waiting to lift you up. Don't sink—take His outstretched hand!

KEY BIBLE TEXT: "I sink in deep mire, where there is no standing. ... But as for me, my prayer is to You, O LORD, in the acceptable time; O God, in the multitude of Your mercy, hear me in the truth of Your salvation. Deliver me out of the mire, and let me not sink" (Psalm 69:2, 13, 14).

Truly Dead

An Amazing Fact: *When Harold West died, his doctor drove a stake through his heart to make sure he was dead. When he was buried, they did not nail his coffin shut just in case he was not completely dead. But West was no vampire; he was just an overcautious banker who deathly feared to be buried alive. When West died at 90, he left a will directing that "my coffin shall not be screwed down and that a surgeon be instructed to pierce my heart with a steel or other instrument to make certain death has occurred."*

There are other strange will bequests to be carried out after people died. Gene Roddenberry, the creator of the Star Trek series on television, had his ashes flown into space on a Spanish satellite and then shot out as the satellite orbited the earth.

Predeceased by his wife and two daughters, John Bowman, from Vermont, was convinced that after his death, in 1891, the whole family would be reincarnated. In anticipation, he left a trust fund for the maintenance of his 21-room mansion, including a demand that servants prepare dinner nightly in case the Bowmans were hungry when they returned. The money ran out in 1950.

For years, critics have said the resurrection never happened because Jesus was not actually dead when they buried Him, but rather in a comatose state from which He revived. Even some pastors are saying that Jesus was not really dead in the tomb, but that He entered a different realm to preach to the lost from past ages. But what does the Bible say?

"Now when evening had come, there came a rich man from Arimathea, named Joseph, who himself had also become a disciple of Jesus. This man went to Pilate and asked for the body of Jesus. Then Pilate commanded the body to be given to him. When Joseph had taken the body, he wrapped it in a clean linen cloth" (Matthew 27:57–59). Even the chief priests testified to Pilate, "Sir, we remember, while He was still alive ..." (v. 63). Christ's own enemies testified that Jesus was truly dead.

But that is not the end of the story...

KEY BIBLE TEXT: "And Jesus cried out again with a loud voice, and yielded up His spirit" (Matthew 27:50).

DAY 87 Real Strength

An Amazing Fact: *The heaviest car ever balanced on a person's head was 352 lbs. On May 24, 1999, John Evans of England balanced a Mini on his head for 33 seconds. John was around six-and-a-half feet tall and weighed 343 pounds at the time. He also had a strong 24-inch neck. The trick was dangerous because if he stumbled, he would not have been able to move quickly enough to push the car aside.*

You might be surprised at the feats of human strength people attempt these days. Tyler Yamauchi holds the world record for Roman Rings hanging duration (32.84 seconds). What are the most push-ups done in one hour—on the back of one's hands? Paddy Doyle did 1,940 reps on November 8, 2007. But some records make you wonder: Zafar Gill of Pakistan broke a record that would hurt your ears. He lifted a 160-pound gym weight with a clamp attached to the lobe of his ear!

The Bible talks about how we should really use our strength. Paul writes, "We then who are strong ought to bear with the scruples of the weak, and not to please ourselves" (Romans 15:1). A chapter earlier, the apostle introduces this idea: "Receive one who is weak in the faith, but not to disputes over doubtful things" (14:1). Evidently, there were Jewish converts who had some doubts about religious practices. Paul calls some of these practices "doubtful things." In other words, there are some practices that are scripturally sound and should be followed (keeping the Ten Commandments, for example), but there are others that are based on traditions of men (how to wash before eating food).

If people are genuinely seeking to follow after the Lord, strong Christians should be considerate of them. They should not use their strength to hammer others over the head. A judgmental attitude might damage other Christians, especially those young in the faith.

You might be tempted to break a world record by lifting a weight with your ear lobe. But it is much better to use your ears to listen to and care for other Christians new in the faith.

KEY BIBLE TEXT: "But beware lest somehow this liberty of yours become a stumbling block to those who are weak" (1 Corinthians 8:9).

The Eagle's Wings

An Amazing Fact: *The wingspan of an eagle can reach up to eight feet, enabling it to reach speeds of 40 miles per hour in flight and 100 miles per hour when diving.*

The eagle has captured people's imaginations for thousands of years. This majestic bird is not the biggest or most powerful bird in the world, but its combination of quickness, strength, and incredible eyesight has caused it to stand head and shoulders above other birds in the human psyche.

When these abilities are combined with their wingspans, it makes for a very impressive specimen—especially when observed in their nests, which can be as much as 13 feet deep and weigh more than a ton. (One record-setting bald eagle's nest in Florida measured in at 20 feet deep, 10 feet wide, and weighed nearly three tons!)

It is no wonder that the Bible often employs the imagery of an eagle to illustrate the character and actions of God. Moses, in Deuteronomy 32:11, 12, describes God's care of Israel in this way: "As an eagle stirs up its nest, hovers over its young, spreading out its wings, taking them up, carrying them on its wings, so the Lord alone led him."

God's "wings" provide the ultimate safety for all who will come under them. They offer optimal protection and unsurpassed security. More than this, they are wide enough and large enough to take in all who would respond to the Spirit's biddings. None need worry whether there is room enough under the wings of heaven's Eagle, for Jesus Himself says, "Come to Me *all you* who are labor and are heavy laden, and I will give you rest" (Matthew 11:28, emphasis added).

KEY BIBLE TEXT: "You have seen what I did to the Egyptians, and how I bore you on eagles' wings and brought you to Myself" (Exodus 19:4).

DAY 89 Rejoicing Always

An Amazing Fact: *Some science studies suggest that happiness might be more important to health than diet or exercise! A few of the benefits of happiness are decreased blood pressure, increased energy, better mental health, improved relationships, and more creativity. Some of the best ways to increase your happiness are: exercise, doing kind things for others, counting your blessings, and praising God.*

David is a prime example of a person who praised God no matter what was happening in his life. Many of the Psalms were written when David was in dire trouble. Psalm 70 seems to be one of these. It starts out with a plea: "Make haste, O God, to deliver me! Make haste to help me, O LORD. Let them be ashamed and confounded who seek my life; let them be turned back and confused who desire my hurt" (vs. 1, 2).

Threatened by enemies who wanted to murder him, David sat down and wrote a song. While it contains urgent pleas for help, it also contains powerful praises to the Lord.

We can see this pattern repeated in many of the Psalms of David. He knew where his strength came from; he knew the Source of his hope. In good times and bad—in all circumstances—he praised the God of heaven.

In spite of the difficulties in life, we have a God who loves us. He is always with us, for we are His children. He promises us forgiveness and eternal life. This gives us hope and a constant reason to rejoice in Him.

KEY BIBLE TEXT: "Let all those who seek You rejoice and be glad in You; and let those who love Your salvation say continually, 'Let God be magnified!'" (Psalm 70:4).

The Great Emancipator

An Amazing Fact: *While attempting to sign the Emancipation Proclamation, which legally freed all the slaves living in the southern states of America, Abraham Lincoln's hand shook so much that he had to put his pen down before adding his signature.*

After discussing the idea of the Emancipation Proclamation for many months with his cabinet, on January 1, 1863, at 11:00 AM, an initial draft of this monumental document was presented to Lincoln. While reading it over, however, Lincoln noticed a technical error that needed correcting, so he sent it back to the State Department.

In the meantime, since it was New Year's Day and the White House was open to the general public back them, Lincoln spent the next three hours shaking peoples' hands. Finally, after the crowds left, the corrected version of the proclamation was presented to him at 2:00 PM. It was then, after picking up the pen to sign it into law, that his hand began to shake.

You see, it wasn't shaking because he was nervous; it was shaking because his arm had become so stiff and numb from shaking hands for three hours. So he put the pen down and gained his composure, saying, "I never, in my life, felt more certain that I was doing right, than I do in signing this paper. ... If my hand trembles when I sign the Proclamation, all who examine the document hereafter will say, 'He hesitated.'"

Abraham Lincoln, who has often been called the "Great Emancipator," is a reflection of the human race's "Great Emancipator," Jesus Christ, who did not hesitate when called upon to liberate and redeem the human race—though His hands, as they were nailed to Calvary's tree, also shook. Thus, Solomon declares of Christ, "For He will deliver the needy when He cries ... and will save the souls of the needy. He will redeem their life from oppression and violence" (Psalms 72:12–14).

KEY BIBLE TEXT: "And one shall say unto him, What are these wounds in thine hands? Then he shall answer, Those with which I was wounded in the house of my friends" (Zechariah 13:6).

DAY 93 Miracles at the Jordan

An Amazing Fact: *The Jordan River begins near Mount Hermon and meanders 156 miles before ending at the Dead Sea. At its widest, the Jordan is about 20 yards across. South of the Sea of Galilee, the river is highly polluted, and some environmentalists fear that part of the river is in danger of dying.*

The Jordan River, which has been flowing for millennia, is one of the best-known waterways. Each year it is visited by thousands of Christian pilgrims from all over the world. The children of Israel had a long history with the Jordan, and it was the site of many miracles.

One of these miracles occurred under Joshua's leadership. The Ark of the Covenant was carried over the Jordan. When the priests' feet touched the water, the river receded and became dry land until all the people had crossed over. God always leads the way.

Though He was sinless, Jesus was baptized by John the Baptist in the Jordan. When He came up from the water, the symbol of the Spirit of God miraculously descended upon Him, and the Father voiced His approval of His Son.

Why was Jesus baptized? He was leading the way for us, setting an example. Baptism is important, a powerful symbol for death and resurrection. A person who is baptized dies to the old, destructive way of life and is resurrected to a new, victorious life in Christ.

KEY BIBLE TEXTS: "Behold, the ark of the covenant of the Lord of all the earth is crossing over before you into the Jordan" (Joshua 3:11). "It came to pass in those days that Jesus came from Nazareth of Galilee, and was baptized by John in the Jordan. And immediately, coming up from the water, He saw the heavens parting and the Spirit descending upon Him like a dove. Then a voice came from heaven, 'You are My beloved Son, in whom I am well pleased'" (Mark 1:9–11).

Jericho

An Amazing Fact: *Archaeological findings in the Middle East sometimes reveal surprising evidence linked to biblical accounts. The ruins of the ancient city of Jericho contain collapsed brick walls, including a small section of wall still standing, which might reflect the story of Rahab!*

In the 1950s, archaeologist Kathleen Kenyon conducted extensive exploration and research in the ruins of the ancient city of Jericho. She concluded that the city contained no evidence of the destruction recalled in the book of Joshua. But later researchers reexamined her work and found that her dating was incorrect. When the correct dates were applied to the findings, collapsed brick walls were found surrounding the city exactly as we would expect.

And what about the story of Rahab? The book of Joshua records that Rahab's home and family were saved from destruction when she followed the instructions of the Israelite spies and hung a scarlet cord from her window. Interestingly, a short stretch of the city's mud brick wall was left standing with houses positioned against it. This portion of the wall was even on the north side of the city, a short distance from the hills to which the spies escaped.

In today's skeptical world, it can be easy to doubt the words of Scripture in the face of cynicism and doubt. But God's Word stands true. Increasingly, the stories of the Bible have been linked with archaeological evidence, revealing that these passages are far more than stories and legends. We can trust that God Himself has spoken to us through His Word. His message for us, from stories of instruction to words of comfort and hope, has been preserved for thousands of years.

KEY BIBLE TEXT: "And when you hear the sound of the trumpet, that all the people shall shout with a great shout; then the wall of the city will fall down flat" (Joshua 6:5).

DAY 95 God's Measure of Intelligence

An Amazing Fact: *How smart are you? IQ tests have been around since 1905. Though there are several different tests, an average IQ score is 100. A high IQ is not necessarily an indicator of wealth, ambition, or career success. It simply indicates that a person has higher-than-average reasoning abilities. The highest recorded IQ score of 250 was by William James Sidis—it's literally off the charts. He entered Harvard at the age of 11.*

Can you actually measure intelligence? Well, it depends on how you define "intelligence." Most would say intelligence is a very general mental capacity that involves the ability to plan, reason, think abstractly, solve problems, grasp complex ideas, learn quickly, and learn from experience. It's not just about being good at taking tests. It reflects a deeper capability of "catching on" and "making sense" of things.

One of the smartest people in the world as measured by IQ is Kim Ung-Yong of Korea. His score is 210, and he's called a genius. At age three he was solving complicated calculus problems. He received a Ph.D. in physics from Colorado State University when he was 16. Other smart people include Christopher Michael Langan (IQ 195), Philip Emeagwalie (IQ 190), Garry Kasparov (IQ 190), and Marilyn Vos Savant (IQ 186). Genius scores begin at 145.

But one thing is clear about the makers of IQ tests: They do not measure character. You can be smart in some ways and dumb in other ways! Character cannot be measured by standards set by mankind. Character is measured by God. The Bible says, "Let no one deceive himself. If anyone among you seems to be wise in this age, let him become a fool that he may become wise. For the wisdom of this world is foolishness with God" (1Corinthians 3:18, 19).

Your brain can weigh up to three pounds. Are you gifted or a genius? Think about how God would answer that question.

KEY BIBLE TEXT: "But the natural man does not receive the things of the Spirit of God, for they are foolishness to him; nor can he know them, because they are spiritually discerned" (1 Corinthians 2:14).

A Universal Theater

DAY 96

An Amazing Fact: *If you were driving in a car going the speed of light, it would take you 30 billion years to go from one end of the universe to the other.*

To say the universe is big would be an understatement. There is barely a word in English to describe the size of it. When measuring distances in the universe, scientists use a unit called "light years." This is the distance light can travel in a year. Since light travels 670 million miles per hour, light travels about six trillion miles in one year. Thus, the size of the universe is roughly 15 billion light years (or about 90 billion trillion miles), and it would take you 30 billion years to travel the distance of the universe if traveling at the speed of light.

Are you up for it?

Of course, perhaps just as fascinating is the number of galaxies—like our Milky Way—that are in the known universe. Scientists estimate there are 100 to 200 billion galaxies in the universe, with each galaxy having as many as 400 billion stars like our sun.

What is not known by scientists is whether life exists anywhere else in the universe. Many have postulated that there is, but thus far, no life has been discovered.

The Bible seems to hint at the idea of life existing beyond this planet—besides heaven, of course. Paul, in 1 Corinthians 4:9, curiously announces that "we have been made a spectacle to the whole universe, to angels as well as to men" (NIV). The Greek word for "spectacle" is literally "theater." Thus, apparently, beings throughout this huge universe are watching this small, little planet, waiting to see what unfolds in the drama between God and Satan.

We all have a critical part to play.

KEY BIBLE TEXT: "For the earnest expectation of the creation eagerly waits for the revealing of the sons of God" (Romans 8:19).

DAY 97 Seeing Our Need

An Amazing Fact: *Matthew was born near the Sea of Galilee. As an adult, he became employed by the Roman government as a collector of taxes. The Jews considered tax collectors "unclean" because of their association with Gentiles. They were also suspected of being thieves since many of them overcharged on taxes so they could keep the excess for themselves.*

"Tax collectors and sinners" was a phrase the Pharisees seemed to repeat during the ministry of Christ. They lumped together those who collected taxes for the Romans and common sinners. In the eyes of the Pharisees, they were some of the lowest forms of life—filthy, contaminated, and to be avoided at all costs. Yet Jesus and His disciples associated with these seedy people, and the Pharisees demanded to know why.

They first asked the disciples, and it would have been interesting to hear their replies. How would they have defended their Master's actions? Were they shocked that Jesus had chosen a tax collector to be one of them?

Jesus overheard the questions and answered the Pharisees, and they couldn't argue with His words. "I came to save the unsaved."

Jesus saw value in the people who were despised by the Pharisees. He saw great potential in the "sinners." Unlike the Pharisees, these outcasts saw their need of Christ and opened their hearts to Him.

KEY BIBLE TEXT: "Now it happened, as He was dining in Levi's house, that many tax collectors and sinners also sat together with Jesus and His disciples; for there were many, and they followed Him. And when the scribes and Pharisees saw Him eating with the tax collectors and sinners, they said to His disciples, 'How is it that He eats and drinks with tax collectors and sinners?' When Jesus heard it, He said to them, 'Those who are well have no need of a physician, but those who are sick. I did not come to call the righteous, but sinners, to repentance'" (Mark 2:15–17).

Generation to Generation

An Amazing Fact: *During the terrifying days of the Spanish Inquisition, many Jews openly converted to Catholicism but practiced parts of their religion underground in secret. Centuries later, some of their descendents began to identify their Jewish heritage as they discovered the history behind family practices—such as lighting candles on Saturday and saying Adonai as they crossed themselves.*

In the 14th and 15th centuries, Spain was a dark place for the Jewish people. Oppression and prejudice had existed for years, but in the wake of the Spanish Inquisition, many Jews converted to Catholicism to protect themselves. They were known as *conversos* or *marranos*. A number of these people continued to practice Judaism underground. They lit Sabbath candles in the darkness of their own homes. They whispered Hebrew blessings during mass. They held their Passover seders outdoors, a safe distance from watching eyes.

Years later, some of their descendents began to recognize that small pieces of their family's religious practices were linked to Judaism. They had never realized that the faith of their ancestors had been passed down through the centuries. History came alive with the knowledge of who their ancestors really were.

In Scripture, the psalmist records a promise to keep faith alive through generations to come. He remembers the sayings and practices of old, learned from his fathers, and vows that his people "will not hide them from their children, telling to the generation to come the praises of the Lord." Like the conversos of Spain, he promises to pass on the knowledge of his God. Sharing the knowledge of God with our children is one of the most powerful ways we can keep our faith alive! The impact of our example will live on for generations.

KEY BIBLE TEXT: "I will utter dark sayings of old, Which we have heard and known, and our fathers have told us. We will not hide them from their children, telling to the generation to come the praises of the LORD, and His strength and His wonderful works that He has done" (Psalm 78:2–4).

DAY 99 Your Inheritance

An Amazing Fact: *There are more than 900 billionaires in the world. Perhaps the most well known in America are Bill Gates ($53 billion) and Warren Buffet ($47 billion). In 2010, 10 billionaires passed away, leaving giant fortunes to family members. For wealthy Americans, 2010 was a good year to die rich since the estate tax had expired.*

Is your dad rich? Some people become wealthy as heirs of their parent's fortunes. Theo Albrecht, a grocery baron from Germany, died in 2010 at age 88, leaving his two sons $14.4 billion—making them new to the Forbes billionaire list.

Sometimes, sorting out who gets how much is messy. Two new Brazilian heiresses spent a decade fighting in court with their deceased father's widow over their inheritance. The widow was 40 years younger than the daughters' father and married him four months before he died. The daughters won in court. Their father, Amador Aguiar, founded Banco Bradesco, one of Brazil's largest banks.

When the children of Israel came to the Promised Land, God divided the territory up and gave each tribe an inheritance. In Joshua 18 and 19, the remainder of the land was divided up and distributed. Jesus likewise promises us, "I go to prepare a place for you" (John 14:2). The writer of Hebrews says of the patriarchs were pilgrims on the earth, "but now they desire a better, that is, a heavenly country" (Hebrews 11:16). There is a heavenly Promised Land that we may look forward to because we are heirs of Christ, who died to assure us of our inheritance.

Is your Father rich? Actually, your Father is very rich. Your heavenly Father owns everything in the universe. And God is now preparing a special place for you, an inheritance beyond measure.

KEY BIBLE TEXT: "But when the fullness of time had come, God sent forth His Son, born of a woman, born under the law. ... Therefore you are no longer a slave but a son, and if a son, then an heir of God through Christ" (Galatians 4:4, 7).

The Great War

An Amazing Fact: *During the First Battle of Bull Run in the American Civil War, citizens from Washington, D.C., were so confident that the Northern army would win effortlessly that they brought picnic baskets and watched the fighting from a nearby hill.*

It was the first major battle in the American Civil War. The Confederate Army had 9,000 troops camped in Manassas, Virginia, just 26 miles outside the nation's capital. With 30,000 Union troops at his disposal, General Irvin McDowell devised a plan to push the Confederate Army back. An easy victory was anticipated by all.

So Washingtonians, confident of the Union Army's superior strength, flocked by the hundreds to a hill outside the capital to watch the presumed victory. Many brought picnic baskets with bread and wine and peered through opera glasses to get a closer look at the battlefield. One woman was overheard saying, "That is splendid! Oh, my! Is not that first-rate? I guess we will be in Richmond this time tomorrow."

By 4:30 in the afternoon, the telegrapher in Washington spread the news that the Union Army had achieved a glorious victory. All were relieved.

But it was premature. In a sudden turn of events, the tide mysteriously changed and the Confederate Army pushed back. By late afternoon, galvanized by the determination of General Thomas "Stonewall" Jackson (who received his nickname as a result of the battle), the Confederates overtook the exhausted Union Army and completely turned them back. It was the bloodiest battle in United States history to that point, and it alerted both sides to the reality that the Civil War would not be a short affair.

Jesus wisely proclaimed that "if a house is divided against itself, that house cannot stand" (Mark 3:25). Yet the universe has been at war for thousands of years—ever since Lucifer rebelled in heaven. The battle has been long. There have been many casualties. But we are not simply bystanders, watching from a distant hill. We are key players, invited by God to lovingly "fight" on His behalf.

KEY BIBLE TEXT: "For we wrestle not against flesh and blood, but against principalities, against powers, against the rulers of the darkness of this world, against spiritual wickedness in high places" (Ephesians 6:12 KJV).

DAY 101 Hearing With the Heart

An Amazing Fact: *There are at least 37 different parables that Jesus told. Some of these stories are repeated in three of the Gospels, but the book of John does not contain any of them.*

People can listen without hearing, but it's impossible to hear without listening. When people truly hear someone, they take the words into their hearts. The words stay with them as they consider the meaning and absorb what was said. Really hearing someone involves a commitment.

The Pharisees listened to Jesus speak, but they didn't really hear Him. Though they might have understood the literal meaning of His stories, they never grasped the deeper concepts about God and His kingdom. His words entered their ears but never made it to their hearts, perhaps because they had decided in advance that they would not believe what He had to say. Their hearts were hardened against Him.

After telling the story of the sower, Jesus explained to His disciples why He spoke in parables. He quoted a prophecy from Isaiah that was fulfilled by the attitudes of the Pharisees who were, by their own choice, spiritually blind and deaf.

God always desires people to turn from their sins and be forgiven. If the Pharisees had been willing to hear Jesus and take His words to heart, God would have been glad to accept them.

KEY BIBLE TEXT: "But when He was alone, those around Him with the twelve asked Him about the parable. And He said to them, 'To you it has been given to know the mystery of the kingdom of God; but to those who are outside, all things come in parables, so that "Seeing they may see and not perceive, and hearing they may hear and not understand; lest they should turn, and their sins be forgiven them"'" (Mark 4:10–12).

The Mustard Seed

An Amazing Fact: *In ancient times, a warring king sent Alexander the Great a threatening bag of sesame seeds in reference to the vast number of his troops. In return, Alexander sent a bag of mustard seeds—smaller, yes, but more numerous and more potent!*

Throughout history, mustard has been popular both for its culinary and healing properties, but also as a symbol. One ancient writer claimed mustard would cure scorpion bites. Another suggested it would improve lazy housewives! Alexander the Great used mustard in the above scenario to represent the size and power of his troops. More recently, scientists have discovered that mustard seeds contain a number of healthy properties, such as magnesium, omega-3 fatty acids, and iron.

Jesus also used mustard as a symbol. In Mark, he compares the kingdom of God to a mustard seed. As Jesus noted, the mustard seed was the smallest seed sown by local Palestinian farmers, yet it commonly grew up to a height of 12 feet.

Similarly, God's kingdom often starts small. If you look back on your life, you can probably identify little instances of a choice or a conversation that began your journey closer to God. The beginning of God's kingdom in our hearts isn't always an impressive event. Many times it is simply small steps and slow growth progressing forward. Our walk with God doesn't develop overnight, but like the mustard plant, it can show incredible growth in time when it is planted in the right soil.

KEY BIBLE TEXT: "To what shall we liken the kingdom of God? Or with what parable shall we picture it? It is like a mustard seed which, when it is sown on the ground, is smaller than all the seeds on earth; but when it is sown, it grows up and becomes greater than all herbs, and shoots out large branches, so that the birds of the air may nest under its shade" (Mark 4:30).

DAY 103 God Protects the Vulnerable

An Amazing Fact: *In 1799, the American sailing vessel Nancy was seized by the British and taken into Port Royal, Jamaica, under suspicion of carrying contraband. Before the Nancy was boarded, her captain had the crew throw the forbidden freight and the ship's cargo papers into the sea. At the trial, the captain and officers were about to be acquitted for lack of evidence when the captain of another ship walked into court with the Nancy's original cargo papers. His men discovered them in the stomach of a shark they harpooned. Consequently, the defendants were convicted. Today, these remarkable documents, called The Shark's Papers, are on exhibit in Kingston, Jamaica.*

The Shark's Papers story is one of the most unusual court cases in history. Captain Briggs of the *Nancy* was quite unhappy with the turn of events and complained of being condemned by a shark. He had defiantly claimed that no papers were burned or tossed overboard, but that was a big lie.

Psalms 82 stands as a plea for justice. "God stands in the congregation of the mighty; He judges among the gods" (v. 1). God then condemns rulers and judges with judging unlawfully, unjustly, or partially. "How long will you judge unjustly, and show partiality to the wicked? Defend the poor and fatherless; do justice to the afflicted and needy. Deliver the poor and needy; free them from the hand of the wicked" (vs. 3, 4). In essence, the Lord tells these judges, "Pronounce fair sentences. Defend the vulnerable and needy."

John writes of a day when nothing shall be hidden. "Then I saw a great white throne and Him who sat on it, from whose face the earth and the heaven fled away... And I saw the dead, small and great, standing before God, and books were opened. ... And the dead were judged according to their works, by the things which were written in the books" (Revelation 20:11, 12).

We may have our records cleaned by the blood of Jesus Christ. But for those who turn away from God, the papers will be laid out. They cannot be hidden, not even in the belly of a shark.

KEY BIBLE TEXT: "Arise, O God, judge the earth; for You shall inherit all nations" (Psalm 82:8).

Running the Race

DAY 104

An Amazing Fact: *The world's longest certified footrace is the Self-Transcendence 3,100 Mile Race. It's held in New York City over a 52-day period.*

Begun in 1996 by Sri Chinmoy, the Self-Transcendence is a remarkable feat, held annually between June and August. Instead of running a straight 3,100 miles, however, runners actually run 5,649 laps around a single city block in Queens, New York, that is just .5488 miles around. Runners must average nearly 60 miles a day to complete the race within the 52-day limit—which takes upwards of 18 hours a day.

Over the course of one day, a runner will consume 10,000 calories, consisting of things like eggs, mashed potatoes, and tofu. And, as can be imagined, each runner will go through as many as 20 pairs of running shoes during the whole race.

Since its inception, fewer than 30 people have completed the race.

One of those 30, Madhupran Wolfgang Schwerk of Germany, is the ecord-holder. In 2006, he ran the race in 41 days and 8 hours, averaging 5 miles per day.

The Bible often compares the Christian's journey to a race. Paul wrote to the believers in Corinth: "Do you know that those who run a race all run, but one receives the prize? Run in such a way that you may obtain it" (1 Corinthians 9:24).

God invites us to follow His lead and aim for the prize—the same prize Jesus pursued—the salvation of souls. But it's not a short race, requiring only a short burst of speed. As we daily respond to God's grace, we can gain strength to run with endurance the race that is set before us.

KEY BIBLE TEXT: "Therefore we also, since we are surrounded by so great a cloud of witnesses, let us lay aside every weight, and the sin which so easily ensnares us, and let us run with endurance the race that is set before us, looking unto Jesus, the author and finisher of our faith, who for the joy that was set before Him endured the cross, despising the shame, and has sat down at the right hand of the throne of God" (Hebrews 12:1, 2).

DAY 105 Enemies Devoured

An Amazing Fact: *The world hosts about 1,400 species of scorpions, with about 40 kinds occurring in the United States. Scorpions, like spiders, have eight legs and belong to the arachnid family. They feed on insects they catch with their two lobster-like claws and kill with a venomous stinger at the end of their segmented, abdominal tail. In most species, the sting is merely painful to humans and not fatal, although the sting of one species found in the states has proved fatal to young children.*

But scorpions have been known to kill and devour their own species, as well as demonstrate vengeful behavior. One experimenter placed a hundred of these arachnids in a large glass vessel, and after a few days only 14 remained. The rest had been killed and eaten by the others. He then put a pregnant female in a glass vessel and observed her as she devoured her young as fast as they were born. One managed to escape, taking refuge on the mother's back, and found revenge by killing the mother scorpion in turn.

The scorpion's behavior reminds us of the story of Gideon's army surrounding the Midianites at night. God called Gideon to be a judge and leader of Israel. When gathering to attack the Midianites, the Lord told Gideon there were too many to face in combat. Eventually, Gideon ended up with only 300 men—who were not even given swords, but a trumpet and a torch! In the middle of the night they surrounded the camp, blew their trumpets, and uncovered their torches. The Bible then says, "And every man stood in his place all around the camp; and the whole army ran and cried out and fled. When the three hundred blew the trumpets, the Lord set every man's sword against his companion throughout the whole camp" (Judges 7:21, 22). Evidently, many Midianites died at the hands of their fellow soldiers.

Satan and his host are enemies to God's people. We can stand against them with the sword of the Lord (our Bibles) and know that God will protect us. Someday these enemies will turn on themselves and be destroyed forever.

KEY BIBLE TEXT: "For the Lord God is a sun and shield; the Lord will give grace and glory; no good thing will He withhold from those who walk uprightly" (Psalm 84:11).

Many Are One

An Amazing Fact: *In Leonardo da Vinci's painting "The Last Supper," Judas is depicted as having his elbows on the table. Some people believe this might have influenced our current etiquette rule that discourages putting elbows on the table during a meal.*

When we come together to remember the great blessing that Christ poured out in sacrificing Himself for us, we are drawn together in powerful ways. We are humbled as we consider the deep love He has, not only for us, but for everyone. Realizing how willingly He forgives us obligates us to forgive each other. This results in reconciliation and unity.

Jesus says that if we accept the sacrifice of His body that was broken for us, we are His body. Millions of believers become "one bread and one body" because we all accept what Christ has done for us, the overwhelming gift He has given.

Paul says that in Christ "we, though many, are one."

What does it mean to be one? It doesn't mean we will all have the same ideas on how to accomplish things. We are individuals for a reason; we have various strengths and gifts. But if we use them together to further Christ's work, we are unified in that and we form one body in purpose.

How important is it to be one? Jesus specifically asks us to love one another. Our unity and love for each other are signs to the world that we really are His disciples.

KEY BIBLE TEXTS: "The cup of blessing which we bless, is it not the communion of the blood of Christ? The bread which we break, is it not the communion of the body of Christ? For we, though many, are one bread and one body; for we all partake of that one bread" (1 Corinthians 10:16, 17). "Therefore, whether you eat or drink, or whatever you do, do all to the glory of God" (1 Corinthians 10:31).

DAY 107 Like an Owl

An Amazing Fact: *Barn owls are excellent hunters, with large eyes that are especially keen under low light. The wise-appearing, forward-facing eyes, which account for five percent of their body weight, offer a wide range of binocular vision. In fact, they're not even eyeballs, but rather elongated tubes like short telescopes held in place by bony structures in the skull. For this reason, an owl cannot "roll" or move its eyes, but only look straight ahead! However, it more than compensates for this with the ability to turn its head around and almost upside-down.*

When a typical bird flies, air rushes over the surface of the wing, creating turbulence, which makes a whooshing or flapping noise. But barn owls are absolutely silent when they fly. A velvety layer on the feather surface muffles sound. In addition, the leading edges of the wing feathers have a fine comb that deadens the sound of the wing beats. The silent flight prevents prey from hearing its approach and aids the owl's hearing, which is extremely acute.

Strangely, its ear openings are at slightly different levels on its head and are set at different angles—one high up near the owl's forehead and the other lower, about level with the bird's nostrils. The lopsided placement helps these hunters precisely pinpoint prey. The ears are also surrounded by feathers that can be opened up to catch the faint sounds of small prey or closed down to protect against loud sounds. They are covered by a flexible ruff made up of short, densely webbed feathers that frames the face, turning it into a parabolic dish-like reflector for sound. This gives the owl very sensitive and directional hearing, with which it can locate small prey even in total darkness.

The Bible teaches us that the eyes of God can see us wherever we are—and His ears can even hear our thoughts. David writes, "Bow down Your ear, O Lord, hear me; for I am poor and needy" (Psalms 86:1). God can hear our faintest cries for help, even in the dark.

KEY BIBLE TEXT: "Give ear, O Lord, to my prayer; and attend to the voice of my supplications" (Psalm 86:6).

Division or Unity?

DAY 108

An Amazing Fact: *According to researcher David B. Barrett, there were 33,830 different Christian denominations worldwide as of 2001.*

Of course, it's hard to know exactly how many different denominations there really are, but nearly 34,000 is a staggering number. These range from Baptists to Roman Catholics to Pentecostals to Latter-day Saints—and everything in between.

And to think that it all started with one Man who lived 2,000 years ago!

Of course, this is the point that so many have made: If all 33,380 of these denominations are all supposedly following the same Person, why is there so much division?

Yet it shouldn't surprise us. It didn't take long for the early Christian church to start dividing into different denominations. In at least two places, the apostle Paul addressed this very issue: "Now I plead with you, brethren, by the name of our Lord Jesus Christ, that you all speak the same thing, and there be no divisions among you" (1 Corinthians 1:10). He then went on to write, "Now I say this, that each of you says, 'I am of Paul,' or 'I am of Apollos,' or 'I am of Cephas,' or 'I am of Christ.' Is Christ divided?" (vv. 12, 13). Later on, while writing about the Lord's Supper, Paul raised the issue again: "For first of all, when you come together as a church, I hear that there are divisions among you" (1 Corinthians 11:18).

It was never Christ's desire for there to be division among His followers, of course. Though He never wanted a surface-level unity that was at the expense of truth, He nevertheless prayed to His Father that all believers would "be one, as You, Father, are in Me" (John 17:21). This is because true unity among Christ's disciples indicates to the world that He is worth following.

KEY BIBLE TEXT: "Behold, how good and how pleasant it is for brethren to dwell together in unity!" (Psalm 133:1)

DAY 109 Samson the Ant

An Amazing Fact: *Ants are incredibly strong compared to humans; they can lift and carry loads up to 50 times their own weight ... and some say it's really 500 times. They will frequently pick up another ant from their colony and give them a ride in their mandibles; an ant is an easy burden compared to some of the large caterpillars and other dead insects they have to bring home.*

Ants are everywhere. Perhaps it is because there are 35,000 different types of them in the world, with 60 species in North America. Ants have two stomachs. One is for them, and one is to feed others from. The ant also has the largest brain in proportion to its size. They are incredible little creatures. And they are strong. Even a conservative estimate of lifting 10 times their body weight is amazing. That means if you had the strength of an ant and weighed 100 pounds, you could lift 1,000 lbs. Not only that, but ants can drag an object far above their body weight! Could you drag more than a ton of weight around?

The book of Judges introduces us to the strongest man who ever lived—Samson. His life is filled with fascinating stories of defeating lions, catching 300 foxes, and killing a thousand men with the jawbone of a donkey. Samson was incredibly strong, but his strength did not come from within himself. The Bible says, "And the Spirit of the Lord came mightily upon him" (Judges 14:6). God was the source of Samson's strength.

You might not be strong compared to other humans or even ants. But like the mighty ant, God can give you strength to deal with your enemies. Unfortunately, Samson did not always use his strength to the glory of God. Learn a lesson from Samson and from the humble ant.

KEY BIBLE TEXT: "Finally, my brethren, be strong in the Lord and in the power of His might" (Ephesians 6:10).

A Deaf Man Hears

An Amazing Fact: *Alexander Graham Bell, inventor of the telephone, worked as a teacher at the Boston School for Deaf Mutes. His mother was almost entirely deaf, and Bell eventually married a deaf woman.*

About 1 in 800 babies are born deaf, but there are dozens of other causes of deafness. Worldwide, about 200,000 deaf people have received cochlear implants, which converts sound into electronic signals. The signals are delivered to the acoustic nerve, which relays them to the hearing center of the brain for interpretation. Though the result is very different from natural sound, it is a great help to many.

Since the deaf man who came to Jesus for help also suffered from a speech impediment, it's likely that he had been deaf from birth or from a young age. Can you imagine how exciting it must have been for him to suddenly have perfect hearing and speech? It's likely that the first thing he heard was the voice of his Healer.

Spiritually, we all have speech impediments (we don't always say the right thing or speak with grace) and we are all deaf to some degree (we don't always listen as carefully as we should). If we ask Him, God will open our ears to His Spirit and loose our tongues so we can speak His truth plainly and with love.

KEY BIBLE TEXT: "Then they brought to Him one who was deaf and had an impediment in his speech, and they begged Him to put His hand on him. And He took him aside from the multitude, and put His fingers in his ears, and He spat and touched his tongue. Then, looking up to heaven, He sighed, and said to him, 'Ephphatha,' that is, 'Be opened.' Immediately his ears were opened, and the impediment of his tongue was loosed, and he spoke plainly" (Mark 7:32–35).

DAY 111 A Heart of Love

An Amazing Fact: *A tenaciously hard-working dynamo, the heart can continue beating even when all surrounding nerves are severed. And what a beat! It thumps an average of 75 times a minute, 40 million times a year, and 2.5 billion times in an average life. With each beat, the adult heart discharges about four ounces of blood. This amounts to about 2,000 gallons a day or 760,000 gallons a year.*

The heart is often associated with love. We eat heart-shaped candies and cakes. We buy cards with cartoon hearts on them for our loved ones. Hearts are scribbled at the bottom of love letters. Understanding the power of the heart makes it even more reasonable to connect it with true love. The heart produces enough energy in one hour to lift a 150-pound man to the top of a three-story building; in 12 hours enough to lift 65-tons one foot off the ground; and enough power in 70 years to lift the largest battleship completely out of the water.

Perhaps the biggest heart of all is found in the blue whale. These giant mammals are not considered full-grown until 10 years of age, when its heart will be as big as a small car and its blood vessels large enough for a human baby to crawl through. If a fast-beating heart represents deep love, then the hedgehog might be a very loving creature. Its heart beats about 300 times per minute.

When Paul explains how spiritual gifts are to function in the body of Christ, he speaks of love. In 1 Corinthians 13 we discover that without love all the gifts in the world are meaningless. Love is the very center of how Christ's church is to live and serve. Without love it is all like a clanging gong.

Despite all the power of a human heart, it is powerless to change itself. We must receive God's love into our hearts. No matter how much blood your heart can pump, it will never be a heart that loves unless it is converted by the love of Christ. Give your heart to Jesus today.

KEY BIBLE TEXT: "And now abide faith, hope, love, these three; but the greatest of these is love" (1 Corinthians 13:13).

Too Much Yeast

DAY 112

An Amazing Fact: *The largest loaf of bread ever baked weighed 3,463 pounds! It was made by Joaquim Goncalves of Brazil in 2008.*

Talk about a lot of bread! On November 13, 2008, in celebration of Guinness World Records Day, Goncalves and a host of others set out to bake the largest loaf of bread ever recorded. Local papers and other members of the press were there to witness it, as well as an official from Guinness World Records. After baking for an hour-and-a-half, the warm, steamy bread came out and the record was declared. A majority of this bread was sent to various charities in the area.

In order to bake a loaf of bread that big, you have to have a lot of yeast!

Interestingly, it was this precise thing that Jesus warned His disciples against—too much yeast! In response to the disciples not having enough bread for a journey upon which they were embarking, Jesus took the opportunity to warn them, "Beware of the yeast of the Pharisees and the yeast of Herod" (Mark 8:15 NRSV).

The disciples were utterly perplexed. They thought Jesus was referring to the fact that they did not have enough bread, but He was talking about something entirely different. The purpose of yeast is to cause dough to rise and expand. It literally puffs bread up.

This is precisely what the Pharisees did and what their teachings encouraged. They were the definition of puffed up. They tried to magnify everything they did, impressing people with their pious prayers and self-righteous ceremonies. And embracing just a tablespoon of their pride-filled teaching would eventually cause the leavening of a whole life.

But Christ's character is altogether different. While man's pride naturally expands, Christ humbles Himself and chooses to become nothing. (See Philippians 2:5–8.) And His followers, when beholding Him, will naturally follow His lead.

KEY BIBLE TEXT: "Your boasting is not a good thing. Do you not know that a little yeast leavens the whole batch of dough? Therefore purge out the old leaven, that you may be a new lump, since you truly are unleavened. For indeed Christ, our Passover, was sacrificed for us" (1 Corinthians 5:6, 7).

DAY 113 Number 70

An Amazing Fact: *There are some interesting facts about the number 70. For instance, Antarctica contains 70 percent of the world's fresh water (in the form of ice). Cheetahs, the world's fastest mammals, can run 70 MPH. Up to 70 percent of vitamin C is lost when vegetables are steam cooked. A game of hockey lasts for 70 minutes. The lowest temperature ever recorded was -70 degrees centigrade in Yakutsk, Russia.*

What's so special about the number 70? Nothing. In fact, all numbers are fascinating. Take the number 9—if you multiply nine by any whole number (except zero) and repeatedly add the digits of the answer until it's one digit, you will end up with nine. For instance, 2 x 9 = 18 (1 + 8 = 9) or 3 x 9 = 27 (2 + 7 = 9) or 9 x 9 = 81 (8 + 1 = 9). It gets even wilder: How about 578,329 x 9 = 5,204,961 (5 + 2 + 0 + 4 + 6 + 9 + 1 = 27 (2 + 7 = 9)). If you really want to stretch your brain (and your calculator), try 482,729,235,601 x 9. It really doesn't matter what number you pick, nine is just a special number!

God invented math since the Lord is the Creator of all things. Numbers are important to God. There were exactly six days of creation followed by a seventh day for rest. The New Jerusalem has 12 foundations. The Godhead is composed of three beings. Judas sold Jesus for 30 pieces of silver.

But most of all, numbers teach us that God sees us and loves us. After all, even the hairs of our head are numbered (Matthew 10:30)!

Psalms 90 speaks of how fleeting the life of people can be. We are like grass that grows in the morning and is cut down at night. Unless we are careful in how we live, the number of our days can be wasted. Psalms 90:10 says, "The days of our lives are seventy years..." Every day is precious. It is another opportunity to learn that you are more than a number to God.

KEY BIBLE TEXT: "So teach us to number our days, that we may gain a heart of wisdom" (Psalm 90:12).

Everybody Ought to Know

An Amazing Fact: *The Bible contains over 100 different names or titles for Christ. Here is a small sample: Son of God, Son of Man, Son of David, Great High Priest, Light of the World, Bread of Life, Lord of Glory, Great Shepherd, Advocate, Morning Star, Heir of All Things, Lamb of God, True Vine, Lion of the Tribe of Judah, Alpha and Omega, Chief Cornerstone, Prince of Peace.*

Jesus' countrymen often debated about who He was. Although their ministries overlapped, some people believed that He was John the Baptist. Even Herod trembled to think that Jesus might be John the Baptist returned to life after Herod had him executed.

Another thought was that Jesus might be Elijah, the prophet whom Moses had spoken of, or still yet another historical prophet.

When Jesus asked His disciples who they believed He was, Peter spoke with conviction, saying, "You are the Christ." Peter recognized Jesus as the Messiah, something he could not have known unless God had revealed it to him.

For 2,000 years people have argued about who Jesus is. For Christians, there is no doubt and no debate. We have overwhelming evidence, in Scripture and in our own lives, that Jesus is the Christ, the Messiah, the Righteous One, the Deliverer, the precious Savior of the world.

KEY BIBLE TEXT: "Now Jesus and His disciples went out to the towns of Caesarea Philippi; and on the road He asked His disciples, saying to them, 'Who do men say that I am?' So they answered, 'John the Baptist; but some say, Elijah; and others, one of the prophets.' He said to them, 'But who do you say that I am?' Peter answered and said to Him, 'You are the Christ'" (Mark 8:27–29).

DAY 115 Eyes to Watch Over You

An Amazing Fact: *Bald eagles primarily eat fish and can live up to 40 years in the wild. Furthermore, they are monogamous and remain faithful to their mate until death. These amazing birds are especially renowned for their excellent eyesight.*

Eagles have two foveae, or centers of focus, in the retina of each eye that allow them to see both forward and to the side at the same time. (Human retinas have only one.) Depending on which way an eagle looks, the lens of its eye focuses an image on one fovea or the other. The rear fovea is for forward, stereoscopic vision, and the other is for looking sideways. Both foveae are more densely lined with rods and cones than those of human eyes, giving them much greater resolving power.

Eagles have color vision, and while their eyes are not as large as a human's, their sharpness is at least four times that of a person with perfect vision. While soaring, gliding, or flapping, they are capable of seeing fish in the water from several hundred feet above the surface or identify a rabbit moving almost a mile away. An eagle flying in a fixed position at an altitude of 1,000 feet could spot prey as small as a mouse over an area of almost three square miles!

David writes in Psalm 91 of the safety we may have in God's presence. "He who dwells in the secret place of the Most High shall abide under the shadow of the Almighty" (Psalms 91:1). Perhaps it was observing the eagle that inspired David to sing, "He shall cover you with His feathers, and under His wings you shall take refuge" (v. 4).

When you choose to dwell in "the secret place of the Most High" you can rest assured that God has His eyes on you, even at night.

KEY BIBLE TEXT: "Behold, He who keeps Israel shall neither slumber nor sleep" (Psalm 121:4).

Take Up Your Cross

An Amazing Fact: *The largest cross in the world is in Escoral, Spain, at the Valley of the Fallen basilica. Made entirely of stone, the cross stands 492 feet tall!*

Construction of the giant basilica and monument started in 1940. It took 18 years to complete and was inaugurated on April 1, 1958. It was built in honor of those who gave their lives on both sides of the fighting during the Spanish Civil War. The cross was designed by architect Diego Mendez and sits on top of a rocky cliff known as Risco de la Nava, which is 4,500 feet above sea level. With a height of 492 feet and the arms stretching out 154 feet wide, the entire cross weighs over 200,000 metric tons.

Talk about a huge cross! Nobody in the world could carry such an enormous cross.

In Mark 8:34, Jesus made quite a perplexing statement about another cross. He said that anyone who "desires to come after Me" must "deny himself, and take up his cross, and follow Me." Jesus wasn't asking us to take up the cross in Escoral, Spain, of course, but the task of taking up our crosses might be as equally a challenging pursuit. The cross Jesus spoke of was not a cross of wood or stone or any other material. The cross Jesus asked us to carry is the denial of self and the extinguishing of our pride.

And this is, indeed, a hard task because we are all born with the desire to gratify self rather than denying it. Our orientations are naturally directed toward getting our own way and doing our own thing. To actually take up our crosses and deny ourselves is a daunting task.

Of course, the task becomes easier, and even a joy, when we see that Christ first took up His cross. When we see that He denied Himself, this pours contempt on our pride and we find ourselves following His lead and taking up our own crosses.

KEY BIBLE TEXT: "He must increase, but I must decrease" (John 3:30).

DAY 117 God's Rest

An Amazing Fact: *Tutankhamun is probably the most famous Egyptian pharaoh and is better known as King Tut. This boy king died in his late teens and remained at rest for more than 3,300 years. But that changed in 1922 when Egyptologist Howard Carter, who was excavating in the Valley of the Kings, discovered the king's tomb.*

Still, the tomb came close to escaping discovery altogether! Carter had been searching for the tomb for a number of years on behalf of English patron Lord Carnarvon, who later decided that enough time and money had been expended with little return. However, Carter managed to persuade his patron to fund one more season, and within days of resuming excavation, the missing tomb was found—full of treasures.

Today the tomb still contains the pharaoh's remains, hidden from view inside the outermost of three coffins. He is believed to be the only pharaoh still residing in the Valley of the Kings. King Tut's tomb has yielded some of the greatest treasures of antiquity, but the most priceless treasure of all time is actually in an empty tomb outside Jerusalem!

Psalm 92 is a song for the Sabbath, a day of rest. It teaches us to praise God for the works of the past and the future. Jesus, after His crucifixion, rested in a tomb on the Sabbath. But Christ rose from the grave and is now in heaven interceding for us. This Psalm teaches us to give glory to the Lord. Some people might praise ancient kings who still lay in their tombs. We praise a living God who is coming again and in whom we can find true rest.

KEY BIBLE TEXT: "Those who are planted in the house of the Lord shall flourish in the courts of our God. They shall still bear fruit in old age; they shall be fresh and flourishing" (Psalms 92:13, 14).

Many Witnesses

An Amazing Fact: *Sir William Ramsay, a renowned archeologist of the late 19th and early 20th centuries, set out to disprove the historicity of the New Testament. Traveling to Asia Minor, he began to uncover evidence. It wasn't what he expected. Each dig provided further indication that the historical accounts of the New Testament were very accurate. Overwhelmed and convicted by the mountain of evidence, Sir Ramsay eventually became a Christian.*

There were a multitude of witnesses to verify the resurrection of Christ. Mary saw and spoke with Him. Peter and the other disciples saw Him, spoke with Him, touched Him, and even ate with Him on multiple occasions. Later, more 500 of His followers saw Him at one time.

Why is it so important to be convinced of the resurrection of Jesus? Paul explains it this way: "And if Christ is not risen, your faith is futile; you are still in your sins! Then also those who have fallen asleep in Christ have perished" (1 Corinthians 15:17, 18).

Without the resurrection of Christ, the future would be hopeless and being a Christian would be pointless. Paul says that if we have hope in Jesus just in this life, "we are of all men the most pitiable" (verse 19).

But we are convinced—through the witnesses in Scripture and through our own life-transforming experiences—that Jesus lives. In Him, our future is secure.

KEY BIBLE TEXT: "Moreover, brethren, I declare to you the gospel which I preached to you, which also you received and in which you stand, by which also you are saved, if you hold fast that word which I preached to you—unless you believed in vain. For I delivered to you first of all that which I also received: that Christ died for our sins according to the Scriptures, and that He was buried, and that He rose again the third day according to the Scriptures, and that He was seen by Cephas, then by the twelve. After that He was seen by over five hundred brethren at once" (1 Corinthians 15:1–6).

DAY 119 Whiter Than Snow

An Amazing Fact: *Brides wear white to symbolize their innocence and purity. White reflects light and is a popular color in decorating and fashion because it is light, neutral, and goes with everything. However, white shows dirt and is therefore more difficult to keep free from stains than other colors.*

What's your favorite color? Some like green, which seems to symbolize nature, a calming and refreshing color. Others enjoy red, which is an emotionally intense color and can actually stimulate your heart to beat faster. Blue represents loyalty, and weight lifters do better in blue rooms. The most romantic color is pink; it's tranquilizing. Yellow is a cheery color, purple is the color of royalty, and brown is a reliable, solid color and is abundant in nature.

One of God's favorite colors in the Bible is white. The robes we will be given in heaven are white (Revelation 3:20). Jesus rides on a white horse (Revelation 19:11). There is a great white throne of judgment (Revelation 20:11). David asked God to cleanse him from sin and said, "I shall be whiter than snow" (Psalms 51:7). It is interesting that white is seen in your eye when all three types of color-sensitive cone cells are stimulated with equal amounts. Perhaps this teaches us that when God is fully present there is no taint of sin.

The Bible talks about Jesus being transfigured. He was changed in appearance, and some of His glory was allowed to shine out. Notice how this is described. "His clothes became shining, exceedingly white, like snow, such as no launderer on earth can whiten them" (Mark 9:3). Jesus was without sin and when His divine nature opened up more fully, the color the disciples saw was a brilliant white. John saw something similar in Revelation 1:14.

No matter what your favorite color is, God wants you to know that when you come with your sin-stained life, the Lord will cleanse you and make you pure, just like Jesus.

KEY BIBLE TEXT: "'Come now, and let us reason together,' says the Lord, 'Though your sins are like scarlet, They shall be as white as snow; Though they are red like crimson, They shall be as wool'" (Isaiah 1:18).

Our Inheritance

An Amazing Fact: *When Ben Rea of the United Kingdom died in 1988, he left $12.5 million of his fortune to his cat Blackie, who became the wealthiest cat in the world.*

Ben Rea was a millionaire recluse. He was an antiques dealer from Dorney, England, who shared his old, musty mansion with 15 cats. Eventually all the cats died off ... except for his favorite, Blackie.

Rea did not have as much affection for humans, however, feeling that everyone was simply out to get his money. By the time he died of a heart attack at age 82, he had worked all his family out of his will. He didn't leave one single cent to any relative; instead, he bequeathed it all to Blackie—who enjoyed a pampered life while Rea's relatives steamed with anger.

Though God shares Rea's affection for furry felines, His attitude toward human beings is a little different. He doesn't look at us with a suspicious eye—but with a longing eye. It was this precise reason that God sent His Son. When we were poor, in need, and without strength, God sent Jesus to this world to die on our behalf—even for His "relatives," whose attitudes toward Him weren't exactly pure. And thus, when Jesus died, He didn't bequeath His inheritance to animals but to humans.

The Psalmist declares, "For the Lord will not cast off His people, nor will He forsake His inheritance" (Psalms 94:14). We can rest in the assurance that God will never turn us away. He will never forsake us. Our inheritance in Him is guaranteed.

KEY BIBLE TEXT: "For you know the grace of our Lord Jesus Christ, that though He was rich, yet for your sakes He became poor, that you through His poverty might become rich" (2 Corinthians 8:9).

DAY 121 The Guardian of Airways

An Amazing Fact: *Your voice box is an amazing organ located at the top of your windpipe. It is a hollow, tubular structure that creates sounds and prevents food from entering your airways. On the upper part of your voice box is a flap called the epiglottis. When you swallow, your voice box rises and your epiglottis forms a lid over its opening. This blocks the passageway to your respiratory tract and prevents food and other foreign substances from entering where they don't belong.*

Inside your voice box (or larynx) there are two bands of tissue that form your vocal cords. When you speak or sing, muscles pull these cords together. The air passing through the cords makes them vibrate. You hear these vibrations as sounds. The shorter your vocal cords are and the faster they vibrate, the higher the pitch you produce. In both girls and boys, the voice box and vocal cords grow during puberty and cause their voices to deepen. In girls, this change can be hardly noticeable with their voices dropping by just a couple of tones. But boys' voice boxes grow considerably. They also tilt to a different angle in the neck and can start to stick out as a prominent "Adam's apple." Boys' voices can drop by as much as an octave.

A man once brought his son to Jesus' disciples because the boy could not speak. When Jesus spoke with the father, He said, "If you can believe, all things are possible to him who believes" (Mark 9:23). The father "found his voice" and blurted out, "Lord, I believe; help my unbelief!" (v. 24). Then Jesus healed the boy, who now had a voice.

Though you also have a voice, you might not always use it to speak in faith. When we believe in God's Word, we will find the voice of our faith growing stronger. Doubt sometimes blocks our voices from speaking truth. We need a "spiritual epiglottis" to guard the airways of our souls. Speak in faith and you will find your true voice.

KEY BIBLE TEXT: "Your watchmen shall lift up their voices, with their voices they shall sing together; for they shall see eye to eye when the Lord brings back Zion" (Isaiah 52:8).

Singing to God

An Amazing Fact: *We all know that birds, bugs, and frogs are natural singers. But other animals that sing include some fish, mice, and bats—usually too high pitched for human ears—humpbacks whales, belugas, and even certain species of ground squirrels. In most instances, it is a male serenading a female with love songs.*

A multitude of research studies confirm that singing is good for humans. To start with, singing releases endorphins—pain-killing hormones that cause happiness—in our brains. Singing can lower stress, improve sleep, and increase the function of the immune system.

Musical therapies, some still in the research phase, are being used to successfully treat patients with dementia, depression, and other medical conditions.

Singing can help to clear the sinuses and respiratory tubes, tone your stomach and facial muscles, improve your posture, and increase your lung capacity and mental alertness.

There's no doubt that singing has many physical and emotional benefits. Music and singing are wonderful gifts from God. And when we use songs to praise God, our spiritual lives benefit as well.

The psalmist encouraged us to sing to our great God, to "come before His presence with thanksgiving," to praise Him as the Creator of all things and "the Rock of our salvation."

KEY BIBLE TEXT: "Oh come, let us sing to the LORD! Let us shout joyfully to the Rock of our salvation. Let us come before His presence with thanksgiving; let us shout joyfully to Him with psalms. For the LORD is the great God, and the great King above all gods. In His hand are the deep places of the earth; the heights of the hills are His also. The sea is His, for He made it; and His hands formed the dry land" (Psalm 95:1–5).

DAY 123 God Is Calling

An Amazing Fact: *Valdemar Poulsen, the Danish telephone engineer and inventor, patented what he called a 'telegraphone' in 1898. The telegraphone was the first practical apparatus for magnetic sound recording and reproduction and enabled telephone conversations to be recorded. This was followed up by Willy Müller, who invented the automatic answering machine in 1935. It was a three-foot-tall machine popular with Orthodox Jews who were forbidden to answer the phone on the Sabbath.*

The telephone has been around since 1892, when Alexander Graham Bell commercialized concepts for phone operation that had been around for years. The greeting he suggested for answering the phone was "Ahoy" (as used in ships). Edison later suggested "Hello."

In the 1970s the various American phone companies requested that TV and film producers use the 555 prefix for fictional numbers to prevent genuine numbers from being accidentally used. This backfired somewhat in the 1980s when a Gary Larson cartoon, depicting Satan's number as 555-1332, was reprinted in Australia—where 555 is a genuine area code. The owner of the number became the subject of harassment and later sued Gary Larson and his syndicate.

Can you imagine receiving a phone call from the Lord? Actually, the Bible tells us that many times God "called" people (just not with a phone). One such story is the calling of the little boy Samuel. In 1 Samuel 3 we read of the young lad, while going to sleep one night, hearing his name called out. He ran to Eli the priest, who realized God was speaking to Samuel. The first message Samuel received from the Lord was a heavy one.

We do not need phones to hear God calling to us. And we certainly do not want to put God on hold. We need to be tuned in to the still, small voice of the Lord speaking to our minds and hearts. When God calls, the best way to answer is Samuel's response, "Speak, for your servant hears" (1 Samuel 3:10).

KEY BIBLE TEXT: "When Israel was a child, I loved him. And out of Egypt I called my Son" (Hosea 11:1).

Blessed Are the Poor

DAY 124

An Amazing Fact: *The richest man in the world is Mexican-born Carlos Slim Helú. At age 71, he is worth an estimated $74 billion, surpassing Bill Gates at $53 billion.*

Born to Lebanese parents in Mexico, Helú made his fortunes in telecommunications. He is chairman of Telmex, a Mexican phone company that controls 80 percent of the landlines in the country. Helú is so wealthy that his net worth is equivalent to over seven percent of Mexico's GDP.

Perhaps what is most remarkable about him, however, is his frugality. Though he is the richest man in the world, he still lives in the same modest six-bedroom house that he has resided in for more 30 years. Not only this, even though kidnapping is prevalent in Mexico, he still drives himself to work.

Of course, most of us probably have the inclination to envy this man. Think of all the things we could do with only a fraction of his wealth! We have our wish lists that contain all the toys we'd like to buy. We have our dream homes and our fantasy vacations.

Yet Jesus gave a stern warning to those who are wealthy and for those who covet wealth. After a young man came to Jesus, asking Him what he had to do to inherit eternal life, Jesus told him to sell everything he had and give his money to the poor. The young man turned away sorrowful, however, because he was too attached to his toys.

It was then that Jesus declared that it "is easier for a camel to go through the eye of a needle than for a rich man to enter the kingdom of God" (Mark 10:25).

KEY BIBLE TEXT: "Blessed are the poor in spirit, for theirs is the kingdom of God" (Matthew 5:3).

DAY 125 Shout to the Lord

An Amazing Fact: *The world's loudest shout belongs to a Northern Ireland grade school teacher. Annalisa Flanagan from Comber had something to shout about when her sensational voice was re-entered into the Guinness Book of Records as the loudest in the world. She's held the record for a decade with a shout that measured at 121 decibels, the equivalent of a jet engine. The word Annalisa shouted when she broke the world record was: "Quiet!"*

Excessive shouting can damage your vocal cords. The strain can cause vocal cord nodules, and misusing your voice by screaming is unwise. Singers know how important it is to warm up their voices and use their diaphragms if they are going to sing loudly. Screaming is actually a vocal technique popular in heavy metal, punk, and hard rock music.

The Bible speaks of God's people shouting. "Shout joyfully to the Lord, all the earth; break forth in song, rejoice, and sing praises" (Psalm 98:4). We can conclude from this passage that there is an appropriate time and place to lift up your voice loudly in praise to God. It is to be marked with a focus on praising God, being joyful and singing—not screaming or drawing attention to yourself. Worship in song was never meant to be wild and uncontrolled. Shouting to the Lord is marked by focus, purpose, and deep appreciation for God's salvation (Psalm 95:1).

God will also one day shout. Paul explains this event of the second coming: "For the Lord Himself will descend from heaven with a shout, with the voice of an archangel, and with the trumpet of God. And the dead in Christ will rise first" (1 Thessalonians 4:16). Sometimes we are too bland and quiet in our prayers and praises to God. There are appropriate times to be earnest and fervent in calling to the Lord. But we must remember that loudness does not make our praises more acceptable to God.

KEY BIBLE TEXT: "Then, as He was now drawing near the descent of the Mount of Olives, the whole multitude of the disciples began to rejoice and praise God with a loud voice for all the mighty works they had seen" (Luke 19:37).

The Things Not Seen

An Amazing Fact: *Since much of the persecution of Christians throughout the world is carried out in remote areas, it is impossible to know accurately how many are being persecuted for their faith. Some estimates run as high as 200 million people in 60 countries. It is also estimated that many thousands of Christians are martyred each year.*

A boy named Peter lived in a country that was taken over by a communist government. His mother and father were Christians. It was forbidden to talk to others about God, but Peter's parents continued to do so. Eventually they were caught and put in prison.

Peter was then sent to a special camp where people tried to train him to forget about God. The other children there were cooperative with their teachers, but Peter would not lay aside his beliefs. The other children shunned him and made fun of him. Separated from his family and desperately lonely, he prayed for help. Each day God gave him the strength to resist the "training."

With Jesus as his best Friend giving him strength, Peter stayed faithful under extreme pressure. Finally, the training camp gave up on him and he was sent back to his family.

Because of his strong belief in "the things which are not seen," Peter would not give up his faith. And because he knew Jesus so much better through his persecution, his trial became a blessing.

KEY BIBLE TEXT: "Therefore we do not lose heart. Even though our outward man is perishing, yet the inward man is being renewed day by day. For our light affliction, which is but for a moment, is working for us a far more exceeding and eternal weight of glory, while we do not look at the things which are seen, but at the things which are not seen. For the things which are seen are temporary, but the things which are not seen are eternal" (2 Corinthians 4:16–18).

DAY 127 Resurrection Bodies

An Amazing Fact: *The water bear, named for its awkward gait, is a tiny animal less than a millimeter long, yet it can withstand the most extreme conditions on earth. Its proper name is a tardegrade, and there are many species found all over the world, from the coldest poles to the warmest jungle. The beast has eight legs, two eyes, a central nervous system, and has piercing mouthparts that it uses to feed on the juices of plants. It is just barely visible to the naked eye.*

So how tough are these guys? They normally live in damp places like mosses and lichens, but these habitats often dry out, get baked in the sun, and freeze in winter. So to survive these un-cozy periods, the water bear has a clever trick. It pulls in its legs, loses some water, shrivels up, and transforms into a "tun," enabling it to withstand all kinds of extremes while hibernating.

Here's a sample of some harsh environments that water bears have survived. Left in a bottle with dried moss for 120 years without water or air—when water was added, they sprang to life. Exposed to minus 458-degrees Fahrenheit, the coldest temperature possible (i.e., one degree above absolute zero). When thawed, they started up again. And in September 2007, tardigrades were taken into low Earth orbit on a space mission and exposed to the vacuum of space for 10 days. After the bugs returned, scientists discovered many of them had survived and laid eggs that hatched normally.

Paul speaks in 1 Corinthians 5 of the assurance believers can have in the resurrection. Followers of Christ are exposed to all sorts of harsh conditions and "groan" (or long for) the day they will have new bodies. The water bear gives us a taste of this amazing Bible teaching of coming back to life after being exposed to extreme situations. Someday, when Jesus comes, we will spring to life. No matter how we died, Christ will restore us with strong bodies, even more durable than the water bear's.

KEY BIBLE TEXT: "For we know that if our earthly house, this tent, is destroyed, we have a building from God, a house not made with hands, eternal in the heavens" (2 Corinthians 5:1).

Looking Unto Jesus

An Amazing Fact: *Abolition of the slave trade in England was delayed for more than 10 years because five pro-abolitionist parliamentarians were at the opera when the vote was being taken.*

William Wilberforce had been working tirelessly for years toward one goal: the abolition of the slave trade in England. In 1796, he felt as if the tide had finally turned in his favor. When he brought the bill before parliament, as he did every year of his political career, he nervously awaited the vote.

Sadly, the pro-abolition side fell short by four votes. Lamenting later in his diary, Wilberforce wrote, "Enough at the Opera to have carried it." It turns out those parliamentarians were attending the opening night of the comic opera I Dui Gobi (The Two Hunchbacks). Unfortunately, it would not be until 1807 that the bill finally passed. During that time, hundreds of thousands of slaves lost their lives.

It is no wonder that David wrote in the book of Psalms, "I will set nothing wicked before my eyes" (Psalm 101:3). The Hebrew word for "wicked" is actually a little less extreme than this, however. It literally means "worthless," or that which doesn't have any real value. Yet how many times do we, like those parliamentarians, set worthless things before our eyes when people all around us are hurting, dying, and desperately needing our help? How many times do we turn on the TV or watch a movie when there are much bigger issues going on that God wants to involve us in?

God graciously invites us to look "unto Jesus" instead. (See Hebrews 12:2). It is there that we will find all that is lovely and, in response, we will seek to live as He lived.

KEY BIBLE TEXT: "Finally, brethren, whatever things are true, whatever things are noble, whatever things are just, whatever things are pure, whatever things are lovely, whatever things are of good report, if there is any virtue and if there is anything praiseworthy—meditate on these things" (Philippians 4:8).

DAY 129 God's Giant Youth

An Amazing Fact: *Robert Wadlow (1918 – 1940) was the tallest person in history for whom there is irrefutable evidence. He was known as the Alton Giant (or Giant of Illinois) because he was born in and grew up in Alton, Illinois. He reached a height of 8 feet, 11.1 inches and weighed 485 pounds at the time of his death at age 22.*

How did Wadlow grow to be so large? Doctors believe it was caused by hypertrophy of his pituitary gland, which results in an abnormally high level of human growth hormone. Robert showed no end to his growth, even at his death. His shoe size was 37AA. Unfortunately, his height had its drawbacks. He needed leg braces in order to walk and had little feeling in his legs and feet. Ten days before his death, while traveling on a tour, his ankle became infected because of a faulty leg brace. On July 15, 1940, he died in his sleep.

The Bible tells us that David fought against a giant named Goliath, who stood about 9-½ feet tall. His staff was "like a weaver's beam," which is the bar to which the long threads are fastened in a cloth-making loom, probably two inches in diameter. The iron spearhead weighed about 15 pounds.

Saul's army stood shaking in their boots every time Goliath came out and defied the God of Israel. But David knew that while the weapons of man are no match for giants, he also understood that God's power can save man. That's true for you as well as you face your own giants.

KEY BIBLE TEXT: "You come to me with a sword, with a spear, and with a javelin. But I come to you in the name of the Lord of hosts, the God of the armies of Israel, whom you have defied" (1 Samuel 17:45).

Overwhelming Forgiveness

An Amazing Fact: *A Gallup Poll once found that 94 percent of Americans would like to be forgiving. But 85 percent felt that they could not be forgiving by themselves; in order to forgive, they needed help from God or something outside themselves.*

Why do most people find it so hard to forgive? Maybe it has something to do with pride. If someone has wounded our feelings, it doesn't seem fair to forgive them quickly and easily. Let them suffer guilt, let them grovel ... then maybe we'll consider it.

Aren't we glad God doesn't treat us that way when we do something wrong? According to Psalm 103, He doesn't deal with us or punish us in the way our sins deserve. It says His mercy is as high as the heavens! As soon as we ask for forgiveness from Him, He graciously removes our sins "as far as the east is from the west" (v. 12).

Jesus said, "And whenever you stand praying, if you have anything against anyone, forgive him, that your Father in heaven may also forgive you your trespasses" (Mark 11:25). The Bible is plain on the subject: We can't be forgiven unless we are willing to forgive.

Recognizing the undeserved, overwhelming forgiveness we receive every day from God should spark deep gratitude in our hearts and make it easier to extend forgiveness to those who have offended us. If we ask Him, God will give us the power to forgive others.

KEY BIBLE TEXT: "The Lord is merciful and gracious, slow to anger, and abounding in mercy. He will not always strive with us, nor will He keep His anger forever. He has not dealt with us according to our sins, nor punished us according to our iniquities. For as the heavens are high above the earth, so great is His mercy toward those who fear Him; as far as the east is from the west, so far has He removed our transgressions from us" (Psalm 103:8–12).

DAY 131 Well Hidden

An Amazing Fact: *For 26 years after the surrender of Japan in 1945, Japanese soldier Shoichi Yokoi hid in the remote jungles of Guam living on berries, nuts, rats, and frogs. Following the creed of soldiers loyal to imperial Japan, he refused to surrender because he did not believe the war was really over. Two local hunters discovered him in January 1972 in a remote jungle. He was wearing a pair of burlap pants and a shirt that he had made from tree bark.*

When found, Yokoi was expecting the worst from his American captors. Instead, they gave him a first-class trip back to Japan. His first words to his people were, "It is with much embarrassment that I return." But instead, the Japanese people welcomed him back as a national hero. He became a popular commentator on survival and even ran for parliament. You can even tour his little cave home in the remote outback of Guam. Yokoi died in September 1997.

When David was being pursued by King Saul, he hid in the mountains with a small army of loyal men. Saul tried repeatedly to capture David but could never lay a hand on him. The wilderness strongholds provided the perfect defense for David's quick and nimble army. Hiding is not an easy thing to do, especially for Yokoi, who initially hid with 10 other Japanese soldiers. Seven of them moved away, and the remaining three were together for several years before they separated. Yokoi later found them dead, apparently from starvation.

In 1 Samuel 23 we read how Saul's army finally encircled David in the wilderness of Maon. Providentially, a messenger called Saul away to fight the Philistines, who had just invaded the land. David was spared, and the place was called "the Rock of Escape."

We too may find a Rock in the wilderness in which to hide from the enemy. Jesus Christ is our sure Protector.

KEY BIBLE TEXT: "For in the time of trouble He shall hide me in His pavilion; in the secret place of His tabernacle He shall hide me; He shall set me high upon a rock" (Psalm 27:5).

The Lord's Anointed

DAY 132

An Amazing Fact: *The same night that John Wilkes Booth assassinated President Abraham Lincoln, assassinations were also attempted against Secretary of State William Seward and Vice President Andrew Johnson.*

Most people don't realize that Booth, when he took the life of Abraham Lincoln, also sought to wipe out Lincoln's entire leadership. On the same night, Lewis Powell attempted to assassinate Secretary of State Seward in his home. Powell was able to gain entry into Seward's home by claiming he was delivering medicine to the ailing man. When he gained entry to his room, he made his attempt.

Though Seward was critically injured by Powell's knife, he did survive. While recovering, he was not told about Lincoln's assassination in fear that it might send him into shock and derail his recovery. While looking out the window from his bed a few days later, however, Seward noticed the American flag flying at half-mast. He said to his attendant, "The president is dead." When the young man tried to deny it, Seward said, "If he had been alive he would have been the first to call on me."

Vice President Andrew Johnson was a little more fortunate. The man who was supposed to kill him at his hotel decided against the plan 15 minutes before he was to carry it out. "I enlisted to abduct the President of the United States," the man later claimed, "not to kill."

Young David, after he was anointed by Samuel to be king but before he did become king, had the chance to take the life of King Saul on two occasions. But David, learning from the ways of his merciful God, refused to do so, saying, "I will not stretch out my hand against my lord, for he is the Lord's anointed" (1 Samuel 24:10). Saul was anything but righteous at that point, yet David felt convicted by God that He had no business taking the life of the king.

KEY BIBLE TEXT: "Do not be overcome by evil, but overcome evil with good" (Romans 12:21).

DAY 133 The Deceiver

An Amazing Fact: *When it comes to disguise, octopuses are the ultimate chameleons. Thanks to special cells in their skin, they have the ability to change color and texture, assuming a thousand combinations. In the blink of an eye, they can fade into the sea floor, appearing to be just another bumpy rock.*

One Pacific Ocean octopus has earned its name from its incredible ability to transform its shape. The mimic octopus has been known to imitate everything from giant crabs and fish to sea snakes. One clever species will even take up residence in a vacant clamshell and use the suction cups on its tentacles to slowly open and close the shell. It will then wiggle the tip of one tentacle like a little worm to attract hungry fish—and whoosh!—the octopus will jet out and seize the unsuspecting victim.

Among the most flexible and versatile of all God's creatures, an octopus can squeeze into amazingly small spaces to hunt or avoid predators. They've been known to hide themselves in soda cans and aspirin bottles! This ability to fit into tight spots pays off when hunting, as octopuses can chase small crabs, shrimp, and fish into tiny cracks, coaxing them out with their long tentacles.

The Bible tells us that when Jesus' disciples asked about signs of the end of the age, Jesus said, "Take heed that no one deceives you. For many will come in My name, saying, 'I am He,' and will deceive many" (Mark 13:5, 6). One of the signs of Christ's soon coming is the work of the deceiver, Satan, who will pretend to be the Messiah and call people to follow him. If we study our Bibles carefully, we will watch and be ready for it. God will give us eyes to spot the master of deception no matter what shape or color he makes himself into. We need not fall into his traps.

KEY BIBLE TEXT: "Let no one deceive you by any means; for that Day will not come unless the falling away comes first, and the man of sin is revealed, the son of perdition" (2 Thessalonians 2:3).

Warning Against Imposters

DAY 134

An Amazing Fact: *In the 19th century, at least five public figures claimed to be Jesus Christ or another messiah. In the 20th century, the number of individuals making similar claims more than quadrupled.*

Ever since Jesus returned to heaven, there have been "false christs" and "false prophets." Knowing this would happen, Jesus specifically warned us about them. Their aim is deception. Jesus told us these imposters would "deceive, if possible, even the elect." It sounds like we need to pray for alertness and wisdom!

How will we recognize the real Jesus Christ when He comes back to Earth? We will be able to tell by the manner of His return. Jesus gives us these details: "Then they will see the Son of Man coming in the clouds with great power and glory" (Mark 13:26). "For as lightning comes from the east and flashes to the west, so also will the coming of the Son of Man be" (Matthew 24:27). The Apostle John tells us, "Behold, He is coming with clouds, and every eye will see Him" (Revelation 1:7).

During this earth-shattering event, it will be obvious to everyone that it's the end of the age. Some will mourn. But for those who belong to Him, it will be an awesome experience of joy as we realize that the fulfillment of all our hope—our Savior—has arrived!

KEY BIBLE TEXT: "Then if anyone says to you, 'Look, here is the Christ!' or, 'Look, He is there!' do not believe it. For false christs and false prophets will rise and show signs and wonders to deceive, if possible, even the elect. ... Then they will see the Son of Man coming in the clouds with great power and glory. And then He will send His angels, and gather together His elect from the four winds, from the farthest part of earth to the farthest part of heaven" (Mark 13:21, 22, 26, 27).

DAY 135 Paradise

An Amazing Fact: *Where is the best place in the world to live? According to an annual survey of the Economist Intelligence Unit, Vancouver, British Columbia, has hit the top for the fifth year in a row. Cities are rated in five areas: stability, healthcare, culture and environment, education, and infrastructure. Second place went to Melbourne, Australia, and third to Vienna, Austria.*

But wait a minute! The United Nations listed Norway as the most desirable country in the world in which to live, followed by Australia and Iceland. At the bottom of its list are Niger, Afghanistan, and Sierra Leone, especially because of war and AIDs epidemics. Except that CNN reports that International Living magazine voted France, for a fifth year in a row, the best place in the world to live! You can get 12 months of paid maternity leave in France, guaranteed by law. Finally, Forbes shares the research of international human resource consulting company Mercer, which puts Vienna, Austria, at the top. In fact, not one place in the United States makes the list.

So where is paradise? Where is the perfect place to live? It depends. Most people are pretty happy right where they are at this moment. The environment is certainly nicer in some parts of the world than others, though toxins have touched our entire planet wherever you go. The biggest problem with finding the perfect place to live is that any place that has a human being will be imperfect, including your own home—that includes the person who looks back at you from the mirror every morning.

Paul writes about an acquaintance who apparently had a vision of paradise (2 Corinthians 12:4), also known as the garden of Eden. This special place was our first home, but our planet has undergone some changes since God first created the perfect place for us to live. Someday Eden will be restored (Revelation 2:7). When that day comes, we will have no doubts about the best place in the world to live.

KEY BIBLE TEXT: "The Lord God planted a garden eastward in Eden, and there He put the man whom He had formed" (Genesis 2:8).

More Precious Than Perfume

An Amazing Fact: *For $215,000, you can buy the world's most expensive perfume. That money will buy a 16.9-ounce bottle of Clive Christian's Imperial Majesty.*

With only 10 bottles of Imperial Majesty in the world, it's not the perfume itself that makes it so expensive—though even the perfume alone at $2,150 an ounce would be more expensive than any other. Instead, what makes Clive Christian's perfume so outrageously expensive is its bottle. The 16.9 ounces of perfume is poured into a Baccarat crystal bottle, complete with a five-carat diamond mounted onto an 18-carat gold collar.

Talk about an expensive Mother's Day gift!

Mark 14 tells of another tale of expensive perfume. While Jesus dined in Bethany at Simon the leper's house a few days before His crucifixion, the dinner party was interrupted by the smell of a distinguished fragrance. Looking all around the room in search of the scent's origin, everyone's eyes settled upon a sinful woman who was washing Jesus' feet with the ointment. It didn't take long for Judas to rally the other disciples in protest of the woman's supposed wastefulness. After all, Judas exclaims, the perfume might have been sold for more than 300 denarii (a year's worth of wages) and given to the poor.

But much to the audience's utter surprise, Jesus commanded everyone to leave her alone, for "she has done a good work for Me" (Mark 14:6). Why the positive response from Jesus—who was ever concerned about the poor? Because the costly ointment being poured out was a picture of His precious, priceless blood that He was about to pour out for the entire world.

KEY BIBLE TEXT: "Knowing that you were not redeemed with corruptible things, like silver or gold, from your aimless conduct received by tradition from your fathers, but with the precious blood of Christ, as of a lamb without blemish and without spot" (1 Peter 1:18, 19).

DAY 137 Respecting the Power

An Amazing Fact: *U.S. National Park Ranger Roy Sullivan has the record for being struck by lightning the most times. Sullivan was struck eight times during his 35-year career. He lost the nail on one of his big toes and suffered multiple other injuries to the rest of his body.*

Lightning is an atmospheric electrostatic discharge between rain clouds or between a rain cloud and the earth seen in the form of a brilliant arc—sometimes several miles long. The discharge creates a sound wave that is heard as thunder. Some strokes might even move from ground to cloud, particularly from mountain peaks and tall objects such as radio towers. Lightning flashes from a cloud to the earth can be less than 3,000 feet in length, while flashes from one cloud to another have been recorded at more than 20 miles long. Only one lightning flash in a hundred ever strikes the earth.

However, contrary to the belief that lightning never strikes the same spot twice, it has been known to strike one object or person many times during an intense electrical storm. During one such storm, the Empire State Building was struck 15 times within 15 minutes. Lightning is also fast and hot. A bolt of lightning can travel up to 140,000 miles per hour and can reach temperatures approaching 54,000 degrees. An estimated 24,000 people are killed by lightning strikes each year around the world.

The most sacred object in Israel was the Ark of the Covenant. When David had the Ark moved to Jerusalem, Uzzah reached out to steady ark when the oxen stumbled, and he instantly died. Uzzah might have had become so familiar with the sacred that he no longer respected God's requirements about touching it. Later, instead of moving the Ark on an oxcart (Philistine-style), it was carried by the priests using poles as God had commanded.

Can we also become so familiar with the sacred that we lose our respect for the things of God?

KEY BIBLE TEXT: "And when Aaron and his sons have finished covering the sanctuary and all the furnishings ... then the sons of Kohath shall come to carry them; but they shall not touch any holy thing, lest they die" (Numbers 4:15).

We Can't Earn It

An Amazing Fact: *The apostle Paul's 35 years of travels took him through Turkey, Greece, Rome, and, of course, Israel and Palestine. Sometimes he journeyed by ship (he was shipwrecked three times!) and sometimes by foot. During his five missionary trips, he traveled a total of 13,000 miles.*

When Paul wrote his letter to the Galatians, he told them plainly that if anyone tried to preach a different gospel to them, that person should be "accursed"—even if it was him or an angel. That was strong language, but Paul needed to get their attention. He had taught them salvation by faith in Christ alone, but someone had been teaching the Galatians something quite different, telling them they needed to do certain other things in order to be saved.

The gospel Paul had preached, he reminded them, was not something he had made up. No human taught or gave him the gospel. He says, "It came through the revelation of Jesus Christ." After Paul's conversion, Jesus Himself revealed the gospel to him.

There is only one gospel. At its core are Jesus Christ and His sacrifice, which reconciles us to God through faith. Nothing we can do could ever earn the salvation that He gives to us as a free gift.

KEY BIBLE TEXT: "But even if we, or an angel from heaven, preach any other gospel to you than what we have preached to you, let him be accursed. ... But I make known to you, brethren, that the gospel which was preached by me is not according to man. For I neither received it from man, nor was I taught it, but it came through the revelation of Jesus Christ" (Galatians 1:8, 11, 12).

DAY 139 Gestures

An Amazing Fact: *Zoosemiotics, the study of animal communication, is a growing field of study of different forms such as gestures, facial expressions, gaze following, vocalization, and olfactory communication. Male humpback whales sing the longest and most complex songs in the animal kingdom. Each song lasts for more than half an hour. These messages can be heard underwater from more than a thousand miles away!*

Gestures are one of the most common forms of animal communication. For instance, the herring gull will present its bill to the chicks followed by a tapping on the ground. The babies see the red spot on the mother's bill and peck at it, which in turn causes the parent to regurgitate food for the young. Dogs have many facial expressions that communicate things like anger, through baring their teeth, for instance.

Vocalizations communicate warnings, conveying food sources, mating rituals, and more. But you can be fooled by animal communication if you are not careful to pick up metacommunication signals. These signals modify certain messages given by the animal. One of the most common examples is when dogs "fight" playfully. Initial "play face" signals and the position of the dog's tail indicate that what follows is more fun than aggressive.

In the garden of Gethsemane, Judas greeted Jesus with a kiss. But his communication was deceptive. On the surface he appeared to be happy to see Christ, but underneath he was sending a signal to the soldiers. "Now His betrayer had given them a signal, saying, 'Whomever I kiss, He is the One; seize Him and lead Him away safely'" (Mark 14:44). Judas likely hoped Christ would display His power and escape. But that didn't happen.

Our Lord allowed Himself to suffer and die in order to communicate a clear message of love and hope to us. His meaning was to the point. "I love you and want you to be with Me in My kingdom forever." Will we receive His gesture of love?

Can we also become so familiar with the sacred that we lose our respect for the things of God?

KEY BIBLE TEXT: "That which we have seen and heard we declare to you, that you may have fellowship with us" (1 John 1:3).

By Beholding ...

An Amazing Fact: *By the time the average American turns 65, he or she will have spent nine years watching television.*

The numbers are astounding. People in America watch a lot of TV. The research is quite extensive. The average American watches about four hours of television a day, which amounts to about two months of straight TV watching each year.

And televisions aren't little boxes anymore! Whereas TVs used to be 18 inches, 20 inches, or maybe 30 inches, the average size of a TV these days is 46 inches—with some people estimating that by 2015 the average TV will be 60 inches! And it's all in high definition now, so everything looks so real.

This means that by the time a child departs elementary school and has witnessed 8,000 murders on TV, and the 200,000 acts of violence by the time they're 18, every single scene will have been as about as realistic as it can get—in true-to-reality, high-definition 60-inch television.

This is not meant to scare you into throwing out your TV. It's a simple reality check. Paul writes in positive terms: "But we all, with unveiled face, beholding as in a mirror the glory of the Lord, are being transformed into the same image from glory to glory, just as by the Spirit of the Lord" (2 Corinthians 3:18).

Thus, we are encouraged to spend our time—maybe even more than nine years—looking into the face of Christ. Because when we look at Jesus through the Word of God, we are transformed into His beautiful, compassionate, and loving image.

KEY BIBLE TEXT: "Therefore, holy brethren, partakers of the heavenly calling, consider the Apostle and High Priest of our confession, Christ Jesus" (Hebrews 3:1).

DAY 141 Crowing Communication

An Amazing Fact: *Roosters do not always crow at the crack of dawn. Some will crow any time during the day. A rooster crows to protect his hens and ward off enemies, and they are very territorial. Since they are active during the day, they are most rambunctious in the morning when their testosterone level is highest.*

"Cock-a-doodle-doo" is the phrase we often think of when a rooster jumps up on a fence post at the crack of dawn to welcome the new day. But lots of other things can set off a rooster to crow, such as a train passing by or a car starting. A cockerel (another name for rooster) is also very protective of his hens and will be quick to fight off any intruders.

Crowing roosters can sometimes be such a bother to neighbors that people look for ways to quiet their "fowl" talk. Locking him up at night, sealing off the cracks in the henhouse that let light in, or using blackout curtains are a few ways to fool him into holding back the crowing. Caponizing (neutering) a rooster will also sometimes help.

There is a familiar story in the Bible about a rooster crowing. Peter was told by Jesus in the upper room that he would deny Christ three times. Peter vehemently rebuked Jesus, saying, "If I have to die with You, I will not deny you!" (Mark 14:31). But it happened in the courtyard of the high priest—Peter denied Christ. "A second time the rooster crowed. Then Peter called to mind the word that Jesus had said to him, 'Before the rooster crows twice, you will deny Me three times.' And when he thought about it, he wept" (Mark 14:72).

How sensitive are we to God's call to our hearts when we sin or deny Christ? How tuned in are we to the Holy Spirit's whisper? Would we hear the Lord wooing us if we heard a rooster crow?

KEY BIBLE TEXT: "And when he brings out his own sheep, he goes before them; and the sheep follow him, for they know his voice" (John 10:4).

Lifting the Needy

An Amazing Fact: *According to the United Nations Food and Agriculture Organization, about 925 million people in the world are undernourished—that's one in seven. Poor nutrition kills at least 5,000,000 children every year.*

Starvation is only one of the heart-wrenching problems that affect the poor and the needy. Clean drinking water and proper medical care are two more critical needs, and there are many others.

Psalm 113 says that God "raises the poor out of the dust, and lifts the needy out of the ash heap, that He may seat him with princes" (vs. 7, 8). This shows the great value God places on the poor. The Bible says, "Has God not chosen the poor of this world to be rich in faith and heirs of the kingdom which He promised to those who love Him?" (James 2:5). The people who suffer in poverty are as important to God as the rulers of the nations. They are just as surely His children.

It's easy to be overwhelmed by the sad statistics, even to be stunned into inaction. After all, what can one person do against such widespread tragedy and desperation? The truth is we can all do something, at least in some small way, to alleviate the suffering in the world.

Love for God obligates us to act. As ambassadors for Christ, we must continue His work of lifting up the needy with our love.

KEY BIBLE TEXT: "Who is like the LORD our God, who dwells on high, who humbles Himself to behold the things that are in the heavens and in the earth? He raises the poor out of the dust, and lifts the needy out of the ash heap, that He may seat him with princes—with the princes of His people" (Psalm 113:5–8).

DAY 143 Which Prisoner?

An Amazing Fact: *The United States has the highest incarceration rate in the developed world. The most recent statistics (2009) show 743 inmates for every 100,000 people. According to the U.S. Bureau of Justice Statistics, 7.2 million people were on probation, in jail or prison, or on parole—or about 3.1 percent of all adults.*

At the end of 2009, there were about 2.3 million inmates in the United States. The three states with the lowest ratio of prisoners per population were Maine, Minnesota, and New Hampshire. The states with the highest ratio were Louisiana, Mississippi, and Oklahoma.

There are different types of facilities to hold inmates. Local city and county jails hold less serious offenders. Prisons hold more serious offenders and range from minimum security to supermax facilities, which house the most dangerous criminals. Prison population charts look fairly level with moderate increases from the 1920s to the 1970s. But in the 1980s until today, the graph spikes upward very quickly.

At Jesus' trial before Pilate, a prisoner named Barabbas was brought out. This hardcore criminal did not forget to pay a parking meter; he had been incarcerated for murder and was likely a member of the violent Jewish party called the Zealots. Pilate felt the pressure of the crowd, who wanted him to unjustly convict Jesus. He remembered the Jewish custom of releasing a prisoner during Passover, and he gave the mob a choice between Jesus and Barabbas.

The guilty man was set free, and the righteous Man was condemned. The true prisoner was unchained, and the One without fault was bound. The murderer got off and the Life Giver got put in. The one who truly deserved death, Barabbas, represents you and me. He was released so that the One who did not deserve death could take on the penalty of sin so that we could be set free.

KEY BIBLE TEXT: "So Pilate, wanting to gratify the crowd, released Barabbas to them; and he delivered Jesus, after he had scourged Him, to be crucified" (Mark 15:15).

Adoption

An Amazing Fact: *Steve Jobs, the founder and former CEO of Apple, was adopted as a baby.*

From Aristotle to Johan Sebastian Bach to Gerald Ford, many famous people have been adopted. Perhaps no adoptee is more relevant to today's culture, however, than Steve Jobs. As the founder and former CEO of one of America's most valuable companies, Jobs is widely considered around the world as the leading innovator.

But it wasn't always easy for him. His unwed birth parents were both graduate students in California—his dad Syrian and his mom American. Unable to take care of him, his mother made arrangements for him to be adopted during her pregnancy by a lawyer and his wife. When plans fell through shortly before he was born, because the first couple decided they wanted a girl instead, Jobs's birth mother was forced to hand him over to another couple, neither of whom had a college degree. In fact, his dad didn't even have a high school education. His mother agreed to give him to Paul and Clara Jobs, contingent upon them promising to send Steve to college some day. They made good on their promise, and 17 years later Steve enrolled in college—only to drop out six months later.

The rest is history. Along with a close friend, Steve went on to start Apple Computers at age 20. Apple is the leading technology brand in the world and flirts with the title of most valuable company in America—switching back and forth with Exxon-Mobile. And all this has been accomplished by a man who was put up for adoption by a mother who couldn't take care of him.

One of the Bible's favorite salvation themes is adoption. Though we were once in bondage and estranged from Christ, Paul says that we have been adopted into the family of God and we are now His sons and daughters. (See Galatians 4:1–7.) And since we are adopted into God's family, we can attain to even greater heights than Steve Jobs!

KEY BIBLE TEXT: "For you did not receive the spirit of bondage again to fear, but you received the Spirit of adoption by whom we cry out, 'Abba, Father'" (Romans 8:15).

DAY 145 Fixed to a Cross

An Amazing Fact: *The word "crucifixion" comes from the Latin meaning "fixed to a cross." It was an ancient method of execution in which the victim's hands and feet were bound and nailed to a cross. It was one of the most horribly painful and disgraceful methods of capital punishment, and as such was primarily reserved for traitors, captive armies, slaves, and the worst of criminals.*

Many Christians carry the symbol of the "cross" stamped on their Bibles or hanging around their necks. But few have explored the depths of the horror of this form of execution. Crucifixion most likely began with the Persians, but later spread to the Assyrians, Scythians, Carthaginians, Germans, Celts, and Britons. Under Alexander the Great, Roman crucifixions became commonplace.

The Romans usually had the victim beaten and tortured, and then they forced the captives to carry their own cross to the crucifixion site. After binding the hands and feet and nailing the criminal with crude iron nails to the wooden cross, a small platform was placed under the feet to allow the victim to lift himself up for an agonizing breath, thus prolonging suffering and delaying death. Unsupported, the victim would hang entirely from nail-pierced wrists, severely restricting breathing and circulation. At times mercy would be shown by breaking the victim's legs, causing death to come quickly. As a deterrent to crime, crucifixions were usually conducted in highly public places, with the criminal charges posted on the cross above the victim's head.

Jesus was crucified with these posted words: "THE KING OF THE JEWS" (Mark 15:26). He was executed in a highly visible place. People mocked him. They laughed at Him, scorned Him, and wagged their heads. "He saved others," they said, "Himself He cannot save" (v. 31). How true. Jesus chose to stay on that wooden cross in order to "save others." Will you receive Him as your Savior?

KEY BIBLE TEXT: "I have been crucified with Christ; it is no longer I who live, but Christ lives in me; and the life which I now live in the flesh I live by faith in the Son of God, who loved me and gave Himself for me" (Galatians 2:20).

The Heavens Are the Lord's

An Amazing Fact: *Our Milky Way Galaxy is part of what astronomers call the "Local Group," which also includes the Andromeda Galaxy, the Triangulum Galaxy, and approximately 30 smaller galaxies. The Andromeda Galaxy, also known as M31, is our nearest neighboring spiral galaxy and is close to 2,500,000 light-years away. It can be seen from Earth's Northern Hemisphere.*

One of the greatest blessings on Earth is the ability to look up into the night sky and gaze upon the beautiful, creative masterpiece that we call the universe. But when we do this, we really have a very weak concept of what we are looking at (even the astronomers among us). There are more mysteries about the cosmos, it seems, than there are stars. Even of our home galaxy we know very little. Nevertheless, stargazing is an awe-inspiring activity. Our hearts are drawn to the Creator as we marvel at such stunning work.

A well-known psalm of David says, "When I consider Your heavens, the work of Your fingers, the moon and the stars, which You have ordained, what is man that You are mindful of him, and the son of man that You visit him?" (Psalm 8:3, 4). It's mind-blowing to realize that the God who knows every intricate detail of such a massive universe cares for us. He who placed and maintains each star and planet and galaxy—and knows them all by name—this same Creator God is very interested in the details of each of our lives because He loves us so much.

KEY BIBLE TEXT: "May you be blessed by the LORD, Who made heaven and earth. The heaven, even the heavens, are the LORD's; but the earth He has given to the children of men" (Psalm 115:15, 16).

DAY 147 The Tallest Tree

An Amazing Fact: *The world's tallest standing tree is a Coast Redwood at 379.1 feet tall, located in Redwood National Park in California. The stoutest tree in the world (the girth of the tree) is an African Baobab, with a circumference of 52 feet. The largest tree (in volume) is a Giant Sequoia named General Sherman located in Sequoia National Park in California.*

There has been much debate over which is the tallest tree in the world. This partly comes from poor methods of measuring and much exaggeration. Perhaps the simplest and most accurate way to measure giant trees is by climbing to the top and dropping down a tape measure. Historical claims of trees growing to 490 or 500 feet tall are now disregarded as unreliable and/or attributed to human error.

The northern coast of California seems to be the ideal location for tall trees to grow. In fact, of the 10 tallest trees in the world, three are in California and one is in Oregon (a Coast Douglas Fir measuring 326 ft.). Yet there are also four record-breaking trees in Tasmania, Australia. The other two countries with the tallest trees are the Philippines and Borneo.

Jesus was crucified on a wooden cross, sometimes referred to as a tree (1 Peter 2:24). When Christ died, it was as if a mighty tree had fallen. "And Jesus cried out with a loud voice, and breathed His last" (Mark 15:37). Actually, something did fall. "Then the veil of the temple was torn in two from top to bottom" (v. 38). This refers to the inner veil that separated the Holy Place from the Most Holy Place in the sanctuary. Only the High Priest could enter beyond the veil to speak with God on behalf of the Lord's people. The rending of this curtain signified that the old order of ceremonies and sacrifices had passed.

Jesus' death on the "tree" of Calvary opened a new era when people could approach God directly through Christ in the heavenly sanctuary. We may now reach new heights because the tallest Tree had been cut down.

KEY BIBLE TEXT: "Christ has redeemed us from the curse of the law, having become a curse for us (for it is written, 'Cursed is everyone who hangs on a tree')" (Galatians 3:13).

The Biggest Cup

An Amazing Fact: *Baskin-Robbins holds the Guinness World Record for the largest cup of ice cream ever made. It weighed in at 8,865 pounds!*

In celebration of its 60th birthday, Baskin-Robbins decided it would create the world's largest cup of ice cream. On September 13, 2005, the company made an 8,865-pound cup of ice cream at its Canton, Massachusetts, headquarters.

Which one of their 31 flavors did they use? Vanilla, of course!

Though that is a huge cup of tasty ice cream, it is nowhere near the size of a cup of something else the Bible mentions. The author of Psalm 116 praises the Lord for "all his goodness to" him (v. 12 NIV). And in return, he says that he will "take up the cup of salvation and call upon the name of the Lord" (v. 13).

Could there be any cup in the universe that is bigger? The "cup of salvation" is big enough for everyone to take from, for God "desires all men to be saved" (1 Timothy 2:4). And Christ has certainly made the way for all to be saved, because as He sweat drops of blood in the garden of Gethsemane, He finally took up that cup after pleading with His Father to take it from Him (Matthew 26:36–46). Only it wasn't 8,865 pounds of vanilla ice cream that He tasted; instead, as He lifted that cup to His quivering lips, the author of Hebrews says that He "tasted death for everyone" (Hebrews 2:9).

Thus, there is no reason why any of us should be lost! Christ has tasted death for every man and every woman and now invites us to drink from the biggest cup in the universe—the cup of salvation. Will you respond to His invitation?

KEY BIBLE TEXT: "And He Himself is the propitiation for our sins, and not ours only, but also for the whole world" (1 John 2:2).

DAY 149 The Brightest Light

An Amazing Fact: *"The Torch" claims to be the world's brightest flashlight. It is currently being tested by the Guinness Book of World Records as the world's most powerful flashlight, with 4,100 lumens of "raw light power." It is supposedly 100 lumens brighter than the previous record holder. It burns so hot that it can ignite paper, melt plastic, and even cook an egg. All yours for only $149!*

Ever since the invention of the light bulb, mankind has continued to make more powerful and brighter lights. One of the brightest lights in the world (claimed by its owners) is the tip of Luxor Hotel in Las Vegas, which contains a fixed-position spotlight that points directly upward. Its beam is supposedly 42.3 billion candlepower.

But you don't need to go to Las Vegas to find the brightest light in the world. David writes in 2 Samuel 22:29, "For You are my lamp, O Lord; the Lord shall enlighten my darkness." From the first day of Creation when God proclaimed, "Let there be light" (Genesis 1:3), to the final book of Revelation, which tells us, "There shall be no more night there: They need no lamp nor light of the sun, for the Lord God gives them light" (Revelation 22:5), there is a clear association between our Lord and light.

Jesus said, "I am the light of the world. He who follows Me shall not walk in darkness, but have the light of life" (John 8:12). Then in John 12:36, Christ admonishes us, "While you have the light, believe in the light, that you may become sons of the light."

The Word of God, the Bible, is also referred to as light. In fact, David says, "Your word is a lamp to my feet and a light to my path" (Psalm 119:105). You do not need the world's most powerful flashlight to find your way to heaven. God provides the light you need through the Bible. Turn on your light every day.

KEY BIBLE TEXT: "But if we walk in the light as He is in the light, we have fellowship with one another" (1 John 1:7).

Don't Bite

An Amazing Fact: *Americans report about 16 shark bites, 8,000 venomous snakebites, 400,000 cat bites, 5 million dog bites, and 70,000 human bites each year. Of these, human bites are the most likely to cause infection because of the types of bacteria that live in our mouths.*

To "backbite" means to say mean, slanderous, or spiteful things about people when they are not present—to talk about them behind their backs. This can be far more malicious than common gossip, and more damaging to our souls. Paul warns, "But if you bite and devour one another, beware lest you be consumed by one another!" (Galatians 5:15).

Backbiting is always destructive. It can wreck friendships and dissolve marriages. It can tear apart a church community. As Christians, backbiting is something we always want to avoid. If we ever find ourselves as part of a conversation attacking another person, the best thing to do is walk away. Or if we know the accusation to be untrue, we might even speak up in defense of the person.

If we really love our neighbors as ourselves, if we have the fruit of the Spirit, if we belong to Christ, backbiting can have no part in our lives. Instead, we must "through love serve one another" (v. 13).

KEY BIBLE TEXT: "For all the law is fulfilled in one word, even in this: 'You shall love your neighbor as yourself.' But if you bite and devour one another, beware lest you be consumed by one another! ... But the fruit of the Spirit is love, joy, peace, longsuffering, kindness, goodness, faithfulness, gentleness, self-control. Against such there is no law. And those who are Christ's have crucified the flesh with its passions and desires" (Galatians 5:14, 15, 22–24).

DAY 151 David's Dream Team

An Amazing Fact: *The 1992 U.S. men's Olympic basketball team, nicknamed the "Dream Team," was the first American Olympic team to feature active NBA players. It was considered one of the strongest team in any sport and beat opponents by an average of 44 points each game. It won the gold against Croatia in the summer games in Barcelona.*

Some of the famous names of this team include Michael Jordan, Scottie Pippen, John Stockton, Karl Malone, Magic Johnson, and Larry Bird. In June 1992 the team made its debut in Portland, Oregon, where they easily beat the Cubans 136 to 57 and prompted their coach, Miguel Calderon Gomez, to say, "You can't cover the sun with your finger."

Fans and opposing players all welcomed the Dream Team to the Olympics and wanted their pictures taken with them. But not everyone liked them. They received death threats and were guarded by soldiers with Uzis. The team was elected to Basketball's Hall of Fame in 2010.

In the Bible, we find a "dream team" in the Old Testament. David had his "mighty men," 37 in all, who were powerful warriors with stories of great victory. God used these soldiers to give Israel victory over its enemies. These are men who fought lions and single-handedly dispatched hundreds of Philistines. Three men broke though a stronghold of Philistines at Bethlehem just to get a drink of water for David.

But victory does not go to men; the glory goes to God. Many times in the Bible you will read, as in 2 Samuel 23, "So the Lord brought about a great victory" (v. 12). David's dream team knew where all the power came from for beating the enemy—strength comes from the Lord. When we face our own enemies, we can be part of a dream team of heavenly hosts who will fight for us.

KEY BIBLE TEXT: "Hear, O Israel: Today you are on the verge of battle with your enemies. Do not let your heart be faint, do not be afraid, and do not tremble or be terrified because of them; for the Lord your God is He who goes with you, to fight for you against your enemies to save you" (Deuteronomy 20:3, 4).

God Speaks

DAY 152

An Amazing Fact: *Albert Einstein did not learn how to talk until after the age of two.*

It's hard to believe that the man who many consider to be one of *the* most brilliant geniuses—if not *the* most brilliant genius—in the history of the world had trouble learning how to talk. But such was the case with theoretical physicist Albert Einstein. His parents were so worried, in fact, that they consulted a doctor about the problem. The problem didn't end after he began to finally talk, however. He was so quirky and slow in his speech that family members dubbed him "der Depperte," or, "the dopey one."

When he did make sense in his speech, he still left people perplexed. Upon seeing his sister Maja for the first time after her birth, he immediately asked, "Yes, but where are the wheels?"

We can be thankful that God has no such problem when it comes to speaking or making sense. This reality caused the psalmist to joyfully proclaim, "I called on the Lord in distress; the Lord answered me and set me in a broad place" (Psalm 118:5). We need not fear that God will not hear us when we cry out or that He will not respond with a voice of truth and peace.

This doesn't mean, of course, that God will always respond to us instantly or even in the way that we want. But we can rest in the assurance that He will speak on our behalf and that His words are powerful enough to bring about amazing things.

KEY BIBLE TEXT: "For as the rain comes down and the snow from heaven, and do not return there, but water the earth, and make it bring forth and bud, that it may give seed to the sower and bread to the eater, so shall My word be that goes forth from My mouth; it shall not return to Me void, but it shall accomplish what I please and it shall prosper in the thing for which I sent it" (Isaiah 55:10, 11).

DAY 153 Covered by His Blood

An Amazing Fact: *Around A.D. 400, the great Coliseum in Rome was often packed as spectators watched violent games in which human beings battled one another or wild beasts until one was killed. People reveled in such sport and found their highest delight when a person was slain. On one such day, a Syrian monk named Telemachus stood up. He was grieved and outraged by the utter disregard for human life and leapt into the arena in the midst of the carnage! He boldly cried out, "This thing is not right! This thing must stop!"*

Telemachus was a daring man. He was willing to stand up and call a spade a spade. Because he was interfering with their entertainment, the authorities commanded for Telemachus to be run through with a sword. Some stories say he was stoned to death by the crowd. But his death kindled a flame in the hearts and consciences of many. History tells us that because of his courageous sacrifice, within a few months these blood baths began to decline and soon ended.

Jesus Christ stepped into the stadium of our planet, where the battles between good and evil was waged over the lives of God's people. Our Lord stood against the tide of evil, placing His own life in the midst of the carnage. The crowds at Jesus' trial were incensed and cried out against Him. They crucified the true King of the Jews. But by His death, redemption and life came to many.

The Bible says, "In Him we have redemption through His blood, the forgiveness of sins, according to the riches of His grace" (Ephesians 1:7). Because Jesus was willing to lay down His life, the battle between life and death has ended for those who choose to follow the Lord and accept His sacrifice for our sins.

KEY BIBLE TEXT: "Or do you not know that as many of us as were baptized into Christ Jesus were baptized into His death? Therefore we were buried with Him through baptism into death, that just as Christ was raised from the dead by the glory of the Father, even so we also should walk in newness of life" (Romans 6:3, 4).

Asking for Wisdom

An Amazing Fact: *In the 17th century people began calling the third molars "the teeth of wisdom." Later, this was shortened to "wisdom teeth." The name has some basis in fact, since these teeth tend to appear during the transition into adulthood and by the time a person's brain reaches its full development, which is about 25 years of age.*

Solomon started out his kingship with the right attitude. He knew he needed discernment in order to be a good king, and he knew only God could provide it. Bowing before the Lord, he humbly prayed for wisdom, referring to himself as "a little child."

In the same sense, we are all little children. We desperately need wisdom and guidance from our heavenly Father for all aspects of our lives. And God is glad to give it to us. "If any of you lacks wisdom," the Bible tells us, "let him ask of God, who gives to all liberally and without reproach, and it will be given to him" (James 1:5). Here's a promise we could claim every day!

Paul prayed that the early Christian believers would receive "the spirit of wisdom and revelation in the knowledge of Him [Jesus]" (Ephesians 1:17). And we know that "the fear of the Lord is the beginning of wisdom" (Proverbs 9:10). Knowing and honoring Christ is where wisdom begins.

KEY BIBLE TEXT: "Now, O LORD my God, You have made Your servant king instead of my father David, but I am a little child; I do not know how to go out or come in. ... Therefore give to Your servant an understanding heart to judge Your people, that I may discern between good and evil" (1 Kings 3:7, 9).

DAY 155 Beautiful Buildings

An Amazing Fact: *The Taj Mahal (meaning "crown of buildings") is a mausoleum located in Agra, India. It was built in 1653 by Mughal emperor Shah Jahan in memory of his third wife, Mumtaz Mahal. It is often recognized as one of the most beautiful buildings in the world.*

Myths and legends surround the construction of the Taj. As one of the seven wonders of the ancient world, there is great interest in this amazing structure. We know it took about 22 years and 22,000 people to construct the building. Some estimate that in today's dollar, it cost about $100 million to construct. Apparently 1,000 elephants were used to transport building materials during construction. The architecture skillfully combines Persian, Islamic, and Indian styles.

The materials used to adorn the Taj Mahal include 28 different varieties of semi-precious and precious stones with exquisite inlay work. Depending on which time of day you view the tomb, you will see different colors—pink in the morning, white in the day, and golden in the moonlight. The pillars surrounding the Taj are slightly tilted outwards so that in the event of an earthquake they will fall away from the tomb itself.

The most beautiful temple in the world built in ancient times was surely Solomon's temple. His preparations are described in 1 Kings chapters 4 and 5. His labor force was 30,000 strong. His father, David, had already assembled a large store of materials. But we find Solomon working with Hiram, king of Tyre, to obtain a large harvest of timber (cedar and cypress logs). Huge stones were quarried, and Solomon paid them well.

Solomon probably would have been unhappy to know that this temple was named after himself. When writing to Hiram, he states, "And behold, I propose to build a house for the name of the Lord my God" (1 Kings 5:5). Even the king of Tyre responds, "Blessed be the Lord this day," giving thanks and glory to God (v. 7). The temple, which represents the life and work of Jesus, was to always point heavenward. Christ now stands in the heavenly sanctuary, alive and serving us. He is not dead in a tomb in Palestine.

KEY BIBLE TEXT: "And let them make Me a sanctuary, that I may dwell among them" (Exodus 25:8).

Sweeter Than Honey

An Amazing Fact: *Honey is the only food that doesn't spoil.*

Honeybees collect a thin, sweet liquid called nectar. Nectar spoils easily, but once ripened into honey, it becomes a stable, high-density, high-energy food. Honey contains more than 20 complex sugars. Small amounts of other substances are also present in honey—flavoring materials, pigments, acids, and minerals—but sugar makes up the majority. This high sugar content is what prevents honey from spoiling. If not sealed in a comb or jar, honey absorbs moisture from the air and eventually crystallizes, but crystallized honey is still usable if melted back into a liquid.

Honey has many internal and external uses. It's a short-term energy booster (although similar to refined sugar, it might come with a corresponding "carb crash"); it treats a sore throat; it enhances vitamin A absorption; it strengthens the colon; it helps remove parasites; local honey can help treat seasonal allergies; and some say a little honey every day even boosts the immune system. Externally, honey is valued in natural skincare as a moisturizer and acne fighter. Thanks to its antiseptic and antibacterial properties, honey helps clean and heal minor wounds.

Whether or not he knew the sweet substance's complexities since revealed by modern science, David knew its value when he compared it to God's law. God's versatile law applies to every life situation you might find yourself in. And like honey, God's law doesn't go bad!

KEY BIBLE TEXT: "The judgments of the Lord are true and righteous altogether. More to be desired are they than gold, yea, than much fine gold: sweeter also than honey and the honeycomb" (Psalm 19:9, 10). "Teach me, O Lord, the way of Your statutes, and I shall keep it to the end" (Psalm 119:33).

DAY 157 Out of the Desert

An Amazing Fact: *During the first Gulf War, a small team of U.S. Navy SEALS created a diversion so convincing that it completely fooled the Iraqi army. About a dozen SEALS stormed the beaches of Kuwait and created such havoc that Iraqi generals believed the U.S.-led attack was coming from the sea. Iraq sent the majority of their army to repel this fake attack—only to find they had been duped as the main U.S. force came through the Saudi Arabian desert! Within hours the war was over, and it all started with less than 20 soldiers!*

We don't think of the desert as a place where exciting things happen, but don't be fooled like the Iraqi army. Deserts are places on our planet characterized by little rain or plant growth. Specifically, they receive less than 10 inches of water per year. They are mostly made up of sand, rocks, and gravel. Deserts cover about one-fifth of all the land in the world. The largest hot desert in the world is the Sahara in North Africa. It covers 3.3 million square miles. Others have names and nicknames like "Death Valley," "The Empty Quarter," and "The Place of No Return."

But did you know that deserts are only second to tropical rain forests in the variety of plants and animals that live there? Even though they have a reputation for supporting little life, they have high biodiversity, including animals that remain hidden during daylight hours to control body temperature.

One of God's greatest soldiers in the Bible was John the Baptist. This prophetic "voice in the wilderness" grew up in the desert. The Bible says, "So the child grew and became strong in spirit, and was in the deserts till the day of his manifestation to Israel" (Luke 1:80). Many scoffed at this "wild man" from the desert, but John caught the attention of a growing number of leaders. His message cut deep. His voice rang true. And he eventually introduced the greatest figure in history, Jesus the Lamb of God.

Don't be surprised at what God can bring out of the desert!

KEY BIBLE TEXTS: "The voice of one crying in the wilderness; Prepare the way of the LORD; Make straight in the desert a highway for our God" (Isaiah 40:3).

Why Shepherds?

An Amazing Fact: *Sheep-herding dogs, such as border collies, are highly intelligent and can easily learn 20 to 30 different commands. These are communicated to the dog by voice, whistling, and/or hand signals. A well-trained working sheep dog is very valuable, with some selling for as much as $10,000 or more.*

Isn't it interesting that a group of shepherds were the first humans selected to visit Jesus after His birth? But why shepherds? Why not someone more prominent like a priest (there must have been a few good ones), or a governor, or some other ruler?

Many heroes in the Bible were shepherds. Abraham, Jacob, Moses, and David all had their flocks. What characteristic did these people all have in common? For one thing, they were all humble.

The shepherds that the angels visited were very humble people. They must have been looking for Him all along, studying the prophecies, praying, and waiting eagerly for their Messiah to arrive.

Jesus says, "And you will seek Me and find Me, when you search for Me with all your heart" (Jeremiah 29:13). Half-hearted looking won't do. We must search for Him without reserve, and with an open, humble heart.

KEY BIBLE TEXTS: "So it was, when the angels had gone away from them into heaven, that the shepherds said to one another, 'Let us now go to Bethlehem and see this thing that has come to pass, which the Lord has made known to us.' And they came with haste and found Mary and Joseph, and the Babe lying in a manger. Now when they had seen Him, they made widely known the saying which was told them concerning this Child. And all those who heard it marveled at those things which were told them by the shepherds. But Mary kept all these things and pondered them in her heart. Then the shepherds returned, glorifying and praising God for all the things that they had heard and seen, as it was told them" (Luke 2:15–20).

DAY 159 Walking With Jesus

An Amazing Fact: *Walking for 30 to 60 minutes a day, five days a week, has many health benefits, such as reducing the chances of cancer, type 2 diabetes, heart disease, anxiety, and even depression. It increases bone health, lowers the more harmful low-density lipoprotein (LDL) cholesterol and raises the more useful good high-density lipoprotein (HDL) cholesterol. Studies have also shown that walking can help prevent Alzheimer's and dementia.*

There is nothing simpler than walking, yet the benefits to the body's health are amazing. Brisk walking can improve your stamina, energy, weight control, life expectancy, and reduce stress. It can also reduce your risk of getting osteoporosis, bowel cancer, high blood pressure, diabetes, strokes, and coronary heart disease. It improves your memory skills, concentration, abstract reasoning—and not to mention that it can uplift your spirit!

There are many different forms of walking. Some people are fitness walkers and use pedometers to track their steps. Others enjoy leisurely strolls, bushwalking, race walking, hiking, hill walking, and Nordic walking. There are many ways to walk! Race walking is a long-distance athletic event that is similar to a running race, except one foot must always be (or appear to be) in contact with the ground. John Butcher once said, "Walking is convenient, it needs no special equipment, is self-regulating and inherently safe. Walking is as natural as breathing."

Walking with Jesus every morning for 30 to 60 minutes of quiet time in your Bible and in prayer is good for your spiritual health and will improve the rest of your day. Perhaps that is what Paul meant when he wrote, "I, therefore, the prisoner of the Lord, beseech you to walk worthy of the calling with which you were called" (Ephesians 4:1).

How is your walk with Christ?

KEY BIBLE TEXT: "And they heard the sound of the LORD God walking in the garden in the cool of the day" (Genesis 3:8).

Poetic Justice

DAY 160

An Amazing Fact: *French statesman Ferdinand Flocon turned the French Civil Code into a poem to make the code more accessible to the people.*

The French Revolution resulted in 14,000 pieces of new legislation. In 1804, Napoleon created the Napoleonic Code out of these and France's older laws. He added the Code of Civil Procedure in 1806, a Commercial Code in 1807, a Criminal Code and Code of Criminal Procedure in 1808, and a Penal Code in 1810. Together these became known as the French Civil Code.

Writer and editor Ferdinand Flocon entered politics in 1848. When he was not reelected the following year, he returned to editing and selling books but continued his political activism, so the French government placed him under house arrest. The democratic wordsmith died poor, nearly blind, and bitter.

Despite his short political career, Flocon knew the law, and he clearly knew words. It is said that he turned the French Civil Code—its 22,892 articles, statutes, amendments, and annotations—into a 170,000-word poem, perfect in rhyme and meter.

Long before Flocon, another law-poem was written. After exile, the Jews returned home and rebuilt the temple. They compiled the Psalms—some old, some new—to sing in the temple. One new one, Psalm 119, dedicates eight verses each to the 22 Hebrews letters. For example, verses 1 thru 8 each start with *aleph*, the first letter of the alphabet. Verses 9 thru 16 all start with the second letter *beth*. Verses 17 thru 24 all start with the third letter, and so on.

Besides alliteration, Psalm 119 repeatedly uses eight words for the law of God: word, saying, statutes, judgments, law, commands, precepts, and testimonies. Psalm 119 uplifts God's wonderful law, and thus God's character. Study for yourself and see how perfect, just, and loving God's law is.

KEY BIBLE TEXTS: "Taste and see that the Lord is good; blessed is the man who trusts in Him!" (Psalm 34:8). "At midnight I will rise to give thanks to You, because of your righteous judgments" (Psalm 119:62).

DAY 161 Good as Gold

An Amazing Fact: *Gold is the most malleable and ductile of all the metals. It can easily be beaten or hammered so thin that it is translucent. Just one ounce of gold can be drawn into a wire more than 50 miles long. This precious metal occurs in seawater to the extent of up to 250 parts by weight to 100 million parts of water. Although the quantity of gold present in seawater is more than nine billion metric tons, the cost of recovering the gold would be far greater than the value of the gold recovered.*

Pure gold has a bright yellow color and luster that it maintains without oxidizing in air or water. It is the least reactive chemical element known. It has been a valuable and highly sought-after precious metal for coins, jewelry, and other arts since long before the beginning of recorded history.

The density of gold is higher than most other metals, making it difficult to pass counterfeits.

Many factors determine the value of a gold coin, such as its rarity, age, condition, and the number originally minted. Gold coins coveted by collectors include the Aureus, Solidus, and Spur Ryal.

In July 2002, a very rare $20 1933 Double Eagle gold coin sold for a record $7,590,020 at Sotheby's, making it the most valuable coin ever sold. In early 1933, more than 445,000 Double Eagle coins had been struck by the U.S. Mint, but most of these were surrendered and melted down following Executive Order 6102. Only a few coins managed to survive.

David speaks of God's law with reference to gold and silver. "The law of Your mouth is better to me than thousands of coins of gold and silver" (Psalm 119:72). And in speaking of God's commandments, he writes, "More to be desired are they than gold, yea, than much fine gold" (Psalm 19:10). Perhaps the density of gold explains why God's law is not corruptible or reactive to elements around it. Do we value God's Word even more than the finest gold coins in the world?

KEY BIBLE TEXT: "And the street of the city was pure gold, like transparent glass" (Revelation 21:21).

Children of Light

DAY 162

An Amazing Fact: *When "solar winds"—electrically charged particles flowing out from the sun—hit our atmosphere, the Earth's magnetic field traps and pushes most of them to the polar regions. The strange and beautiful light shows of the aurora borealis and aurora australis (northern and southern lights) are the result. These can be seen as a glow or as curtains or arcs. Green is the most common color, but they can also be pink, red, yellow, blue, or a combination.*

Light is an essential gift from God. "Let there be light" was His first command of creation. He knew how important it would be for us. A lack of light or low levels of light can cause depression in humans and animals. We need regular exposure to strong light for our physical and emotional well-being.

The same is true in our spiritual lives. Without a regular supply of strong spiritual light, we can easily become discouraged and lose our way.

The Word of God provides this light. "Your word is a lamp to my feet, and a light to my path" (Psalm 119:105).

In John 8:12, Jesus says, "I am the light of the world. He who follows Me shall not walk in darkness, but have the light of life." Because of Him we can "walk as children of light ... finding out what is acceptable to the Lord" (Ephesians 5:8, 10). We don't need to stumble around in the dark. Jesus promises to light our way.

KEY BIBLE TEXT: "For you were once darkness, but now you are light in the Lord. Walk as children of light (for the fruit of the Spirit is in all goodness, righteousness, and truth), finding out what is acceptable to the Lord" (Ephesians 5:8–10).

DAY 163 Beyond the Honeymoon

An Amazing Fact: *The honeymoon was an accepted practice of Babylon weddings as early as 4,000 years ago. For a month after the nuptials, the bride's father supplied his son-in-law with all the mead he could drink. Mead is a honey beer, and because their calendar was lunar based, this period was called the "honey month"—or what we know today as the "honeymoon."*

Not all marriages find the first month after the wedding to be the sweetest. At odds with Pope Clement VII's refusal to annul his marriage to Catherine of Aragón, King Henry VIII sent a delegation to the Vatican in an effort to patch up the political differences between himself and the pope. The Earl of Wiltshire led the delegation—he also took his dog.

As was customary, the earl prostrated himself before the pope and was about to kiss the pontiff's toe. The pope, always willing to receive the homage, thrust his foot toward the earl, but the earl's watching dog mistook the action and went to defend his master. Instead of a kiss, the pope received a bite on the toe!

This so enraged the Swiss Guard that they instantly killed the poor dog. Terribly angered, the earl stormed away and refused to proceed with the mission to reconcile England with Rome. After the earl's return, King Henry took permanent steps to separate the Church of England from the jurisdiction of Rome. The Anglican Church was born.

Paul speaks of a union between a bride and groom as a depiction of Christ and the church. The mutual submission and sweet love between a husband and his bride will live beyond the honeymoon when there is a sacrificial love that goes beyond self. "Nevertheless let each one of you in particular so love his own wife as himself, and let the wife see that she respects her husband" (Ephesians 5:33). Let the special attentions of the honeymoon continue beyond the first month and into the rest of your married lives.

KEY BIBLE TEXT: "When a man has taken a new wife, he shall not go out to war or be charged with any business; he shall be free at home one year, and bring happiness to his wife whom he has taken" (Deuteronomy 24:5).

A Still Small Voice

DAY 164

An Amazing Fact: *The highest wind speed ever recorded on earth occurred at Barrow Island, Australia. During typhoon Olivia, the wind reached 253 miles per hour.*

For more than 60 years, the Mount Washington Observatory in New Hampshire boasted that it had recorded the fastest wind speed on Earth. In 1934, the observatory recorded a wind speed of 231 miles per hour. But in 1996, during typhoon Olivia, Barrow Island in Australia recorded a wind speed of 253 miles per hour. The amazing—and somewhat puzzling thing—is that it took the World Meteorological Organization 14 years to recognize a new record had been set. As they were scouring through some old data, they came across the record-setting wind speed.

It didn't take long for news to spread about the new record. And the Mount Washington Observatory reluctantly conceded that the data had to be recognized, though they were still suspicious of why it took 14 years for the new record to be declared. Of course, whether it is 253 or 231 miles per hour, we wouldn't want to be facing such powerful winds!

Interestingly, the prophet Elijah faced some very strong winds after escaping from evil Jezebel and waiting to hear from God. He also faced an earthquake and fire. But 1 Kings gives us some interesting insight into God's glory and power. There we read that God was not in the wind, not in the earthquake, not in the fire. Instead, He spoke to Elijah in a "still small voice" (1 Kings 19:12).

This is how God prefers to speak and interact with us. He doesn't want to overwhelm us with grandeur. He doesn't desire to impress us with splendor. He wants to come close and converse with us as with a friend.

KEY BIBLE TEXT: "Be still, and know that I am God" (Psalm 46:10).

DAY 165 God's Body Armor

An Amazing Fact: *Kevlar is a synthetic fiber developed in 1965 and was first used commercially in the early 1970s as a substitute for steel racing tires. It has a high tensile strength-to-weight ratio, making it five times stronger than steel. It is used for making a variety of items such as canoes, racing sails, and bicycle tires. It's most well-known application is in body armor.*

When Stephanie Kwolek first invented poly-paraphenylene terephthalamide, the solution was a cloudy substance that was usually thrown away. But she decided to persuade the technician she was working with, Charles Smullen, to test the solution. They were amazed to find the solution did not break like nylon. Her supervisor and lab director realized her discovery was significant because it opened the door to a new field called polymer chemistry.

In body armor, Kevlar fibers actually "catch" a bullet in a multilayer web of woven fabrics. Different layers in the weave perform different tasks. The "engaged fibers" absorb and disperse the energy of the impact, transferring it to other fibers at "crossover points" in the weave of the body armor. Of course, if you don't wear the vest, it won't protect you. The Department of Justice estimates that 25 percent of state and local police are not issued body armor. Of the 1,200 officers killed in the line of duty since 1980, more than 30 percent could have been saved by body armor. The risk of dying from gunfire is 14 times greater for an officer not wearing body armor.

Paul writes, "Put on the whole armor of God, that you may be able to stand against the wiles of the devil" (Ephesians 6:11). The bullets we face are not ballistic missiles from guns. We need body armor that cannot be pierced by Satan because "we wrestle not against flesh and blood" (v. 12). God offers you something stronger than poly-paraphenylene terephthalamide. Take time today to put on the protective gear that will withstand the most powerful fire of the enemy.

KEY BIBLE TEXT: "Therefore take up the whole armor of God, that you may be able to withstand in the evil day, and having done all, to stand" (Ephesians 6:13).

The Beauty of Persistence

An Amazing Fact: *In the late 1800s, engineer Washington Roebling and his father set out to build a bridge from New York to Long Island. This was highly criticized as "impossible." After a construction accident paralyzed Washington and killed his father, the project was stopped, but Washington never gave up. Although he could only move one finger, he worked out a way to communicate instructions to his wife; she translated these for engineers who again started working on the bridge. After 13 years, the Brooklyn Bridge was completed.*

Human persistence is a noble quality.

Consider Henry Ford, who went broke five times before he founded the Ford Motor Company. Thomas Edison's teachers called him "too stupid to learn anything," and he was fired from his first two jobs. Dr. Seuss's first book was rejected by 27 different publishers. Beethoven's music teachers thought he was hopeless as a musician and composer. Before becoming prime minister at age 62, Winston Churchill was defeated in every election. Abraham Lincoln was demoted during his military service, was not very successful at business, and lost many runs for public office. But these people all persisted and eventually achieved success.

As motivating as human persistence can be, however, God's persistence is greater and more inspiring. Because of the persistence of His love for us, He will complete the good work that He has begun in us. He will not give up on us. As long as we seek His help with an honest heart, He will never turn us away.

KEY BIBLE TEXT: "I thank my God upon every remembrance of you, always in every prayer of mine making request for you all with joy, for your fellowship in the gospel from the first day until now, being confident of this very thing, that He who has begun a good work in you will complete it until the day of Jesus Christ; just as it is right for me to think this of you all, because I have you in my heart, inasmuch as both in my chains and in the defense and confirmation of the gospel, you all are partakers with me of grace" (Philippians 1:3–7).

DAY 167 God's Fishermen

An Amazing Fact: *Researchers studying walleye vision found that orange is the color most visible to walleyes, followed by yellow and yellow green. Surprisingly, red is the least visible color. No wonder you find so many orange and chartreuse lures in the tackle boxes of savvy walleye anglers.*

Another interesting fact about walleye fish is that a sudden decrease in light level triggers them to bite. That explains why the fish usually turn on just as the sun is disappearing below the horizon and the light intensity is rapidly decreasing. It also accounts for the biting that starts when the dark clouds preceding a thunderstorm roll in.

The very best time to catch a trophy walleye is five to seven weeks after the fish have completed spawning. That's when the big females, famished after not having eaten for nearly two months, go on the prowl for food. And with the natural supply of baitfish at its annual low, they're likely to hit almost anything you throw at them.

Maybe you can't think of anything more boring than fishing, but many of Jesus' first disciples were fishermen. The first time they heard Jesus, He asked them to push their boats out into the lake and let down their nets. Inside they laughed, "What does He know about fishing? You don't catch much fish in the daytime!" But they agreed to do it anyway. "And when they had done this, they caught a great number of fish, and their net was breaking" (Luke 5:6).

Peter appropriately responded to the amazing catch of fish. "When Simon Peter saw it, he fell down at Jesus' knees, saying 'Depart from me, for I am a sinful man, O Lord!'" (v. 8). Jesus replied, "Do not be afraid. From now on you will catch men" (v. 10). The proud fisherman was not ready to serve the Master fisherman until he was humbled. We are best prepared to go fishing when we recognize our limitations and listen to the Creator of fish and men.

KEY BIBLE TEXT: "So when they had brought their boats to land, they forsook all and followed Him" (Luke 5:11).

Brought Back to Life

An Amazing Fact: *During the Middle Ages, individuals with leprosy were often required to witness their own funerals.*

Ever since Bible times, people with leprosy have been stigmatized. They have been labeled "unclean" and banished from contact with other human beings, often sent to leper colonies to live out a sad, lonely, and miserable existence. This is because many believed that leprosy is highly contagious and that lepers were being punished by God for their sins.

Perhaps the most unfortunate treatment toward lepers came during the Middle Ages, when many were actually required to witness their own funerals. The infected person was brought before a priest and declared dead. This was often done while the leper stood in an empty grave as friends and family mourned. The "funeral" ended by having a shovel full of dirt tossed upon the living leper, signifying finality.

You can imagine the psychological effect this would have on someone who tragically came down with leprosy! For all intents and purposes, the person was "dead." The Bible also takes a very negative view of leprosy. This is because leprosy served as an illustration of what it looks like to be spiritually dead.

Fortunately, the Bible also shares a number of glorious stories about individuals who were mercifully cured of this dreadful disease. Not surprisingly, many of them reacted with overwhelming joy. And this serves as a picture of the gospel. Though all of us have been dead in our sins, the Bible teaches that God "made us alive together with Christ ... and raised us up together, and made us sit together in the heavenly places in Christ Jesus" (Ephesians 2:5, 6).

KEY BIBLE TEXT: "But God, who is rich in mercy, because of His great love with which He loved us, even when we were dead in trespasses, made us alive together with Christ (by grace you have been saved), and raised us up together, and made us sit together in the heavenly places in Christ Jesus" (Ephesians 2:4–6).

DAY 169 Bowing the Knee

An Amazing Fact: *The largest and most complicated joint in the human body is the knee. It is a mobile pivotal hinge joint that permits flexion and extension. It is capable of slight turns that change the whole movement of the rest of the body. At birth babies do not have a conventional kneecap, but a growth formed of cartilage. It becomes a normal kneecap for girls at age three and for boys at age five.*

It is much easier to reach the ground when you are kneeling. Bending over to pick up an object on the floor can stress your lower back. If you spent a couple of hours weeding your garden by bending over, you would feel the horrible results the next morning.

Kneeling also demonstrates submission, reverence, and obedienc Humility can be demonstrated by a kneeling posture. The apostle Pa writes, "Let this mind be in your which was also in Christ Jesus. ... t humbled Himself and became obedient to the point of death, even death of the cross" (Philippians 2:5, 8). Paul practiced humility himse referring to himself as "the least of the apostles" (1 Corinthians 15:9 took great humility for Christ to take the form of a "bondservant" and co "in the likeness of men" (Philippians 2:7).

On a visit to the Beethoven museum in Bonn, a young American stud became fascinated by the piano on which Beethoven had composed some o his greatest works. She asked the museum guard if she could play a few bars on it; she accompanied the request with a lavish tip, and the guard agreed. The girl went to the piano and tinkled out the opening of the "Moonlight Sonata." As she was leaving she said to the guard, "I suppose all the great pianists who come here want to play on that piano."

The guard shook his head. "Paderewski [a famed Polish pianist] was here a few years ago and said he wasn't worthy to touch it." It is much easier to reach God when you are kneeling. Bow on your knees before the Lord today and remember who is most worthy of praise.

KEY BIBLE TEXT: "To me, who am less than the least of all the saints, this grace was given" (Ephesians 3:8).

The Boy-King

DAY 170

An Amazing Fact: *Two of history's youngest monarchs were King Henry VI, who became king at eight months and 25 days of age; and Mary, Queen of Scots, who became queen at the age of six days.*

The wicked queen Athaliah had a plan; she tried her best to wipe out any other heirs to the throne, including her own grandsons. Heir after heir fell to her ruthless plot. From a human standpoint, she seemed destined to succeed.

But God had another plan. Providence caused one young heir to the throne to be rescued by his aunt and safely hidden away in the house of the Lord for six years. At the right moment Joash, the secret heir, was proclaimed king. The seven-year-old was crowned, and his supporters held great celebration.

When she saw what had happened, Athaliah screamed, "Treason! eason!" The guards had to drag her away.

Although he was only a small child, Joash loved God. Because he and supporters chose a righteous path and committed themselves to keep 's law, the Lord caused them to prevail. He can do the same for you too.

KEY BIBLE TEXTS: "When Athaliah the mother of Ahaziah saw that her son was dead, she arose and destroyed all the royal heirs. But Jehosheba, the daughter of King Joram, sister of Ahaziah, took Joash the son of Ahaziah, and stole him away from among the king's sons who were being murdered; and they hid him and his nurse in the bedroom, from Athaliah, so that he was not killed. So he was hidden with her in the house of the LORD for six years, while Athaliah reigned over the land" (2 Kings 11:1–3). "I am small and despised, yet I do not forget Your precepts. Your righteousness is an everlasting righteousness, and Your law is truth" (Psalm 119:141, 142).

DAY 171 Repairing the Temple

An Amazing Fact: *Carpenter ants damage wood in building construction. They prefer dead, damp wood in which to build nests. Unlike termites, they do not eat wood but leave behind sawdust-like material called frass. The most likely culprit in North American homes is the black carpenter ant. However, there are over 1,000 species of carpenter ants, including the famous "exploding ants" of Southeast Asia.*

Whether it is carpenter ants, carpenter bees, or wood boring beetles, insects can cause a lot of damage to building structures. Termites, of course, rank at the top of the list of wood-damaging insects. There are more 4,000 species. Most are actually valuable to the environment, but about 10 percent are pests that destroy buildings and cost about $2 billion annually. They live in colonies of several hundred to several million and use "swarm intelligence" to find and consume food. Perhaps their damage is so great because they eat 24 hours a day, 7 days a week.

Neglecting the care of a building for 100 years is a long time. That's about how long Israel neglected to care for God's temple since it was dedicated by Solomon. The new King Joash noticed the temple was in disrepair and decided to do something about it. "And Jehoash (Joash) said to the priests, 'All the money of the dedicated gifts that are brought into the house of the Lord. ... Let the priests take it themselves ... and let them repair the damages of the temple, wherever any dilapidation is found" (2 Kings 12:4, 5).

Whether damage happens by termites or tornadoes, we should honor the Lord's house by keeping it in good repair. It demonstrates our loyalty and respect for our places of worship when we keep them cleaned and in good condition. Let us have the spirit of Joash and repair our churches if they have been damaged. Follow the example of the boy-king of whom it is written, "Jehoash did what was right in the sight of the Lord" (2 Kings 12:1).

KEY BIBLE TEXT: "Then everyone came whose heart was stirred, and everyone whose spirit was willing, and they brought the Lord's offering for the work of the tabernacle of meeting" (Exodus 35:21).

Junk or Jesus?

An Amazing Fact: *America's largest landfill is Apex Regional Landfill, 20 miles northeast of Las Vegas. It has over 3,199,653 tons of garbage.*

Talk about a lot of trash! The Apex Regional Landfill takes in over 9,000 tons of trash a day. Back in 2007, it was getting as much as 15,000 tons of trash a day. And, spanning 2,200 acres, the dump could keep taking trash at the same rate for the next 200 years.

It's hard to believe, but this particular landfill is just one of many landfills that contribute to America's burgeoning trash industry. All told, the trash industry in America does about $50 billion worth of business a year!

Perhaps just as hard to believe is what the apostle Paul considered to be trash. In Philippians 3:8 he says that he considered all things to be "as garbage" compared to gaining Christ and knowing Him (NLT). And Paul had a lot to cling to, humanly speaking. He was born into the right family, trained at the best institutions, and was zealous for law keeping. He had a lot going for him. Yet in the grand ledger of his life, he counted all his accomplishments as "debits" and knowing Jesus as a "credit."

This is because he saw a vision of Jesus that made everything else in the world fade. He had been saved from his former life of persecuting God's people. He had been redeemed from trying to earn his own salvation by performing good works. He had been granted a new heart and a new life. Thus everything else in this world was utter trash in Paul's estimation.

What about us? Have we caught the same vision that Paul caught—thus causing all else in life to leave us dissatisfied in light of God's glory and grace?

KEY BIBLE TEXT: "For I determined not to know anything among you except Jesus Christ and Him crucified" (1 Corinthians 2:2).

DAY 173 Good Poverty

An Amazing Fact: *At least 80 percent of people around the world live on less than $10 a day. The poorest 40 percent of the world's population accounts for just five percent of global income. The richest 20 percent accounts for three-quarters of the world's income. And according to UNICEF, 22,000 children die each day due to poverty.*

Children are often the quiet sufferers in poverty. They die quietly in some of the poorest villages on Earth, far from the awareness and conscience of the world. Being weak and meek in life makes these dying masses even more invisible in death. Measles, malaria, and diarrhea are the three biggest killers of children, and they are all preventable. HIV/AIDS has created more than 14 million orphans; 92 percent of them live in Africa.

So how could Jesus say, "Blessed are you poor, for yours is the kingdom of God" (Luke 6:20)? Doesn't Christ have a heart for the poor, especially children? Jesus absolutely cares about the underprivileged. He spent almost all of His ministry reaching out in kindness and love to the sick and dying. Then what does Christ mean when He says, "Blessed are you poor"?

Our Lord is not speaking of physical poverty, but of spiritual poverty. In other words, the kingdom of heaven belongs to those who recognize that there is nothing they can bring to God to ensure salvation except their outstretched hands. No works, no money, no pilgrimages, no "nothing," will impress God to save you. When we stand before the Lord, we are all "dirt poor." And that's a good thing, because to acknowledge our great spiritual need is the first step in receiving God's free gift of salvation.

KEY BIBLE TEXT: "Listen, my beloved brethren: Has God not chosen the poor of this world to be rich in faith and heirs of the kingdom which He promised to those who love Him?" (James 2:5).

Forget What's Behind

DAY 174

An Amazing Fact: *There are many types of amnesia. One of the more unusual types is prosopamnesia, which causes an inability to remember faces. Lacunar amnesia involves loss of memory about a specific event. Dissociative amnesia can be caused by repressed memories following psychological trauma. The most popular type portrayed in Hollywood is retrograde amnesia, in which a person loses past memories due to a traumatic injury.*

In his letter to the Philippians, Paul advised "forgetting those things which are behind and reaching forward to those things which are ahead" (Philippians 3:13). What did he mean by forgetting those things that are behind?

Paul obviously didn't mean that we should forget everything in our past history. After all, remembering the way God has led us helps us spiritually. But there are things in our pasts that could hinder us spiritually. Dwelling on our past sins, endlessly mulling over our mistakes, and contemplating our failures can be self-destructive.

After we have confessed our sins to God and accept His forgiveness, it should be a closed subject. Sometimes, though, we reprocess those sins; sometimes the enemy throws them in our faces. Either way, it can be very discouraging.

"Leave them in the past," is Paul's wise advice. Instead of rehashing our failures, we should reach forward to the things that are ahead, pressing toward the spiritual victory that God will give us.

KEY BIBLE TEXT: "But I press on, that I may lay hold of that for which Christ Jesus has also laid hold of me. Brethren, I do not count myself to have apprehended; but one thing I do, forgetting those things which are behind and reaching forward to those things which are ahead, I press toward the goal for the prize of the upward call of God in Christ Jesus" (Philippians 3:12–14).

DAY 175 Like a Bear

An Amazing Fact: *Found along the coasts and islands of the northernmost regions, polar bears are the largest land carnivores. In fact, one adult male polar bear weighed more than 2,200 pounds! Yet the young are only about 25 ounces when born.*

Adult polar bears also have very large stomachs with a capacity for more than 150 pounds of food, which allows them to go weeks between meals. They are also great roamers, covering up to 50 miles a day and 100,000 square miles during a lifetime in a constant search for seals.

Strong swimmers, polar bears paddle with their large front paws and use their rear paws as rudders to steer. They swim an average of six miles per hour and can go as far as 60 miles without a pause. Polar bears are also excellent divers, remaining submerged for up to two minutes and attaining a depth of 15 feet. They have also been observed leaping out of the water up to eight feet in the air to surprise a seal resting on an ice floe.

King Hezekiah was one of the better kings of Judah. Most of them were evil. His name means "the LORD strengthens." Hezekiah was like a strong bear, but not because he was physically large or intellectually sharp. The Bible says, "And he did what was right in the sight of the LORD" (2 Kings 18:3). One of his strongest moments was when he destroyed the bronze snake that Moses made in the wilderness. It had become an idol for God's people, and they even offered incense to it.

We do not need to swim 60 miles without a pause in order to be strong. We can be strong by being obedient to the Lord, just like Hezekiah. "He trusted in the LORD God of Israel, so that after him was none like him among all the kings of Judah, nor who were before him" (v. 5).

KEY BIBLE TEXT: "Let the weak say, 'I am strong'" (Joel 3:10).

Citizens of Another World

An Amazing Fact: *There has been one United States president who, when he died, was no longer a citizen of the United States. It was the country's tenth president— John Tyler.*

John Tyler served in office from 1841 to 1845. But more than being an American, Tyler was a Virginian. And so when Virginia, along with the other southern states, seceded from the union, Tyler stayed true to his home state and joined them, renouncing his U.S. citizenship.

Tyler had actually served as the chair of the Virginia Peace Convention, which was held in 1861 in Washington, D.C. It was an effort to prevent a civil war. When no compromise was achieved, however, he viewed secession as the only option and joined Virginia and the other states in abandoning their citizenship.

From there, he was elected to the House of Representatives of the Confederate Congress, but it was a position he would never fill. He died on January 18, 1862, before ever serving one day in office. And thus, he is the only president in the history of the United States to die as a former citizen.

Paul, in his letter to the Philippians, shares some interesting news about our citizenship: "For our citizenship is in heaven, from which we also eagerly wait for the Savior, the Lord Jesus Christ" (Philippians 3:20). Though we might have been born in America or Canada or some other part of the world, as Christians, our true citizenship is in heaven. Thus, we are invited to renounce our allegiance to the world and respond to God's invitation to take up the mission of our heavenly home—which is to spread the good news to the citizens of this world.

KEY BIBLE TEXT: "Jesus answered, 'My kingdom is not of this world. If My kingdom were of this world, My servants would fight, so that I should not be delivered to the Jews; but now My kingdom is not from here'" (John 18:36).

DAY 177 Metrology

An Amazing Fact: *When it came to measuring things in ancient times, the body ruled. At first an inch was the width of a man's thumb. A hand was approximately five inches across. A span was the length of an outstretched hand. And a foot was the length of a foot, or about 11 inches. Today a foot is 12 inches.*

There is a science to measuring things. Metrology literally means "the study of measurement." It is broken into three fields: science, industry, and law. Calibration is a process in which metrology is applied to equipment and processes to ensure conformity with a standard of measurement. Without precise measurement, commerce would be a mess. Nine out of 10 people who work with measurements are employed in commercial applications.

Defined measurements sometimes were determined by kings. King Edward II of England ruled that one inch equaled three grains of barley placed end to end lengthwise. King Henry I of England fixed the yard as the distance from his nose to the thumb of his out-stretched arm. Lest you think such early measurements were silly, consider that dividing things into units occurred in ancient times and still impacts us today. The Romans used units of 12, and today we have 12 inches in a foot and 12 months in a year.

Jesus once said, "Give and it will be given to you: good measure, pressed down, shaken together, and running over will be put into your bosom. For with the same measure that you use, it will be measured back to you" (Luke 6:38). You might wonder at how some foods are measured. Have you ever purchased and opened a cereal box only to find that it was half full? It's disappointing, isn't it—but don't judge too quickly, as the contents have merely settled.

God encourages us to be generous in how we "measure" things. Don't judge others too quickly. Believe the best of them. That's just how the Lord treats us, giving us more than we ask for. It's like the baker's dozen.

KEY BIBLE TEXT: "For judgment is without mercy to the one who has shown no mercy" (James 2:13).

Defeating Deceit

DAY 178

An Amazing Fact: *Among Americans polled about honesty, 52 percent said lying is never justified; yet 65 percent said it was sometimes okay to lie to keep from hurting someone's feelings. Twelve percent of adults admit that they lie sometimes or occasionally. However, when asked, "Are you a liar?" 97 percent said "No." The three percent who admitted to lying were tested to evaluate their actual honesty and were found to be 28 times more honest than the people who denied lying.*

Very few people—if any—are honest 100 percent of the time. Even Christians and other people who are committed to being honest sometimes are caught off guard and speak something that is less than the truth in the confusion of the moment—sometimes to keep from hurting another person's feelings. Other times, perhaps, they are not completely honest with themselves.

We deal with dishonest people all the time. And all of us, at some time in our lives, have been dishonest. Many times dishonesty hurts other people; sometimes it only hurts the dishonest person.

But dishonesty always hurts God because one of His characteristics is truth. The Bible says, "Lying lips are an abomination to the LORD, but those who deal truthfully are His delight" (Proverbs 12:22).

Lying comes naturally to humans. "The heart is deceitful above all things, and desperately wicked; who can know it?" (Jeremiah 17:9). The only way to conquer a deceitful heart is to allow God to replace it with the pure heart of our Savior. He is willing to transform us today.

KEY BIBLE TEXT: "In my distress I cried to the LORD, and He heard me. Deliver my soul, O LORD, from lying lips and from a deceitful tongue" (Psalm 120:1, 2).

DAY 179 Never Slumbers

An Amazing Fact: *One U.S. president was said to have slept through his entire term of office! He was David Rice Atchison, but you probably haven't heard of him and very few have.*

Here's how it supposedly happened: James Polk's term as the 11th president expired on Saturday, March 3, 1849. President-elect Zachary Taylor did not want to be inaugurated on a Sunday; he preferred the ceremonies to be held on Monday, March 5. Yet the United States could not be without a leader, even for 24 hours, so the next person in line was President Pro-tem of the Senate, who happened to be Senator David Rice Atchison. He, therefore, took over the office for that Sunday.

Atchison later explained his "sleeping term" by saying that his last day of work in congress was so heavy and busy that he went to bed very late Saturday night exhausted. He slept soundly, even snoring, all through the day that he was president—March 4, 1849. How sad to be president for a day and not remember a single minute!

The Bible tells us we can trust on help coming from God, who made heaven and earth. David writes, "He will not allow your foot to be moved; He who keeps you will not slumber. Behold, He who keeps Israel shall neither slumber nor sleep" (Psalm 121:3, 4). Jesus demonstrated that same tenacity in the garden of Gethsemane before the crucifixion. Weighed down with the sins of the world, Christ asked His disciples to pray for Him, but they fell asleep.

We can trust our Lord to stay awake and watch over us. God doesn't fall asleep on us, not even for a single minute.

KEY BIBLE TEXT: "When you lie down, you will not be afraid; yes, you will lie down and your sleep will be sweet" (Proverbs 3:24).

Never Too Young

An Amazing Fact: *The youngest reigning monarch today is King Oyo. At 19 years of age, he rules the Kingdom of Toro, which is one of four kingdoms in the country of Uganda.*

King Oyo—whose real name is Rukirabasaija Oyo Nyimba Kabamba Iguru Rukidi IV—actually ascended to the throne when he was just three years old. Born in 1992, he was forced to become ruler of the kingdom in 1995 when his father unexpectedly passed away. Upon his ascension, he became the 13th ruler in the kingdom's 180-year history and, not surprisingly, he became—and still is—the youngest monarch in the world.

As can be expected, he was aided in his rule by three regents—his mother, aunt, and godmother—until he was 18. These three ladies helped rule over the affairs of the kingdom and trained him to be king. At age 19, he had full control over all the affairs of Toro, a task that is large for anyone, never mind a 19 year old!

The Bible details a number of young rulers as well. One of those was King Josiah who, at the age of eight, became king of Judah. What was most remarkable about Josiah's reign, however, was not that he was so young. What was most remarkable was the fact that he "did what was right in the sight of the Lord" (2 Kings 22:2) and restored true worship among God's people.

This is particularly noteworthy because Josiah's reign came during a dark period in Israel's and Judah's history. Thus, this young man was able to restore—at least for a season—the worship of the true God when all else seemed hopeless.

Josiah's example should be encouraging to all of us—whether young, old, or anywhere in between. Enabled by God's grace, we can stand tall for Him.

KEY BIBLE TEXT: "Let no one despise your youth, but be an example to the believers in word, in conduct, in love, in spirit, in faith, in purity" (1 Timothy 4:12).

DAY 181 Focusing

An Amazing Fact: *Each day you are bombarded with billions of bits of sensory input, most of which you ignore. If you tried to focus on every sound, noise, light, picture, word, smell, and talk coming your way, you'd go crazy. You were created with a special filtering system in your brain called the Reticular Activating System (RAS), which allows you to focus on what is most important.*

Imagine yourself walking through a busy airport. There are hundreds of people walking past you, lots of noise from talking, announcements being made over loudspeakers, jet airplanes taking off, lights flashing, little shops advertising their goods, and small restaurants with the smell of food wafting about. How much of this do you notice? Probably not much, especially if you are focused on getting somewhere. Suddenly, over the PA system, your name is announced. Amidst all of that noise and confusion your brain picks up this one bit of information. How can it do this?

Thanks to a bundle of nerves the size of your finger that runs from your upper spinal cord deep into your brain stem, God created you with an internal secretary that helps filter millions of bits of information coming at you at any given moment. The RAS helps you to be awake, to focus, and to set goals. When you decide you need to get to a certain destination, this part of your brain helps keep you on track. It is also tuned into "red flags" or "danger" input that catches your attention and protects you.

The Lord has given us the ability to learn to focus on what is most important. We are not helpless victims of our environments. We can choose to think about the right things. Paul writes about this when he says, "Finally brethren, whatever things are true, whatever things are noble, whatever things are just, whatever things are pure, whatever things are lovely, whatever things are of good report, if there is any virtue and if there is anything praiseworthy—meditate on these things" (Philippians 4:8).

The devil has plenty of stimuli to send your way today. What will you focus on?

KEY BIBLE TEXT: "The things which you learned and received and heard and saw in me, these do, and the God of peace will be with you" (Philippians 4:9).

The Centurion's Faith

An Amazing Fact: *Centurions of ancient Rome were usually in charge of a unit consisting of 80 men, though some controlled larger groups. A centurion was recognized by the sword on his left side and the dagger on his right, the sideways horsehair crest on his helmet, an armored shirt, and metal awards displayed on his chest.*

Where did the centurion get his faith? Raised in a heathen nation and trained in a brutal military system, he was hardly the type of person you would expect to have faith in Jesus.

The centurion had a tender heart, for he loved his sick servant. He wanted him well and sought out Jesus to heal him. He had a love for the Jewish nation too; he had built them a synagogue.

He was also a humble man. The centurion sent this message to Jesus: "I'm not worthy to have You come into my house, Lord. Just say the word, and my servant will be well."

Jesus was amazed by the centurion's belief in Him. He hadn't seen "such great faith, not even in Israel!"—not even among the people who were taught the Scriptures from childhood, the people who were supposed to be the most godly on Earth.

The centurion was a man of authority, but he recognized a far greater authority in Jesus. His eyes of faith saw that Jesus was the Commander of the universe.

KEY BIBLE TEXT: "And when He was already not far from the house, the centurion sent friends to Him, saying to Him, 'Lord, do not trouble Yourself, for I am not worthy that You should enter under my roof. Therefore I did not even think myself worthy to come to You. But say the word, and my servant will be healed.' ... When Jesus heard these things, He marveled at him, and turned around and said to the crowd that followed Him, 'I say to you, I have not found such great faith, not even in Israel!'" (Luke 7:6, 7, 10).

DAY 183 God's Many Children

An Amazing Fact: *Multiple births of humans are fairly common with two or three babies at a time, known as twins and triplets. Siblings of multiple births result either from a single egg (monozygotic) that splits into two or more embryos and are identical. Siblings from multiple eggs (dizygotic) are referred to as fraternal. Polyzygotic multiples represent a combination of identical and fraternal siblings.*

One way for a family to grow rapidly is through multiple births. Imagine mom coming home from the hospital with three babies instead of one! Multiple births of as many as eight babies have been born alive, the first set on record to the Chukwu family in Texas in 1998; one died and seven survived. In 2009, a second set, the Suleman octuplets, was born in Bellflower, California. To date, all eight have survived. There have been a few sets of nonuplets (nine) in which a few babies were born alive, though none lived longer than a few days. Twins are the most common type of multiple births and happen in one out of 80 pregnancies. Triplets happen about every 8,000 births.

The book of 1 Chronicles begins with a genealogy of Adam's family down through many generations. In this family tree the most popular set of twins in Scripture is identified, Esau and Jacob. The list culminates with the most important figure, Jacob, who is considered the most prominent patriarch. Why? The 12 tribes of Israel were established from his children. Chronicles relates the history of Israel from its ancestral roots, showing how God has a plan for His children.

Whether you were born as a singleton (single birth) or a quintuplet (five births), you are a precious child of God and are part of a royal lineage that will live forever. As you read through the family tree lists in Scripture, remember that you are part of a very large family!

KEY BIBLE TEXT: "Behold what manner of love the Father has bestowed on us, that we should be called children of God!" (1 John 3:1).

The Royal Line

An Amazing Fact: *The Queen of England owns all the whales, dolphins, and sturgeons for three miles off the coast of the United Kingdom. This has been the case for British royalty since the statute of 1324 was issued during the reign of King Edward II.*

The Royal Family's reign spans 37 generations and 1,209 years. All of the monarchs are descendants of King Alfred the Great, who reigned in 871. Their history includes everything from knights in shining armor and beheadings to Queen Elizabeth II and her current total of nine thrones—one at the House of Lords, two in Westminster Abbey, and six in Buckingham Palace's Throne Room. Many are intrigued by royalty—in fact, many roused early to watch the wedding between Prince William and his princess.

In light of the line of this regal family, think about this: Your King has existed forever, not just some 1,200 years. God's throne is in the throne room of all throne rooms. He owns the whole world. He *made* the whole world! He has chosen you and trusts you to be His light in the world, His ambassador (2 Corinthians 5:20). Because of Jesus:

- You are important—your name is written in heaven (Luke 10:20).
- You are His friend (John 15:14).
- You are clean through the word that Jesus has spoken to you (John 15:3).

Jesus gave Himself for you to impart His perfect life to you. What's more, He would have given Himself *just for you.* When you give your heart and life to Him, you become a part of His lineage. What will you do with this inestimable value He has placed on you?

KEY BIBLE TEXT: "A record of the genealogy of Jesus Christ the son of David, the son of Abraham: ... and Jacob the father of Joseph, the husband of Mary, of whom was born Jesus, who is called Christ. ... and you are to give him the name Jesus, because he will save his people from their sins" (Matthew 1:1, 16, 21).

DAY 185 Brought Back

An Amazing Fact: *Believe it or not, in January 1942, Russian Lieutenant Chisov survived a 22,000-foot fall without a parachute from his badly damaged plane. He providentially fell on the edge of a ravine covered with snow and, because he struck it glancingly, slid as he landed. He was badly injured but survived and eventually returned to his duties.*

An even more incredible escape happened to U.S. Flight Sergeant Alkemade in 1944, when he jumped from his blazing bomber over Germany without a parachute. He fell 18,000 feet, but a fir tree broke the fall as he continued downwards into a knee-high bank of snow. The damage? None!

On July 9, 1960, Roger Woodard became the first person known to survive a plunge over Niagara Falls without a barrel. He and a friend were boating above the falls when the motor failed. A huge wave overturned the boat, throwing both into the swift current. Roger's companion vanished, while he, wearing a life jacket, was swept over the 162-foot precipice. The tourist boat Maid of the Mist happened to be at the bottom of the falls, and the captain heard Roger crying, "Help!" A year later Woodard accepted Christ as his Savior, and said, "I guess the Lord saved me the first time so that I could be saved the second time."

David writes about the joyful return of God's people to Zion. "When the Lord brought back the captivity of Zion, we were like those who dream. Then our mouth was filled with laughter, and our tongue with singing. Then they said among the nations, 'The LORD has done great things for them'" (Psalm 126:1, 2).

Don't wait for a near-death experience to return to God. The Lord welcomes you with joy. Perhaps it seems like a dream now, but when we walk into the New Jerusalem, we will surely sing, "The LORD has done great things for us, and we are glad!" (v. 3).

KEY BIBLE TEXT: "But if you return to Me, and keep My commandments and do them, though some of you were cast out to the farthest part of the heavens, yet I will gather them from there, and bring them to the place which I have chosen as a dwelling for My name" (Nehemiah 1:9).

A Greater Liberty

An Amazing Fact: *Fireworks are believed to have originated in China more than 2,000 years ago. They became very popular in Europe during the Renaissance and were brought to America by the 1600s. The first Independence Day celebration included some fireworks, and they have become standard for the occasion. The record for the most firework rockets launched in 30 seconds is over 56,000!*

Over 200 years ago, the American colonies adopted the Declaration of Independence and seceded from Great Britain. The war for independence began in 1775 and ended eight years later. Sacrifice and bloodshed were required in order to gain liberty. The new nation was at stake.

More than 2,000 years ago, a far greater war was waged, a far greater liberty obtained. Sacrifice and bloodshed were required. The survival of the human race was at stake. Redemption for every human hung in the balance.

Jesus left His home in heaven and came to Earth to fight for us, to rescue us. He paid the price for our sins by sacrificing Himself. We were dead in our trespasses, but "He has made us alive together with Him" (Colossians 2:13). In Jesus we can have true liberty, freedom, and independence from sin for all eternity.

KEY BIBLE TEXT: "And you, being dead in your trespasses and the uncircumcision of your flesh, He has made alive together with Him, having forgiven you all trespasses, having wiped out the handwriting of requirements that was against us, which was contrary to us. And He has taken it out of the way, having nailed it to the cross. Having disarmed principalities and powers, He made a public spectacle of them, triumphing over them in it" (Colossians 2:13–15).

DAY 187 Big Winds

An Amazing Fact: *Many wanted to build a bridge to connect San Francisco to Marin County. San Francisco was the largest American city still served primarily by ferryboats. Experts said that a bridge couldn't be built across the 6,700-foot strait. It had strong, swirling tides and currents, water 500 feet in depth at the center of the channel, and frequent strong winds. They also said ferocious winds and blinding fogs would prevent construction and operation.*

When construction began on the Golden Gate Bridge on January 5, 1933, Joseph B. Strauss, chief engineer, was adamant about using the most rigorous safety precautions in the history of bridge building. Hard hats, not commonly used, with glare-free goggles were specially designed for workers. Special hand and face cream protected the workers against the constant biting wind. The most conspicuous precaution was the safety net, suspended under the entire floor of the bridge from end to end. During construction, the net saved the lives 19 men who became known with affection as the Half-Way-to-Hell Club.

Weather conditions have closed the bridge three times: December 1, 1951, because of gusts of 69 mph; December 23, 1982, because of winds of 70 mph; and December 3, 1983, because of wind gusts of 75 mph.

Jesus' disciples once found their lives at risk because of strong winds while sailing across a lake. "As they sailed ... a windstorm came down on the lake, and they were filling with water, and were in jeopardy" (Luke 8:23). But the winds did not stop Christ from sleeping in the boat. "Then He arose and rebuked the wind and the raging of the water. And they ceased, and there was a calm" (v. 24).

Experts said a bridge couldn't be built across a deep channel of sin and raging winds. But Christ became a bridge to heaven. Jesus laid down His life that we could cross over in safety to a better land. I'm glad our Lord didn't listen to the experts!

KEY BIBLE TEXT: "So the men marveled, saying, 'Who can this be, that even the winds and the sea obey Him?'" (Matthew 8:27).

This Light of Mine

DAY 188

An Amazing Fact: *Chips, a mixed-breed canine hero of World War II, participated in the invasion of Sicily. When his handler's infantry unit was pinned down by gunfire, Chips broke away and charged the machine gun team. The Italian unit abandoned their fortification and was captured. For bravery in this and other circumstances, Chips was awarded the Distinguished Service Cross, Silver Star, the Purple Heart, and eight battle stars. These were later revoked by a new policy stating that animals could not receive military decorations.*

During World War II, some of America's cities ordered citywide blackouts because of the bomb threat. Windows were covered with black shades, cars drove without headlights, and men were not to smoke a cigarette outside—it was said a lighted match could be seen from the air miles away. One family was instructed to extinguish the fire in their fireplace because of the glow from the chimney. The block warden warned, "One small light could change everything."

In the darkness of that long-ago night in Bethlehem, Jesus became that one small light. He changed everything. He said, "I am the light of the world. He who follows me shall not walk in darkness, but have the light of life" (John 8:12). He proclaims, "You are the light of the world" (Matthew 5:14). You and I are the ones He depends on to show His love to a dying world.

"God is light; in him there is no darkness at all. ... If we walk in the light, as he is in the light, we have fellowship with one another, and the blood of Jesus, his Son, purifies us from all sin" (1 John 1:5–7 NIV). That's it—fellowship with one another! That's how we share the light.

Some believe that those who have won many to righteousness will shine as the stars forever and ever. But unlike Chips, those stars won't be taken away.

KEY BIBLE TEXT: "But you are a chosen generation, a royal priesthood, a holy nation, His own special people, that you may proclaim the praises of Him who called you out of darkness into His marvelous light" (1 Peter 2:9).

DAY 189 Big Songs

An Amazing Fact: *You might have noticed that often the smallest birds have the most interesting songs. The various wrens, for example, are among the smallest birds in North America, but they have incredibly loud voices and many complex songs. On the other hand, while bald eagles are among the largest of all birds, their "song" and calls are unremarkable unless threatened by some predator. Eagles are indeed loud, but they have a limited vocabulary.*

Have you ever noticed in early summer that the hills are alive with the sound of birds singing? These beautiful creatures made for our enjoyment actually sing for many different reasons. There are basically two categories of bird sounds: songs and calls. Singing primarily happens around mating and nesting season. Calls happen all the time and mainly communicate messages to other birds, often in shorter and clipped chirps. Songs are usually longer and more complex.

Birds sing to stake out their territory, defend their turf, identify themselves, attract the opposite sex, stimulate nest building, and encourage the female to incubate her eggs. Some studies also show that birds sing just because they like to sing! Biologists have also discovered that birds have accents; the same cardinal in Indiana might sound slightly different than one in Florida.

Paul writes, "Let the word of Christ dwell in you richly in all wisdom, teaching and admonishing one another in psalms and hymns and spiritual songs, singing with grace in your hearts to the Lord" (Colossians 3:16). "Admonish" means to warn or notify. It can also mean to reprove gently or to counsel against wrong practices. Singing can be more than expressing thanks to the Lord, it can guide and instruct us as well.

Perhaps we can learn from the songs of the birds. When the enemy intrudes on our territory, we can sing to drive him away. When the devil tells us lies ("You are a no good, worthless person...") we can identify ourselves in song as God's beloved children. When a friend is discouraged, we can sing words to point them to Jesus.

KEY BIBLE TEXT: "Look at the birds of the air, for they neither sow nor reap nor gather into barns; yet your heavenly Father feeds them. Are you not of more value than they?" (Matthew 6:26).

Salted Speech

An Amazing Fact: *In ancient times, salt was a valuable trade item. The price of salt was so high during the Middle Ages that people sometimes called it "white gold." Up until the 1900s, people in Ethiopia used one-pound bars of salt as currency.*

Jesus said, "You are the salt of the earth" (Matthew 5:13). What did He mean by this metaphor? Well, salt is a seasoning. Jesus' disciples are meant to add a flavor of godliness to the world. Salt is also a preservative. By living pure lives and influencing those around them, true disciples of Christ help to preserve the world from moral decay.

In Paul's writings to the early Christians, he urged them to "walk in wisdom toward those who are outside" so they might have a positive influence on those around them—so they might be good witnesses for Christ (Colossians 4:5).

He also emphasized the importance of a believer's speech toward unbelievers. Words can help or hurt. They can build others up or tear them down. Paul advised, "Let your speech always be with grace, seasoned with salt, that you may know how you ought to answer each one" (Colossians 4:6).

Speaking with grace involves kindness, compassion, and a forgiving spirit in our communication with another person.

Seasoning our conversation with salt can mean using Christian tact, comforting and encouraging someone who is hurting, and flavoring our words so that the other person might be prompted to consider spiritual truth or learn more about God.

KEY BIBLE TEXT: "Continue earnestly in prayer, being vigilant in it with thanksgiving. ... Walk in wisdom toward those who are outside, redeeming the time. Let your speech always be with grace, seasoned with salt, that you may know how you ought to answer each one" (Colossians 4:2, 5, 6).

DAY 191 Big Numbers

An Amazing Fact: *There are a lot of big numbers in the world. Americans spend $300,000,000 per day on clothes. The human body contains 70,000 miles of blood vessels. And the earth weights approximately 6,58 8,000,000,000,000,000,000,000 tons!*

Numbers are fascinating, and people enjoy counting things. For instance, more than 15,000,000,000 prizes have been given away in Cracker Jack's boxes. People have about 100,000 hairs growing on their heads (some of us have a few less!). There are 31,536,000 seconds in a year. And there are about 8,000,000 words in the English language.

The largest number in the English language with a word naming it is googolplex. This number is equal to 10 to the power of a googol, or $10^{10\char`^100}$, which would be written as 1 followed by 10100 zeroes. There are fewer particles in the entire universe than this huge number. The words "googol" and "googolplex" were both suggested in the 1930s by the nine-year-old nephew of mathematician Dr. Edward Kasner.

As technology has increased, the methods of "people counting" has also become more sophisticated. Pointing at people as they walk by was replaced with handheld tally counters to count people. Now you can use infrared beams, computer vision, thermal imaging, and even synthetic intelligence to count people.

According to the Bible, King David was tempted to count people when it was not the Lord's will. "Now Satan stood up against Israel, and moved David to number Israel" (1 Chronicles 21:1). It appears David felt threatened by a military opponent, and instead of consulting with God, he counted the size of his army. Even Joab, his commanding officer, didn't like the idea.

We can be tempted to count out big numbers to make ourselves look better than we are. It can lead us to trust in our own power, our own money, or our own things instead of realizing that our numbers will never add up to what God can provide. You can count on the Lord!

KEY BIBLE TEXT: "After these things I looked, and behold, a great multitude which no one could number" (Revelation 7:9).

Truth Matters

An Amazing Fact: *Victor Lustig was one of the most talented tricksters who ever lived. His master con was pretending to be a government official and sending six scrap metal dealers invitations to discuss the sale of the Eiffel Tower. He told them the upkeep on the tower was too costly and the city wanted to sell it for scrap. He actually sold it to one of the dealers and took a train to Vienna with a suitcase full of cash! A year later, his luck ran out—he was arrested for counterfeiting and eventually died in prison in 1947.*

One day a mother-in-law was playing with her granddaughter, who evidently had tried to win a game with a deceptive move. The woman gave a careful admonition to the little girl not to ever, in any way, do or say anything that *even hinted* at being untrue or deceitful.

What a wonderful piece of advice.

It's pretty clear when God says, "You shall not steal. You shall not bear false witness against your neighbor" (Exodus 20:15, 16). We also might hear the oft-used quote, "Honesty is the best policy." Here's another one: "Love truthfulness and honesty. These are sacred treasures." A character in Shakespeare's *Hamlet* says, "To thine own self be true ... thou canst not then be false to any man."

Can you be trusted? Let's be of more character than Victor Lustig. Let's strive to be like Paul, worthy of imitation: "Therefore I urge you to imitate me. I am sending to you Timothy. ... He will remind you of my way of life in Christ Jesus, which agrees with what I teach everywhere in every church" (1 Corinthians 4:16, 17 NIV).

KEY BIBLE TEXT: "Truthful lips endure forever, by a lying tongue lasts only a moment. The Lord detests lying lips, but he delights in men who are truthful. The tongue that brings healing is a tree of life, but a deceitful tongue crushes the spirit" (Proverbs 12:19, 22; 15:4).

DAY 193 The Greatest

An Amazing Fact: *Jackie Robinson is one of the greatest sports heroes of all time. An African-American baseball player, he is regarded as a sporting legend. In 1947 he became the first black player in major league baseball. He was elected the National League's most valuable player in 1949. He was also inducted into the Baseball Hall of Fame in 1962, the first black person to gain this honor.*

Who is the greatest sport athlete of all-time? There are lots of opinions, of course, but some of the top stars might include Michael Jordan, Babe Ruth, Johnny Unitas, Nile Kinnick, Magic Johnson, Larry Bird, Joe DiMaggio, Billie Jean King, and the entire 1980 U.S. Olympic hockey team. But how could we forget David Robinson, Walter Payton, Hank Aaron, Muhammad Ali, Wilt Chamberlain, Cal Ripken, Lance Armstrong, Jesse Owens, Arnold Palmer, Arthur Ashe, or Ted Williams?

There are many lists of greatest sports heroes of all time, and it's interesting that none of them exactly agree. Almost all of them are about adult men and women who can throw the farthest, jump the highest, hit the hardest, or run the fastest. How do you judge who is the greatest sports hero? By the number of trophies or touchdowns? Perhaps it is by the number of medals or records broken.

Jesus overhead His disciples arguing one day about "who is the greatest." "And Jesus, perceiving the thought of their heart, took a little child and set him by Him, and said to them, 'Whoever receives this little child in My name receives Me; and whoever receives Me receives Him who sent Me. For he who is least among you all will be great'" (Luke 9:47, 48).

God's measurement of the greatest is different from man's. Our Lord sees greatness in humble service. You put yourself at the top of His list by bowing low in service. You are lifted up when you kneel down. The next time you think about the greatest sports heroes of all time, think about how many are willing to sacrifice self in order to lift up others.

KEY BIBLE TEXT: "But many who are first will be last, and the last first" (Matthew 19:30).

Fire From Heaven

An Amazing Fact: *In Jesus' day, the Samaritans were a large group. Through the years, wars such as the Third Samaritan Revolt and other calamities reduced their numbers a great deal. It is estimated that there are now just over 700 people remaining who are descended from the biblical Samaritans.*

On His last journey to Jerusalem, Jesus planned to stay in a Samaritan village. He sent James and John ahead to prepare the way. But because He was headed for Jerusalem, the prejudiced Samaritans didn't want Him there.

This infuriated James and John. "Lord, do You want us to command fire to come down from heaven and consume them, just as Elijah did?" James and John thought they were doing Jesus a favor. In their "righteous" indignation, they thought it was a good idea to just wipe these people off the map!

Imagine their surprise when Jesus rebuked them. "You do not know what manner of spirit you are of. For the Son of Man did not come to destroy men's lives but to save them" (Luke 9:55, 56).

When Jesus is rejected, He doesn't take revenge. He will not force people to accept Him. But someone who rejects Him today could still bow at His feet tomorrow. He waits with patience and mercy because He wants everyone to be saved.

KEY BIBLE TEXT: "And as they went, they entered a village of the Samaritans, to prepare for Him. But they did not receive Him, because His face was set for the journey to Jerusalem. And when His disciples James and John saw this, they said, 'Lord, do You want us to command fire to come down from heaven and consume them, just as Elijah did?' But He turned and rebuked them, and said, 'You do not know what manner of spirit you are of. For the Son of Man did not come to destroy men's lives but to save them'" (Luke 9:51–56).

DAY 195 Kings of the Earth

An Amazing Fact: *According to legend, Gordius was a Greek peasant who became king of Phrygia—because he was the first man to drive into town after an oracle had commanded his countrymen to select as ruler the first person who would drive into the public square in a wagon!*

In gratitude, Gordius dedicated his wagon to the god Zeus and tied the tongue of the wagon securely in the temple grove with a thick strong rope. The knot was so intricately entwined that no one could undo it. Many tried, but all failed. Yet a prophet said that whoever succeeded in loosing the difficult knot would become the ruler of all Asia. Hearing this, Alexander the Great unsuccessfully attempted to untie the complex Gordian knot, so he drew his sword and cut it through with a single stroke. Alexander, of course, went on to become the ruler of Asia and beyond. The expression "to cut the Gordian knot" is now used for resolving a difficult problem by a quick and decisive action.

But Alexander the Great had another difficult problem. He was ruler of Macedonia at age 16, a victorious general at 18, and king at 20—and then what happened to the great king? After Alexander began a second night of carousing in Babylon with 20 guests, he drank to the health of every person at the table. For Proteas, a Macedonian in his company, Alexander called for Hercules' cup, which had a huge capacity. After filling it, he drank it all down. Soon he fell to the floor, was fever stricken, and—a few days later—dead. He had conquered the then-known world, but not himself.

There is little to praise in the kings of the Earth. David looked forward to a future time when, "All the kings of the earth shall praise You, O LORD, when they hear the words of Your mouth. Yes, they shall sing of the ways of the LORD, for great is the glory of the LORD" (Psalm 138:4, 5).

Join your voice in praising the Ruler of our universe and make the Lord the king of your heart.

KEY BIBLE TEXT: "Great and marvelous are Your works, Lord God Almighty! Just and true are Your ways, O King of the saints!" (Revelation 15:3).

Bedrock

An Amazing Fact: *Hoover Dam is located on the border between the states of Arizona and Nevada. Enough rock was excavated in its construction to have built the Great Wall of China. The dam was built to last 2,000 years—the concrete in it will not even be fully cured for another 500 years.*

Though workers probably experienced a great deal of elation over the completion of Hoover Dam, it can't even compare with the gratification, pleasure, thrill, and worship associated with Solomon's completion of the temple of the Lord. "The trumpeters and singers were as one, to make one sound to be heard in praising and thanking the Lord ... the house of the Lord was filled with a cloud, so that the priests could not continue ministering because of the cloud; for the glory of the Lord filled the house of God" (2 Chronicles 5:13, 14).

Have you ever built something with your hands? You know, there are ways to build other than excavating, pouring concrete, framing, putting up rafters, or pounding nails. Every one of us does it every day in some way. We either build up or tear down.

Actually, by giving ourselves to God, we are in His workshop. We all need our rough edges removed, the uneven surfaces smoothed, to become ready for heaven. God desires everyone who confesses Him to become an earnest worker for Him, building upon the rock of Jesus Christ. Dig deep—avoid the sand bed, hunt for the rock, and lay your foundation on Him. When trials come to test you, your foundation will be sure.

Praise the Lord for His work in your life. May His glory fill us like the temple of old.

KEY BIBLE TEXT: "But everyone who hears these words of mine and does not put them into practice is like a foolish man who built his house on sand. The rain came down, the streams rose, and the winds blew and beat against that house, and it fell with a great crash (Matthew 7:26, 27 NIV).

DAY 197 A Purity Plea

An Amazing Fact: *The word "porn" is the fourth-highest ranked search term by children under seven years old, and the average age when a person first views porn is only 11 years old. About 40 million adults visit pornographic websites daily. It shouldn't be a surprise that nearly half of all divorces list porn as a contributing factor.*

The statistics on what some call "the most destructive force in our culture" are staggering. More than 11 million Americans have a sexual addiction. Child porn generates about $3 billion annually. At least 25 percent of all employees who use the Internet look at porn do so at work. It truly is a road to hell with broken people lying all over the place. Our society continues to wave the "freedom" banner while millions walk into slavery, looking for love in all the wrong places.

The apostle Paul does not turn a blind eye to the problem of sexual addiction. He makes a plea for purity. "For this is the will of God, your sanctification: that you should abstain from sexual immorality; that each of you should know how to possess his own vessel in sanctification and honor, not in passion of lust, like the Gentiles who do not know God; that no one should take advantage of and defraud his brother in this matter" (1 Thessalonians 4:3–6). The Roman culture to which Paul wrote was sexually permissive. His challenge to instill the notion of purity in their culture would be even more relevant today.

If you struggle with sexual addiction, you need to face this ugly sin with a passion of someone going to war to conquer an enemy. Consider these three steps: Admit you have a problem, get help with accountability, and remove all impurity from your life. Make a clean break and begin filling your mind with the pure things of God. You cannot find victory on your own. Your battle is really an obsession with self. Growing in Christ is learning to live for others, not your feelings. Your choices do not affect only you, they negatively impact those around you. So choose purity and experience real freedom.

KEY BIBLE TEXT: "Therefore put to death your members which are on the earth: fornication, uncleanness, passion, evil desire, and covetousness, which is idolatry" (Colossians 3:5).

Treasuring the Words of Jesus

DAY 198

An Amazing Fact: *The original biblical town of Bethany, home of Mary, Martha, and Lazarus, is believed to have been situated on the southeastern slope of the Mount of Olives, less than two miles from Jerusalem. Historians believe the town was the site of an almshouse for the poor. Its name is derived from words in at least two languages that mean "house of the poor" or "house of poverty."*

According to the Bible, Martha welcomed Jesus and His disciples into her house. That apparently launched her into a frenzy of activity. She probably felt a little overwhelmed at having to prepare food and accommodations for all those men. Under the stress of the moment, she accused her sister, Mary, of leaving her to serve alone.

Unlike the "distracted" Martha, Mary realized this was the opportunity of a lifetime. The Messiah, the very Son of God, had come to her house to visit. She could sit at his feet and listen to soul-rousing truths that she had never heard before, at least not the way Jesus told them.

As Jesus made clear to the sisters, while there's nothing wrong with serving, there is something more vital. What Martha needed, we all need—more attention to the things of God, the things that last forever. We need to sit at the feet of Jesus and treasure His every word.

KEY BIBLE TEXT: "Now it happened as they went that He entered a certain village; and a certain woman named Martha welcomed Him into her house. And she had a sister called Mary, who also sat at Jesus' feet and heard His word. But Martha was distracted with much serving, and she approached Him and said, 'Lord, do You not care that my sister has left me to serve alone? Therefore tell her to help me.' And Jesus answered and said to her, 'Martha, Martha, you are worried and troubled about many things. But one thing is needed, and Mary has chosen that good part, which will not be taken away from her'" (Luke 10:38–42).

DAY 199 Persistence

An Amazing Fact: *If you put a buzzard in a 6-foot-by-8-foot pen that's entirely open at the top, the bird, despite its ability to fly, will be an absolute prisoner. Why? A buzzard always begins flight with a run of 10 to 12 feet. Without this runway, it will not even attempt to fly—but will remain a prisoner for life, waddling around in a small jail with an open top.*

Another animal that will not persist in trying to fly is the common bat. It is a remarkably nimble night creature in the air, but it cannot take off from a level place. If it's placed on flat ground, all it can do is shuffle about, helplessly and painfully, until it reaches some slanted ground from which to launch itself.

On the other hand, a common little insect teaches us a great deal about effort. The bumblebee, if dropped into an open glass tumbler, will stay there until it dies. It never sees the means of escape at the top but persists in trying to find some way out through near the bottom. It will continue to seek until it completely destroys itself through exhaustion.

Jesus tells a story of persistence. He spoke of a friend coming at midnight who was hungry. So this man went to his neighbor to ask for three loaves of bread so he could feed his friend. The neighbor did not want to be bothered. It was late, and he was already in bed! But notice, "I say to you, though he will not rise and give to him because he is his friend, yet because of his persistence he will rise and give him as many as he needs" (Luke 11:8).

Christ teaches us that we need to be more like a bumblebee than a bat or buzzard. When we pray to the Lord we are much too quick to give up. "What's the use," we think, "It doesn't matter." But Jesus tells us that when it comes to prayer, persistence matters! Instead of ending up in the bottom of a jar, we will find a way out—and the direction of escape is above!

KEY BIBLE TEXT: "Then He spoke a parable to them that men always ought to pray and not lose heart" (Luke 18:1).

Spreading the Good News

DAY 200

An Amazing Fact: *Did you know there is a Peanut Butter of the Month Club? You can gift a friend with 12 "limited-production, specialty-flavored peanut butters from boutique peanut butter producers nationwide." Who knew there was such a thing as a "boutique peanut butter?" For the price of $215, you can spend the whole year telling your friends that you're really into raspberry white chocolate peanut butter, cinnamon currant peanut butter, or ...*

God has gifted each of us with abilities and talents that can be used for building His kingdom. In daily life we come into contact with many different people, each with their own set of "flavors" as different as the assortment of peanut butter. Physical attributes vary: height, weight, strength, hair color, color of the skin—not one person is exactly the same.

Some individuals are well read and can converse intellectually on many subjects. Some are not and cannot. Attitudes differ—one is positive, the other negative. There might be similar or opposing views on almost any subject. Some don't hesitate to verbalize, while others are silent.

But woven into each life is a common thread: "You are the body of Christ, and members individually. There are diversities of gifts, but the same Spirit. There are differences of ministries, but the same Lord. And there are diversities of activities, but it is the same God who works all in all ... distributing to each one individually as He wills (1 Corinthians 12: 27, 4–6, 11). Have you discovered your gifts? It's exciting to know that every one of them can be used for Jesus.

He said, "He who is not with me is against me, and he who does not gather with me, scatters" (Luke 11:23). What an awesome opportunity we have to be a gatherer with Jesus. What a tremendous blessing to have a part in the salvation of others. He is calling you. Answer quickly, "Here am I, send me."

KEY BIBLE TEXT: "For this reason I remind you to fan into flame the gift of God" (2 Timothy 1:6 NIV).

DAY 201 Big Castles

An Amazing Fact: *The Prague Castle is the biggest castle in the world, measuring 1,870 feet in length and 426 feet in width. It has been home to kings of Bohemia, Holy Roman Emperors, and presidents of the Czechoslovakia and Czech Republic since about the 9th century. It could house 87 White Houses or six Buckingham Palaces.*

Castles were basically European inventions of the 9th century. Nobles built castles to control territories, and castles were both defensive and offensive in nature. They were bases of military from which raids could be launched but also provided protection from enemies. Common in the medieval period, castles were used for a variety of purposes, including military, administration, and domestic. The advent of the cannon seemed to diminish castles use as military bases. So instead, they became places to exhibit wealth and impress others. The Prague Castle houses several churches, monasteries, homes, gardens, palaces, and defense towers. Today there are several museums, art collections, and exhibitions on display.

Castles are often, but not always, fortresses. They were originally built to protect people inside. Moats surrounded castles, and drawbridges pulled up made it more difficult for the enemy to penetrate. Arrow slits (or loopholes) were openings that provided archers places to fire on attackers. Other common features were baileys (fortified enclosures), the keep (a central fortified tower), curtain walls (defensive walls surrounding a bailey), and gatehouse (to control entry).

God has been spoken of in the Bible as a fortress. David wrote, "Blessed be the LORD my Rock, who trains my hands for war, and my fingers for battle—my lovingkindness and my fortress, my high tower and my deliverer, my shield and the One in whom I take refuge, who subdues my people under me" (Psalm 144:1, 2). David found strength from the Lord to do battle, as well as protection ("refuge") in God. So we may turn to our mighty heavenly Father for help in times of trial as well as safety from our enemy.

Turn to Jesus as your true source of power and protection. Our God is like a mighty fortress in which we can find shelter from the storms of life.

KEY BIBLE TEXT: "I will say of the LORD, 'He is my refuge and my fortress; my God, in Him I will trust'" (Psalm 91:2).

The Inward Part

An Amazing Fact: *In a recent poll, many Americans showed extreme greed in response to the question: "What would you do for 10 million dollars?" About 25 percent would abandon their family or their church, 16 percent would walk away from their marriage, and 13 percent would allow their children to be put up for adoption.*

The Pharisees were quick to criticize Jesus and His disciples for not observing their manmade rules. One of the points of disagreement was ceremonial washing. The Pharisees were ready to condemn people who disregarded their washing traditions; they thought it was a terrible sin.

Jesus responded, "Now you Pharisees make the outside of the cup and dish clean, but your inward part is full of greed and wickedness" (Luke 11:39).

Appearance was everything to the Pharisees. As long as they "looked good" they were pleased with themselves. But Jesus pointed out that what is inside a person is the most important thing. The Pharisees, who made such a show of washing in a particular way, had neglected to clean their hearts. Jesus saw right through them, as He always does. He saw the greed and sin, and He knew what they really needed: generous, giving hearts.

KEY BIBLE TEXT: "And as He spoke, a certain Pharisee asked Him to dine with him. So He went in and sat down to eat. When the Pharisee saw it, he marveled that He had not first washed before dinner. Then the Lord said to him, 'Now you Pharisees make the outside of the cup and dish clean, but your inward part is full of greed and wickedness. Foolish ones! Did not He who made the outside make the inside also? But rather give alms of such things as you have; then indeed all things are clean to you'" (Luke 11:37–41).

DAY 203 Food for All

An Amazing Fact: *Bees are very social insects, and mutual feeding seems to be the order of their existence. The workers feed the helpless queen, who cannot feed herself. They feed the drones and, of course, they feed the young. They seem to actually enjoy this social act. One bee always seems ready to feed another bee, even if that bee is from a different colony.*

The bee has been aptly described as busy. To produce one tablespoon of honey for our toast, the little bee makes 4,200 trips to flowers. A worker bee will fly as far as eight miles in search of nectar. He makes about 10 trips a day to the fields, each trip lasting 20 minutes and covering 400 flowers. To produce just one pound of clover honey, the bee must visit 56,000 clover heads. Since each head has 60 flower tubes, a total of 3,360,000 visits are necessary. In the end, that worker bee will have flown the equivalent of three times around the world. And they never sleep!

The impact of the honeybee on your food goes beyond honey. This little wonder of God's creation is responsible for 80 percent of all insect pollination; if it didn't do its job it would significantly decrease the yield of fruits and vegetables.

Psalm 145 is a song of praise to the Creator. "Great is the LORD, and greatly to be praised; and His greatness is unsearchable" (Psalm 145:3). As we look at the amazing honeybee, we can join David in saying, "I will meditate on the glorious splendor of Your majesty, and on Your wondrous works" (v. 5). When we consider the immense number of flowers it takes to make one pound of honey, it seems an impossibility, yet the Bible says, "The eyes of all look expectantly to You, and You give them their food in due season. You open Your hand and satisfy the desire of every living thing" (v. 15, 16).

Thank God for the honeybee!

KEY BIBLE TEXT: "Give us day by day our daily bread" (Luke 11:3).

Our God of Detail

An Amazing Fact: *Hair is one of the fastest-growing tissues in the body, second only to bone marrow. In fact, the average adult scalp grows more than 100 feet of hair per day!*

Though this fact seems incredible, consider that the average adult scalp has 100,000 hairs. That means that each hair only needs to grow about a third of a millimeter per day to reach a total of over 100 feet. The average life of a hair is four to seven years. Each time a hair falls out, a new one usually grows in its place. This can happen up to 20 times for each hair follicle.

Another interesting fact is that redheads have an average of only 80,000 hairs, while black- and brown-haired persons average 100,000. Blondes top the list at 120,000. Though you might feel alarmed after brushing to see your brush full of hair, it is doubtful that the average 100 hairs that you lose per day would make any visible difference. In fact, a person must lose over 50 percent of his hair to have any noticeable difference in his appearance.

At times we might feel that God is distant or takes little notice of the affairs of our lives. But this is a lie from the enemy. Our loving heavenly Father knows all about us. We are told that He not only "knows our frame" (Psalm 103:14), but He has numbered the very hairs of our head (Luke 12:7). Not only does He know and understand the big picture—what makes us who we are, but He is fully aware of the little details of our lives. By telling us that He knows the number of hairs we have, He is letting us know that He is also aware of the bigger, more difficult details of our lives. When we are tempted to feel alone or unimportant, let's remember that God loves us with an everlasting love (Jeremiah 31:3), and is just waiting for us to experience the joy of total dependence upon Him.

KEY BIBLE TEXT: "Your Father knows the things you have need of before you ask Him" (Matthew 6:8).

DAY 205 The Deceiver

An Amazing Fact: *The Australian lyrebird is a copycat (or shall we say "copy bird"?). It is best known for its superb ability to mimic the sounds of other birds in the forest. It has also been heard to copy the sounds of chainsaws, car alarms, barking dogs, crying babies, and even camera shutter clicks.*

In the 1930s, a Mrs. Wilkinson befriended a lyrebird in her back yard ("James") by feeding him scraps. The bird bonded with her and would often perform long courtship dances accompanied by the calls of a dozen or more birds whenever she was around. Included in his repertoire were the sounds of automobile horns honking, a nearby rock crushing machine, and the sound of a hydraulic ram.

How can the lyrebird make such an incredible array of sounds? Its secret is in a very complex syrinx (vocal organ), the most complex of all song birds, giving it an extraordinary ability to copy the sounds of other birds and noises. A researcher once recorded flute-like sounds of a lyrebird near the New England National Park, as did a park ranger in New South Wales. After doing some research they discovered that a flute player living near the park used to play his flute for his lyrebird. This happened about 40 years earlier!

The Bible warns us of a deceiver who will appear to be what he is not. "Let no one deceive you by any means; for that Day will not come unless the falling away comes first, and the man of sin is revealed, the son of perdition, who opposes and exalts himself above all that is called God or that is worshiped, so that he sits as God in the temple of God, showing himself that he is God" (2 Thessalonians 2:3, 4). But he is not God.

The apostle Paul warns us this deceiver seems like the real thing. "The coming of the lawless one is according to the working of Satan, with all power, signs, and lying wonders" (v. 9). He might sound "just like the real thing," but we are told not to be led astray. Study the call of the True Master. You will recognize His voice.

KEY BIBLE TEXT: "Let no one deceive you with empty words" (Ephesians 5:6).

Real Wealth

An Amazing Fact: *In the year 1800, about 90 percent of Americans were farmers. By 1900, that number dropped to a little over 40 percent. Currently, only about two percent of Americans are farmers.*

The rich farmer in Jesus' parable was apparently neither satisfied with nor thankful for the riches he had. He wanted more. He displayed no concern for others. He was self-absorbed and coveted a life of luxury and ease. Most tragic of all, he showed no interest in God who had blessed him with so much.

Jesus said, "One's life does not consist in the abundance of the things he possesses." There is no future in a covetous life. Any treasures that a covetous person manages to accumulate might give him a false sense of security, an illusion of invincibility. But riches can't protect him from disaster, they can't save his life, and they can't give him lasting joy or an eternal future.

Real wealth isn't found apart from God. The spiritual life is what matters most. Only God can give us the eternal treasure of life with Him in His kingdom of love.

KEY BIBLE TEXT: "And He said to them, 'Take heed and beware of covetousness, for one's life does not consist in the abundance of the things he possesses.' Then He spoke a parable to them, saying: 'The ground of a certain rich man yielded plentifully. And he thought within himself, saying, "What shall I do, since I have no room to store my crops?" So he said, "I will do this: I will pull down my barns and build greater, and there I will store all my crops and my goods. And I will say to my soul, 'Soul, you have many goods laid up for many years; take your ease; eat, drink, and be merry.'"' But God said to him, 'Fool! This night your soul will be required of you; then whose will those things be which you have provided?' So is he who lays up treasure for himself, and is not rich toward God" (Luke 12:15–21).

DAY 207 Count the Stars

An Amazing Fact: *Looking up at the clear night sky, you can see about as much of the universe as a single-cell amoeba might see of the ocean in which it swims. The moon, the planets, and the few thousand stars that are visible to us are merely a single drop of water in the boundless sea of the universe. The distance from our galaxy to the next nearest one is almost one-and-a-half million light years. And the known universe is believed to be about 10 to 12 billion light-years long.*

The disc-shaped galaxy to which our sun belongs is called the Milky Way, which is a family of 200 to 400 billion stars and 50 billion planets. Each planet is a separate island in space, and about 500 million are estimated to be in the habitable zone of their parent star. But then, there could be as many as 200 (some say 500) billion galaxies in the universe, and each of which could have as many or more stars as the Milky Way. Multiply those two numbers together and you'll see that there could be as many as 2×10^{23} stars in the observable universe. That's 200,000,000,000,000,000,000,000.

With so many stars out there, it's amazing to consider the vast distances involved. The closest star to Earth is Proxima Centauri, located 4.2 light years away. In other words, it takes light itself more than four years to complete the journey from the star to the Earth. If you hitched a ride on the fastest spacecraft ever launched from Earth, it would still take you more than 70,000 years to get there from here. Traveling between the stars just isn't feasible right now. But someday, in heaven, it will be!

When David sings praises to God, he writes, "He counts the number of the stars; He calls them all by name. Great is our Lord, and mighty in power; His understanding is infinite" (Psalm 147:4, 5). Truly, as we behold the wonder of the stars on a dark night, we will join the psalmist in giving praise to our awesome Creator.

KEY BIBLE TEXT: "The heavens declare the glory of God; and the firmament shows His handiwork" (Psalm 19:1).

One Big Mess

DAY 208

An Amazing Fact: *The Deepwater Horizon oil spill (also known as the BP oil spill) is the largest accidental marine oil spill in the history of the petroleum industry. It flowed for three months in 2010 before being capped on July 15, 2010. It released about 4.9 million barrels of crude oil.*

The Deepwater Horizon oil spill created a big mess. Wildlife and marine life were destroyed. Hundreds of miles of shoreline were contaminated. The fishing industry was shut down. Today, tar balls continue to show up in fishermen's nets. Oil sheens are still observed in many places. By July 2011 about 490 miles of coastline in Louisiana, Mississippi, Alabama, and Florida are still contaminated.

Who is responsible for the mess? The U.S. Government is holding British Petroleum (BP) accountable for all clean-up costs and damage. In June 2010, BP set up a $20 billion fund to compensate those hurt by the spill. Over one million claims have been submitted, and thousands still come in each week.

Hezekiah also had a big mess to clean up. "In the first year of his reign, in the first month, he opened the doors of the house of the Lord and repaired them" (2 Chronicles 29:3). Then he said to the Levites, "Now sanctify yourselves, sanctify the house of the Lord God of your fathers, and carry out the rubbish from the holy place. For our fathers have trespassed and done evil in the eyes of the Lord" (vs. 5, 6). From the start of his reign, Hezekiah tackled what was most important—caring for the house of the Lord.

Our own lives are a mess. Without Jesus, the temples of our hearts are filled with rubbish. Like Hezekiah, we have a big mess to clean up. Billions of dollars won't do the job. We don't need skimmers or disbursement chemicals. The sacred work of heart cleansing comes only through a broken spirit that allows the Holy Spirit to come inside and clean house. Why not invite the Spirit to come in and start cleaning your heart today?

KEY BIBLE TEXT: "Search me, O God, and know my heart; Try me, and know my anxieties; And see if there is any wicked way in me" (Psalm 139:23, 24).

DAY 209 Run Swiftly

An Amazing Fact: *The 100-meter dash is one of the most popular running sports at the Olympics. It is also the shortest. The reigning 100m Olympic champion is thought of as the fastest man or woman in the world.*

Historically, the 10-second barrier has been a measurement of men's performances, while the best female sprinters take eleven seconds or less to complete the race. Currently, the men's world record is 9.58 seconds, set by Jamaica's Usain Bolt, while American Florence Griffith-Joyner holds the women's world record of 10.49 seconds. Of the top-12 fastest runners in the world among men, four are from Jamaica, five from the United States, two from Canada, and one from Nigeria. The fastest foot speed recorded is 27.79 miles per hour during a 100-meter sprint by Usain Bolt.

There are many different types of "runs," such as track running, road running, or cross-country running. Distances are clustered by the terms sprint, middle distance, and long distance. A marathon is 26 miles and 385 yards. The event began in commemoration of the fabled run of the Greek soldier Pheidippides, a messenger from the battle of Marathon to Athens. The current marathon record holder is Haile Gebrselassie from Ethiopia, who broke the record in September 2008 in Berlin by clocking in at 2 hours, 3 minutes, and 59 seconds.

The apostle Paul was a man on the move for Jesus. He once wrote, "Finally, brethren, pray for us, that the word of the Lord may run swiftly and be glorified, just as it is with you, and that we may be delivered from unreasonable and wicked men; for not all have faith" (2 Thessalonians 3:1, 2). Sometimes Paul literally ran out of town when he was chased away. But his goal was not to lift up himself, but to glorify God.

How does the Word of God run swiftly? Through people like you and me who are determined to share Christ with others. Today, put on your running shoes and help spread the good news about Jesus.

KEY BIBLE TEXT: "Therefore we also, since we are surrounded by so great a cloud of witnesses, let us lay aside every weight, and the sin which so easily ensnares us, and let us run with endurance the race that is set before us" (Hebrews 12:1).

Watching and Ready

An Amazing Fact: *Most biblical lamps were made of clay pottery and were oval-shaped or round and were squeezed on one end to form a channel for the wick, which was normally made from flax. Oil lamps were often engraved with symbols. The most commonly used fuel was olive oil, although nut oil, fish oil, and other types of oil were sometimes used.*

Jesus advised His disciples to keep their lamps burning, to keep the light shining. This light represents the presence of the Light of the world. We need the continuous presence of Jesus, through His Holy Spirit, in order to share the gospel message with others and to prepare us for His return.

Jesus promises a great blessing to those who consistently watch for their Master. "Assuredly, I say to you that he will gird himself and have them sit down to eat, and will come and serve them." They will be welcomed into heaven with a feast of celebration. Can you imagine being served a special dinner by the Lord of the universe?

Though it might be tempting to sleep in the darkness, we need to stay sharp, focused, and ready for Christ's return. After all, He is "coming at an hour you do not expect" (Luke 12:40). Spending time with Him in regular Bible study and prayer will keep your lamp burning bright.

KEY BIBLE TEXT: "Let your waist be girded and your lamps burning; and you yourselves be like men who wait for their master, when he will return from the wedding, that when he comes and knocks they may open to him immediately. Blessed are those servants whom the master, when he comes, will find watching. Assuredly, I say to you that he will gird himself and have them sit down to eat, and will come and serve them. ... Therefore you also be ready, for the Son of Man is coming at an hour you do not expect" (Luke 12:35–37, 40).

DAY 211 Singing New Songs

An Amazing Fact: *Zebra finches are teaching scientists about how humans learn to sing. Like human babies, new finches start out babbling. Through trial and error they eventually learn the rhythms and syllables of their parents' vocalizations. Almost all animals make sounds instinctively. A cat raised by a dog will still meow. A deaf dog will still bark. But some animals must learn to sing.*

Some animals must learn their vocalizations. These include bats, whales, and three types of birds (parrots, hummingbirds, and songbirds). Zebra finches songs are easy to study because they are short and simple and do not change. When a zebra finch is hatched, it has about 4 to 12 weeks during a "sensitive" period in which to learn "Dad's" song (only the males sing). It listens to the song and then babbles. After awhile it begins to piece together parts of the song correctly but still has errors. Eventually, it will sing the song perfectly and will never change its tune.

But if a zebra finch is raised by a bird from a different species (cross fostering), it will learn a new song, though it will have an "accent" similar to its own species. There is some genetic influence, but experience shapes the wiring of the brain. The finch can learn to sing a new song. Of course, the younger you are, the easier it is for your brain to re-wire itself.

Our heavenly Father has songs to teach us. Our personal experiences with God provide a rich new repertoire of music that we can use to praise the Lord. David writes, "Sing to the LORD a new song, and His praise in the assembly of saints. Let Israel rejoice in their Maker; let the children of Zion be joyful in their King" (Psalm 149:1, 2).

Someday we will stand on the sea of glass and sing praises to Jesus. Let us practice singing those new songs on this Earth so we will be ready to lift our voices in praise in heaven.

KEY BIBLE TEXT: "And they sang a new song, saying: 'You are worthy to take the scroll, and to open its seals; for You were slain, and have redeemed us to God by Your blood'" (Revelation 5:9).

The Renewing Fire

An Amazing Fact: *Some plants have leaves naturally coated in flammable oils in order to encourage fast, intense fires. Not by accident, these plants have heat-activated seeds that require fire or intense heat in order to open and germinate.*

This fact reveals the useful purpose that fire is intended to play in nature. But it has not always been viewed this way. Prior to 1910, forest fires burned as much as 50 million acres annually in the United States. As awareness and interest in national parks increased, lawmakers established rules and funding to protect these national treasures from this perceived threat. A law enacted in 1908 permitted deficit spending in the case of emergency fire situations. As a result, in 1910 the Forest Service acquired a $1 million deficit due to emergency fire suppression efforts. Public education campaigns, such as Smokey the Bear, trained the general public to perceive all wildfire as a threat to civilized society and natural resources.

Beginning in the 1970s however, perception of fire management began to shift. In spite of increased funding, massive wildfires continued to be prevalent across North America. It was discovered that, in actuality, suppression of fire in certain ecosystems not only *increases* the likelihood of a wildfire, but also increases the intensity of those wildfires. Allowing the natural cycle of fire kept the underbrush clean, thus making for shorter, less intense fires, which in turn allowed the bigger trees to survive.

Jesus said, "I am come to send fire on the earth" (Luke 12:49). Though unpleasant, fire is important. As seen in nature, it is necessary for purification and regeneration. The same is true in our lives. Instead of perceiving our trials as a threat, let's view them as messengers of God to either remove the dross from our life or, by our patience in suffering, to display His faithfulness to others.

KEY BIBLE TEXT: "Beloved, do not think it strange concerning the fiery trial which is to try you, as though some strange thing happened to you; but rejoice to the extent that you partake of Christ's sufferings, that when His glory is revealed, you may also be glad with exceeding joy" (1 Peter 4:12, 13).

DAY 213 God's Signature

An Amazing Fact: *Forrest R. Smith III, 48, of Exeter, Pennsylvania, was sentenced to 33 months in prison and to pay $120,000 in restitution after getting busted for forging author signatures in books by Truman Capote, Michael Crichton, Tom Clancy, Kurt Vonnengut, and Anne Rice and then selling them on eBay.*

Smith had obtained documents containing authentic signatures of each author and had ink-based stamps made for the signatures. Assistant U.S. Attorney Mark Dubnoff said someone in the book-selling field initially uncovered Smith's scheme and alerted authorities. Another bookseller noticed that someone was buying up first-edition books and a short time later those same books were being put up for sale—but as signed copies of a book whose author was dead.

Signatures serve many purposes. One is to identify a document. Another is to indicate the purpose of a document. That's why a signature is often located at the end. Signatures of famous people are often called autographs and tend to be artistic in nature and are usually given as souvenirs.

What are some of the most valuable signatures in the world? Try purchasing one of only five known copies of William Shakespeare's signature and you will pay about $5 million. In 1991 someone purchased Abraham Lincoln's signature that defended the Emancipation Proclamation; it went for $748,000.

Paul had to deal with an apparent forgery. His benediction at the end of his second letter to the church at Thessalonica ends with, "The salutation of Paul with my own hand, which is a sign in every epistle; so I write" (2 Thessalonians 3:17). Paul not only identifies himself but indicates this letter is not a forgery. It is authentic. Apparently another letter was circulating (2:2) from a false teacher. So Paul warns his friends to not be led astray but to be faithful to the truths he communicated with them.

As we study our Bibles, we can know that the signature of God is in the inspired word. We will not be fooled if we stick with the message of Scripture.

KEY BIBLE TEXT: "All Scripture is given by inspiration of God, and is profitable for doctrine, for reproof, for correction, for instruction in righteousness" (2 Timothy 3:16).

Why Keep the Commandments?

An Amazing Fact: *In the days when many public schools in America displayed the Ten Commandments, a higher percentage of the population was familiar with them. Now, according to one poll, less than 60 percent of Americans know the commandment regarding murder and only 34 percent are familiar with the Sabbath commandment.*

Paul said, "The law is not made for a righteous person, but for the lawless and insubordinate, for the ungodly" (1 Timothy 1:9). The Ten Commandments show people who are sinning where they are going wrong.

"Now the purpose of the commandment is love," he adds. The Ten Commandments show us how to live in a way that reflects the love of our Creator.

Since "the law is not made for a righteous person," does this mean that morally upright people don't need to bother with keeping the law? Of course not. It means they are already keeping it!

God wrote the Ten Commandments on stone to signify their unchanging nature. While He was on Earth, Jesus always upheld the commandments as a reflection of His character of love; they were part of His teaching. And He says to all His disciples, "If you love Me, keep My commandments" (John 14:15).

KEY BIBLE TEXT: "Now the purpose of the commandment is love from a pure heart, from a good conscience, and from sincere faith, from which some, having strayed, have turned aside to idle talk, desiring to be teachers of the law, understanding neither what they say nor the things which they affirm. But we know that the law is good if one uses it lawfully, knowing this: that the law is not made for a righteous person, but for the lawless and insubordinate, for the ungodly and for sinners, for the unholy and profane, for murderers of fathers and murderers of mothers, for manslayers, for fornicators, for sodomites, for kidnappers, for liars, for perjurers, and if there is any other thing that is contrary to sound doctrine" (1 Timothy 1:5–10).

DAY 215 God's Makeover

An Amazing Fact: *Extreme Makeover: Home Edition is a reality television series that provides home renovations for less fortunate families. Over eight seasons, different teams of volunteers have helped restore or completely rebuild more than 180 homes for people who have suffered tragedies in their lives.*

How would you like to wake up some morning to hear that you were going to get a new house? After being interviewed about your family's needs and preferences, you'd also be given a free one-week vacation while your house was totally renovated at no cost to you. One week later, before your eyes, would be your completely renewed home, with all-new furniture, electronics, and landscaping too. It would be a tearjerker moment, wouldn't it?

The program receives thousands of applications for families in need. The producers look for truly deserving families who are the type to give back to their communities. Sometimes the family has a father who was critically injured, a child who is extremely ill, or several foster children. Some have lost loved ones in car accidents or have been victims of domestic violence.

The Bible talks about a renovation project that brought tears to the eyes of some and shouts of joy from others. It was the renovation of the temple in Jerusalem after the Babylonian captivity. When the foundations for the temple were laid, the Bible says, "Many of the priests and Levites and heads of the fathers' houses, old men who had seen the first temple, wept with a loud voice when the foundation of this temple was laid before their eyes. Yet many shouted aloud for joy" (Ezra 3:12). In fact, the shouting was so loud you could not distinguish joy from weeping.

Someday God is going to do an extreme makeover of this Earth. Our home will be completely made new—not modified, not touched up, not just surface changes, but a brand-new creation. It will be just like it was in the beginning. Jesus will someday swing wide the gates of heaven and say, "Welcome home!"

KEY BIBLE TEXT: "Now I saw a new heaven and a new earth, for the first heaven and the first earth had passed away" (Revelation 21:1).

Sleeping Peacefully

An Amazing Fact: *A great Danish army invaded Scotland many years ago. They crept stealthily over the border and prepared to make a night attack on Scottish forces. There lay the camp of the Scots, silent in the starlight, never dreaming that danger was so near. The Danes, to make their advance quieter, came forward barefooted. Big mistake!*

As the Danes neared the sleeping Scots, one unlucky soldier set his broad foot down squarely on a bristling thistle. Consequently, a roar of pain followed, and it rang out like a trumpet blast through the sleeping camp. In a moment, the Scottish soldiers all grabbed their weapons and the Danes were thoroughly routed. From that time, the thistle became the national emblem of Scotland!

Have you ever had a difficult time going to sleep at night? Perhaps you moved into a new home and as you tried to drift off to sleep every little noise disturbed you. Some people find it difficult to sleep because of worry. They spend their time doing "work" in their heads. One counselor said, "If you can't get to sleep, go mop your kitchen floor, then lay down. If you still can't get to sleep, go mop it again. Eventually you will be happy to go to sleep!" Maybe that's not the best method, but there is one thing for sure, God cares about your sleep.

The Bible says, "When you lie down, you will not be afraid; Yes, you will lie down and your sleep will be sweet" (Proverbs 3:24). The Lord promises to watch over us as we close our eyes to rest at night. We can put our confidence in those protective angels that stand guard, not only over our bodies, but our minds as well.

Proverbs continues, "Do not be afraid of sudden terror, Nor of trouble from the wicked when it comes; For the Lord will be your confidence, And will keep your foot from being caught" (vs. 25, 26). In the case of the sleeping Scots, they were protected when the enemy's foot got "caught" by stepping on a thistle! When you lay down to sleep tonight, put your confidence in the Lord.

KEY BIBLE TEXT: "For so He gives His beloved sleep" (Psalm 127:2).

DAY 217 The Lowest Place

An Amazing Fact: *The Kola Superdeep Borehole in Russia is the deepest hole ever drilled and the deepest artificial point on Earth. For two decades it was also the longest borehole at more than seven-and-a-half miles. Drilling began in 1970 and ended in 1992 when the extreme heat made it impossible to run the equipment any deeper.*

The original goal of the borehole was 49,000 feet while seeking to break through the Earth's crust. There are basically three layers to our planet: the crust, the mantle, and the core. Geologists have been trying to drill down to the mantle, about 18 to 20 miles deep. (In the ocean, it is only about three miles deep.) So far no one has drilled through the elusive "Moho," a nickname for the boundary between the crust and mantle.

There are other huge holes made by people: gigantic pits made for mining. Chuquicamata is an open-pit copper mine in Chile with the largest total production of copper in the world; it has a depth of 2,788 feet. The Udachnaya Pipe is a diamond mine in Russia at over 1,968 feet deep. But the Bingham Canyon Mine, a copper mine in the Oquirrh Mountains of Utah, is 3,937 feet deep and 13,123 feet wide (2.5 miles). It is the world's largest manmade excavation.

God actually wants us to be at the lowest place. No, not in a hole in the Earth, but in our attitudes. Jesus told a story explaining how people often go to banquets and want to sit in the highest place. Sometimes the host asks them to move, and it is embarrassing to go down to the lowest place. You should "go to the lowest place" that you might be moved to the highest. Then Christ states, "For whoever exalts himself will be humbled, and he who humbles himself will be exalted" (Luke 14:11).

God's physics are different than man's. The Lord tells us that going down lifts you up. So why not bow down in prayer for the One who will someday exalt you?

KEY BIBLE TEXT: "Therefore humble yourselves under the mighty hand of God, that He may exalt you in due time" (1 Peter 5:6).

Blessed by a Heathen King

An Amazing Fact: *King Artaxerxes had a surname that translates to "Longimanus" in Latin, supposedly because he had a right hand that was noticeably longer than his left hand.*

Artaxerxes, ruler of Persia, displayed compassion that amazed the prophet Ezra, who gave praise to God for putting it in the king's heart to be merciful to him and to the Jewish people.

The king commissioned Ezra to return to Jerusalem, taking with him as many people as wanted to return, and to continue work on the temple of God. He even gave Ezra generous gifts of silver and gold for the temple and advised him to buy many offerings to sacrifice to God. He told him to take from the king's treasury anything else he might need to help with the temple, and he gave Ezra the power to collect from his treasurers "beyond the river." He also advised him and empowered him to enforce the law of God and the law of the king and to teach anyone in his region who didn't know the law.

This was all quite astonishing; apparently God had blessed this heathen king with wisdom from above. Artaxerxes recognized the supreme authority of God and didn't hesitant to bow to that authority, even in front of his counselors and princes. Because of his respect for the true God, the people of the Lord were greatly blessed.

KEY BIBLE TEXT: "Blessed be the LORD God of our fathers, who has put such a thing as this in the king's heart, to beautify the house of the LORD which is in Jerusalem, and has extended mercy to me before the king and his counselors, and before all the king's mighty princes" (Ezra 7:27, 28).

DAY 219 Walking on Coals

An Amazing Fact: *Fire walking is the act of walking barefoot over a bed of hot coals or stones. It has been used as a rite of passage to test a person's strength, courage, or faith. Some believe it requires supernatural power, but modern physics has debunked this idea.*

Can a person walk barefoot over hot coals and not burn their feet? It depends. Several factors are involved. First, the length of time the foot is in contact with coals is usually not enough to induce a burn. Some try to run through the coals but are burned because the coals are pressed hard against their feet. Second, coals are not very good conductors of heat. If a person walked through hot coals and stepped on a piece of metal, his or her feet would burn. Another factor is that coals reach their flash point (hottest temperature) and then begin to cool down, so you must choose carefully when to walk through the fire.

But it's not really a good idea to walk through a bed of hot coals. You will probably burn your feet! It is not a matter of supernatural power (though the devil can do lots of tricks). It is just not a smart thing to do. And that's the point Solomon is making when he writes, "Can a man take fire to his bosom, and his clothes not be burned? Can one walk on hot coals, and his feet not be seared?" (Proverbs 6:27, 28). It's a rhetorical question intended to get the answer, "Of course not!"

That is what the wise man teaches about the person who thinks adultery is something that is innocent and will not hurt you. "Whoever commits adultery with a woman lacks understanding; he who does so destroys his own soul" (v. 32). Will breaking the seventh commandment leave you unscathed? Of course not! Be wise and do not go down the senseless and destructive path of sexual sin. It is driven by a passion that will burn and destroy you forever.

KEY BIBLE TEXT: "Marriage is honorable among all, and the bed undefiled; but fornicators and adulterers God will judge" (Hebrews 13:4).

All We Like Sheep

An Amazing Fact: *In July 2005, Turkish shepherds, while they ate breakfast, watched in stunned and helpless silence as their entire flock of 1,500 sheep followed each other one by one over a cliff. In all, only 450 sheep died ... the later ones being cushioned by the earlier ones.*

Sheep have a strong instinct to follow the one in front of them without "thinking." Also, if a sheep gets tipped over and ends up on its back, it often cannot get back on its feet. Because of these and other strange tendencies, many people have assumed that sheep are dumb animals. However, sheep are very intelligent. They can recognize more than 50 other sheep's faces for up to two years. A study in the journal *Nature* suggests they might be nearly as good as people at distinguishing faces in a crowd.

You might be wondering how a sheep gets stuck when it tips over. Interestingly, it is usually the sheep that are fat or laden with a heavy coat of wool that get stuck. A sheep might lie down in a comfortable little hollow after eating, roll on its side, and stretch out to get a little more comfortable. If it a large sheep, its feet will be unable to reach the ground. The sheep then panics and flails its feet around, which often makes it flip over on its back. In this position the sheep is likely to die if the shepherd does not find it soon.

Luke 15 tells us that Jesus takes notice of the missing sheep and leaves the 99 safe ones to go and find the one that has gotten itself into trouble. Notice that it is the fat, extra-woolly sheep that usually gets into trouble. Let us learn the lesson. When things appear to be going well and we are getting comfortable, this is the time of greatest danger. A loving Shepherd often directs His sheep to less comfortable places in order to keep them safe.

KEY BIBLE TEXT: "When thou hast eaten and art full ... Beware that thou forget not the LORD thy God ... Lest when thou hast eaten and art full ... Then thine heart be lifted up, and thou forget the LORD thy God" (Deuteronomy 8:10–14 KJV).

DAY 221 Are You in Prison?

An Amazing Fact: *Paul Geidel (1894–1987) was the longest serving American inmate whose sentence ended with his release. After being convicted of second-degree murder in 1911, Geidel served 68 years and 245 days in various New York state prisons. He was released on May 7, 1980, at the age of 86.*

Geidel was born to an alcoholic saloonkeeper who died when the boy was only five years old. He spent most of his childhood in an orphanage and eventually worked in menial jobs. One day he decided to rob a wealthy broker who was staying in a hotel where Geidel worked. He suffocated the man and got away with a few dollars. Two days later he was arrested and convicted of second-degree murder and sent to prison for 20 years to life.

He was almost released in 1926 but was found to be legally insane. In 1974 he was granted parole, but the 80-year-old inmate did not want to leave prison. With no family, he thought he wouldn't make it on the outside, so he chose to stay in for six more years. Finally, on May 7, 1980, he was released having served the longest prison sentence in American history. He lived out the remainder of his days in a nursing home.

Prison is about "serving" time and "putting in" labor for crime. Yet some people relate to God like they are serving time. In the story of the prodigal son, Jesus tells about the older son angrily talking with his father about the return of his younger brother. He said, "Lo, these many years I have been serving you; I never transgressed your commandment at any time; and yet you never game me a young goat that I might make merry with my friends" (Luke 15:29).

It is possible to serve God and still be trapped in a prison in your heart. Salvation is not about "having to serve time," it is about rejoicing in the free gift. Don't stay in prison. God wants to release you.

KEY BIBLE TEXT: "And he said to him, 'Son, you are always with me, and all that I have is yours'" (Luke 15:31).

Worldly Wisdom vs. God's Wisdom

DAY 222

An Amazing Fact: *Scientists have discovered a way to "jam" a part of the human brain related to wisdom. In the experiments, people were exposed to a social situation that they would normally consider unfair. While a part of their prefrontal cortex was "jammed," by a purportedly harmless pulse of electromagnetic energy, people were unable to act in response to the unfair situation. (Any volunteers?)*

William Shakespeare once wrote, "The fool doth think he is wise, but the wise man knows himself to be a fool." This rings similarly to Paul's advice: "If anyone among you seems to be wise in this age, let him become a fool that he may become wise" (1 Corinthians 3:18).

It is true that we, in ourselves, have no wisdom. All the education and philosophy in the world can't give it to us. Because of our fallen nature, wisdom has to come from outside ourselves.

The world's concept of wisdom is very different from God's view. "For the wisdom of this world is foolishness with God" (1 Corinthians 3:19). The world wants wisdom without God, but it doesn't exist.

The wisdom that comes from God is a treasure worth finding. "How much better to get wisdom than gold!" (Proverbs 16:16). Godly wisdom will guide us in every aspect of our existence and help us to understand the Bible and God's will for our lives. All we need to do is ask Him for it.

KEY BIBLE TEXT: "Give instruction to a wise man, and he will be still wiser; teach a just man, and he will increase in learning. 'The fear of the LORD is the beginning of wisdom, and the knowledge of the Holy One is understanding. For by me your days will be multiplied, and years of life will be added to you. If you are wise, you are wise for yourself, and if you scoff, you will bear it alone'" (Proverbs 9:9-12).

DAY 223 The Great Wall

An Amazing Fact: *The Great Wall of China is the longest manmade structure in the world. It stretches (with all its branches) more than 5,500 miles. It is a myth that it is one continuous wall built all at once. Pieces of the wall were constructed over several dynasties. Actual wall length combined is 3,889 miles.*

The Great Wall is one of the seven wonders of the medieval age and was originally built in the 5th century BC on the northern borders of the Chinese empire to keep out nomadic groups. Pieces of the wall were constructed all the way to the 16th century. The first walls were made by stamping gravel and earth between board frames. Later the use of stone and brick was found to be easier to work with and more durable.

The wall itself is 16 to 26 feet in height, 15 to 30 feet wide at the base, and 9 to 12 feet wide at the top. It is more than a wall. There are guard towers, beacon towers, stairways, bridges, and battlements. It is quite an old wall at 2,232 years old, and much of it is gone. Erosion, construction, and people "using" parts of the wall for their own construction have left much of it in disrepair. It is believed that millions of Chinese peasants who helped build the wall were buried under it as they died from their hard labor.

An incredible story is told of building a wall in the Bible. Nehemiah came to Jerusalem to inspect the broken down walls and was heartbroken. He undertook to rebuild the wall. Breaking it into 40 sections, people of all classes joined in different parties to repair it. This was not just a political project. The walls were actually consecrated to the God of Israel, who was bringing back a remnant. (See Nehemiah 3:1.)

Someday we will see the walls of the New Jerusalem (Revelation 21:12) as God's chosen people, rejoicing that our Lord has given us a great wall of protection; it is a wall that will never crumble.

KEY BIBLE TEXT: "In that day this song will be sung in the land of Judah: We have a strong city; God will appoint salvation for walls and bulwarks" (Isaiah 26:1).

A Spirit of Power

DAY 224

An Amazing Fact: *Because of its grace, strength, and sheer size, the bald eagle was chosen to symbolize the United States. Baby eagles (eaglets) begin their lives high in a tree nest typically five feet in diameter. After making the first break in the shell, it can take an eaglet 12 to 48 hours to completely hatch out.*

The parents provide well for their offspring, and the young birds grow rapidly—they add one pound every five days. But eventually, they must learn to fly and hunt for themselves. The mother teaches her eaglets to fly by making the nest very uncomfortable. She rips up the soft padding to expose sharp sticks, bones, and rocks. Then she stops bringing food, but she'll frequently fly by the nest of hungry eaglets sporting fresh fish or rabbits to tempt them. The little eaglets become so hungry and uncomfortable they are eventually compelled to leave the nest and commit themselves to the unknown world of air outside.

It's incredibly dangerous, as approximately 40 percent of young eagles do not survive their first flight. It's believed that only about 1 in 10 eagles survive to adulthood (five years old). Some of the primary reasons are gunshot wounds by hunters that kill for feathers and talons to sell on the black market and lead poisoning from eating wounded ducks, rabbits, and other game that eluded the hunter but later died. It can be tough to be an eagle; in fact, they were once declared an endangered species. But they've since made a comeback.

Paul encouraged young Timothy, "For God has not given us a spirit of fear, but of power and of love and of a sound mind" (2 Timothy 1:7). Perhaps Timothy was timid and needed encouragement to "get out of the nest" and spread his wings. Certainly the eagle depicts power as well as risk that we all eventually experience in our Christian growth.

KEY BIBLE TEXT: "For you did not receive the spirit of bondage again to fear, but you received the Spirit of adoption by whom we cry out, 'Abba, Father'" (Romans 8:15).

DAY 225 Forgiveness and Pardons

An Amazing Fact: *An item in the May 2, 1985, Kansas City Times describes the attempt by some fans of O. Henry, the short-story writer, to get a pardon for their hero, who was accused in 1898 of embezzling $784.08 from the bank where he was employed. The question was raised, "Can you give a pardon to a dead man?"*

Back in 1830 George Wilson was convicted of robbing the U.S. Mail and was sentenced to be hanged. President Andrew Jackson issued a pardon for Wilson, but the convict refused to accept it. The matter went to Chief Justice Marshall, who concluded that Wilson would have to be executed. "A pardon is a slip of paper," wrote Marshall, "the value of which is determined by the acceptance of the person to be pardoned. If it is refused, it is no pardon. George Wilson must be hanged."

The court stated: "A pardon is a deed, to the validity of which delivery is essential, and delivery is not complete without acceptance. It may then be rejected by the person to whom it is tendered; and if it is rejected, we have discovered no power in this court to force it upon him."

A pardon is a form of forgiveness for a crime or cancellation (in whole or part) of the penalty associated with it. Sometimes forgiveness focuses more on letting go of resentment, indignation, or anger. Jesus spoke of forgiving a brother who sins against you. "If your brother sins against you, rebuke him; and if he repents, forgive him" (Luke 17:3). In fact, Christ says, "And if he sins against you seven times in a day, and seven times in a day returns to you, saying, 'I repent,' you shall forgive him" (v. 4).

George Wilson was offered forgiveness but refused to accept it. Christ has offered forgiveness and pardon for our sins. Not only would it be wise to accept this gracious offer but also to have this attitude toward others as well. How much better it is to offer it to people who are alive and can accept the pardon.

KEY BIBLE TEXT: "And forgive us our debts, as we forgive our debtors" (Matthew 6:12).

Generosity Blesses the Giver

DAY 226

An Amazing Fact: *Many children raised money to help the victims of the 2010 earthquake in Haiti. Few were as young as Will Merchant, who was only six years old when he learned about other kids raising money and came up with his own plan. By selling his original artwork, Will raised $500 to help earthquake victims. He was asked why he wanted to help people he'd never met. His answer: "God led me in my heart to do that."*

There are many different motivations for helping others. Sometimes it comes from a desire for public recognition, but this is not generosity. True generosity springs from empathy, kindness, and love.

Being generous always blesses the giver. The generous person might not benefit in ways that are obvious to others. In fact, their gift might be spurned or unappreciated. But even then, there is something positive that happens inside the heart of the person who gives.

On the other hand, according to the proverb, being stingy has an opposite outcome—it leads to poverty. This is always true, not necessarily in material things, but at least in a spiritual sense.

The Bible says, "The generous soul will be made rich, and he who waters will also be watered himself" (Proverbs 11:25). This doesn't mean that generous people will necessarily receive material gain in return for their generosity, though that sometimes happens; yet they can count on other forms of enrichment.

There are definite emotional, physical, and spiritual benefits to giving. People who give out of generosity report more happiness; negative emotions are lessened and positive emotions are strengthened, which can support good health. The spiritual blessing of giving comes from God, the Ultimate Giver.

KEY BIBLE TEXT: "There is one who scatters, yet increases more; and there is one who withholds more than is right, but it leads to poverty. The generous soul will be made rich, and he who waters will also be watered himself" (Proverbs 11:24, 25).

DAY 227 Be Kind to Animals

An Amazing Fact: *Around 63 percent of all U.S. households (71.1 million) have pets, and more than half of these households have more than one animal. The two most popular pets in most Western countries are cats and dogs. In the United States, a 2008 survey showed that dog-owning households outnumbered those owning cats—but that the total number of pet cats was higher than that of dogs.*

Pets are household animals that people keep for enjoyment or companionship. There are health benefits to keeping a pet. They have been shown to help relieve stress and lower blood pressure. In fact, there are medically approved "therapy animals" used to visit people who are confined. Walking your dog gives you exercise, fresh air, and sunshine (and perhaps some social interaction). The most popular pets are, of course, dogs and cats. Worldwide there are about 202 million cats owned (can you own a cat?) and about 171 million dogs who have owners.

In case you are looking for something a little more interesting than a dog or cat, here are a few strange pets that people own. How about a hedgehog? They are nocturnal, so you'll need to stay up late to play with them. Some people have enjoyed skunks as pets. But one of the most interesting is the Madagascar hissing cockroach. They don't bite, sting, or fly ... but they do hiss when you poke them!

The Bible talks about how to care for your animals. Whether it is livestock for your livelihood or pets for pleasure, the Bible says, "A righteous man regards the life of his animal, but the tender mercies of the wicked are cruel" (Proverbs 12:10). In other words, be kind to animals. They are God's creatures made for our enjoyment. Someday we will enjoy even greater freedom to interact with animals in an earth made new, a place where we will not have to worry about getting hurt.

KEY BIBLE TEXT: "You shall not muzzle an ox while it treads out the grain" (Deuteronomy 25:4).

Mystery of the "Lady Be Good"

An Amazing Fact: *In 1959 a British Petroleum survey crew, while looking for oil in the North African desert of Libya, spotted the wreckage of a B-24 bomber. Upon investigation, it proved to be the remains of the "Lady Be Good," a WWII bomber that had returned from a mission in Italy but had never reached the airbase. Mysteriously, the plane was empty.*

What caused the "Lady Be Good" to miss her base, landing more than 400 miles away in the north Sahara desert, has remained an unsolved mysteries and caused much controversy. Upon the first examination of the plane, Air Force investigators made some startling discoveries. First was the fact that the crew of nine was neither in the plane nor anywhere nearby. Second, the navigator made no log entries after the initial bombing mission was aborted. Third, the navigator's equipment and charts were stored in their cases. How could the navigator give directions to the pilot with the equipment in storage?

Over a period of several years after the discovery of the plane, the bodies of all but one of the crewmen were discovered in the desert—over 80 miles from the plane. The crew apparently had parachuted from the plane as it ran out of fuel. Though a diary found in the clothes of one of the crewmen told of the harsh desert conditions and of having only a half a canteen of water and no food between them, it gave no clue as to the cause of the accident.

Proverbs 12:15 says, "The way of a fool is right in his own eyes, but he who heeds counsel is wise." After removal from the plane and testing, all the instruments were found to be operational. One of the hypotheses is that, due to a severe tailwind that night, the plane might have passed the base earlier than expected. In this case, the crew would be forced to decide between following the radio beacon or their own calculations as to how long the trip should have taken.

Being right in our own eyes can be fatal, not only physically, but, more important, spiritually. Let us allow the infallible Word of God to be our beacon, whether it always makes sense to us or not.

KEY BIBLE TEXT: "There is a way that seems right to a man, but its end is the way of death" (Proverbs 14:12).

DAY 229 Starting Out Well

An Amazing Fact: *Blaise Pascal (1623–1662) was a French mathematician, physicist, and religious philosopher who wrote a treatise on vibrating bodies at nine years old; his first proof, on a wall with a piece of coal, at 11 years old; and a theorem by 16 years old.*

A child prodigy is someone under the age of 18 who masters one or more skills beyond their expected level of maturity. Such giftedness shows levels of a highly skilled adult in an area that is demanding. People debate whether nature (natural giftedness) or nurture (environment) plays a larger role in child prodigies. Stories of different talented children and youth seem to indicate it can be both.

For instance, George Frederic Handel loved music, but his father wanted him to study civil law. In fact, he was strictly forbidden to touch any musical instruments. But Handel found a way to move a small clavichord to the uppermost room in their home and play after everyone else was fast asleep. At an early age he became skilled on the clavichord and organ, and we still listen to his music today!

Can we get a head start in our walk with God, even at a young age? Paul wrote to young Timothy, "But you must continue in the things which you have learned and been assured of, knowing from whom you have learned them, and that from childhood you have known the Holy Scriptures, which are able to make you wise for salvation through faith which is in Christ Jesus" (2 Timothy 3:14, 15).

The Bible made Timothy wise in the most important field of endeavor we can pursue—the science of salvation. You can be gifted by the Holy Spirit in many different areas but do not neglect the foundation for all the skills you acquire: a thorough knowledge of the Word of God. It is a book worth mastering, even at an early age.

KEY BIBLE TEXT: "And these words which I command you today shall be in your heart. You shall teach them diligently to your children, and shall talk of them when you sit in your house, when you walk by the way, when you lie down, and when you rise up" (Deuteronomy 6:6, 7).

The Crown No Human Deserves

An Amazing Fact: *Some of the finest gems in the world are in the crown jewels of England. The king's crown weighs more than 39 ounces. It was made in 1838 and contains many jewels from older crowns, some dating back hundreds of years. It has almost 300 pearls, 2,818 diamonds, plus magnificent rubies, sapphires, emeralds, and other gems.*

"Then the soldiers of the governor took Jesus into the Praetorium and gathered the whole garrison around Him. And they stripped Him and put a scarlet robe on Him. When they had twisted a crown of thorns, they put it on His head" (Matthew 27:27–29).

Jesus' crown while on Earth was a crown of thorns fashioned by the cruel hands of the Roman soldiers. In contrast, the apostle John describes what it will be like when Jesus returns. "Then I looked, and behold, a white cloud, and on the cloud sat One like the Son of Man, having on His head a golden crown" (Revelation 14:14).

Paul wrote about the "crown of righteousness" that was laid up for him, which God would present to him and to everyone who is happy to see Christ return. This crown will be far more special and well designed than any crown jewels the world has ever seen!

What have we done to deserve such a reward? Absolutely nothing—we don't deserve it. We're not righteous, but Jesus is. In mercy He has redeemed us and reconciled us to God, and it is His desire to give us the crown that only He deserves.

KEY BIBLE TEXT: "Finally, there is laid up for me the crown of righteousness, which the Lord, the righteous Judge, will give to me on that Day, and not to me only but also to all who have loved His appearing" (2 Timothy 4:8).

DAY 231 Can You See?

An Amazing Fact: *The Mexican tetra (or blind cave fish) is a freshwater fish found in southern Texas and the central/eastern parts of Mexico. There are about 30 distinct populations of this fish that are blind and live in deep caves where there is no light. The eyed and eyeless forms of this fish come from the same species. When born, all have eyes—but those in dark caves lose their ability to see.*

Blind tetras can still find their way around by means of their "lateral lines," which are highly sensitive to water pressure. Their eyes, which are not used, simply degenerate and skin grows over them. Modern genetics have shown that a lack of use of a part of the body does not necessarily mean it will completely disappear. More recently, some scientists have discovered that blind cave fish can "see" (at least in some small way) light because of the pineal gland in their brain.

One day Jesus was walking through Jericho and a blind man called out, "Jesus, Son of David, have mercy on me!" (Luke 18:38). Others tried to quiet him down, but he only cried the louder. Jesus heard his cry and asked to see him. After being asked by Jesus what he would like, he said, "Lord, that I may receive my sight" (v. 41). Then Jesus said to him, "Receive your sight; your faith has made you well" (v. 42).

Someone once said, "Faith is seeing what you cannot see." If that is the case, then this blind man could "see" before he could see! He knew that Christ was the Son of the living God and could heal him.

Sometimes people who see well with their natural eyes are blind with their spiritual eyes. They cannot discern truths of Scripture or sense the working of the Holy Spirit in their lives. They need to be healed of their spiritual blindness. Like blind tetras, they need to be taken out of dark places and brought into the light.

KEY BIBLE TEXT: "For the hearts of this people have grown dull ... their eyes they have closed, lest they should see with their eyes and ... understand with their hearts" (Acts 28:27).

Never Too Short

An Amazing Fact: *Junrey Balawing is the world's shortest adult. As of June 2011, he was measured at 23.5 inches tall. He takes over the previous record holder, Khagendra Thapa Magar from Nepal, who measured 26 inches tall.*

According to his family, Junrey stopped growing the first year of his life. Balawing has difficulty walking because of pain, cannot attend school, and stays home where he needs constant attention and care. The son of a poor blacksmith, the family's luck turned for the better after Junrey was born and his father found work. His birthday is the same day as the Philippines independence day, so his village south of Manila has a double celebration. When he was born, his mother says he was about the size of a one-liter Coke bottle. She knew something was wrong, and the doctor gave her vitamins to help strengthen his bones. But he didn't grow. The family hopes media attention will bring medical help for their son.

Zacchaeus was not very tall ... but certainly taller than Junrey. And that didn't stop Zacchaeus from his work as a tax collector, nor his desire to see Jesus. "Then Jesus entered and passed through Jericho. Now behold, there was a man named Zacchaeus who was a chief tax collector, and he was rich. And he sought to see who Jesus was, but could not because of the crowd, for he was of short stature" (Luke 19:1–3). You know the rest of the story. He climbed a tree and when Jesus passed by, the Lord stopped and noticed the little man.

Sometimes we feel short and unnoticed in life. But Christ sees us. He notices us no matter how tall or short we are of stature. God's eyes are upon us. We can know that our faintest cries for help are heard. Any effort we make to turn toward Jesus will be noticed, even if that means having to climb a tree.

KEY BIBLE TEXT: "Behold, the Lord's hand is not shortened that it cannot save; Nor His ear heavy that it cannot hear" (Isaiah 59:1).

DAY 233 Royal Pain

An Amazing Fact: *Henry VIII, the 16th century king of England, is best remembered for his shocking treatment of his many wives. He married Catherine of Aragon in 1509 and had the marriage annulled in 1533. He married Ann Boleyn in 1533 and had her beheaded in 1536. He married Jane Seymour in 1536. She died in childbirth in 1537. He then married Anne of Cleves in 1540 and divorced her that same year. He married Catherine Howard in 1540 and had her beheaded in 1542. Finally, he married Catherine Parr in 1543, and she survived him.*

The current British monarch, Queen Elizabeth II, is the fifth longest serving British monarch (54 years). Only four other kings and queens have served longer: Queen Victoria (63 years), King George III (59 years), James VI of Scotland and James I of England (58 years), and King Henry III (56 years). The queen and Duke of Edinburgh have been married for 60 years. They were married on November 20, 1947, in Westminster Abbey. Both the queen and duke are great, great grandchildren of Queen Victoria.

One of the most famous queens in the Bible is Queen Esther. But her story began with one of the most "not so famous" queens, Queen Vashti. King Ahasuerus reigned over Persia from 486 to 465 B.C. On the seventh day of a great feast, the drunken king asked Queen Vashti to appear so that he could show off her beauty. She refused to come. The king was furious at her act of rebellion. She was demoted, and a new queen was sought.

The book of Esther shows us, in interesting ways, elements of the story of salvation. In one sense, Lucifer is cast down (demoted) and Christ (who had a humble birth) is lifted up to a glorious place. It's like a 'rags to riches' story with many reversals. Though many kings and queens have behaved in less than honorable ways, we know from the Bible that the King of Kings will be honored by the entire universe as righteous.

KEY BIBLE TEXT: "Great and marvelous are Your works, Lord God Almighty! Just and true are Your ways, O King of the saints!" (Revelation 15:3).

Words Matter

DAY 234

An Amazing Fact: *In a poll of Americans, 39 percent of people aged 35 and over and 62 percent of people aged 18 to 34 admitted to swearing at least a few times a week. Three-quarters of the individuals polled said they frequently encounter profanity or swear words, and two-thirds said they are bothered when they hear other people swear in public (even if they swear themselves).*

The words we speak are very important, more so than we usually realize. Whether our conversations are public or private, our words influence ourselves and others for good or for not-so-good. They can hurt or help, encourage or discourage, build up or tear down those around us.

Our words can affect our physical and emotional health or the health of others: "A wholesome tongue is a tree of life, but perverseness in it breaks the spirit" (Proverbs 15:4). "There is one who speaks like the piercings of a sword, but the tongue of the wise promotes health" (Proverbs 12:18).

Words can calm or enrage others. "A soft answer turns away wrath, but a harsh word stirs up anger" (Proverbs 15:1). Words can kill; words can save. "Death and life are in the power of the tongue" (Proverbs 18:21).

In casual conversation, it's sometimes tempting to let our words run uncensored. But the Bible puts great importance on our speech. In Proverbs 21:23 we read, "Whoever guards his mouth and tongue keeps his soul from trouble."

Next time you're tempted to speak a rash or unkind word, remember the psalmist's words: "For there is not a word on my tongue, but behold, O LORD, You know it altogether" (Psalm 139:4). The best use for our tongues is praising God.

KEY BIBLE TEXT: "A soft answer turns away wrath, but a harsh word stirs up anger. The tongue of the wise uses knowledge rightly, but the mouth of fools pours forth foolishness. A wholesome tongue is a tree of life, but perverseness in it breaks the spirit" (Proverbs 15:1, 2, 4).

DAY 235 The Red Carpet

An Amazing Fact: *The first reference in history of a "red carpet" being rolled out to welcome a dignitary was in the play Agamemnon by Aeschylus, written in 458 B.C. The title character returned from Troy and was greeted by his wife Clytemnestra, who offered him a red path to walk upon. He hesitated to walk upon colors that only the 'feet of the gods' should tread.*

A red carpet is traditionally used to mark the path taken by heads of state on formal occasions. The first president in the United States to receive the "red carpet treatment" was James Madison in 1821. Since then it has been expanded and used by everything from the Academy Awards to United Airlines, which established "Red Carpet Clubs" for VIP lounges.

Renaissance paintings often show oriental carpets, patterned with red as the main color, laid on the steps to a throne or on a platform where rulers reign. Actually, purple is considered the color of royalty since it was one of the most expensive dyes to create.

Jesus once received a royal welcome. Unfortunately it was not by the dignitaries of state. The Jewish leaders were actually upset at Christ's triumphal entry into Jerusalem. His followers stepped in and led the ceremony. Christ rode on a colt as prophesied in Zechariah 9:9, 10. The Bible says, "And as He went, many spread their clothes on the road" (Luke 19:36).

The pathway Christ took into Jerusalem was different from the pathway He took out. Jesus was appropriately welcomed as a king by people willing to lay down their best coats to show homage. But on Friday, the Lord walked out of Jerusalem on a "red carpet," as it were—a bloodstained path to Calvary. The path to the cross was the path to glory. We are called to walk that same royal road as followers of Jesus. When we get to heaven, the gates of the great city will swing open wide and we will receive another "red carpet" welcome. Will you be there?

KEY BIBLE TEXT: "The twenty-four elders fall down before Him who sits on the throne and worship Him who lives forever and ever, and cast their crowns before the throne" (Revelation 4:10).

Slow Mover

DAY 236

An Amazing Fact: *The sloth is such a slow-moving animal that it is common for algae to grow in its fur. Their main predator is the eagle. Moving very slowly in the trees makes them less visible. Though they hardly move at all during the daytime, they actually sleep very little.*

There are six species of sloths—four species of three-toed sloths and two of the two-toed variety. Most of the sloths you find in zoos are the two-toed variety, which are easier to feed than their three-toed cousins (who are very picky eaters). They mainly eat leaves and buds and are built with special claws for climbing around trees. Their slow digestive system is adapted for the challenge of gaining energy from leaves.

Sloths can actually move quickly if they want to. More than one biologist has had a quick nip from a sloth that decided to defend its territory. When they do move fast, they burn up lots of energy. Their muscle mass is only about a third that of other mammals of the same size. They are very content to hang upside down in trees all day long, eating, sleeping, and even giving birth in that position. In fact, the sloth's fur grows in a different direction than most mammals, which suits them well by protecting them from the elements in the upside down position.

The Bible says there are times to be slow and times to be fast. "A wrathful man stirs up strife, but he who is slow to anger allays contention" (Proverbs 15:18). When you are feeling angry, it's a good time to be more like a sloth—move slowly and deliberately; don't be reactive. On the other hand, the very next verse says, "The way of the lazy man is like a hedge of thorns, but the way of the upright is a highway" (v. 19). Obviously, we can move so slowly that we are not diligent in our work. A slothful worker finds life can be more difficult.

KEY BIBLE TEXT: "He who is slothful in his work is a bother to him who is a great destroyer" (Proverbs 18:9).

DAY 237 Stones Crying Out

An Amazing Fact: *One of the earliest types of radio was called a crystal radio and did not require any power source. It got its name because it had a tiny piece of crystalline mineral, usually galena, in its electrical circuit. This enabled it to receive signals and "amplify" them in early earphones before modern diodes were invented. Today most radios amplify the incoming radio signal with a battery or other power source.*

It is truly amazing to see how far and fast technology has come in the last 90 years since radio was first introduced. We can mention not only radio and television, but sonar, radar, microwave, and cell phones. Medical technology has also made breathtaking breakthroughs in non-invasive imaging techniques such as CT and MRI (magnetic resonance imaging). But probably one of the most influential technological developments has been the personal computer.

At the heart of all of these electronic devices is again another mineral, this time not galena, but silicon. Silicon is a semi-conductor, which means it partially restricts the flow of electricity. When sandwiched into electronic "chips" in the right way, silicon can act as a variable "gate" to control the flow of electricity in response to small input voltages. This results in a very precise control of electricity that is needed in most electronic devices today, and it's why integrated circuits (made of silicon) are essential in amplifiers of just about every kind of electronic device, including modern-day radios.

When Jesus was riding on the colt into the city, the crowd of disciples began singing and praising God. The watching Pharisees told Jesus to rebuke His disciples. But Jesus responded by saying, "I tell you that if these should keep silent, the stones would immediately cry out." (Luke 19:40) Was this a prophecy? Today, the rocks *are* truly crying out. There are literally millions of tiny pieces of silicon faithfully crying out the gospel message through radio, TV, computer, and other devices.

As God's people, let us be faithful to not only use the technology He has so miraculously provided for us near the close of Earth's history, but to be personal, living, breathing witnesses to God's faithfulness in our lives.

KEY BIBLE TEXT: "You are My witnesses, says the LORD, And My servant whom I have chosen" (Isaiah 43:10).

According to His Mercy

DAY 238

An Amazing Fact: *A New York man was about to stop at a diner before going home for the evening when a teenager pulled a knife and asked for his wallet. As the boy was walking away, the man offered him his jacket. The teen was baffled by the kindness but accepted the man's offer of a meal. After they ate together, the teenager returned the wallet and the man gave him $20. In return, the teen gave the man his knife.*

Mercy, if it is accepted, changes everything. "But when the kindness and the love of God our Savior toward man appeared, not by works of righteousness which we have done, but according to His mercy He saved us" (Titus 3:4, 5).

Our "righteousness" doesn't impress God; the Bible says, "But we are all like an unclean thing, and all our righteousnesses are like filthy rags" (Isaiah 64:6). It's only through God's mercy that we are saved. Only by His grace are we justified. Only by His grace does He give us eternal life.

Since God has shown us such overwhelming mercy, we should do the same for others. This all goes back to the Golden Rule. How do we carry it out in our lives?

The Bible tells us, "So speak and so do as those who will be judged by the law of liberty. For judgment is without mercy to the one who has shown no mercy. Mercy triumphs over judgment" (James 2:12, 13).

KEY BIBLE TEXT: "But when the kindness and the love of God our Savior toward man appeared, not by works of righteousness which we have done, but according to His mercy He saved us, through the washing of regeneration and renewing of the Holy Spirit, whom He poured out on us abundantly through Jesus Christ our Savior, that having been justified by His grace we should become heirs according to the hope of eternal life" (Titus 3:4–7).

DAY 239 The Banquet Table

An Amazing Fact: *Westminster Abbey in London is one of Great Britain's most-famous churches. This splendid edifice was built in stages beginning in the 11th century, and it enshrines many of the traditions of the British people. English monarchs since William the Conqueror have been crowned in the abbey, and most are buried in its chapels. Famous citizens like Isaac Newton and David Livingstone are also buried there. But one of the most amazing people buried in the abbey is a farmer named Thomas Parr.*

Born in 1483 during the reign of King Richard III, Thomas is reported to have lived to the age of 152, witnessing the seating of 10 sovereigns on the throne during his long life—including the entire 50-year reign of Queen Elizabeth I.

In 1635, King Charles I invited Thomas to the palace that he might meet this remarkable man. The king inquired as to what did Thomas owe his long life; he answered that he lived a simple life, eating mostly potatoes and oatmeal. While at the palace, old Thomas feasted on the rich food served at the palace. He was not used to this food, and that night after dining on the king's delicacies, he became very ill and died. King Charles felt so terrible having killed Britain's oldest citizen with his food that he commanded Thomas to be buried in Westminster Abbey.

There is a story in the Bible about a king, a banquet, and honor bestowed on a man. Queen Esther found favor before the king, who offered to grant her any wish. She knew a man named Haman who wanted to destroy the Jews, especially a man named Mordecai. In a turn of events, the king actually had Haman show honor to Mordecai instead. Then, at a banquet for the king and Haman, Esther revealed Haman's plot to destroy the Jews. The king ordered him hanged on the gallows.

Banquets can be places where events lead some to life and others to death. Old Tom Parr didn't survive a royal banquet very well. But someday, we can enjoy a banquet with the King of Kings, a meal that leads us into everlasting life.

KEY BIBLE TEXT: "He brought me to the banqueting house, and his banner over me was love" (Song of Solomon 2:4).

Your Family Tree

An Amazing Fact: *The family tree of Confucius has been maintained for more than 2,500 years and is listed in the Guinness Book of World Records as the largest existing family tree.*

Genealogy is one of the fastest-growing hobbies in North America. More and more people are fascinated in tracing their roots back as far as they can. Are you related to royalty, or were your ancestors horse thieves? Some people want to carve out a place for their family in history. Others want to preserve history and story for their relatives and children. Still others are motivated by religious reasons.

Your ability to trace your ancestors has exploded with the use of the Internet and computer software. You can even hire a professional genealogist to do research for you. A new field of study that has recently opened is genetic analysis, as your DNA gets passed down from your ancestors with relatively little change. Two people can have a DNA test to determine if they are related within an estimated number of generations.

The Confucius Genealogy Compilation Committee is the group that has collected, collated, and published the 2,500 years worth of data. It was most recently printed in 2009. The previous printing was in 1930. Kong Deyong, a 77th generation descendant set up the committee and began work in 1998. Several volumes cover almost 80 generations and list over two million members.

Paul warned Titus, "But avoid foolish disputes, genealogies, contentions, and strivings about the law; for they are unprofitable and useless" (Titus 3:9). Some people were motivated to pursue family trees in order to give themselves status. This false sense of importance created divisions in the church and was harmful to unity in the body of Christ.

As Christians, our status in Christ makes us children of God (1 John 3:1), and there is no greater position than knowing your true Father.

KEY BIBLE TEXT: "As I urged you when I went into Macedonia—remain in Ephesus that you may charge some that they teach no other doctrine, nor give heed to fables and endless genealogies, which cause disputes rather than godly edification" (1 Timothy 1:3, 4).

DAY 241 The Signet Ring

An Amazing Fact: *Sigillography is the study of seals used to impress a figure into clay or wax or embossing paper with the purpose of authenticating a document. Devices with molds for making a mirror image on a document have been mounted on rings and used by kings since ancient times.*

In ancient Mesopotamia clay cylinders were used for marking documents or items by rolling them across a piece of wet clay, thereby embossing the product. But one of the more common seals was made by rings. Usually the embossing piece on the ring was carved from gemstones. Metal was also used but it created a weaker material.

A signet ring was worn to show a person's authority and power and has been an important part of the regalia of many monarchies. Their mark was binding and indicated the rights of the official. Today we do not use signet rings to indicate our signature, but people still wear them to demonstrate their family lineage or connection with an organization, such as a class ring.

The signet made a deep impression in clay or wax forming an official seal. The imprinted seal carried the full authority of the office it represented. You did not dare question it. The royal official's design was well known. The symbol was not doubted and could be recognized by citizens as authentic. There would be the pain of death to those who violated seals.

King Ahasuerus gave Queen Esther authority to protect the Jews. He even went so far as to say, "You yourselves write a decree concerning the Jews, as you please, in the king's name, and seal it with the king's signet ring; for whatever is written in the king's name and sealed with the king's signet ring no one can revoke" (Esther 8:8).

What a beautiful illustration of God's seal on our lives. When we are "stamped" with God's seal, we are safe and secure, protected under the authority of the mightiest power in the universe. When you give yourself to God, the impression of Christ is made upon your life.

KEY BIBLE TEXT: "And do not grieve the Holy Spirit of God, by whom you were sealed for the day of redemption" (Ephesians 4:30).

Heart Test

An Amazing Fact: *Gold has been treasured by mankind for a long time, with gold bars and jewelry dating as early as 4000 B.C. It also has some very interesting properties. For instance, a cubic foot of gold weighs about half-a-ton, and a one-ounce piece of gold can be pressed to cover 300 square feet.*

Gold is refined to remove its impurities. This usually involves a lengthy process of heating and cooling cycles. Gold is tested with heat; it is made pure by going through the fire.

Just as most gold is naturally impure, humans in their natural state are filled with impurities. The Bible says, "The heart is deceitful above all things, and desperately wicked; who can know it?" (Jeremiah 17:9). And the answer follows: "I, the Lord, search the heart, I test the mind, even to give every man according to his ways, according to the fruit of his doings" (v. 10).

We can't determine the purity of a piece of gold by just looking at it; neither can humans be judged by what is on the outside. While our actions can give a clue to our characters, only God can read our thoughts and see inside our hearts. Only He can judge our content with accuracy.

What are we made of? What is in our characters? "The Lord tests the hearts" (Proverbs 17:3). None of us are perfect, but God doesn't abandon us. When necessary He allows trials to come our way. Through the heat of these trials our hearts are refined—if our faith is in God.

KEY BIBLE TEXT: "The refining pot is for silver and the furnace for gold, but the Lord tests the hearts" (Proverbs 17:3).

DAY 243 Whose Image?

An Amazing Fact: *The Lydian Lion is considered by many to be the oldest coin in the world. It was minted in Lydia, Asia Minor (present-day Turkey), out of a gold and silver alloy about 2,700 years ago (600 B.C.). The Lydian bears the head of a roaring lion. It only has a design on one side due to the primitive methods of stamping out coins when it was made. There is some debate about whether it was a coin used for monetary exchange or simply a badge or ceremonial object used by priests in a temple.*

Roman currency was used during the time of Jesus. The first Roman denarius was minted in 211 B.C. It was a small silver coin and one of the most common in circulation.

Jesus once used one of these coins to teach a lesson. Spies had been trying to trick Christ into making a statement that would get Him into trouble with the Roman authorities. "Is it lawful for us to pay taxes to Caesar or not?" (Luke 20:22). He was Jesus' wise response. "'Why do you test me? Show me a denarius. Whose image and inscription does it have?' They answered and said, 'Caesar's.' And He said to them, 'Render therefore to Caesar the things that are Caesar's, and to God the things that are God's'" (vs. 23–25).

Christ could not be cornered. Jesus turned the spies' trap into a sermon on supporting our ruling government. Of course, there is a limit to our allegiance to man's laws. Our first allegiance is to God's law. When the two laws conflict, we must honor God's reign above all else. Unfortunately the Jewish nation did not first render obedience to God, and this led them to be subject to a foreign power represented by the insignia and image of the common denarius.

KEY BIBLE TEXT: "But they could not catch Him in His words in the presence of the people. And they marveled at His answer and kept silent" (Luke 20:26).

Deep Devotion

An Amazing Fact: *French angelfish are completely devoted to their partners and mate for life. They are found in the warm tropical parts of the Atlantic Ocean and spend all of their time together—traveling, hunting, sleeping, and protecting their territory. Mature French angelfish are rarely seen alone. If they are, their mate has likely died. They do not "remarry."*

Swans are another species that will keep their mates for life. There have been occasional reports of swans "separating," but only when there has been a nesting failure or loss of young. Perhaps their strong commitment to each other is why pictures of swans conjure up images of romance. On the other hand, the black vulture might not seem like a romantic bird, but it is one of the most faithful animals in the entire animal kingdom. They are so intolerant of "infidelity" that they have been observed attacking other vultures that were unfaithful to their partners!

The PDSA organization (UK) gives certificates to animals for bravery and devotion. Toby, a black Labrador Retriever, was stabbed four times in the chest and legs by an armed burglar in April 2009 in Lancashire. He successfully chased the burglar off the property. Wicker, a pet German Shepherd, aided his owner's son by fetching help when the boy had an epileptic seizure. Dotty, a donkey, helped her stable mate (a sheep) when it was attacked by a Pit Bull. And Piper, a Labrador Retriever guide dog, defended his blind owner who was attacked and then safely walked his injured owner home. What devotion!

The Bible says, "A friend loves at all times, and a brother is born for adversity" (Proverbs 17:17). We can learn much from our animal friends, but our greatest example is found in Jesus Christ, who was made "like His brethren" and declared, "For whoever does the will of God is My brother and My sister and mother" (Hebrews 2:17; Mark 3:35).

Jesus, the divine Son of God, was truly a friend who sticks closer than a brother when He gave His very life on Calvary for you. When you face the enemy today, know that there is a Friend who stands beside you and will never leave you alone.

KEY BIBLE TEXT: "A man who has friends must himself be friendly, but there is a friend who sticks closer than a brother" (Proverbs 18:24).

DAY 245 Every Student Is a Teacher

An Amazing Fact: *According to the U.S. Census Bureau, 27 percent of the population over the age of three is enrolled in school. That means there are 76 million students in schools of all kinds, from preschool to university. In comparison, there are 7.2 million teachers in those schools.*

In our society, the teacher and the student are usually two different individuals. However, God seemed to have something different in mind for His chosen nation. The first two chapters of Isaiah contain two invitations to learning. The first is from God: "'Come now, and let us reason together,' Says the LORD, 'Though your sins are like scarlet, They shall be as white as snow. ... If you are willing and obedient, You shall eat the good of the land'" (Isaiah 1:18, 19). This invitation to reason with God was for the people of Judah and Jerusalem, whom the Lord called a "sinful nation" and a "brood of evildoers" (Isaiah 1:4). God wanted to forgive their sins and teach them to "do good" (Isaiah 1:17). He planned on calling Jerusalem "the city of righteousness" (Isaiah 1:26).

The second invitation is from one Gentile to another: "Come, and let us go up to the mountain of the LORD, To the house of the God of Jacob; He will teach us His ways, And we shall walk in His paths" (Isaiah 2:3). God knew that if His people learned to do good, people from "all nations" would come to them, hoping to learn about God's ways.

As we enter the month of September, which has traditionally been the start of the school year, the most important lessons we can learn are in God's school: "Learn to do good; Seek justice, Rebuke the oppressor; Defend the fatherless, Plead for the widow." And the beauty of God's school is that each student becomes a teacher!

KEY BIBLE TEXT: "Let your light so shine before men, that they may see your good works and glorify your Father in heaven" (Matthew 5:16).

Roaring Lions

An Amazing Fact: *For nine months, between 1898 and 1899, the two infamous "man-eater lions of Tsavo" terrorized workers employed in the construction of a railway bridge in Africa. As the death toll rose, construction was brought to a virtual standstill. Workers refused to continue until protection could be provided.*

In March 1898 the British started building a railway bridge over the Tsavo River in Kenya. During the next nine months of construction, two male lions stalked the campsite, dragged workers from their tents at night, and devoured them. Crews tried to scare off the lions. They built campfires and thorn fences around their camp to keep the man-eaters out. It didn't work.

The construction on the bridge came to a dead halt. A hunter named Colonel Patterson was hired to set traps and tried several times to ambush the lions at night from a tree. He failed many times but finally shot the first lion on December 9, 1898. Three weeks later, the second lion was found and killed. The first lion killed measured nine feet, eight inches from nose to tip of tail. It took eight men to carry the carcass back to camp. The construction crew soon returned and completed the bridge in February 1899.

How many people were killed by the lions? Over the years, Patterson gave several different figures. He once claimed there were 135 victims, but recent research speculates that the number was probably closer to 35—that's still a large number!

The Bible says, "The king's wrath is like the roaring of a lion, but his favor is like dew on the grass" (Proverbs 19:12). Satan is described like a roaring lion looking for people to devour (1 Peter 5:8). He is driven by hatred and revenge. But Christ is also described as "the lion of the tribe of Judah" (Revelation 5:5) whose messages can be like a roaring lion (Revelation 10:3).

God is not driven by hatred. When we choose Christ as our Savior, we need not fear the roar of the lion.

KEY BIBLE TEXT: "For we do not wrestle against flesh and blood, but against principalities, against powers, against the rulers of the darkness of this age" (Ephesians 6:12).

DAY 247 An Undying Hero

An Amazing Fact: *On April 12, 1961, cosmonaut Yuri Gagarin became the first person in space when his Vostok spacecraft lifted off in the early morning. Although the mission lasted less than two hours and consisted of just one rotation around the earth, the journey ushered in the era of human spaceflight.*

A soviet fighter pilot, Yuri Gagarin was just 27 years old when he made his first and only trip into space. He became a national treasure ... and too valuable to the Soviet propaganda machine to send up on another dangerous mission.

It's a sad irony, then, that when Gagarin was finally scheduled to ascend to the cosmos once more, he died in a crash during a routine training exercise. Gagarin remained a hero after the fall of the Soviet Union; statues of him were preserved while monuments to Russia's Communist leaders were torn down.

God sent another man to usher in a new era for the world: Jesus Christ. He radically transformed the world's understanding of God and the way human beings should treat each other. He removed the separation between man and God by bearing the world's sins and dying on the cross. He was raised from the dead and lives on, even today, at the right hand of God. He will soon finish the work He began by coming to Earth and taking His children home to heaven.

Although Christ left the Earth to minister in the heavenly sanctuary, His followers continue His work until He returns. With the aid of the Holy Spirit, Christ's people turned the ancient world "upside down" (Acts 17:6), have permanently left their mark on history, and will continue to spread the love and forgiveness of God until the very last day.

God honors the people who labor for Him, both in this life and in the eternal life to come. He will one day say, "Well done, good and faithful servant" (Matthew 25:21). In what ways have you served God lately?

KEY BIBLE TEXT: "I heard the voice of the Lord, saying: 'Whom shall I send, And who will go for Us?' Then I said, 'Here am I! Send me'" (Isaiah 6:8).

Do Business Till I Come

An Amazing Fact: *On May 19, 1780, New Englanders were shocked when it became as dark as night at noon. Many people believed that Judgment Day had come, and some in the Connecticut State Senate moved that their work be adjourned for the day. However, a preacher's son by the name of Abraham Davenport opposed this suggestion. John Greenleaf Whittier, in a poem called "Abraham Davenport," presents Davenport's response this way:*

> *... "This well may be*
> *The Day of Judgment which the world awaits;*
> *But be it so or not, I only know*
> *My present duty, and my Lord's command*
> *To occupy till He come. So at the post*
> *Where He hast set me in His providence,*
> *I choose, for one, to meet Him face to face,*
> *No faithless servant frightened from my task,*
> *But ready when the Lord of the harvest calls;*
> *And therefore, with all reverence, I would say,*
> *Let God do His work, we will see to ours.*
> *Bring in the candles." And they brought them in.*

Many people are frightened when they consider the coming end of the world, just as Jesus predicted: "Men's hearts failing them from fear and the expectation of those things which are coming on the earth" (Luke 21: 25). However, God's faithful do not need to fear. When we see signs of Jesus' return, we should be encouraged in our work "because [our] redemption draws near" (Luke 21:28). So instead of being afraid while we wait, we should do as Jesus instructed in the parable: "A certain nobleman went into a far country to receive for himself a kingdom and to return. So he called ten of his servants, delivered to them ten minas, and said to them, 'Do business till I come'" (Luke 19:12, 13).

KEY BIBLE TEXT: "For God has not given us a spirit of fear, but of power and of love and of a sound mind. Therefore do not be ashamed of the testimony of our Lord ... but share with me in the sufferings for the gospel according to the power of God" (2 Timothy 1:8).

DAY 249 Never Caught

An Amazing Fact: *Long before such a feat of engineering was thought possible, Lockheed Aircraft designed and built the most impressive aircraft to ever roam the skies. The first flight of an SR-71 "Blackbird" took place in 1964. For years, the Blackbird's maximum speed and altitude was kept top secret. But we now know the aircraft set two world records for absolute speed (2,193 miles per hour) and altitude (more than 85,068 feet).*

For more than 30 years, the SR-71 flew with impunity. With a normal cruising speed of Mach 3 and altitude of 80,000 feet, no missile or plane, then or now, could catch it. As a result, despite hundreds of reconnaissance missions over hostile enemy territory, not a single aircraft was lost to enemy fire.

The Blackbird could fly from Los Angeles to Washington D.C. in one hour! It flew so fast that to refuel in-flight, the sleek jet had to fly as slow as possible and the refueling aircraft as fast as it could to prevent from being run over! The capabilities of the steel bird have not been surpassed: It could survey 100,000 square miles per hour. The SR-71 was retired in 1990, although it saw temporary reinstatement after Gulf War reconnaissance shortcomings. Even with all the amazing advances in modern aviation technology since, no aircraft can fly faster or higher than the Blackbird.

We would do well to learn from the Blackbird. The Bible encourages us to watch carefully and not be caught off guard regarding Christ's second coming. "But take heed to yourselves, lest your hearts be weighed down with carousing, drunkenness, and cares of this life, and that Day come on you unexpectedly. For it will come as a snare on all those who dwell on the face of the whole earth" (Luke 21:34, 35).

When we take time every day to study our Bibles and live with an awareness that these are the last days, not a single Christian will be "lost to enemy fire." Like the Blackbird, we will never be caught off guard.

KEY BIBLE TEXT: "Watch therefore, and pray always that you may be counted worthy to escape all these things that will come to pass, and to stand before the Son of Man" (Luke 21:36).

Falling Stars

DAY 250

An Amazing Fact: *A falling star (also called a shooting star) is not really a falling star at all. It is the path you see on a dark night of a meteoroid as it enters the Earth's atmosphere. Then it becomes a meteor. If it does not completely burn up and actually lands on the ground, it is then called a meteorite.*

Meteoroids range in size from a particle of sand to the size of boulders. Millions of them enter our atmosphere every day. Most are only the size of a pebble. And most, when they enter our atmosphere at great speeds, burn up and disintegrate. The composition of a meteoroid can actually be determined by its trajectory and the light spectrum it gives off. If a cluster of meteoroids enter the atmosphere somewhat close together, we call that a meteor shower. A fireball is a brighter-than-usual meteor. One of the brightest ever filmed was the Peekskill Meteorite of October 9, 1992.

"Falling Star" is a very popular phrase that has been used by rock bands, television shows, children's games, and novels. Perhaps you know Perry Como's "Catch a Falling Star." But the Bible talks about the most significant falling star, Lucifer. "How you are fallen from heaven, O Lucifer, son of the morning! How you are cut down to the ground, You who weakened the nations! For you have said in your heart: I will ascend into heaven, I will exalt my throne above the stars of God" (Isaiah 14:12, 13). Satan wanted to take the place of God.

When Satan was cast out of heaven, "His tail drew a third of the stars of heaven and threw them to the earth" (Revelation 12:4). The falling star took others with him. Do not give yourself over to the enemy. Do not fall with him. Rather, shine for Christ by inviting Him into your heart today.

KEY BIBLE TEXT: "Those who are wise shall shine Like the brightness of the firmament, And those who turn many to righteousness Like the stars forever and ever" (Daniel 12:3).

DAY 251 The Power of the Tongue

An Amazing Fact: *The tongue isn't really the strongest muscle in the body, as some claim. In fact, it isn't a single muscle at all. The tongue is made up of eight different muscles; four of these attach the tongue to bone, while the other four control its shape and size. The tongue's ability to change its shape, size, and position is an important part of speech.*

In fact, the position of the tongue is so important to speech that vowels are put into categories based on the position of the tongue required to make that particular sound. For example, high vowels are vowels that require the tongue to be in a high position in the mouth. The tongue is flexible enough that the International Phonetic Alphabet recognizes seven different vowel heights—from high to mid to low—and five different categories—from front to central to back.

Even more amazing than the tongue's contribution to speech is the correlation between speech and the safety of the soul. Proverbs repeatedly makes the connection: "Whoever guards his mouth and tongue Keeps his soul from troubles;" "He who guards his mouth preserves his life;" and finally, "Death and life are in the power of the tongue" (Proverbs 21:23, 13:3, 18:21). James tells us that if a person could control the tongue they would be perfect—but that "no man can tame the tongue" (James 3:2, 8). Jesus tells us that "by your words you will be justified, and by your words you will be condemned" (Matthew 12:37). But there is hope! Jesus also tells us that the mouth speaks from "the abundance of the heart"—and Jesus himself is the cleanser of hearts (Matthew 12:34).

KEY BIBLE TEXT: "If we confess our sins, He is faithful and just to forgive us our sins and to cleanse us from all unrighteousness" (1 John 1:9).

Humblebees

DAY 252

An Amazing Fact: *Once called humblebees because of their good nature, bumblebees rarely have it in them to sting. But young children struggled to say humblebee, often resorting to "bumblebee." Because of the bumblebee's seemingly awkward movements, the adults adopted the new name.*

Bumblebees are among the few insects that can control their body temperature. In cold weather, queens and workers can shiver their flight muscles to warm themselves. Their large size and heat-conserving hairy coats also help them stay warm, allowing them to fly and work in colder climates and lower temperatures than most other insects.

One day Jesus' disciples were busy arguing about who would be the greatest in the kingdom of heaven. Christ rebuked them gently and said, "The kings of the Gentiles exercise lordship over them, and those who exercise authority over them are called 'benefactors.' But not so among you; on the contrary, he who is greatest among you, let him be as the younger, and he who governs as he who serves" (Luke 22:25, 26).

Like the "humblebee," Christ measures true greatness by humility, not aggressiveness. The nature of a follower of Jesus is to be more like a good child—not busy working to be at the top, but simply living a life of service toward others. It seems impossible that a person could be great by being the least. It also seems impossible for the bumblebee, with their small wings and fat bodies, to fly. Perhaps we can learn a lesson from this simple little insect.

KEY BIBLE TEXT: "For who is greater, he who sits at the table, or he who serves? Is it not he who sits at the table? Yet I am among you as the One who serves" (Luke 22:27).

DAY 253 Beyond Ruts

An Amazing Fact: *The distance between train-track rails, better known as the U.S. railroad gauge, is an odd 4 feet, 8.5 inches. Why? Because that's the way they built them in England, and English expatriates built the U.S. railroads.*

But why did the English build them that size? Well, the first rail lines were built by those who built horse-drawn tramways, and they simply used the same gauge. And they used that gauge because the people who built the tramways used the same jigs and tools used for building wagons—which use that wheel spacing.

But why did the wagons use that odd wheel spacing? If they tried to use any other spacing, the wagons wheels would break because they did not fit in the old road ruts. So who built these old rutted roads? The first long-distance roads in Europe were built by Imperial Rome for the benefit of their legions. And the ruts? They were first made for Roman war chariots—and they used the 4 feet, 8.5 inches measurement. They were all alike in the matter of wheel spacing.

But why that width? They were made to be just wide enough to accommodate the back-ends of two warhorses. Alas, the influence of old ruts tends to live on forever. The writer of Hebrews warns us about the perils of not moving forward in our Christian lives. "Therefore, leaving the discussion of the elementary principles of Christ, let us go on to perfection" (Hebrews 6:1). The word "perfection" can mean "fullness" or "maturity."

As we choose to walk with Jesus every day, we will grow and develop. We will not follow old paths without making sure we know and understand those ways. Practicing a tradition might seem right, but if it does not square with the Bible, we might be doing something only because "that's the way we've always done it before." That's how train track rails were once laid. So ask yourself, "Am I going down the right track?"

KEY BIBLE TEXT: "But also for this very reason, giving all diligence, add to your faith virtue, to virtue knowledge" (2 Peter 1:5).

When God Swore an Oath

An Amazing Fact: *George Fox, the founder of the Religious Society of Friends, or Quakers, was famous for his refusal to swear an oath. At the time, a person could be imprisoned for refusing to swear their loyalty to the king, and Fox was sentenced to prison for this offense multiple times. On one occasion, Fox challenged the judge to find a place in the Bible where either Christ or the apostles had sworn an oath—if the judge could find one, he would swear his loyalty. In his journal, Fox says that though there were several priests present, none of them offered to speak. Nevertheless, Fox was returned to jail.*

Both Jesus and the apostle James make it quite clear that the Christian should not swear an oath. Jesus instructs us, "Do not swear at all ... let your 'Yes' be 'Yes,' and your 'No,' 'No'" (Matthew 5:34–37). James repeats this instruction almost exactly.

Even so, in Hebrews we find that God himself swore an oath.

Hebrews tells us that since humans consider an oath a confirmation that they're telling the truth, and because God wanted to show us "more abundantly" that His word was reliable, God decided to confirm His promise with an oath. What was this promise that was so important that we understand? We find the answer in the story of Abraham offering Isaac as a sacrifice.

Just after God stopped Abraham from killing Isaac, He called to Abraham a second time, saying, "By Myself I have sworn. ... In your seed all the nations of the earth shall be blessed, because you have obeyed my voice" (Genesis 22:15–18). In other words, the promise of the Messiah was so important that God swore an oath to give us a "strong consolation ... both sure and steadfast" (Hebrews 6:18, 19).

KEY BIBLE TEXT: "This hope we have as an anchor of the soul, both sure and steadfast, and which enters the Presence behind the veil, where the forerunner has entered for us, even Jesus" (Hebrews 6:19, 20).

DAY 255 Fatal Drinks

An Amazing Fact: *Two fatal drinks changed history. On the last day of Lincoln's life, the great emancipator said: "We have cleared up a colossal job. Slavery is abolished. After reconstruction, the next great question will be the overthrow and suppression of the legalized liquor traffic."*

That evening, Friday, April 14, 1865, John Wilkes Booth stopped by a saloon to fill himself with liquor to nerve himself for his evil plan. That same night, Lincoln's bodyguard left the theater for a drink of liquor at the same saloon! While he was away, Booth shot Lincoln. These two drinks were among the most costly in American history.

The Bible warns us, "Do not mix with winebibbers, Or with gluttonous eaters of meat; For the drunkard and the glutton will come to poverty, And drowsiness will clothe a man with rags" (Proverbs 23:20, 21).

Getting enough sleep is also very important to our lives. Your driving capability after having been awake for 18 hours is the same as driving after you have had two alcoholic drinks. When you have been awake for 24 hours, you're driving no differently than if you've had six drinks! Getting enough sleep is important when it comes to performance, but Jesus said there is a time to stay awake at any cost.

The guidance of Solomon is worth following. "Hear, my son (and daughter), and be wise; And guide your heart in the way" (v. 19). Don't let alcohol guide you. Don't allow sleep deprivation to lead you.

KEY BIBLE TEXT: "Who has woe? Who has sorrow? Who has contentions? Who has complaints? Who has wounds without cause? Who has redness of eyes? Those who linger long at the wine, Those who go in search of mixed drinks. ... At the last it bites like a serpent, And stings like a viper" (Proverbs 23:29, 30, 32).

Obsolete Laws

An Amazing Fact: *As of 2011 in California, a woman may not drive a vehicle while wearing a housecoat and sunshine is legally guaranteed to the masses.*

Many states and countries have official laws that are rarely enforced and do not seem to make sense from a modern perspective, yet they remain "on the books." Regardless of the original reasons justifying the passage of these laws, they seem silly or arbitrary by today's standards.

So why do they remain in the legal code? Sometimes they get forgotten as society progresses. Sometimes the effort to repeal the laws is greater than the value of repealing them. Yet the bottom line remains: Silly laws remain legal, and though they are rarely enforced, they can be.

God had a law that became obsolete. The Bible says that Jesus nailed this law to the cross (Colossians 2:14). Some believe this law is the Ten Commandments, but Hebrews 7:11 says this obsolete law came to the people under the ministry of the Levitical priesthood. The Ten Commandments were given at Mt. Sinai before the Levitical priesthood was established! Rather, the obsolete law contained the rites and rituals for the sanctuary service, all of which foreshadowed Christ's sacrifice and ministry for humanity. Once Jesus died, these rituals lost their meaning. There was no more reason to sacrifice a lamb in the temple out of faith in the coming Messiah when the Messiah had already become the ultimate sacrifice!

We can be thankful that Jesus fulfilled this law on the cross and God abolished it afterward. Imagine if God had left this law intact after the cross. Even though the rituals would be meaningless, we would still have to obey them. Aren't you glad you don't have to kill an animal when you go to church?

KEY BIBLE TEXT: "Circumcision is nothing and uncircumcision is nothing, but keeping the commandments of God is what matters" (1 Corinthians 7:19).

DAY 257 Rain in the Desert

An Amazing Fact: *The Swiss company Meteo Systems claims that it has created the technology to generate rain in the desert. Meteo Systems takes credit for an unusually high number of rainstorms in the desert region surrounding Abu Dhabi in the summer of 2010. According to the company, their umbrella-style towers in the desert produce negatively charged ions. These ions attract dust and other particles. Eventually, moisture condenses around these particles and rainclouds are formed.*

Many scientists who work in the weather modification field are skeptical of Meteo Systems' project. There can be no doubt that the ability to create rain in the desert would be revolutionary and incredibly lucrative, but according to most scientists, it hasn't really happened yet.

Nevertheless, the Christian can be confident that, at some point, the desert really will have plenty of water. The Bible promises that "the desert shall rejoice and blossom as the rose" and that God will make the desert like the garden of Eden (Isaiah 35:1; 51:3). When will this happen? These promises are connected with promises of "everlasting joy," and Isaiah says that "sorrow and sighing shall flee away" (Isaiah 35:10). Revelation predicts that the end of pain and sorrow will come when God moves the New Jerusalem down to the Earth made new in order to live with us (Revelation 21:1–4). What an amazing promise!

This must be why Isaiah tells us to encourage each other with this promise: "Say to those who are fearful-hearted, 'Be strong, do not fear! Behold, your God will come with vengeance. ... He will come and save you.' Then ...waters shall burst forth in the wilderness, And streams in the desert" (Isaiah 35:4–6). Salvation, everlasting joy, and a God who wants to live with us are so much more than scientists could ever promise!

KEY BIBLE TEXT: "For the LORD will comfort Zion, He will comfort all her waste places; He will make her wilderness like Eden, And her desert like the garden of the LORD; Joy and gladness will be found in it, Thanksgiving and the voice of melody" (Isaiah 50:3).

Facing Death

An Amazing Fact: *The Black Death is a particularly nasty form of bubonic plague and killed tens of millions of people since it first appeared in the 14th century. It is caused by the bacterium carried by infected fleas and rats. In most cases, the infected victim suffers from fever, chills, fatigue, and painfully swollen lymph nodes. It carried away a greater proportion of the world's people than any other disease or war in history. It literally transformed European society—reducing the population by one-third.*

The Black Death was traced to the Gobi Desert in the 1320s. By 1400, it invaded China and reduced the population there from 125 million to 90 million. It then followed trade routes west to India, the Middle East, and finally into Europe. In Cairo, Egypt, a city of 500,000, at the height of the epidemic, 7,000 people died each day. By 1349, the plague had killed one-third of the population of the Muslim world.

In 1347, Eurasian nomads deliberately infected a European community with the disease. While laying siege to a Genoese trading post in the Crimea, they lobbed plague-infected corpses into the town by catapult. From the Crimea, the Genoese inadvertently brought the disease to Sicily in a ship carrying infected rats. The disease then swept through Sicily in 1347; North Africa, Italy, France, and Spain in 1348; Hungary, Austria, Switzerland, England, Germany, and the Low Countries in 1349; and reached Scandinavia in 1350. Some 25 million Europeans were killed by the initial onslaught of the Black Death; whole villages were wiped out.

King Hezekiah once faced death. The prophet Isaiah told him to set his house in order for he would die. "Then Hezekiah turned his face toward the wall, and prayed to the Lord" (Isaiah 38:2). Not only did the Lord miraculously intervene, but He gave an amazing sign: "Behold, I will bring the shadow on the sundial ... ten degrees backward" (v. 8).

When we are facing life-threatening illness, we would do well to cry out to God. The Lord hears our prayers. We might be miraculously healed. And if not now, we know someday there will be no more death.

KEY BIBLE TEXT: "Then Death and Hades were cast into the lake of fire" (Revelation 20:14).

DAY 259 Never Growing Faint

An Amazing Fact: *Bruce Lee, a martial artist and film star who lived from 1940 to 1973, was said to be one of the strongest and fastest men alive at the time. Among his amazing feats was his ability to strike an object from three feet away in only .05 of a second. He could reportedly do push-ups using only his thumbs.*

Bruce Lee was not a very big man, but he was very powerful. Not only were his physical achievements unparalleled, but his charisma made him very attractive as well. He was a very influential actor too, popularizing the martial arts movie genre for the Western audience. He was thoroughly dedicated to his physical and artistic work.

On July 20, 1973, however, Lee died. He was reportedly not feeling well earlier in the day, and the official cause of death was labeled a cerebral edema caused by a reaction to a medication he had taken for a headache. In the end, his strength and power could not stop excess fluid from building up in his brain.

God, on the other hand, has limitless power and strength. The Bible says that He never grows faint or weary. His strength never subsides, and He never gets tired or needs to rest. He holds the same power today as He did when He created the Earth and all that is in it. He will never die or decay. He will reign throughout eternity with unfathomable power.

Though God is the only one with inherent immortality, He imparts that immortality to us as a free gift. From our position of sin and mortality, we can only imagine bodies that do not grow weary and strength that never fades. But the Bible promises that, when we trust in the Lord and wait on Him, we will "run and not be weary" and will "walk and not faint." Because of Christ's sacrifice for us, we can look forward to life without end with strength and power that rivals and exceeds even the most amazing feats demonstrated by Bruce Lee during his life.

KEY BIBLE TEXT: "For the wages of sin is death, but the gift of God is eternal life in Christ Jesus our Lord" (Romans 6:23).

From Cave Dwellers to Billionaires

An Amazing Fact: *Zsolt and Geza Peladi are two brothers who were so poor that they lived in a cave near Budapest, Hungary. To support themselves they sold whatever scraps they could find on the street. But in early 2009, their lives took a dramatic turn. Their maternal grandmother left them and their sister a portion of a seven billion dollar fortune.*

The two boys knew that their mother came from a wealthy family, but their mother was estranged from her family. Later, they even lost track of their mother. Upon the death of their wealthy grandmother in Germany, German law required that the estate be given to the next of kin. No surviving relatives were known, so the authorities started genealogical research. They discovered that the brothers' mother had died and that the Peladi brothers were the direct descendents.

Only the deaths of their grandmother and mother could have released the brothers from their extreme poverty, especially since their grandmother never knew them. After all, a will cannot be executed until a death has taken place: "For where there is a testament, there must also of necessity be the death of the testator" (Hebrews 9:16). In a way, we're in the same situation. Estranged from God by our sin, only Christ's death could connect us to the riches of salvation. Just as the authorities searched for descendents, Jesus searches for us: "For the Son of Man has come to seek and to save that which was lost" (Luke 19:10). But while the Peladi brothers could lose their fortune, our inheritance in Christ will not fade away.

KEY BIBLE TEXT: "Blessed be the God and Father of our Lord Jesus Christ, who according to His abundant mercy has begotten us again to a living hope through the resurrection of Jesus Christ from the dead, to an inheritance incorruptible and undefiled and that does not fade away, reserved in heaven for you" (1 Peter 1:3–5).

DAY 261 Sun Creator

An Amazing Fact: *The sun is a fantastically hot cosmic radiation powerhouse. It has a surface temperature of about 11,000 degrees, and its interior temperature is estimated as high as 18 million degrees. The sun is so colossal in size that it contains 99.8 percent of the total mass of our solar system. Jupiter consists of about 0.2 percent, which means Earth is a pretty small speck.*

Our sun is so huge, it would take more than a million Earths to fill its core. Because it's some 93 million miles away, it takes the light from the sun about eight minutes and 20 seconds to reach us.

The pressure at the center of the sun is about 700 million tons per square inch. It's enough to smash atoms, expose the inner nuclei, and allow them to smash into each other and produce light and warmth. In fact, the material at the core of the sun is so hot that if you could capture enough of it to cover a pinhead, it would radiate enough heat to kill a man one mile away.

Without the sun there would be no life on this planet. It gives off light and heat that makes it possible for us to survive and for plants to grow. The sun is not unique, however, and is a star among billions of other stars. Still, it's pretty bright. If you compared the closest 50 stars to Earth, our sun would rank fourth brightest. Because of its massive size, a person who weighs 150 pounds on Earth would weigh 4,200 pounds on the sun because the sun's gravity is 28 times that of our planet.

Isaiah writes a prophetic message to future King Cyrus, who needed to remember the power of the one true God. "I am the Lord, and there is no other; There is no God besides Me. ... They may know from the rising of the sun to its setting That there is none besides Me. I am the Lord, and there is no other; I form the light and create darkness" (Isaiah 45:5–7).

Ancient people have worshiped the sun. But we know that there is only one Son to worship—Jesus Christ, the one who made the sun.

KEY BIBLE TEXT: "I—My hands—stretched out the heavens, And all their host I have commanded" (Isaiah 45:12).

A Satisfied Soul

An Amazing Fact: *Born on June 15, 1950, Michel Lotito was a Frenchman with a very unusual diet. He consumed large quantities of metal and glass since he was nine years old. He was known to have eaten supermarket carts, television sets, bicycles, chandeliers, razor blades, bullets, nuts and bolts, lengths of chain, phonograph records, computers, and an entire Cessna 150 light aircraft (which took him nearly two years to consume).*

Mr. Lotito was an entertainer nicknamed Monsieur Mangetout, or "Mister Eat All Things." It seems that his body adjusted to this unusual diet, as he ate nearly two pounds of metal every day. His technique included lubricating his digestive tract with mineral oil, cutting the parts into bite-size pieces, and then consuming a large quantity of water while eating this junk.

What is most amazing is that he didn't seem to suffer any unusual side effects from eating materials usually considered poisonous. He did once say that bananas and hard-boiled eggs made him sick. Some believe that between 1959 and 1997, Mr. Lotito consumed about one ton of metal. He said he had a complex as a child about being thin. He started eating nails, bottles, and plates to win bets. He once said while eating a bicycle chain that he liked it because it had "taste." Michel died of natural causes on June 25, 2007, ten days after his 57th birthday.

The Bible says, "A satisfied soul loathes the honeycomb. But to a hungry soul every bitter thing is sweet" (Proverbs 27:7). Is your soul satisfied? Is your heart so filled with contentment in your relationship with Jesus that you do not need to be driven by appetite or passion to fill the longings deep within? When you are at peace with God, addictions to external things like drugs, sex, money, food, or power will have no appeal. If you are really hungry in your soul, do not turn to nails and glass. Turn to Jesus. He will fill you with bread that will satisfy.

KEY BIBLE TEXT: "And Jesus said to them, 'I am the bread of life. He who comes to Me shall never hunger, and he who believes in Me shall never thirst'" (John 6:35).

DAY 263 Buried Alive by Laziness

An Amazing Fact: *On November 19, 1856, The New York Times ran a story on a man named Thomas Burns, who was semi-buried as a punishment for laziness. Burns was a prisoner at a penitentiary in New York City and was expected to work in the quarry. The article reports that Burns' consistent refusal to work at anything but a snail's pace so irritated the quarry-master that Burns was buried up to six inches above his knees and then left there for two days!*

According to the deputy warden, Burns was so lazy that he had "tired out" the superintendents of all the prison work departments. It was reported that Burns seemed to enjoy the irritation of his supervisors, appeared in good health, and was quite active when it was mealtime. Burns himself admitted that he felt the world "owed him" food and lodging and that the only thing he owed in return was to wear the prison's "striped pantaloons." He'd been in and out of prison several times—his repeated crime was "vagrancy" or wandering idly. The article made no mention of whether the punishment had any effect on his work ethic.

As harsh and unconventional as this punishment might sound to our ears today, Solomon seems to understand the feeling of Burns' supervisors: "As vinegar to the teeth and smoke to the eyes, So is the lazy man to those who send him" (Proverbs 10:26). Proverbs even predicted Burns' situation: "The hand of the diligent will rule, But the lazy man will be put to forced labor" (Proverbs 12:24).

Solomon presents to us the alternative to laziness—diligence. He says that those who are diligent in their work "shall have enough ... for the food of [their] household" (Proverbs 27:27). How much better it is to be considered one of the diligent than one of the slothful!

KEY BIBLE TEXT: "Be diligent to know the state of your flocks, And attend to your herds; For riches are not forever, Nor does a crown endure to all generations" (Proverbs 27:23, 24).

The Unrecognized King

DAY 264

An Amazing Fact: *Naples was on the verge of insurrection against the Italian monarchy when King Humbert took the throne. Politicians urged violent measures to force the city into submission, but King Humbert refused. However, in 1884, Naples was soon hit by an outbreak of cholera, and the dreaded disease raged with deadly fury. Ignoring his advisors, the young king made an amazing move of devotion toward even his disloyal subjects.*

Shocking his counselors, Humbert left the palace and went alone through the crowded hospitals of Naples, ministering to his subjects. He ventured without a guard into the slums and among the sick. Many of the suffering breathed prayers of gratitude for this young medical servant, not knowing it was the very king they'd spurned. When the plague was finally checked, many learned his true identity. Naples then became a conquered city—conquered by the love of a monarch it once refused. From that time forward, the people of Naples were among Humbert's most loyal subjects.

Another King once left His throne to walk among the sick and dying. Jesus came from heaven's royal kingdom to pass unrecognized through the streets of our world and reach out with love. The Bible says, "He is despised and rejected by men, A Man of sorrows and acquainted with grief, And we hid, as it were, our faces from Him; He was despised, and we did not esteem Him" (Isaiah 53:3). He loved and served many, yet Christ was not accepted by the powers of His day. The religious politicians despised him and eventually had Him killed.

Today, Jesus calls us to walk the road of servanthood, even though we might be despised and rejected. Someday, when heaven's gates open, we will be forever accepted.

KEY BIBLE TEXT: "Then they spat on Him, and took the reed and struck Him on the head" (Matthew 27:30).

DAY 265 The Empty Tomb

An Amazing Fact: *In 1980, an archeological dig in Israel unearthed the Talpiot Tomb, which contained several ossuaries (bone boxes) dating back to biblical times. In 2007, a documentary produced by acclaimed filmmaker James Cameron asserted that this tomb was, in fact, the family tomb of Jesus of Nazareth.*

Neither the archeological team that found the tomb nor the filmmakers behind the first documentary on the subject, released in 1996, found anything of special merit in this tomb. The more recent documentary, however, calls into question the death and resurrection of Jesus as recorded in the Bible. In the wake of some claims made in the popular novel *The Da Vinci Code*, the Talpiot Tomb discovery suddenly seemed relevant and popular.

Many archeological and theological scholars have disputed the claims made by the documentary. Even the author of the original excavation report, Amos Kloner, said of the documentary, "I think it is very unserious work. I do scholarly work ... [This film] is all nonsense." William Dever, an expert on near eastern archaeology and anthropology, who has worked with Israeli archeologists for five decades, said that the film "would be amusing if it didn't mislead so many people."

As Christians, we don't need to be misled. A world tainted by sin will always try to discredit and malign God, but the faithful can stand strongly on the sure Word of God. The Gospels clearly testify of an empty tomb where Jesus had been laid before His resurrection. They record a group of women first bearing witness to it, followed by Peter's corroboration later on. The Bible also tells us that more than 500 people saw the risen Christ with their own eyes, including many of the authors of the Bible itself.

The world will become increasingly false and misleading as we approach the return of Jesus, but we will never be misled if we put our faith in the Bible and trust what it says.

KEY BIBLE TEXT: "After that He was seen by over five hundred brethren at once, of whom the greater part remain to the present, but some have fallen asleep" (1 Corinthians 15:6).

A Better Promise

An Amazing Fact: *Each year, 171,000 Christians are martyred for their faith, and 100 million Christians endure arrest and interrogation. Persecution is especially severe in North Korea. Worship of anyone other than the "dear leader" is illegal. Parents are unable to share their faith at home until their children are old enough to understand the risks. There are an estimated 50,000 to 70,000 Christians in labor camps. Yet Christianity is growing there, with an estimated 400,000 believers.*

Hebrews 11, commonly called the faith chapter, ends its chronicle of Bible heroes with this statement: "And what more shall I say? For the time would fail me to tell of Gideon and Barak and Samson and" (Hebrews 11:32). The author goes on to catalog the things that have been done to people of faith, including persecution and death: "Others were tortured, not accepting deliverance, that they might obtain a better resurrection. ... They were stoned, sawn in two, were tempted, were slain with the sword" (vs. 35, 37). Yet in spite of the things these faith heroes suffered, Hebrews makes it clear that they haven't received their reward quite yet: "And all these, having obtained a good testimony through faith, did not receive the promise" (v. 39). The promise referred to is what God promised Abram: the land of Canaan. The land of Canaan never became the paradise for the Jews that God intended. Why would God make these faithful wait?

The answer becomes clear when we consider how the persecution of God's people continues today. God chose not to reward some of the faithful until all of the faithful could enjoy the promise together, and thus decided on an even better promise than the earthly land of Canaan: "God having provided something better for us, that they should not be made perfect apart from us" (vs. 39, 40). Instead of the earthly Canaan, God has prepared the heavenly New Jerusalem.

KEY BIBLE TEXT: "But now they desire a better, that is, a heavenly country. Therefore God is not ashamed to be called their God, for He has prepared a city for them" (Hebrews 11:16).

DAY 267 High and Holy Places

An Amazing Fact: *The bristlecone pine is the oldest living single organism on our planet. One tree called "Methuselah" is estimated to be 4,789 years old. Its location in the White Mountains of eastern California is undisclosed to protect the tree from vandalism.*

Bristlecone pines are a group of small trees believed to live for about 5,000 years. There are three species: Rocky Mountain (Colorado, New Mexico, and Arizona), Great Basin (Utah, Nevada, and eastern California), and the Foxtail (California). They grow in isolated groves at or just below the tree line. Because of high winds, dry soils, and cold temperatures, seasons are very short and the trees grow very slowly. The bristlecone's wood is dense and resinous, so it is resistant to pests like insects and fungus.

These special trees can remind us of a Bible verse about the Lord: "For thus says the High and Lofty One Who inhabits eternity, whose name is Holy: I dwell in the high and holy place, With him who has a contrite and humble spirit, To revive the spirit of the humble, And to revive the heart of the contrite ones" (Isaiah 57:15).

Perhaps we can learn from the humble bristlecone pine. It can live at such a high elevation because it stays low and close to the rock, sending its roots deep down so it can hang on during the storms that strike the mountain. We, too, can come close to the "High and Holy One" when we are humble. When you are blown about by winds of strife, bow down like the bristlecone pine. Send your roots deep down into Jesus and hang on to Him as you grow slowly and strongly.

KEY BIBLE TEXT: "Those who are planted in the house of the Lord shall flourish in the courts of our God" (Psalm 92:13).

Destruction by Fire

An Amazing Fact: *On April 18, 1906, a powerful earthquake struck off the coast of San Francisco. While the quake was felt from Oregon to Los Angeles and as far inland as Nevada, it was the resulting fires that did most of the damage. The fires raged for four days and nights and left 490 city blocks charred—a total area of about 4.5 square miles.*

According to the San Francisco Museum, the fires initially started because of ruptured gas lines and toppled stoves resulting from the earthquake. However, subsequent fires were started by firefighters improperly demolishing buildings to create firebreaks and by property owners burning their own buildings in an attempt to collect insurance money that would otherwise be denied if the damage had been caused only by the quake. Thus, already horrifying destruction was exacerbated both by greed and by well-intentioned but poorly executed attempts to stop the fires' progression.

The Bible tells us that "scoffers set a city aflame" while "wise men turn away wrath" (Proverbs 29:8). The San Francisco fires demonstrate mankind's natural tendency toward destruction, both by accident and on purpose, but this Proverb warns us that "scoffing" can make that tendency worse and result in total destruction. Scoffing is a form of mocking or jeering. Such behavior often stirs up the wrath of the person being scoffed at, and the results can be violent.

God calls us to behave wisely by turning away wrath whenever possible. This means avoiding mockery and scoffing in our own lives but also speaking gently toward others to diffuse potentially disastrous situations. This kind of wisdom comes only through the process of sanctification, when we surrender our hearts to Jesus and allow Him to live through us. We must surrender anew each day. Have you surrendered to God today?

KEY BIBLE TEXT: "I have been crucified with Christ; it is no longer I who live, but Christ lives in me; and the life which I now live in the flesh I live by faith in the Son of God, who loved me and gave Himself for me" (Galatians 2:20).

DAY 269 By His Stripes

An Amazing Fact: *As many as 2.5 percent of people suffer from prosopagnosia, or face blindness. Someone with prosopagnosia might not be able to recognize his or her spouse, long-time colleagues, or his or her own children. For example, author Heather Sellers once tried to kiss the wrong man at the airport—she thought she recognized her husband's distinctive gait.*

On another occasion, Sellers introduced herself to a new professor at the university where she taught, only to find that he'd been working across the hall from her for 15 years. People with prosopagnosia often work very hard to recognize people based on their clothing, hair color, body shape, voice, and other characteristics.

It seems that quite a few Bible characters had momentary face blindness when first meeting Jesus after His resurrection. Mary Magdalene met Jesus at the tomb but didn't recognize Him until He spoke her name (John 20:14). The disciples saw Him on the shore while they were fishing and didn't know it was Him until their nets were miraculously filled with fish (John 21:4). And the two disciples on the road to Emmaus didn't recognize Him until they saw Him break the bread. What was it about that simple act of breaking bread that opened their eyes?

Let's consider the story closely. Jesus reached out for the bread, took it in His hands, broke it into pieces, and then handed it to each disciple. As they took the bread, the disciples must have taken a second look at His hands ... and the scars from the nails of His crucifixion. Perhaps they knew Him when they saw His scars.

Then and for all eternity, Jesus' scars are a reminder of what He suffered for our sake.

KEY BIBLE TEXT: "But He was wounded for our transgressions, He was bruised for our iniquities; The chastisement for our peace was upon Him, And by His stripes we are healed" (Isaiah 53:5).

The Perfect Home

An Amazing Fact: *Biosphere 2 was a state-of-the-art greenhouse built on three acres in the Arizona desert. It was a giant, computer-controlled environment intended to be a miniature version of the much larger biosphere 1, better known as Earth. Completed in 1991 at a cost of $200 million, it included five wilderness areas, ranging from a rainforest to a desert, and was stocked with thousands of exotic plants and animals.*

Eight humans ("biospherians") were to learn how to live off the land, isolated from the outside world except for communications. The designers envisioned Biosphere 2 as the first step toward human colonization of Mars.

But when this landlocked Noah's Ark set sail for its two-year voyage of discovery from 1991 to 1993, it ran aground from a host of unforeseen environmental and human disasters. Oxygen levels inside the complex dropped so low that emergency oxygen was pumped in—violating the main tenet of isolation. And crop production was so poor that the starving crew got hungry enough to steal food from one another or have it smuggled in. Nearly all the birds and animals that were supposed to thrive inside died—except for "crazy ants" and cockroaches that now fill the place. Their proud vision of man making utopia on Earth became a joke—today Biosphere 2 is a tourist attraction masquerading as science.

The Bible describes the restoration of God's people and land. It depicts the perfect home for us in which to thrive. "The glory of Lebanon shall come to you, the cypress, the pine, and the box tree together, to beautify the place of My sanctuary; And I will make the place of My feet glorious" (Isaiah 60:13).

Someday, when Jesus returns, He will restore our planet to its state before the fall of mankind. We will enjoy the ideal environment, where all of our needs will be abundantly provided. There will be no need for stealing food. Death will be gone. The air will be pure. And we will live forever.

KEY BIBLE TEXT: "The wilderness and the wasteland shall be glad for them, and the desert shall rejoice and blossom as the rose" (Isaiah 35:1).

DAY 271 Safety in the Rock

An Amazing Fact: *The rock hyrax is a terrestrial mammal that resembles a guinea pig and is found in Israel. As its name reveals, it lives among rocks in which it can quickly escape from predators. The animals are especially known for using sentries that send out alarm calls from high points if a predator comes close.*

Hyraxes (called "conies" or "rock badgers" in the Bible) typically live in groups of 10 to 80. Their ability to regulate body temperature is limited, so their activity is related to seasons and times of day. They are short and squatty with a weight of about nine pounds and a length of almost 20 inches. Their thick fur ranges from a dark brown color to a lighter gray, depending on the climate.

Hyrax herds are often subdivided into smaller groups of 5 to 15, with a dominant male who defends and watches over the group. In Africa they are preyed upon by leopards, cobras, adders, wild dogs, and eagles. Yet in Israel the rock hyrax is rarely preyed upon by terrestrial predators because of their excellent system of sentries. This combined with living among the rocks and crags gives them considerable protection.

The Bible says, "There are four things which are little on the earth, But they are exceedingly wise" (Proverbs 30:24). Besides the ant, locust, and spider, the hyrax is listed: "The rock badgers (hyrax) are a feeble folk, Yet they make their homes in the crags" (v. 26).

If you have ever felt small, take heart! Wisdom has nothing to do with our size or strength. We can learn a few lessons from the rock hyrax. The first is to live for others. Be willing to be a "sentry" and share warnings to those you love. And second, learn to live in the shelter of the Rock. Jesus will protect you from the predator (Satan) who is seeking to take you down.

KEY BIBLE TEXT: "The Lord is my rock and my fortress and my deliverer" (2 Samuel 22:2).

Clay Fit for a King

An Amazing Fact: *Ceramics are classified based on the temperature used to fire them—the higher the heat, the more durable the ceramic piece will be. Porcelain is a high-fire ceramic, fired at temperatures ranging from 2,000 to 2,500 degrees Fahrenheit. As a result, it is pressure resistant to 5,000 kilograms per centimeter squared. In other words, a railroad car weighing around 11 tons could be placed on top of a two centimeter square piece of porcelain without breaking the porcelain.*

The process of making a piece of fine porcelain—a product as strong as it is beautiful—is anything but comfortable. First, a piece is molded or turned on a wheel. Then an artisan removes sharp edges, such as seams, from a mold. Next a piece is annealed (heated and gradually cooled), which leaves it as hard as leather. Then it is glazed and fired in the kiln. After firing, rough patches are polished. Sometimes accents are added, like a metallic trim on fine china.

The results of this uncomfortable process are fantastic! Porcelain tiles have graced the walls of palaces, and fine china has decorated the tables of kings.

God's process with His people is similar. Just as the artisan is in complete control of the clay, God is in complete control of our lives: "O Lord, You are our Father; We are the clay, and You our potter; And all we are the work of your hand" (Isaiah 64:8). Just as the clay must be fired before it is useful, God's people must repent of their sins before they can become all He intends. Isaiah recognized this and pled with God: "Do not be furious, O Lord, Nor remember iniquity forever; Indeed, please look—we are all Your people!" (Isaiah 64: 9). Just as fine porcelain eventually becomes both beautiful and strong, God will not give up on His people until they have become what He desires for them.

KEY BIBLE TEXT: "Being confident of this very thing, that He who has begun a good work in you will complete it until the day of Jesus Christ" (Philippians 1:6).

DAY 273 Above Rubies

An Amazing Fact: *Ruby is a pink to blood-red colored gemstone. Chromium causes the color red, and a ruby's value is determined by the four C's: color, cut, clarity, and carat weight. The Smithsonian received as a gift one of the world's finest and largest ruby gemstones—a 23.1-carat Burmese ruby. Known as the "King of Gems," rubies have sometimes been priced seven times higher than diamonds.*

The beautiful gemstone in the Smithsonian was mined in Burma (now Myanmar) in the 1930s and was donated by Peter Buck in memory of his late wife. It displays a richly saturated red color along with exceptional transparency.

Rubies and sapphires come from the same family. The red ones are called rubies, and the others are called sapphires. Like many gemstones, rubies are often heat-treated to improve their color. A well-cut ruby can come close to the brilliance and sparkle of a diamond.

As early as 200 B.C. there is record of rubies being transported along the North Silk Road of China. Rubies have been held as very precious in Asian countries for centuries. They were used as jewelry and as ornaments on armor. Some were even placed underneath the foundations of buildings as good fortune. They are extremely hard, only slightly softer than diamonds, and have a melting point of 3,711 degrees Fahrenheit.

The Bible says this about rubies. "Who can find a virtuous wife? For her worth is far above rubies" (Proverbs 31:10). When you study how rubies are measured for value, you see how the description applies to the character of a good wife. Her beauty is more than exterior. It comes from the clarity from within.

Perhaps even the most valuable rubies, which are rich in a red color, might describe the value we can have in Christ when our sins are covered by His blood.

KEY BIBLE TEXT: "She [wisdom] is more precious than rubies,
And all the things that you may desire cannot compare with her"
(Proverbs 3:15).

A Gift That Keeps Giving

An Amazing Fact: *Senator Joseph Lieberman of Connecticut is an observant Jew who has made a practice of observing the Sabbath since the early days of his political career. He wrote a book, released in August 2011, about his faith and political career in which he emphasized the beauty of the Sabbath.*

Senator Lieberman describes his observance of the Sabbath as "according to the Jewish practice," which includes not turning on lights or driving a car during the holy hours. He also turns off his cell phone and electronic devices, only leaving his home's landline active in case of emergencies. He spends the time with his family and, he says, tries to enjoy a Sabbath afternoon nap.

Jesus affirmed His belief in observing the Sabbath both by claiming ownership of it as "Lord of the Sabbath" (Mark 2:28) and by faithfully observing it Himself through corporate religious worship (Luke 4:16). However, unlike Senator Lieberman, He chose not to observe the rabbinical teachings about the Sabbath, calling them "the commandments of men" (Matthew 15:9). Instead, He focused on worship, healing, and sustenance.

Many people in today's world believe that the seventh-day Sabbath has been abolished, replaced instead by an alternate day of worship. While many people with this belief are sincere lovers of God, the Bible tells us not only that the Sabbath remains in effect today, but it will also stay that way throughout eternity. Isaiah 66:23 tell us, regarding God's kingdom, "And it shall come to pass That from one New Moon to another, And from one Sabbath to another, All flesh shall come to worship before Me."

KEY BIBLE TEXT: "If you turn away your foot from the Sabbath, From doing your pleasure on My holy day, And call the Sabbath a delight, The holy day of the LORD honorable, And shall honor Him, not doing your own ways, Nor finding your own pleasure, Nor speaking your own words, Then you shall delight yourself in the LORD; And I will cause you to ride on the high hills of the earth, And feed you with the heritage of Jacob your father. The mouth of the LORD has spoken" (Isaiah 58:13, 14).

DAY 275 My Impediment Is No Hindrance

An Amazing Fact: *Winston Churchill struggled for much of his life to overcome a lisp. As a young man, he consulted a specialist who told him that all he needed was practice and perseverance. At one time, he believed he had an extra ligament that no one else had that was causing his problem. He worked doggedly to overcome the lisp, repeating phrases like, "The Spanish ships I cannot see for they are not in sight." Many years later he was able to say, "My impediment is no hindrance."*

One of the most common fears is glossophobia—the fear of public speaking. Nearly 75 percent of people report some fear of public speaking. How much worse might that fear be if one suffered from a speech impediment? Or what if the speaker was too young to be respected? Or what if the content of the speech was sure to anger the audience?

In Jeremiah's case, both of the last two scenarios were true. His message was intended to "root out and to pull down, To destroy and to throw down" before he could "build" and "plant" (Jeremiah 1:10). Messages of destruction don't often win friends, and, indeed, Jeremiah laments that he is a "man of contention to the whole earth" and that "every one of them [curse him]" (Jeremiah 15:10). In addition, Jeremiah was under the age of 25 and perhaps only 18 or 20 at his calling to the ministry. It's no wonder that Jeremiah objected, saying, "Ah, Lord God! Behold I cannot speak, for I am a youth."

In spite of the circumstances, God insisted Jeremiah follow His command, then encouraged and enabled him: "Do not be afraid of their faces, For I am with you to deliver you. ... Behold, I have put My words in your mouth" (Jeremiah 1:8, 9). No matter what our impediment, God wants to make it no hindrance.

KEY BIBLE TEXT: "My grace is sufficient for you, for My strength is made perfect in weakness" (2 Corinthians 12:9).

Straight Highways

An Amazing Fact: *The Chunnel is a 31.4-mile undersea rail tunnel that connects Great Britain with northern France. The idea of a tunnel under the English Channel began in the 18th century, but that seemingly impossible dream finally became reality in 1994.*

The channel tunnel is in fact three tunnels—one service tunnel with two passenger tunnels on either side. The main tunnels are 25 feet in diameter and are at an average of 130 feet beneath the channel's seabed. The Chunnel was constructed with 1,000-ton, laser-guided machines that dug 15 feet an hour as they also built retaining walls. These machines were so precise that after the first tunnel was completed, they discovered they were only a few centimeters off course.

The $13.5 billion, seven-year Chunnel is considered one of the wonders of the modern world. Work began in 1988 and took more than six years to complete. It came in at 80 percent over budget. Fires have disrupted service, and illegal immigrants have attempted to use the tunnel to enter England.

The first proposal for a channel tunnel came in 1802 when a French mining engineer made plans that included illumination by oil lamps, horse drawn coaches, and an artificial island in the middle for changing horses. Over the years many more proposals came and went until the dream finally came true.

When John the Baptist was asked, "Who are you?" one of his responses came from a quote from Isaiah 40:3, "The voice of one crying in the wilderness: Make straight the way of the Lord" (John 1:23). When kings traveled through their territories in ancient times, it was common for servants to "prepare the way" for his carriage or chariot by straightening out and smoothing the roadway. John sought to make the pathway to Christ clear for people to receive the Lord.

Like the precision of the Chunnel, we are called to accurately prepare the way of the Lord for people who do not know Jesus. May our lives be like a passageway for others to come to Christ.

KEY BIBLE TEXT: "Behold, I send My messenger, And he will prepare the way before Me" (Malachi 3:1).

DAY 277 Treasure You Never Lose

An Amazing Fact: *In December 2010, U.S. President Barack Obama signed the December 2010 Tax Relief Act, which established the estate tax code for fiscal years 2011 and 2012. Under this law, estates of deceased persons with values of $5 million or greater would be subject to 35 percent taxation before their remainder is passed on to beneficiaries.*

The federal estate tax has been around for a long time, although the various rates and rules of the tax keep changing. Some states also levy an estate tax in addition to the one imposed by the federal government. Moreover, some states have an additional inheritance tax levied against the amount received by the heirs, meaning a given estate might be taxed up to three times before the various governments are finished taking their shares.

The author of Ecclesiastes understood very well that a man's wealth stays behind after his death and is enjoyed by other people. The thought of his wealth, the fruit of his life's labors, belonging to someone else who could be "wise or a fool" (Ecclesiastes 2:19) deeply troubled him, so much so that he considered the accumulation of wealth as "vanity"—and this was before federal or state estate taxes or inheritance taxes!

Jesus knows how deeply many people value their worldly treasures, despite the knowledge that it remains behind after death. Instead of spending our lives accumulating wealth, which can be stolen or destroyed and which will pass to another person after we die, Jesus asks us to focus on heavenly wealth: eternal life and freedom from sin. These are the divine treasures that, once we have them, can never be lost or taxed.

KEY BIBLE TEXT: "Do not lay up for yourselves treasures on earth, where moth and rust destroy and where thieves break in and steal; but lay up for yourselves treasures in heaven, where neither moth nor rust destroys and where thieves do not break in and steal. For where your treasure is, there your heart will be also" (Matthew 6:19–21).

Eternity in Their Hearts

DAY 278

An Amazing Fact: *Our bodies run on a complex internal clock that affects more than just waking and sleeping. Almost every bodily function works according to this circadian rhythm. For example, certain medications are more effective at certain times of day: aspirin and antihistamines are best in the morning, while some chemotherapy might be best at night.*

But humans aren't the only life form with an internal clock; animals, plants, and even fungi have them too! For instance, the only time flies come out of their pupae is the early morning. Some plants will continue to move as if tracking the sun even in a dark room. Animals' heartbeats, body temperatures, and hormonal changes have a daily rhythm as well.

It seems Solomon's observation in Ecclesiastes is just as true for the animal kingdom as it is for humanity: "To everything there is a season, A time for every purpose under heaven" (Ecclesiastes 3:1). In this poetic passage, Solomon describes a cycle of life than is inescapable. The harvest can't come before planting, a new building can only be erected after the old one has been torn down, and, of course, each individual has both a "time to be born, And a time to die" (v. 2). All God's creation is orderly and logical—everything is "appropriate in its time" (v. 11 NASB).

Nevertheless, God has given humanity something that supersedes this cycle: "He has put eternity in their hearts" (v. 11). In spite of internal clocks and the inevitability of death, some part of us knows that there is something more out there. We have been created in God's image, and, without being told, something inside us knows that there is more to life than gaining and losing, keeping and throwing away. There is eternity to be won.

KEY BIBLE TEXT: "Fight the good fight of faith, lay hold on eternal life, to which you were also called" (1 Timothy 6:12).

DAY 279 Good Eyesight

An Amazing Fact: *Contrary to popular belief, bats are not blind. In fact, many bats have exceptionally good eyesight designed for low levels of light.*

Bats are nocturnal creatures and can be found all over the world, from Canada to warm tropical climates. To get around in the dark, many bats rely on a sophisticated form of sonar known as echolocation. With this detection method, bats emit short pulses of high-frequency sounds that are usually well above the threshold of human hearing. The sound waves spread out in front of the bat, striking any objects in its flight path and bouncing back in the form of an echo. By using this God-given radar, bats are able to discern the direction, distance, speed, and in some instances, the size and density of the objects around them.

Jesus surprised His disciples when they discovered the Lord's ability to see things beyond what they could see. Philip invited Nathanael to meet Jesus. Though skeptical, he went and met Christ, who said, "Behold, an Israelite indeed, in whom is no deceit!" (John 1:47). Nathaniel asked, "How do you know me?" Jesus answered, "Before Philip called you, when you were under the fig tree, I saw you" (v. 48).

God is not blind. He does not lose track of us. Jesus still sees us in the secret places of our lives. Even in the darkest night, when we cry out to our heavenly Father, the Lord sees us ... even in the dark.

KEY BIBLE TEXT: "If I say, 'Surely the darkness shall fall on me,' Even the night shall be light about me" (Psalm 139:11).

Taming the Tongue

An Amazing Fact: *Walter Mondale, a vice president under Jimmy Carter, ran for president in 1984 against incumbent Ronald Reagan. Upon accepting the Democratic Party nomination for president, he said, "Mr. Reagan will raise taxes, and so will I. He won't tell you. I just did." He proceeded to lose the election by one of the worst Electoral College landslides in history, gaining electoral votes only from Minnesota and the District of Columbia.*

The United States had a massive budget deficit under the first Reagan administration, and Mr. Mondale pledged to cut it by two-thirds. To do this, he anticipated having to raise taxes. He issued the statement at his nomination in an effort to demonstrate his honesty with the voters, implying that his opponent would not be as honest. However, it was largely understood as a pledge to raise taxes. This was one of the factors that led to his massive defeat.

What would have happened if Mr. Mondale had said something different? We will never know. The story only shows us how important it is to carefully consider the words we use and how easy it is for our tongues to get us into trouble!

The apostle James has strong words of warning about the danger of having an untamed tongue. He says it is an "unruly evil, full of deadly poison" (James 3:8). Without God's help, we can never tame our tongues, but even converted Christians must be careful. If we turn away from the Lord's guidance for even a moment, our words can harm us in unimaginable ways.

When you are tempted to speak rashly, consider saying nothing at all. Silence is often the wisest choice you can make. By holding your tongue, you may spare yourself and others from a lot of pain.

KEY BIBLE TEXT: "In the multitude of words sin is not lacking, But he who restrains his lips is wise" (Proverbs 10:19).

DAY 281 Cleansing the Temple

An Amazing Fact: *As church attendance has dropped and the population has shifted from cities to suburbs, hundreds of church buildings worldwide have been turned into community centers, museums, offices, and residences. In Pittsburgh, the St. John the Baptist Church has been turned into the Church Brew Works. Pews were shortened to fit next to tables, and merchandise is sold from the old confessional. The steel and copper brewing tanks are located on the altar.*

It would be distressing to almost anyone to see his or her old church turned into a bar. In Jesus' time, although the temple hadn't been closed or converted, the presence of the moneychangers and merchants changed the worshipful atmosphere to one of a busy marketplace. Jesus was incensed. After making a whip, he chased out the merchants with their animals and overturned the moneychanger's tables. When the Jews asked Him to give a sign of His authority to do this, Jesus spoke in a parable: "Destroy this temple, and in three days I will raise it up" (John 2:19). He wasn't talking about the physical temple, but Himself—the Jewish leaders would have Him killed, and He would be resurrected three days later. As the Messiah, He had the authority to cleanse the temple.

But the temple is not only symbolic of Jesus' mission. It is also a symbol of the Christian: "Do you not know that you are the temple of God and that the Spirit of God dwells in you?" (1 Corinthians 3:16). Just as the merchants and shoppers crowded the temple of old, sin can crowd the worship from our hearts, and only Christ can cleanse the heart.

KEY BIBLE TEXT: "The Lord, whom you seek, Will suddenly come to His temple. ... But who can endure the day of His coming? And who can stand when He appears? For He is like a refiner's fire. ... He will purify the sons of Levi. ... That they may offer to the LORD An offering in righteousness" (Malachi 3:1–3).

Twice Saved

An Amazing Fact: *A wealthy family in England took their children to the country where they went swimming. When one of their boys began to drown, the son of a local gardener bravely jumped in to rescue him. The parents were so grateful for this deed, they asked the gardener what they could do for the young hero. The gardener said that his son desperately wanted to go to college to become a doctor, but he could not afford the tuition. The family gladly agreed to pay the courageous boy's way through school for saving their son.*

Years later, after the Teheran Conference, the prime minister was stricken with pneumonia. The King of England instructed that the best doctor be found to save the gravely ill leader. The doctor chosen was Sir Alexander Fleming, the developer of penicillin and Nobel laureate, who nursed Winston Churchill back to health. "Rarely," said Churchill to Fleming, "has one man owed his life twice to the same rescuer." You see, it was Fleming who had saved Churchill from drowning in his youth.

This incredible story can remind us of something Jesus once said to a famous leader in Israel who needed to be saved. The curious teacher complimented Christ, but the Lord turned the subject to a message that Nicodemus needed to hear. "Most assuredly, I say to you, unless one is born again, he cannot see the kingdom of God" (John 3:3). The teacher missed the point. He asked, "How can a man be born when he is old? Can he enter a second time into his mother's womb and be born?" (v. 4). For a man who supposedly was a master of ideas, Nicodemus was lost on this one.

Christ was patient in leading His student to truth. "Do not marvel that I said to you, 'You must be born again'" (v. 7). We have all been "born" once. But in order to receive salvation, we must be born twice. It's like Winston Churchill's experience of being saved twice. It seems like a rare and impossible experience, but with God, it is the doorway to life everlasting. Have you been rescued from sin and been born again?

KEY BIBLE TEXT: "Whoever has been born of God does not sin, for His seed remains in him; and he cannot sin, because he has been born of God" (1 John 3:9).

DAY 283 God Is Nigh

An Amazing Fact: *In 1862, following a Civil War battle near Harrison's Landing, Virginia, during the night, Union Captain Robert Ellicombe heard the moans of a soldier who lay severely wounded on the field. Not knowing if the man was a Union or Confederate soldier, Captain Ellicombe decided to risk his life to bring the stricken man back for medical attention. Crawling on his stomach below the gunfire, the captain reached the wounded soldier and began pulling him toward his encampment.*

When the captain finally reached his own lines, he discovered it was a Confederate soldier. But the soldier was dead. The captain lit a lantern. He went numb with shock. In the dim light, he recognized the young soldier as his own son. The boy had been studying music in the south when war broke out. Without telling his father, the boy had enlisted in the Confederate Army.

The following morning, the heartbroken father asked his superiors for permission to give his son a military burial. His request for a group of Army band members was only partially granted since his son was a Confederate. Out of respect, they offered one musician. The captain chose a bugler, whom he asked to play a series of musical notes he had found on some paper stuffed in the pocket of his dead son's uniform. Later, bugler Oliv Wilcox Norton played the melody, now known as "Taps." It is now used all military funerals. Some words written for the tune go like this: "Day done, Gone the sun, From the lakes, From the hills, From the sky. All is wel safely rest. God is nigh."

God the Father lost His one and only Son, Jesus Christ, in a battle between good and evil. Our Lord chose to die "on the other side." Jesus willingly took sin upon Himself. He became, as it were, the enemy, in order that we might be set free. Our heavenly Father was heartbroken, yet God was willing to suffer this grief that we might receive the gift of eternal life. Have you received this costly gift?

KEY BIBLE TEXT: "For God so loved the world that He gave His only begotten Son, that whoever believes in Him should not perish but have everlasting life" (John 3:16).

Wealthy Oppressors

An Amazing Fact: *The rich get richer, and the poor get poorer. This is an old truism, but a 2010 study by Norton and Ariely shows that people don't realize how true it is. Researchers asked more than 5,000 respondents to identify a pie chart that looked like it represented wealth distribution in America. About 90 percent of respondents thought the top 20 percent of society owned 60 percent of the wealth, and most said the bottom 40 percent owned 8 to 10 percent. They were wildly incorrect. The top 20 percent of society actually controls 85 percent of wealth, and the bottom 40 percent—120 million Americans—control only 0.3 percent.*

Being wealthy is not a sin, but the Bible does have some strong words for those who have gotten their wealth dishonestly: "The wages of the laborers ... which you kept back by fraud, cry out; and the cries of the reapers have reached the ears of the Lord of Sabaoth" (James 5:4). Literally, that last phrase is "the Lord of Hosts" or "armies"—in other words, wealthy oppressors should watch out because the cries of the oppressed have been heard by the commander of a great army.

How does this apply to those who aren't among the richest 20 percent of Americans? Consider this: Even the poorest five percent of Americans are still wealthier than almost 70 percent of the world population. Do we contribute to the relief of the poor from their oppression? Are we content with what we have or have we been drawn to the "pleasure and luxury" of the rich? After all, James compares their luxury to the fattening of an animal for slaughter and says the inevitable corrosion of their wealth is a "witness against them" (v. 5). How much better it is to store up treasure in the heavenly bank!

KEY BIBLE TEXT: "Do not lay up for yourselves treasures on earth, where moth and rust destroy and where thieves break in and steal; but lay up for yourselves treasures in heaven, where neither moth nor rust destroys and where thieves do not break in and steal. For where your treasure is, there your heart will be also" (Matthew 6:19–21).

DAY 285 Perseverance

An Amazing Fact: *In 2005, an unlikely dance team was formed when ballerina Ma Li met bicyclist Zhai Xiaowei and the two practiced to perform together for a national dance competition. The amazing part? Ma Li is missing her right arm, and Zhai Xiaowei is missing his left leg, yet the two performed in beautiful unity!*

When ballerina Ma Li lost her right arm in a car accident as a teenager, her life was shattered. Her boyfriend left her, and she was forced to suddenly re-learn everyday physical tasks. Life was not easy, but she persevered and eventually returned to ballet. In 2005, she met Special Olympics bicyclist Zhai Xiaowei, who had lost his left leg as a child in a farming accident. The two came together and, with incredible perseverance and hours of practice, began preparing to compete nationally. Their performance was an inspiration to thousands, not only for its beauty, but also for their example of persistence in the face of difficult odds.

In scripture, the apostle James also reminds us to persevere. He points to our examples in biblical history, from the prophets to Job. "We count them blessed who endure," he says. The blessings of persistence aren't immediate. As Christians walking with God in a sinful world, we often face frustration, temptation, and even suffering. It requires perseverance to choose right in the face of wrong, especially when wrong seems like the easy choice. But God promises compassion and mercy. When we choose persistence like Mai Li and Zhai Xiaowei in the face of difficult odds, we will also see a beautiful ending to our story.

KEY BIBLE TEXT: "My brethren, take the prophets, who spoke in the name of the Lord, as an example of suffering and patience. Indeed we count them blessed who endure. You have heard of the perseverance of Job and seen the end intended by the Lord—that the Lord is very compassionate and merciful" (James 5:10, 11).

Thirsting for Truth

An Amazing Fact: *An adult human body is made up of approximately 70 percent water. The recommended water intake is about eight cups per day, though a healthy person can drink up to three gallons depending on the environment and activity. By the time a person feels thirsty, more than one percent of the total amount of water in the body has been lost.*

It is very difficult to drink too much water. Although you can be seriously harmed and even killed by drinking too much water too quickly, it is rare. Water intoxication occurs when the amount of water coming into your body dilutes the sodium levels in your bloodstream and causes an imbalance of water in your brain. This happens mostly during periods of intense athletic activity because of the rapid loss and replenishing of water.

Most people do not drink too much water; they drink too little. Everyone has been thirsty at one time or another, and many people in the world do not have enough fresh water to drink on a regular basis. Most people would love to never thirst again. This was the case with the woman at the well in Samaria.

Christ promised her a kind of water that would keep her from thirsting again. He told her that God the Father desires honest worship from the heart, not from a specific location like Jerusalem. All "true" worshipers, according to Jesus, worship "in spirit and truth." Such worship will spring forth into everlasting life. When we have Jesus, we will never spiritually thirst again.

KEY BIBLE TEXT: "And the Spirit and the bride say, 'Come!' And let him who hears say, 'Come!' And let him who thirsts come. Whoever desires, let him take the water of life freely" (Revelation 22:17).

DAY 287 A Necessity and a Pleasure

An Amazing Fact: *Prahlad Jani, a holy man from India, claims he hasn't had anything to eat or drink since 1940. To test his claims, he has been observed at a hospital in Ahmedabad, India, on two occasions. In 2010, after 15 days of reportedly not eating or drinking, researchers said he was still in good health. Medical professionals in the West have been skeptical of these claims. The estimated amount of time a person can go without food is around 30 to 40 days.*

Food is necessary to life, and most people consider eating to be one of life's pleasures. But life is much more than food. In the story of the woman at the well, Jesus' disciples left Him to rest while they went to purchase food. They returned just as the woman was leaving. When they pressed Him to eat, He made a startling statement: "My food is to do the will of Him who sent Me, and to finish His work" (John 4:34). Doing God's work was both a necessity and a pleasure for Jesus, just as food is for us. We feel satisfied after a good meal; Jesus felt satisfied after introducing someone to the Savior.

Jesus then turned His disciples' attention to the nearby fields with an object lesson. Speaking of the people of Samaria, He said, "Look at the fields, for they are already while for harvest! And he who reaps receives wages, and gathers fruit for eternal life, that both he who sows and he who reaps may rejoice together" (John 4:35, 36). Jesus was inviting His disciples to share His work and His joy in saving lost people. Jesus makes the same invitation to His disciples today, and it's a meal too tasty to miss!

KEY BIBLE TEXTS: "For what is our hope, or joy, or crown of rejoicing? Is it not even you in the presence of our Lord Jesus Christ at His coming?" (1 Thessalonians 2:19). "I delight to do Your will, O my God, And Your law is within my heart" (Psalm 40:8).

Message in a Bottle

An Amazing Fact: *In 1493, while in the West Indies, Christopher Columbus tossed a bottle overboard that contained a message for Queen Isabella I of Spain. In 1852, 359 years later, the bottle was found by the captain of an American ship and delivered to Queen Isabella II of Spain.*

Putting a message in a bottle and tossing it into the ocean is nothing new. The first record of messages in bottles is found in 310 B.C., when Greek philosopher Theophrastus conducted an experiment to show that the Mediterranean Sea was formed by the inflowing of the Atlantic Ocean.

An amazing story of a message in a bottle was a letter written by Private Thomas Hughes, a British World War I soldier. In 1914 he wrote a letter to his wife, placed it in a green ginger beer bottle, and tossed it into the English Channel. In 1999 a fisherman found the bottle. Hughes wife had died in 1979, but they located his 86-year-old daughter in New Zealand and sent her the message.

The Bible tells of a message, not in a bottle, that was written on a scroll. Jeremiah had a message from God for Jehoiakim, King of Judah. As it was read to the king, he took a scribe's knife, cut up the message, and burned it in a fire. God then instructed Jeremiah, "Take yet another scroll, and write on it all the former words ... which Jehoiakim the king of Judah has burned" (Jeremiah 36:28).

God has a message in Scripture sent for us to read. It is an old yet personal message. Rather than destroying the message, we would do well to think of it as a treasured letter in a bottle. Open the message today. Take it to heart.

KEY BIBLE TEXT: "Take a scroll of a book and write on it all the words that I have spoken to you ... that everyone may turn from his evil way, that I may forgive their iniquity and their sin" (Jeremiah 36:2, 3).

DAY 289 The Meaning of Life

An Amazing Fact: *Dr. William Breitbart of Memorial Sloan-Kettering Cancer Center of New York developed a psychological treatment program for stage 3 and 4 cancer patients called "meaning-centered psychotherapy." The purpose of the program is to help cancer patients find meaning and purpose for their lives during the time between their diagnoses and their eventual deaths, whenever that might be.*

Dr. Breitbart's program is based in part on the writings of Viktor Frankl, an Austrian psychiatrist who survived the Auschwitz concentration camp during World War II. Dr. Frankl emerged from his horrific experience with the conviction that people can endure any type of suffering if they know their lives have meaning. When applied to cancer patients, this principle helps them endure the physically and emotionally draining experiences of chemotherapy, strained relationships, and facing their own mortality.

The question of life's true meaning has perplexed many people throughout time, but the Christian should know without hesitation that his or her life has meaning. The author of Ecclesiastes spends the entire book lamenting about the futility of life, because no matter what happens during a person's life, death eventually comes. Death comes to the proud and humble alike. Death is the great equalizer. However, after 12 chapters of lamentations, the author sums up the book with a powerful declaration about life's meaning: "Let us hear the conclusion of the whole matter: Fear God and keep His commandments, For this is man's all" (Ecclesiastes 12:13).

The Bible's position on the meaning of life is simple. Our purpose is to obey God. Why? Without this, we are all subject to death and will be erased from memory forever. With God, however, we have the hope of a life to come that begins at Christ's return. Therefore, the biggest purpose of this life is to ensure, as much as possible, that our death will not be our end.

Today, why don't you ask Jesus to strengthen your relationship with Him? Having the assurance of salvation and eternal life is the greatest achievement this world has to offer.

KEY BIBLE TEXT: "And we know that all things work together for good to those who love God, to those who are the called according to His purpose" (Romans 8:28).

I Do Nothing of Myself

DAY 290

An Amazing Fact: *Rick Hoyt has participated in 68 marathons, six Ironman triathlons, and nearly 1,000 other endurance events. What's even more incredible is that Rick has cerebral palsy, is confined to a wheelchair, and speaks through a computer system that he operates with his head. What makes this possible is the other member of Team Hoyt: Dick Hoyt, Rick's father.*

Team Hoyt began when 15-year-old Rick told his dad how much he wanted to run in a five-mile benefit event for an athlete who had been paralyzed. After the race, Rick said, "Dad, when I'm running, it feels like I'm not handicapped." Now, more than 30 years and 1,000 races later, Team Hoyt is dedicated to the inclusion of the disabled in all parts of daily life. Their motto is "Yes You Can!"

Just as Rick's ability to run in a marathon is because of his relationship with his father, Jesus attributed His works to His Father: "Most assuredly, I say to you, the Son can do nothing of Himself, but what He sees the Father do; for whatever He does, the Son also does in like manner" (John 5:19). The book of John returns often to the theme of oneness between Father and Son, and Christ's sacrifice is offered as proof that the Son relies completely on the Father: "When you lift up the Son of Man, then you will know ... that I do nothing of Myself" (John 8:28).

The oneness between the Father and Son is an example of how we can be one with Christ. Jesus says, "As the Father loved Me, I also have loved you; abide in my love. If you keep My commandments, you will abide in My love, just as I have kept My Father's commandments and abide in His love" (John 15:9, 10). Though disabled by sin, with Jesus we can finish the race!

KEY BIBLE TEXT: "Let us lay aside every weight, and the sin which so easily ensnares us, and let us run with endurance the race that is set before us, looking unto Jesus, the author and finisher of our faith" (Hebrews 12:1, 2).

DAY 291 Service

An Amazing Fact: *In 1896, Sir Albert Cook journeyed to Uganda as a medical missionary. In his lifetime, he founded the oldest hospital in East Africa, trained countless native medical workers, began a midwifery school, and established a treatment center for STDs and sleeping sickness, as well as a school for medical assistants!*

In an era of discrimination and prejudice against native Africans, British medical missionary Sir Albert Cook stood out as an unusual example of equality and service. After beginning medical work in Africa, he recognized the desperate need for trained local medical workers and decided to take action. For Cook, missionary work meant recognizing the needs of those around him and doing what he could to serve them.

His actions reflect the words of the apostle James. "If a brother or sister is naked and destitute of daily food, and one of you says to them, 'Depart in peace, be warmed and filled,' but you do not give them the things which are needed for the body, what does it profit?" Sharing God's love often starts with action. In the United States, the need for food and medical attention might not be as desperate as it is overseas, but people also have emotional needs. Showing others that we care, taking an interest in their lives, and being a difference to them is frequently the best first step of evangelism.

KEY BIBLE TEXT: "If a brother or sister is naked and destitute of daily food, and one of you says to them, 'Depart in peace, be warmed and filled,' but you do not give them the things which are needed for the body, what does it profit? Thus also faith by itself, if it does not have works, is dead" (James 2:15–17).

Passing Through the Fire

An Amazing Fact: *The ancient pagan cultures of the world worshiped many false gods, often in connection with the worship of the sun. One such god was named Milcom, alternatively called Molech, Moloch, or Malcham. This god was said to require human sacrifice, often of children and preferably first-born children, as a condition of replenishing the heat and strength of the sun.*

Various accounts of ancient Milcom worship depict statues of the god hollowed-out to allow for a fire to burn within. The sacrificial child would be placed in the statue's mouth to fall into the flames—or be placed upon the statue's outstretched hands to slowly roast the child from the heat within. The cries of the anguished child would be drowned out by loud drums and music. These rituals were collectively called "passing through the fire."

Human sacrifice is abhorrent to the God of Israel. Mankind was made "in the image of God" (Genesis 1:27), and God holds human beings accountable when they shed human blood; by killing another human, they are killing the image of God. (See Genesis 9:6.)

When foretelling of His triumphant restoration of Israel after their captivity in Babylon, God not only pronounces judgment on the surrounding pagan nations, but also of their gods. He declared that "Milcom shall go into captivity With his priests and his princes together" (Jeremiah 49:3). To allow a religion to survive when it requires human sacrifice was unacceptable to the Lord.

God promises to protect His children from passing through spiritual fires as well. Like the faithful Hebrews thrown into the fiery furnace in Daniel chapter 3, God will protect His faithful followers when they face fiery trials of their own.

KEY BIBLE TEXT: "When you pass through the waters, I will be with you; And through the rivers, they shall not overflow you. When you walk through the fire, you shall not be burned, Nor shall the flame scorch you" (Isaiah 43:2).

DAY 293 Saved by a Storm

An Amazing Fact: *Camp Sumter was a Confederate prisoner-of-war camp originally designed to hold only 10,000 men; however, it was eventually used for more than 30,000. The stream running through the middle of the camp was the only water source, and it was used for everything—bathing, laundry, drinking. Plus, the latrines were only three feet away. Dysentery was rampant. In August of 1864, a heavy rainstorm washed away much of the camp's waste. Lightning struck, and a spring of pure water bubbled up. The prisoners called it "Providence Spring."*

Would it be so hard to believe that God used the storm at Camp Sumter to provide water and save the lives of many prisoners? In comparing the accounts of the storm on the Sea of Galilee, it becomes apparent that there were really two storms that evening, and God used one of them to save the disciples.

The people were so impressed by the miracle of the loaves and the fish that they were ready to make Jesus king by force (John 6:15). John says that when He realized their intentions, Jesus went away by Himself to pray. He adds that Jesus immediately "made His disciples get into the boat ... while He sent the multitude away ... they had not understood about the loaves, because their heart was hardened" (Mark 6:45, 52). The disciples got into the boat under protest because they didn't understand Jesus' refusal to accept an earthly kingdom.

The storm in their hearts was overshadowed by the storm on the sea. Their anger faded as they saw Jesus walk on water, as the wind ceased when He got into the boat, and as the boat instantly arrived on the other side. With both storms now calmed, they worshipped Him with a new spirit, saying, "Truly You are the Son of God" (Matthew 14:33).

KEY BIBLE TEXT: "By awesome deeds in righteousness You will answer us, O God of our salvation. ... You who still the noise of the seas, The noise of their waves, And the tumult of the peoples" (Psalm 65:5, 7).

Heavenly Bread

An Amazing Fact: *The fastest "bun" in the West goes to a team of bakers from Wheat Montana Farms and Bakery, who reclaimed the Guinness World Record in 1995. They harvested and milled wheat from the field and then mixed, scaled, shaped, and baked a loaf in exactly 8 minutes and 13 seconds.*

Bread is a basic staple food in the diet of most every culture in the world. Each American consumes, on average, 53 pounds of bread per year. Assuming a sandwich was eaten for breakfast, lunch, and dinner, it would take 168 days to eat the amount of bread produced from one bushel of wheat. A family of four could live 10 years off the bread produced by one acre of wheat.

One bushel of wheat will produce 73 one-pound loaves of bread. It takes nine seconds for a combine to harvest enough wheat to make about 70 loaves of bread. In 1997, Kansas wheat farmers produced enough wheat to make 36.5 billion loaves of bread, or enough to provide each person on Earth with six loaves of bread.

One day a crowd of people went looking for Jesus. The Lord had performed a miracle feeding a multitude with bread, and they wanted more. We, too, go searching for material blessings from God and miss the spiritual blessings He also intended. Jesus sought to correct their understanding of what He meant by "bread from heaven." The crowd said, "Lord, give us this bread always." Jesus said, "I am the bread of life. He who comes to Me shall never hunger, and he who believes in Me shall never thirst" (John 6:34, 35).

If you would know Christ, spiritual bread should be a basic staple of your daily diet. Take time every day to eat from the Word of God and you will never go hungry.

KEY BIBLE TEXT: "Why do you spend money for what is not bread, And your wages for what does not satisfy?" (Isaiah 55:2).

DAY 295 God's Eyes

An Amazing Fact: *To simulate one-hundredth of a second of the complete processing of even a single nerve cell from the human eye requires several minutes of processing time on a supercomputer. The human eye has 10 million or more such cells constantly interacting with each other in complex ways. This means it would take a minimum of 100 years of supercomputer processing to simulate what takes place in your eye many times every second.*

The visual cortex is the part of the brain that processes visual information. It is located in the occipital lobe in the back of the brain. Though computers are getting faster, there is still a level of complexity in processing that doesn't even come close to the fascinating combination of input from the retina into the visual cortex. The average number of neurons in an adult's primary visual cortex in each hemisphere is estimated at 140 million. In reality, your eye does not see; it is your brain that "sees!"

Let's think for a moment about the partnership of the brain and the eye. This helps us understand just how intricate these two organs work together. The brain receives images from both retinas, combines these two pictures, calculates depth of field, recognizes lines and boundaries, analyzes color, determines luminosity, controls the pupil's diameter, controls eye movement with muscles, reassembles all the pieces into a visual image that is then compared with visual memory, reverses the upside-down image, and even fills in blank spots to make sense of the picture!

As one studies the details of eye/brain function, it affirms the role of a Great Designer in the creation of vision. It would seem utterly impossible to imagine all of these pieces and processes randomly coming together by chance and working. Thank God for our eyesight!

This same loving Creator sees you. "For the eyes of the Lord are on the righteous" (1 Peter 3:12). Isn't it good to know that we are watched by One who can see all things?

KEY BIBLE TEXT: "I will instruct you and teach you in the way you should go; I will guide you with My eye" (Psalm 32:8).

Bread From Heaven

DAY 296

An Amazing Fact: *In medieval times, bakers who sold bread that was lighter than they claimed could be severely punished. In England, on a first offense, the baker would be paraded through the dirtiest streets from the town hall to his home with the loaf tied around his neck. A second offense would earn him an hour in the pillory. A third offense meant he would be unable to sell bread in that town again. But it was worse still in Turkey and Egypt—where the baker's ear would be nailed to the doorpost of his shop.*

The feeding of the 5,000 inspired the people around Jesus—they hoped He could feed them just like their forefathers had been fed with manna. But Jesus wanted them to know that eternal life is more important than physical life: "Your fathers ate the manna in the wilderness, and are dead. ... I am the living bread which came down from heaven. If anyone eats of this bread, he will live forever" (John 6:49–51).

Jesus did not want this symbol of Himself to be misunderstood, so He gave them the interpretation of His actions as well: "Most assuredly, I say to you, he who believes in Me has everlasting life. I am the bread of life. ... He who eats My flesh and drinks My blood abides in Me, and I in Him" (John 6:47, 48, 56). "Eating" Christ's flesh really meant to abide in Him—to believe in Him as their Savior from sin.

In spite of the plainness of His message, many of His disciples complained that "this [was] a hard saying; who can understand it?" (John 6:60). Many of Jesus' followers were not ready to accept this kind of Messiah. They would rather have kept their sins and got rid of the Romans. What kind of Savior do we want today?

KEY BIBLE TEXT: "And this is His commandment: that we should believe on the name of His Son Jesus Christ and love one another. ... Now he who keeps His commandments abides in Him, and He in him" (1 John 3:23, 24).

DAY 297 Beloved

An Amazing Fact: *According to one contest and survey, the longest-married couple in the United States has been married for 82 years!*

Worldwide Marriage Encounter, a faith-based marriage enrichment program, recently sponsored this contest to find the longest-married couple in America. More than 300 couples were nominated. About 150 couples had been married for 60 to 69 years; 100 couples had been married for 70 to 79 years; and three couples had been married for more than 80 years! The winning couple, Marshall and Winnie Kuykendall, has been married for 82 years. They reside in New Mexico where they celebrated their 82nd anniversary on February 14, 2011. In our divorce-ridden culture, their marriage stands out as an example of faithfulness!

In the Song of Solomon, the Shulamite woman is asked by her friends, "What is your beloved more than another beloved, O fairest among women?" In other words, how is your love different than anyone else? Her response is certain: "My beloved is white and ruddy, chief among ten thousand." She goes on to describe her beloved's beauty and ends by stating that he is her friend. There are many men, but for the Shulamite woman, hers stood out among ten thousand. She had made her choice, and her eyes did not stray from him. Her beloved was *hers,* and none could compare. It is this kind of faithfulness that God can give a marriage that has built its foundation on Him.

KEY BIBLE TEXT: "What is your beloved more than another beloved, O fairest among women? What is your beloved more than another beloved, that you so charge us? [The Shulamite:] My beloved is white and ruddy, chief among ten thousand" (Song of Solomon 5:9, 10).

Betraying Love

An Amazing Fact: *In October 1950, Soviet dictator Joseph Stalin led a persecution against the people of the Russian city Leningrad. The political leadership of the city was disbanded, and around 2,000 people were exiled or imprisoned. This treatment by a leader against his own people was brutal, but it helped him consolidate his political position.*

The reasons for Stalin's betrayal of Leningrad are varied and complex, dating back to a Nazi siege of Leningrad during World War II and even before. But regardless of his motivations, the bottom line is that Stalin turned on his own people for his personal and political gain, without being provoked.

Betrayals are sometimes baffling, and they always lead to hardship for the person or people being betrayed. Betrayal involves the abuse of trust. If someone knows he will be betrayed, he normally would not enter into a position of trust with the would-be betrayer.

But Jesus Christ was no ordinary person. As the Son of God, He was in constant connection with the Holy Spirit and often knew the future before it came to pass. In order to fulfill the prophecies concerning Himself and to demonstrate God's love for even the worst sinners, Christ chose Judas Iscariot to be one of His 12 disciples. Despite His knowledge that His association with Judas would result in death, He allowed Judas to learn the principles of heaven and salvation and treated Him with love and kindness for several years.

Like Judas, we all have a choice to accept Christ or reject Him, and Christ is willing to dwell with us and teach us even if He knows in advance that we will reject Him and betray His love for us. Today, let's ask Jesus to come into our lives and prevent Satan from leading us astray.

KEY BIBLE TEXT: "Jesus answered, 'It is he to whom I shall give a piece of bread when I have dipped it.' And having dipped the bread, He gave it to Judas Iscariot, the son of Simon. Now after the piece of bread, Satan entered him. Then Jesus said to him, 'What you do, do quickly'" (John 13:26, 27).

DAY 299 Celebrating Suffering

An Amazing Fact: *When Steven Pete was a toddler, he broke his foot at a hospital—but no one noticed until more than a day later. Steven and his brother have congenital analgesia, meaning they don't feel pain. Parenting was a monumental challenge for their mother, Janette Pete. As children, they had to be watched 24 hours a day to make sure that they didn't injure themselves. Janette recalls how she had to take away their bikes because Steven would lie on the ground and let his brother ride over him. Sometimes Steven would melt keys in electrical outlets because he liked the vibrations in his arm.*

Just as pain is a necessary warning system for the body, suffering for Christ is a sign that a person has chosen to turn their backs on sin. Before a person is converted, they spend their time seeking earthly pleasure and gain: "For those who live according to the flesh set their minds on the things of the flesh" (Romans 8:5).

When a person who used to live for pleasure begins to "suffer for righteousness' sake" it is a clear sign that they are not living the way they used to live (1 Peter 3:14). Peter puts it this way: "For he who has suffered in the flesh has ceased from sin, that he no longer should live the rest of his time in the flesh for the lusts of men, but for the will of God" (1 Peter 4:1, 2).

Christians know what the worldly do not: The rewards of living for God are worth any price. When we consider it this way, suffering for God is no longer a burden but a celebration—it is evidence of a changed life.

KEY BIBLE TEXT: "For to be carnally minded is death, but to be spiritually minded is life and peace. ... I consider that the sufferings of this present time are not worthy to be compared with the glory which shall be revealed in us" (Romans 8:6, 18).

Perfect Time

An Amazing Fact: *Physicists at the National Institute of Standards and Technology (NIST) have built the world's most accurate clock. Since aluminum is known to be a better timekeeper than mercury, the team based the clock on a single atom of aluminum. It's accurate to one second in about 3.7 billion years.*

Atomic clocks are the most accurate measurements of time in the world. Basically, they use the microwave signal that electrons give off when they change energy levels. The first atomic clock was built in 1949 and was less accurate than a quartz clock. They have become much more accurate since, especially through cooling the atoms to near absolute zero so that they move more slowly and can be measured more accurately.

The new clock is the second version of NIST's quantum logic clock. It beats the NIST-F1 cesium fountain clock—the U.S. civilian time standard—which loses a second every 100 million years. But because the international definition of the second is based on the cesium atom, cesium remains the 'ruler' for official timekeeping. The new clock is based on a single aluminum ion, trapped by electric fields and vibrating at ultraviolet light frequencies that are 100,000 times higher than the microwave frequencies used in NIST-F1.

Jesus' brothers once encouraged Him to go to Judea during the Feast of Tabernacles. Jesus knew the Jewish leaders sought to kill Him. His unbelieving brothers pressed Him to "show Yourself to the world" (John 7:4). But Jesus said, "My time has not yet come, but your time is always ready" (v. 6). Jesus had perfect time. He knew when to show Himself and when to hold back. His brothers were not driven by the same clock. The frequency by which Christ measured His steps was based on the signals of His Father in heaven.

How tuned in are you to the timing of God's plans for your life?

KEY BIBLE TEXT: "For when we were still without strength, in due time Christ died for the ungodly" (Romans 5:6).

DAY 301 An Eternal Marriage

An Amazing Fact: *According to a book about marriage published in 2007, a first marriage has a 20 percent chance of ending in divorce within five years. After 10 years, the number climbs to 33 percent.*

Marriages are supposed to be a lifelong commitment between two people, a covenant to love and support each other through thick and thin. But divorce all too often preempts these promises from being fulfilled. Though divorce has existed for thousands of years, with God even providing rules governing divorce to the ancient Hebrews, our modern society seems to have taken divorce to a new level. Some statistics suggest that as many as half of all marriages in the United States end in divorce.

God likens His relationship with His people as a marriage. Jesus is the bridegroom, and His church is the bride. The Song of Solomon reveals the depth of God's commitment to His church through poetry and figurative language and reveals the kind of relationship to God He expects His church to have. The female figure in the story represents the church, and she states plainly, "I am my beloved's, And his desire is toward me" (Song of Solomon 7:10).

Have you given your life entirely to Jesus? Can you call Him "my beloved" and honestly declare that you are His? The Bible promises already that "His desire is toward" the church. Won't you be a faithful spouse today and give your life entirely to Him?

Unlike so many marriages on Earth, the marriage between Christ and His bride will last for eternity and never come to an end. His atonement on the cross provided the means for this marriage to occur, and He invites you today to participate in this divine union. All you have to do is say yes.

KEY BIBLE TEXT: "Husbands, love your wives, just as Christ also loved the church and gave Himself for her" (Ephesians 5:25).

As Faithful as the Morning

An Amazing Fact: *The ancient Egyptians believed that the sun god Ra made a daily trip across the sky in the Boat of Millions of Years. At night, it was said that Ra was traveling in the evening boat through the underworld. Every night, Ra battled with the serpent Apep. If Ra was successful, he was reborn at sunrise. In order to keep the sun rising every morning, Egyptian priests performed complicated rituals to help Ra overcome the serpent every night.*

For the Egyptians, even something as regular as the sun rising every morning was fraught with uncertainty. Without the proper rituals, Apep might capture Ra, causing an eclipse or terrible storm. On the other hand, the God of the Israelites used the regularity of the sun to describe the endurance of His righteousness: "The LORD is righteous in her midst. ... Every morning He brings His justice to light; He never fails" (Zephaniah 3:5). The daily predictability of the sun was also a metaphor for the Messiah: "His name shall endure forever; His name shall continue as long as the sun" (Psalm 72:17).

The enduring nature of God should be a great comfort to His people—especially in times when everything else seems uncertain. The prophet of Lamentations, in the middle of his anguish over the destruction of the city of Jerusalem and the captivity of his people, sees the inevitability of morning as a reminder of God's compassion: "Through the LORD's mercies we are not consumed, Because His compassions fail not. They are new every morning; Great is Your faithfulness. ... It is good that one should hope and wait quietly For the salvation of the LORD" (Lamentations 3:22, 23, 26). Even when everything is coming apart at the seams, the sun will still rise and our God will still be faithful.

KEY BIBLE TEXT: "For His anger is but for a moment, His favor is for life; Weeping may endure for a night, But joy comes in the morning" (Psalm 30:5).

DAY 303 Lifting Power

An Amazing Fact: *Among the fastest of all insects, dragonflies have been clocked at more than 25 miles per hour. Fossils also tell us that before the flood, some dragonflies had wingspans of about 30 inches. And they're strong too! About half of their body mass is devoted to flight muscles, and they have the ability to lift more than twice their bodyweight ... a feat that no manmade aircraft has ever come near!*

Dragonflies can also take off backwards, accelerate quickly, and then stop in an instant. They can also execute an un-banked turn as if on a pivot, summersault in the heat of combat, and fly virtually any maneuver using a nearly endless combination of four wings.

Not only can the dragonfly out maneuver anything else with wings, it can also see better too! Its wrap-around compound eyes contain more than 30,000 lenses, providing a 360-degree field of view. In fact, a dragonfly can see a gnat three feet away, dart from his nest, seize and devour the prey, and then return to its perch all in about one second. The U.S. Air Force has even studied the amazing flight versatility of dragonflies in wind tunnels, hoping to uncover the secret of its incredible aerodynamic abilities.

The Bible tells us that God can lift us up and care for us under any circumstance. "Humble yourselves, therefore, under God's mighty hand, that he may lift you up in due time" (1 Peter 5:6 NIV). There is no situation too difficult, no trial too big, no problem too complex, that the Lord cannot carry you through it. God's angels surpass in strength and skill to anything you can imagine, including dragonflies. They quickly accelerate at our call and God's command to pick us up.

But there is a secret to being lifted up. It is to first bow down in humility. Unless we acknowledge our helplessness, we cannot be open to receive the incredible help that the Lord is ready to provide.

KEY BIBLE TEXT: "Cast all your anxiety on him because he cares for you" (1 Peter 5:7 NIV).

A People Remembered

An Amazing Fact: *On May 14, 1948, following a United Nations resolution the year before, the nation of Israel declared its independence and Jews from around the world had a nation of their own for the first time in nearly two millennia.*

Following the Jewish revolt against the Romans in A.D. 66, several years of warfare culminated in the destruction of the temple and the city of Jerusalem. Though smaller populations of Jewish people remained in the area for a few hundred years, the nation was never the same again. Yet against all odds, Israel was restored after World War II and remains to this day.

Israel's history is a cycle of conquest, defeat, and national restoration. Time and again, even when the nation's survival seemed totally hopeless, God delivered them from their troubles and set them up again. Even in the midst of conquest by Babylon, which was the worst horror Israel had seen until that point, when the Jews were starving and dying, God's promise to them was still, "The punishment of your iniquity is accomplished, O daughter of Zion; He will no longer send you into captivity" (Lamentations 4:22).

As Israelites by faith, Christians can have the same assurance of deliverance. God only turns away from His children because of their sins. When we repent and turn back to God, He is faithful to forgive our sins and turn back to us. As Christians, we don't look forward to the establishment of an earthly Christian kingdom. Rather, we long for the New Jerusalem, "a better, that is, a heavenly country" (Hebrews 11:16), and God will deliver us to that land.

KEY BIBLE TEXT: "And you will seek Me and find Me, when you search for Me with all your heart. I will be found by you, says the LORD, and I will bring you back from your captivity; I will gather you from all the nations and from all the places where I have driven you, says the LORD, and I will bring you to the place from which I cause you to be carried away captive" (Jeremiah 29:13, 14).

DAY 305 The Hunter vs. the Humble

An Amazing Fact: *Lions are fierce hunters. Lionesses usually hunt for the pride in coordinated groups. They cannot sustain high speeds for long, so they stalk their prey, relying on cover or darkness to reduce visibility. While lions weigh between 260 and 400 pounds, their usual prey weighs between 400 and 1,200 pounds, such as wildebeests and zebras. When prey is scarce, they have even been known to attack men and even elephants.*

The Bible warns us that the devil is like a lion: "Your adversary the devil walks about like a roaring lion, seeking whom he may devour" (1 Peter 5:8). Just as lions prefer to hunt in the dark or from nearby cover, the devil often uses deception to conquer his prey. Revelation says Satan is the one "who deceives the whole world" (Revelation 12:9). But the Christian need not be deceived: "To the law and to the testimony! If they do not speak according to this word, it is because there is no light in them" (Isaiah 8:20). We can avoid his deceptions by carefully searching the Scriptures.

Just as man-eating lions are often either sickly or desperate, the devil knows that his time is short (Revelation 12:12). He is desperate, but he can be resisted. However, it is a mistake to think that we can withstand him on our own. James makes it clear that humility is our best defense: "God resists the proud, But gives grace to the humble. Therefore submit to God. Resist the devil and he will flee from you" (James 4:6, 7). When we resist the devil by humbly submitting our will to God, the devil will flee.

KEY BIBLE TEXT: "Therefore humble yourselves under the mighty hand of God. ... Be sober, be vigilant; because your adversary the devil walks about like a roaring lion, seeking whom he may devour. Resist him, steadfast in the faith" (1 Peter 5:6–9).

Scorpions and Prophets

DAY 306

An Amazing Fact: *Under normal conditions in the wild, a scorpion appears in various shades of brown and black. But under ultraviolet light, for reasons yet to be discovered, a scorpion turns fluorescent—making it easier for scientists to study them at night.*

As a venomous insect with a tough exterior and pointy stinger, a scorpion's appearance is rather threatening. The insect is also very robust and has even survived being frozen over night; the next morning it thawed and walked away unharmed. It can even live on very little food for extended periods of time, but as a carnivorous insect able to survive in many environments, it can eat just about anything it wants.

In the Old Testament, God uses the image of a scorpion to illustrate a point to the prophet Ezekiel, who had been called to prophesy to Israel. In the face of an angry, rebellious nation, Ezekiel must have faced a great deal of fear, but God reassured him. "Do not be afraid of them or their words, though briers and thorns are with you and you dwell among scorpion. ... Do not be afraid of their words or dismayed by their looks, though they are a rebellious house."

Israel's response to God's words through His prophet was likely very threatening, so the image of a poisonous scorpion was indeed accurate! But God assured Ezekiel not to be afraid. When God calls us to a task, He will always walk beside us.

KEY BIBLE TEXT: "And you, son of man, do not be afraid of them nor be afraid of their words, though briers and thorns are with you and you dwell among scorpions; do not be afraid of their words or dismayed by their looks, though they are a rebellious house. You shall speak My words to them, whether they hear or whether they refuse, for they are rebellious" (Ezekiel 2:6, 7).

DAY 307 Submission to God's Will

An Amazing Fact: *In April 2003, Aron Ralston had a serious accident while hiking alone in Canyonlands National Park in Utah. His right arm became pinned by an 800-pound boulder that had become dislodged. After being trapped for six days, he performed a partial amputation of his arm with a multi-purpose tool to save himself. He then climbed out of the canyon, repelled down a 65-foot wall, and began an eight-mile hike to safety before he was found.*

Mr. Ralston's story is surely incredible—they even made a Hollywood film about it—but there are many other awesome stories of human survival against all odds. These stories demonstrate the amazing drive that people have to survive.

Satan knows about this drive. In the second chapter of Job, he challenges God to test his servant, claiming that "all that a man has he will give for his life" (Job 2:4). Satan was sure that Job would curse God if his life and health were threatened. To demonstrate Job's loyalty, God permits this test, demanding only that Satan "spare his life" (Job 2:6).

This heavenly controversy shows us a lot about what occurs in the spiritual realm beyond our sight. It demonstrates, for one, that bad things that occur on Earth are not caused by God but are permitted by Him. While that can be difficult to understand in the midst of calamity, we must remember that God never permitted anything to happen to Job that was beyond Job's ability to handle. Neither were Job's trials arbitrary. A heavenly purpose was served, and countless people have benefitted from the written account of Job's ordeal since that time.

When calamity strikes us, we should surrender to God's will. He is in control of all circumstances, so we are never alone in our trials. Our struggle will strengthen our faith, and that of others too.

KEY BIBLE TEXT: "No temptation has overtaken you except such as is common to man; but God is faithful, who will not allow you to be tempted beyond what you are able, but with the temptation will also make the way of escape, that you may be able to bear it" (1 Corinthians 10:13).

Learning to Cry

An Amazing Fact: *Studies show that women cry 30 to 60 times a year, while men cry 6 to 17 times per year. However, there is no difference between genders until adolescence, indicating that emotional tears are a learned response. Another study showed that infants pick up cues about how to cry from their parents' language: French infants tend to wail with a rising pitch, while German infants cry with a falling pitch.*

After viewing the abominations of the city of Jerusalem, Ezekiel sees six men with weapons come into the temple, one of whom also carries a writer's inkhorn. The Lord instructs this man to put a mark on "the foreheads of the men who sigh and cry over all the abominations" in the city (Ezekiel 9:4). He then instructs the other five to follow behind and kill everyone who isn't given the mark. This idea—that God's people mourn over the sins of others—is repeated throughout Scripture. The Psalmist records, "Rivers of water run down from my eyes, Because men do not keep Your law" (Psalm 119:136).

Jeremiah, expecting the people might not turn from their wickedness, said, "My soul will weep in secret for your pride; My eyes will weep bitterly And run down with tears, Because the LORD's flock has been taken captive" (Jeremiah 13:17). The reason for these holy tears is twofold: Not only has God's law been violated, but the sinners will soon suffer the consequences.

When Jesus wept over Jerusalem, this was His lament: "If you had known ... the things that make for your peace! But now they are hidden from your eyes. For days will come upon you when your enemies will build an embankment around you" (Luke 19:42, 43). Jesus was mourning that His people refused to know Him and that they would soon suffer the consequences of rejecting Him. Ultimately, Jesus wants His followers to learn to make His tears for His people their own.

KEY BIBLE TEXT: "My eyes overflow with rivers of water For the destruction of the daughter of my people" (Lamentations 3:48).

DAY 309 The Power of Light

An Amazing Fact: *Photosynthesis is the process by which chlorophyll-containing organisms—such as green plants, algae, and some bacteria—capture energy in the form of light and convert it to chemical energy. Virtually all the energy available for life on Earth is made available through photosynthesis.*

To produce the same amount of energy that trees and plants produce from sunlight in one day would require all the coal in 20,500,000 coal cars—or the equivalent of a coal train that wraps around the world six times! It takes almost nine minutes for a photon of light to travel the 93 million miles from the sun to the Earth, but a plant needs only a few trillionths of a second to capture the light energy, process it, and store it in the form of a chemical bond!

The bread we eat, the air we breathe, and even the wood we use to build our homes comes through this miraculous process—lasagna, lumber, and air for our lungs come from sunlight. NASA scientists have studied this process for years, knowing that it is the secret to long-term space travel. However, so far man has been unable to duplicate what God does so easily through plants!

There is another life-giving process that God has created through the Light of the World. The beams from the Son of Righteousness have energy and transforming power to change your life. "Then Jesus spoke to them again, saying, 'I am the light of the world. He who follows Me shall not walk in darkness, but have the light of life'" (John 8:12).

When Christ shines into your heart, there is a miraculous process of change. A sin-hardened heart becomes soft. A proud spirit becomes humble. A selfish life begins to think about others. Like the photosynthesis process that captures energy, we can receive life from Jesus that changes our characters. Without the Light of the World, we are without hope of change.

KEY BIBLE TEXT: "This is the message which we have heard from Him and declare to you, that God is light and in Him is no darkness at all" (1 John 1:5).

Marveling at God Through Nature

An Amazing Fact: *The driest place on Earth is the Atacama Desert near the Pacific coastline of Chile. The average rainfall in these desert mountains is less than .004 inches per year. There are even some locations within the desert where no rain has fallen for more than 400 years. Yet even in this arid wasteland, there is some water. There are some salt lakes throughout the region, and in some elevations, where the temperature never exceeds freezing, snow still remains from previous storms.*

Without the Earth's constant cycle of evaporation and rainfall, life as we know it could not exist. The natural rain cycles keep land and plants irrigated, constantly recycle water around the world, and bring precipitation to even the driest lands. It is amazing to think that the diverse and extensive balance of life on Earth, including human life, is totally dependant upon rainfall, which is beyond mankind's ability to control.

God's people know that rain does not happen by accident. God is the creator of nature, and He is in charge of executing its natural and physical laws. When water comes to even the driest places on Earth, God's people see Him at work. When Job declares that God "gives rain on the earth, And sends waters on the fields" (Job 5:10), he cites this as an example of how God "does great things, and unsearchable, Marvelous things without number" (Job 5:9).

When we behold the wonders of nature, even the rain, we can easily see the majesty of God. God loves His creation, and He takes care of it. We should be confident that God will take the same care of His children too.

KEY BIBLE TEXT: "... that you may be sons of your Father in heaven; for He makes His sun rise on the evil and on the good, and sends rain on the just and on the unjust" (Matthew 5:45).

DAY 311 61 Years Late

An Amazing Fact: *In 1946, Robert Probach wrote a prize-winning essay for the Gonzaga University's student paper. When Robert tried to collect the $20 of prize money, the editor told him to come back later. On each succeeding visit, he got the same message—come back later. He never received the prize money. By 2007, the story had become family lore, and Robert's son Gregg decided to see what would happen if he contacted the university about the matter. On May 18, 2007, the university president handed Robert a check for $512 dollars—$20 plus 61 years of interest. Robert donated the check back to the university.*

Christians have been expecting the Lord's soon return almost since Jesus' ascension nearly 2,000 years ago. Is the Lord like an unfaithful newspaper editor–promising a reward that will never come?

Peter warns his readers that in the last days "scoffers" will come saying exactly that. Peter reminds us that God has an eternal perspective on time: "With the Lord one day is as a thousand years, and a thousand years as one day" (2 Peter 3:8). The psalmist corroborates this: "For a thousand years in Your sight Are like yesterday when it is past, And like a watch in the night" (Psalm 90:4). Peter also reassures us that this apparent delay is not because He's unwilling to keep His promise or has changed His mind: "The Lord is not slack concerning His promise, as some count slackness, but is longsuffering toward us, not willing that any should perish but that all should come to repentance" (2 Peter 3:9).

God is waiting to give out the prize so that as many people as possible can receive it. In the meantime, perhaps we can do what Robert Probach did once he finally received his prize money–share it with as many people as possible.

KEY BIBLE TEXT: "Therefore the LORD will wait, that He may be gracious to you. ... For the LORD is a God of justice; Blessed are all those who wait for Him" (Isaiah 30:18).

A Great Noise

An Amazing Fact: *One of the loudest sounds in world history was the terrific volcanic explosion of Krakatoa in Indonesia in 1883. The blast's power was equivalent to about 100 megatons of dynamite and could be heard more than 3,000 miles away! The sound could be heard by the human ear over 1/10th of the earth's surface.*

As a result of this explosive eruption, more than 36,000 people were killed, and 165 coastal villages were destroyed—mostly by giant sea waves that reached heights of 120 feet. The deadly waves roared at 316 miles per hour, devastating everything in their path and hurling coral blocks ashore that weighed as much as 600 tons.

In addition, the tremendous explosion blew five cubic miles of debris into the atmosphere and settled over an area of 300,000 square miles. The massive dust cloud blocked out sunlight, plunging Jakarta (100 miles away) into complete darkness. For more than three years, the residual produced some of the most beautiful, unusual, and brilliant-red sunsets the world has witnessed. In fact, three months after the eruption, the vivid flaming sunsets were still so intense that fire engines were often called out to quench imaginary infernos.

The Bible says, "But the day of the Lord will come as a thief in the night, in which the heavens will pass away with a great noise, and the elements will melt with fervent heat; both the earth and the works that are in it will be burned up" (2 Peter 3:10). God once destroyed the Earth with water, but the Bible tells us that at the end of time it will be cleansed by fire. The Krakatoa volcano blast gives us only a small taste of that great and dreadful day.

Will you be with the Lord on that day?

KEY BIBLE TEXT: "Then I saw a great white throne and Him who sat on it, from whose face the earth and the heaven fled away" (Revelation 20:11).

DAY 313 Impaired to the Glory of God

An Amazing Fact: *Louis Braille (1809–1852) is the inventor of the Braille system of reading for the blind. Through a series of organized bumps that represent letters, this system allows people with no light perception to enjoy the same written materials as people with normal sight. Mr. Braille was not born blind, however. He became blind after accidentally stabbing himself in the eye with his father's awl.*

Though it was a personal tragedy, Mr. Braille's unfortunate accident led him to develop the Braille system, which is still widely used today. Countless numbers of blind and visually impaired people have benefitted from the invention. Thus, his accident led to a much larger good that has served many people since.

Jesus was called to heal a blind man who was begging. His disciples asked whether it was his own or his parents' sin that caused him to be blind. Christ's answer was that neither party's sin caused the blindness, but rather that he was born blind so "the works of God should be revealed in him" (John 9:3). God does not permit His children to suffer unwarrantedly. Though the blind man surely suffered throughout his life, his blindness caused Him to "see" Jesus for who He really was, and it led to his salvation. Additionally, his story has strengthened the faith of many Bible students throughout time.

When tragedy strikes, we must remember that God is bigger than the tragedy and that He must have a larger purpose in mind—or else He would have prevented the tragedy from occurring. Like Mr. Braille and the blind man in Jesus' day, we should allow God to use our suffering to His glory. Great good, and even salvation, can come from surrendering to God in the midst of hardship.

KEY BIBLE TEXT: "In that day the deaf shall hear the words of the book, And the eyes of the blind shall see out of obscurity and out of darkness" (Isaiah 29:18).

Marvelous Light

An Amazing Fact: *In Svalbard, Norway—a chain of islands halfway between mainland Europe and the North Pole—the sun stays up for just over 130 days, from late April to late August. The summer temperatures average around 40 degrees Fahrenheit, but luckily for the nearly 3,000 residents, the North Atlantic Current moderates winter temperatures, which average around 3 to 10 degrees Fahrenheit. One effect of the persistent light is that people often find it difficult to fall asleep; some also say it can cause hypomania, a persistent euphoric and energetic mood.*

In the Bible, light is a symbol of the Word of God and God's law (Psalm 119:105; Proverbs 6:23). Yet light is often used to describe the experience of salvation too. For example, the psalmist exclaims that the "LORD is my light and my salvation" (Psalm 27:1). Paul's encounter with light on the road to Damascus is another example—he saw "a light from heaven, brighter than the sun," and soon afterward he was given a mission to the Gentiles: "to turn them from darkness to light, and from the power of Satan to God, that they may receive forgiveness of sins" (Acts 26:13, 18).

Even though Paul describes God as "dwelling in unapproachable light," Revelation tells us that the New Jerusalem is "illuminated" by "the glory of God" (1 Timothy 6:16; Revelation 21:23). John helps to make the matter simple: "God is light," but it is possible for us to "walk in the light as He is in the light" when we "confess our sins" and allow Jesus "to cleanse us from all unrighteousness" (1 John 1:5, 7, 9). There's nothing that can lift the spirits better than that kind of light!

KEY BIBLE TEXT: "But you are a chosen generation, a royal priesthood, a holy nation, His own special people, that you may proclaim the praises of Him who called you out of darkness into His marvelous light" (1 Peter 2:9).

DAY 315 No Match

An Amazing Fact: *For the first 5,800 years of human history, if a man wanted to start a fire he had to rub two sticks together or make sparks with a flint and steel.*

But in 1826, John Walker, an apothecary in England, was attempting to develop a new explosive in his lab. As he stirred this new mixture of chemicals, a drop of the substance dried on the end of the stirring stick. While cleaning the crusty lump off the stick, John wiped it on the floor and it ignited.

John made several of the matches to amuse friends but somehow missed their practical value. A man named Samuel Jones saw this demonstration and realized the commercial worth and went into a booming match business. Jones called his matches "Lucifers."

Early matches had a number of problems. The flame was unsteady, and the initial reaction was quite violent. Also, the odor produced by the burning match was unpleasant. Lucifers reportedly could ignite explosively, sometimes throwing sparks a considerable distance. The other problem with early matches was the use of white phosphorus, which would stick to the skin. It was toxic and, therefore, banned from use in many countries.

Lucifer also refers to a beautiful and powerful angelic being who fell from heaven. Ezekiel 28 describes this brilliant cherub: "You were the anointed cherub who covers; I established you; You were on the holy mountain of God; You walked back and forth in the midst of fiery stones. You were perfect in your ways from the day you were created, Till iniquity was found in you" (vs. 14, 15). It says of the destruction of this being, "Therefore I brought fire from your midst; It devoured you, And I turned you to ashes upon the earth In the sight of all who saw you" (v. 18).

Someday Lucifer, the toxic and fallen angel, "shall be no more forever" (v. 19). He will no longer throw sin around at "a considerable distance." His flame will be extinguished for all time.

KEY BIBLE TEXT: "How you are fallen from heaven, O Lucifer, son of the morning!" (Isaiah 14:12).

Loving the World

An Amazing Fact: *The Federal Aviation Administration is in charge of many things relating to air travel in the United States. Among its duties is providing statistics about air travel to both the general population and the airlines. In 2004, the group increased its estimate of the weight of an average male passenger from 170 to 184 pounds, underscoring the general trend toward obesity in the American public.*

Obesity doesn't typically happen by accident. Although there are legitimate medical conditions that result in excessive weight gain, most obesity results from people's choices to eat unhealthy foods in large quantities. Obesity can result in serious medical conditions that can threaten lives and raise medical costs for the people affected and, through increased insurance rates to compensate for the high cost of medicine, the entire society.

The Bible outlines very specific dietary guidelines for God's people to follow. These guidelines don't exist as a test or as a means to earn salvation, but rather because God cares about His people and wants them to be healthy. Additionally, Paul challenges believers to understand, "Do you not know that you are the temple of God and that the Spirit of God dwells in you?" (1 Corinthians 3:16). When we take poor care of our bodies, we disallow God's Spirit from dwelling within us.

Though our physical health will likely improve if we follow God's dietary principles, we can follow a more general principle for all areas of our lives. First John 2:15, 16 tell us not to "love the world or the things in the world, because those things, the lust of the flesh, the lust of the eyes, and the pride of life" are not from the Father. If we allow God to control our appetites for worldly things, including food, He will improve our lives and draw us into a closer relationship with Him.

KEY BIBLE TEXT: "Adulterers and adulteresses! Do you not know that friendship with the world is enmity with God? Whoever therefore wants to be a friend of the world makes himself an enemy of God" (James 4:4).

DAY 317 One Shepherd

An Amazing Fact: *Today, protecting sheep from wolves is not simple because wolves are endangered. In the European Union, it is illegal to shoot a wolf without special permission. Even then, the wolf must be especially dangerous, and shootings are limited to six wolves per year. In one case, authorities authorized killing a wolf that had eaten 10 sheep and killed another 62 by frightening them over the edge of a ravine. In America, the grey wolf was removed from the endangered species list in 2011. American ranchers have always been able to shoot a wolf attacking their flock, but now they can shoot a wolf on sight.*

In the Bible, wolves symbolize various dangers. Jesus warned His disciples that He was sending them out into the world "as sheep in the midst of wolves," or men who would persecute them (Matthew 10:16). Jesus also called false prophets wolves: "Beware of false prophets, who come to you in sheep's clothing, but inwardly they are ravenous wolves" (Matthew 7:15). While instructing the overseers of the Ephesian church, Paul warned of another problem: shepherds behaving like wolves. "After my departure savage wolves will come in among you. ... Also from among yourselves men will rise up, speaking perverse things, to draw away the disciples after themselves" (Acts 20:28–30).

Nevertheless, Jesus will not leave His sheep at the mercy of ravenous wolves or untrustworthy shepherds. God promises that He will gather together all the scattered sheep: "And I will bring them out from the peoples and gather them from the countries, and will bring them to their own land. ... I will establish one shepherd over them, and he shall feed them ... You are My flock, the flock of my pasture; you are men, and I am your God" (Ezekiel 34:13, 23, 31). That one shepherd is Jesus, "the good shepherd" (John 10:11).

KEY BIBLE TEXT: "And other sheep I have which are not of this fold; them also I must bring, and they will hear My voice; and there will be one flock and one shepherd" (John 10:16).

Great and Mighty Things

An Amazing Fact: *The blue whale is a giant sea creature that eats tons of food a day but has no teeth, lives in the ocean all its life but breathes air, and is the largest of Earth's animals but is endangered. It's also smaller than the head of a pin when it's conceived, but 11 months later it will weigh more than two tons and be 24 feet long!*

For the first eight months, the mother provides its only food. Her milk is so rich that the baby blue whale can gain up to nine pounds in one hour. After that, the blue whale will grow longer than a greyhound bus. Blue whales eat mostly a shrimp-like creature called krill. An adult whale will eat one to two tons a day.

The blue whale makes a unique four-note call to signal other whales of danger. At more than 150 decibels, this call is the loudest sound made by any living creature and can be heard hundreds of miles away.

Job was a man who called on God in his despair. When his friends tried to give him advice, he said, "But now ask the beasts, and they will teach you. ... And the fish of the sea will explain to you. Who among all these does not know That the hand of the Lord has done this, In whose hand is the life of every living thing. And the breath of all mankind?" (Job 12:7–10).

When Job felt like giving up (with no help from his friends), he wrote, "Then call, and I will answer; Or let me speak, then You respond to me" (v. 22). There is a call we can make to God in prayer. It doesn't need to be the loudest for the Lord to respond.

KEY BIBLE TEXT: "Call to Me, and I will answer you, and show you great and mighty things, which you do not know" (Jeremiah 33:3).

DAY 319 Loyalty Unto Death

An Amazing Fact: *Thomas Becket was the Archbishop of Canterbury under the reign of King Henry II, and the two men didn't get along. Under orders supposedly from the king, several knights assassinated Becket in 1170. According to an eyewitness account, Becket was struck three times before declaring, "For the name of Jesus and the protection of the Church, I am ready to embrace death."*

Unfortunately, the history of the Christian church is saturated with the blood of martyrs. Christians were persecuted for as long as the church existed, first by the Jews, then the Romans, and eventually even from within the church itself during the Dark Ages. Though these deaths are tragic, the martyrs' last words often reveal an unwavering faith in the God they served, for whom they ultimately gave their lives.

Whether we face death from violence or disease, we should stand firm in the knowledge that Christ remembers us and will raise us from the dead when He returns to Earth. Even before the days of Jesus, the patriarch Job demonstrated this type of faith by declaring boldly, "Though [God] slay me, yet will I trust Him. Even so, I will defend my own ways before Him" (Job 13:15). Job had this faith even before the cross; how much more should we have this kind of faith looking back on the cross!

The Bible promises a time of tribulation before Jesus returns, and living during this time will not be easy. But even if God calls us to die for our faith, we have hope. God promises to remember every time a person sheds another's blood. (See Genesis 9:6.) He also promises justice for His fallen children and everlasting life as a reward for remaining true to Him.

KEY BIBLE TEXT: "And they overcame him by the blood of the Lamb and by the word of their testimony, and they did not love their lives to the death" (Revelation 12:11).

Feuding in Church

An Amazing Fact: *The Beulah Baptist Church of Gibson, Louisiana, spent the spring of 2011 embattled in a feud that resulted in a restraining order and an arrest. The seven members against whom the restraining order was filed claim that the church was violating its charter by using pastoral appointments to fill church offices instead of election by the trustee board. They also allege that the pastor is not properly accounting for church finances or allowing member oversight.*

The conflict between the seven members and the rest of the church became so intense, the pastor filed a restraining order to prevent the seven from harassing, threatening, and following other members. At a court hearing for the restraining order, a judge admonished church members to resolve their disputes in a Christian manner. Nevertheless, days later, one of the seven was arrested after making multiple phone calls to and visiting another member's place of work.

Church feuds are not as uncommon as they should be—churches feud with other community groups or businesses, with other churches, and even within themselves. Even more common still are strained relationships between members and hurt feelings kept under wraps. The apostle John has a blunt message regarding this behavior: "We know that we have passed from death to life, because we love the brethren. He who does not love his brother abides in death" (1 John 3:14). John calls us from protecting our own interests to self-sacrifice: "By this we know love, because He laid down His life for us. And we also ought to lay down our lives for the brethren" (1 John 3:16). Self-sacrificing love is so important that Jesus told the disciples that the world would know they were His disciples by their love for each other (John 13:35). Can the world tell if you are His disciple?

KEY BIBLE TEXT: "My little children, let us not love in word or in tongue, but in deed and in truth" (1 John 3:18).

DAY 321 Re-entry

An Amazing Fact: *The Space Shuttle's main engines weighed less than 7,000 pounds apiece, but each one put out almost a half-million pounds of thrust. Pound for pound, they were the world's most powerful rocket engines. In fact, each engine was as powerful as seven Hoover Dams! After the solid rocket boosters fell away, these three main engines clustered at the rear end of the orbiter continued to provide thrust. They fired for only eight minutes for each flight—just until the shuttle reached orbit.*

However, for its fiery reentry, the underbelly of the orbiter was protected by 24,000 heat-resistant tiles that had to be installed individually by hand. These silicate fiber tiles were incredibly lightweight, about the density of balsa wood, but could last 100 missions before requiring replacement. Each tile could dissipate heat so quickly that a white-hot tile with a temperature of 2,300 degrees could be taken from an oven and held in bare hands seconds later without injury!

John describes an incredible "re-entry" of Jesus' friend, Lazarus, who had died. "Jesus said, 'Take away the stone.' Martha, the sister of him who was dead, said to Him, 'Lord, by this time there is a stench, for he has been dead four days.' Jesus said to her, 'Did I not say to you that if you would believe you would see the glory of God?'" (John 11:39, 40).

Shuttle blastoffs and reentries were glorious to behold. But nothing will match the spectacular coming of Jesus when He shall call forth all the saints from their graves. Those who are dead in Christ will "rise" again and be lifted up to heaven. The power to raise the dead cannot compare to the world's most powerful engines.

KEY BIBLE TEXT: "Now when He had said these things, He cried with a loud voice, 'Lazarus, come forth!'" (John 11:43).

The Glory of the Lord

An Amazing Fact: *The temple of God in Jerusalem was destroyed by the kingdom of Babylon when it conquered Judah. It was rebuilt after the Jewish exile ended, but the new temple was smaller and less grand than the former. Herod the Great ordered a massive renovation of the temple, which began in about 20 B.C., and construction continued until about A.D. 64. However, the temple was once again destroyed, this time by the Romans, in A.D. 70.*

The Bible says that the visible presence of God, sometimes called the Shekhinah glory, was manifest above the portable sanctuary the Israelites had during their wanderings in the desert and in the early days of the nation of Israel; that presence also dwelled at the temple built by Solomon. The prophet Ezekiel sees this presence depart from the temple in a vision he has prior to the destruction by Babylon.

The Bible does not record the presence of God returning to the temple even after it is rebuilt. Though Jesus came into Herod's temple during His ministry, there is no record of a pillar of cloud or fire resting on any temple after the days of Babylon.

Yet Ezekiel has another vision of a rebuilt temple that runs through most of the latter part of his book. In chapter 43, he sees the "glory of the God of Israel" return to this temple. That there is no biblical or historical evidence of this happening demonstrates that the temple Ezekiel saw in vision never became a reality.

However, the Bible does promise that the presence of God will again dwell with His people. In the New Jerusalem, the city of heaven, God's people will dwell with God Himself forever. Though Ezekiel's vision never became a reality on Earth, it acts as a prophecy of the heavenly kingdom to come.

KEY BIBLE TEXT: "But I saw no temple in it, for the Lord God Almighty and the Lamb are its temple. The city had no need of the sun or of the moon to shine in it, for the glory of God illuminated it. The Lamb is its light" (Revelation 21:22, 23).

DAY 323 Living Water

An Amazing Fact: *Water is essential to life and to nearly all functions of the human body. Water helps to keep tissues in the eyes, nose, and mouth moist. It helps protect body organs and lubricate joints. Water dissolves the minerals and nutrients in food, making them accessible to the body, and water also helps carry those nutrients throughout the body. Recent studies have shown that drinking five or more glasses of water per day can even reduce the risk of heart attack by around 50 percent over drinking two or fewer glasses of water.*

It is no secret that people, animals, and plants must have water to live. In Ezekiel's vision, a man "with the appearance of bronze" showed him a stream of water flowing from the temple that is even more necessary to life than the water from a faucet. When the stream, which quickly became a river, reached the ocean, the waters of the sea were healed. Along the banks of the river grew trees that never withered and bore new fruit every month. Most amazingly, the man told Ezekiel that "everything will live wherever the river goes" (Ezekiel 47:9).

Jesus wants His people to be sustained by "water From the wells of salvation" (Isaiah 12:3). Once we experience the water of salvation, a new miracle occurs. Jesus said, "He who believes in Me, as the Scripture has said, out of his heart will flow rivers of living water" (John 7:38). Ezekiel's stream, at first only ankle deep, kept getting wider and deeper until it was "a river that could not be crossed" (Ezekiel 47:5). Jesus wants His gospel message to be spread the same way—from person to person until the whole world has access to His living water.

KEY BIBLE TEXT: "How precious is Your lovingkindness, O God! Therefore the children of men put their trust under the shadow of Your wings. ... And You give them drink from the river of Your pleasures. For with You is the fountain of life" (Psalm 36:7–9).

His Blood Ran

DAY 324

An Amazing Fact: *Do you know why barbershops have a red, blue, and white spiral out front? It's not from patriotic roots. During the Middle Ages, dentistry in Europe was practiced by "barber-surgeons." These community professionals served the townspeople by performing a wide variety of services, which ranged from cutting hair, extracting teeth, and bloodletting.*

For hundreds of years, physicians would bleed people with fevers believing they had too much blood. Sometimes light bleeding was accomplished by applying leaches! For more intense bleeding, the patient would hold the top of a ceramic pillar with their hand while the physician made an incision in the wrist, allowing the blood to drain down the pillar where they measured it in a basin. Physicians would examine the blood's color and quality as it ran spiraling down the pole into the basin. The reason for the two colors on the pole is because veins are generally blue and arteries red.

Gradually, dentistry and surgery were taken over by specialists and the barber was left with his scissors and comb. But the spiral pole still endures. It makes us shudder to think that people once believed bloodletting would bring healing!

Yet John writes, "This is He who came by water and blood—Jesus Christ; not only by water, but by water and blood. ... And there are three that bear witness on earth: the Spirit, the water, and the blood; and these three agree as one" (1 John 5:6–8).

Some Bible students believe water symbolized the beginning of Christ's ministry with baptism in the Jordan and that blood symbolized His final work on the cross of Calvary. The blood of Christ, which ran down the cross, has most definitely brought healing forgiveness to our world. Because Jesus let His own precious blood flow, we may have eternal life. Christ's blood bears witness. Remember this the next time you see a barber's pole.

KEY BIBLE TEXT: "Then He took the cup, and gave thanks, and gave it to them, saying, 'Drink from it, all of you. For this is My blood of the new covenant, which is shed for many for the remission of sins'" (Matthew 26:27, 28).

DAY 325 Step It Up

An Amazing Fact: *There are 18 doctors in the United States with the name Dr. Doctor; there is also a Dr. Surgeon; Dr. Rash, a dermatologist; Dr. Couch, a psychiatrist; and an anesthesiologist by the name of Dr. Gass.*

It seems popular these days to do whatever it takes to be healthy. Simply starting out the day with a cereal box in view can give you information like "Whole Grain Guaranteed;" "Low Fat, Naturally Cholesterol Free, Excellent Source of Fiber, No Salt Added;" "Whole grains have powered people from London to Los Angeles and everywhere in between;" "Add banana and almonds for more calcium and Vitamin E—staying full until lunchtime is easy with this fuel efficient combo!" The media is full of all kinds of advice on diet, exercise, rest, and many other ways to maintain health and fitness, including medications meant to cure any ill.

In the first two chapters of the book of Daniel, the prophet and his three friends made a proposal and stuck to a healthy diet in the king's palace. They were judged to be healthier and better nourished than any of the other young men who ate the royal food. Why not make your own plan to encourage improved health of body and mind? God is not going to work any miracle to counteract your bad habits. It takes work on your part to stay fit.

Keep in mind the words of David: "I will praise You, for I am fearfully and wonderfully made" (Psalm 139:14). We need to stay that way! "Do you not know that you are the temple of God and that the Spirit of God dwells in you?" (1 Corinthians 3: 16, 17). If we want God to dwell in us, we need to make sure we're providing Him a well-maintained home. Plus, there will be fewer visits to Dr. Doctor, Dr. Surgeon, Dr. Rash, Dr. Gass, and Dr. Couch!

KEY BIBLE TEXT: "Beloved, I pray that you may prosper in all things and be in health, just as your soul prospers" (3 John 1:2).

Nebuchadnezzar the Proud

An Amazing Fact: *Tarquin the Proud was the last king of Rome. He became king by murdering his father-in-law, Servius Tullius. He earned the name "Tarquin the Proud" by refusing to bury Tullius' body and killing several prominent senators known to have supported Tullius. The tyranny that characterized his reign was passed on to his son, Sextus Tarquinius. At his father's suggestion, Sextus brought down an enemy city by falsely condemning leading citizens to death. The pride and cruelty of this father-son duo was eventually their downfall. Sextus' rape of a beautiful kinswoman led to a revolt that resulted in the overthrow of Tarquin the Proud and the creation of a Roman republic.*

Like Tarquin, Nebuchadnezzar's pride is legendary. He created a statue similar to the statue in his dream that predicted the fall of his empire—only instead of a head of gold, the entire image was gold. (See Daniel chapters 3 and 4.) Nebuchadnezzar was claiming his kingdom would continue forever despite God's revelation to the contrary. God gave him a dream warning of the consequences of his pride: "Your dwelling shall be with the beasts of the field ... till you know that the Most High rules in the kingdom of men" (Daniel 4:25).

Nevertheless, Nebuchadnezzar returned to his prideful ways, saying, "Is not this great Babylon, that I have built ... for the honor of my majesty?" (Daniel 4:30). Only after spending seven years eating grass could Nebuchadnezzar recognize that "[God] does according to His will in the army of heaven And among the inhabitants of the earth" (Daniel 4:35).

Nebuchadnezzar's experience needn't be our own. Though "God resists the proud," He also "gives grace to the humble" (1 Peter 5:5). Just as Nebuchadnezzar needed to learn that God was in control of his kingdom, we need to learn to give God control of our lives. Let's learn to echo Nebuchadnezzar's prayer, as Jesus taught His disciples to do: "Your will be done On earth as it is in heaven" (Matthew 6:10).

KEY BIBLE TEXT: "Pride goes before destruction, And a haughty spirit before a fall. Better to be of a humble spirit with the lowly, Than to divide the spoil with the proud" (Proverbs 16:18, 19).

DAY 327 Liberty Stands

An Amazing Fact: *The Statue of Liberty is one of the most honored symbols in America. It came to the United States after 20 years of dedication and at a cost of more than $4 million. French sculptor Frederic Bartholdi was inspired to build the enormous monument after seeing the colossi in Egypt. After examining different candidates, he chose his mother as the statue's model.*

The statue was built in France, then dismantled and packaged into 200 massive crates for transport to New York. A French warship transported the gift across the Atlantic. On the way, a terrible storm threatened to sink the vessel. The crew begged the captain to dump the heavy crates into the sea to lighten the load, but the captain responded, "This ship will sink before I give up liberty."

"Liberty" stands at 151 feet tall. From the bottom of the pedestal to the tip of the torch, it rises 305 feet high. Her hand is more than 16 feet long, and her nose is 4-½ feet in length. Over 60,000 pounds of copper and 250,000 pounds of steel were used to create her.

Symbolism is wrapped all around the statue. From the torch that is to light the world with freedom, to the tablet in her hand that is inscribed with the date July 4, 1776, to the broken chains at her feet representing release from bondage, Lady Liberty has welcomed travelers to the land of freedom since 1886.

Job longed for freedom from his sorrow and pain. He wrote, "Oh, that my words were written! Oh, that they were inscribed in a book! That they were engraved on a rock With an iron pen and lead, forever!" (Job 19:23, 24). Then out of his deep anguish rose faith: "For I know that my Redeemer lives, And he shall stand at last on the earth" (v. 25).

Like Lady Liberty who stands on Bedloe's Island in New York Harbor, someday Christ will stand above the broken chains of sin and proclaim liberty from the shackles of death. Will you accept Jesus as Lord of your life?

KEY BIBLE TEXT: "Stand fast therefore in the liberty by which Christ has made us free, and do not be entangled again with a yoke of bondage" (Galatians 5:1).

Like a Lion

An Amazing Fact: *A lion's roar can be heard five miles away and can even reportedly raise dust.*

Lions have always been admired for their power, strength, and courage. But along with their voices, their hearing is also so good that they can hear prey from a distance of one mile. Moreover, a lion's sense of smell is so sharp that it can tell if prey is nearby or even ascertain how long ago it was in the area. Finally, the eyesight of a lion is five times better than that of a human's.

There were many lions in the area of Palestine during Bible times, and the Bible tells many stories about how dangerous and aggressive they were, killing both people and cattle. "Like as the lion and the young lion roaring on his prey, when a multitude of shepherds is called forth against him, he will not be afraid of their voice, nor abase himself for the noise of them" (Isaiah 31:4 KJV). Our adversary, the devil, is also compared to a roaring lion. Lions have been known to make hidden dens, covered by branches and grass, where unsuspecting animals, wandering by, are attacked and eaten. Psalm 10:9 says, "He lies in wait secretly, as a lion in his den; He lies in wait to catch the poor; He catches the poor when he draws him into his net."

During Daniel's time, the Babylonians used fire for punishment (the fiery furnace), but the Persians used lions. Even though Daniel was far away from his beloved home, he trusted implicitly in his God. Like Daniel, even though we can at times feel surrounded by the agents of the enemy, we can also trust in God's power to keep us from both physical and spiritual harm. Let us do our part, however, to keep as far away as we can from the lion's den.

KEY BIBLE TEXT: "No lion shall be there, Nor shall any ravenous beast go up on it; It shall not be found there. But the redeemed shall walk there" (Isaiah 35:9).

DAY 329 Rich in Generosity

An Amazing Fact: *In America, the poor tend to out give the rich in terms of the percentage of their income. This is also the segment of society that relies more on public transportation and rent their homes. They tend to be students, elderly, women, minorities, and recent immigrants.*

People have proposed many reasons for the poor's generosity. For one, the poor know what it's like to need help, aren't afraid of poverty, and are satisfied with what little they have. But researchers say that faith is probably the biggest factor. Poor people are more likely to attend church, and churchgoers give more to secular and religious charities. The poor are also more likely to attend tithing churches than non-tithing churches.

Third John introduces a man named Gaius. Gaius was a very common name, and little is known about the man John writes about. But John's letter makes two things clear. First, Gaius "[walked] in the truth" (3 John 3). Second, Gaius was generous and hospitable. Although he doesn't give specifics, John indicates that Gaius helped traveling missionaries. On the other hand, Third John also introduces Diotephes—a proud man given to slandering the apostles. Diotephes was not generous to traveling missionaries: "He himself does not receive the brethren, and forbids those who wish to, putting them out of the church" (3 John 10). Even during the apostles' time, faithful Christians were more generous than others—but let's not allow the facts to pat us on the back. After all, John didn't just commend Gaius' generosity; he encouraged him to continue in it. How can you continue in generosity and hospitality?

KEY BIBLE TEXT: "But this I say: He who sows sparingly will also reap sparingly, and he who sows bountifully will also reap bountifully. So let each one give as he purposes in his heart, not grudgingly or of necessity; for God loves a cheerful giver" (2 Corinthians 9:6, 7).

The Devourer

An Amazing Fact: *The smallest animal in the world also has the biggest appetite—the mouse-like shrew. One variety in northern Europe, called the "least" shrew, which is rarely longer than an inch-and-a-half, can consume the equivalent of its own weight every three hours. In fact, the appetite of the shrew is so voracious and its metabolism so fast that if they do not eat for two hours, they might starve to death.*

Shrews have small eyes and usually poor eyesight but are very active animals, because each day a shrew must consume 80 to 90 percent of its body weight to survive. In its desperate quest to feed its ravenous hunger, the little shrew will attack and eat almost anything that moves—including creatures twice its size! Their fierce reputation is probably one reason it symbolizes feistiness in literature, such as in Shakespeare's *Taming of the Shrew.*

The Bible speaks of a feisty creature much larger than the shrew. It was a beast that came up out of the sea. In vision, Daniel describes it: "After this I saw in the night visions, and behold, a fourth beast, dreadful and terrible, exceedingly strong. It had huge iron teeth; it was devouring" (Daniel 7:7). Later in the chapter it says, "The fourth beast shall be a fourth kingdom on earth, which shall be different from all other kingdoms, and shall devour the whole earth" (v. 23).

More ferocious than a giant shrew, this beast devours whatever is in its path. Out of its head grew ten horns, then from among them one horn that "was making war against the saints, and prevailing against them" (v. 21). So thank God for the next verse: "Until the Ancient of Days came, and a judgment was made in favor of the saints of the Most High" (v. 22).

KEY BIBLE TEXT: "But the court shall be seated, and they shall take away his dominion, to consume and destroy it forever" (Daniel 7:26).

DAY 331 The Blessing of Pain

An Amazing Fact: *Leprosy is an insidious disease that attacks the peripheral nerves, resulting in numbness and loss of pain sensors in the extremities.*

One of the common myths regarding leprosy is that it is the direct cause of the loss of fingers, toes, hands, feet, and occasionally even a nose. However, the loss of these extremities is a secondary result of the disease. Since leprosy attacks the peripheral nerves, the body no longer receives pain signals from these extremities, and injuries such as burns and cuts are not properly recognized and cared for. The result is often infection, which can then progress to the death and eventual loss of the extremity.

Many would love to live in a world without pain. This is reflected in the fact that one of the fundamental values of our modern society is the avoidance of pain—pain-free dentistry, pain-free surgery, pain-free living. As much as we don't like it, however, pain for now is our friend, at least to alert us when there is a problem in our bodies.

In Daniel 8, the Bible describes in detail the cunning and deceitful actions and attributes of the little horn power. Then verse 25 gives this amazing warning to God's people, "By peace (he) shall destroy many." The word "peace" can also be translated "prosperity."

One of the greatest dangers of God's people is to believe that "I'm OK; you're OK," when in fact we don't feel our great need. After the Lord told Jeremiah that every one of the children of Israel was given to covetousness and "from the prophet even to the priest, everyone deals falsely," He said, "They have also healed the hurt of My people slightly, saying, 'Peace, peace!' when there is no peace" (Jeremiah 6:13, 14). We desire honesty from a physician after a physical examination, don't we? Would we want anything different from our loving heavenly Father? Sometimes the honesty of our friends might seem painful to us, but we are admonished "Faithful are the wounds of a friend" (Proverbs 27:6). True friends have the courage to tell us the truth about our wrongdoing.

KEY BIBLE TEXT: "Let the righteous strike me; It shall be a kindness. And let him rebuke me; It shall be as excellent oil; Let my head not refuse it" (Psalm 141:5).

True Religious War

An Amazing Fact: *In 1850, Hong Xiuquan started a conflict that erupted into a widespread Chinese civil war. Xiuquan believed he was the brother of Jesus, selected to overthrow the Qing Dynasty and establish the heavenly kingdom. During the 14-year war, known as the Taiping Rebellion, approximately 20 million people died, making it one of the deadliest wars in history. Incredibly, Xiuquan named his short-lived kingdom the Heavenly Kingdom of Great Peace.*

The Taiping Rebellion is one of many religious wars that non-believers point to as a reason the world would be better without religion. Yet Jude exhorts us to "contend earnestly for the faith" (Jude 3). Is Jude encouraging religious war?

Lest we misunderstand it, Jude quickly explains: False doctrine had been creeping into the church "unnoticed" (Jude 4). How should the church handle the promoters of these false doctrines? Jude gives this answer: The Lord saved Israel and destroyed the Egyptians, the Lord will judge the angels who defected, and the Lord sent fire on Sodom. Jude suggests we follow Michael the archangel's example—when contending with the devil himself, He said only "The Lord rebuke you" (Jude 9).

If we aren't to fight with a religious war, how should we fight? Jude includes these instructions: "But you, beloved, building yourselves up on your most holy faith, praying in the Holy Spirit, keep yourselves in the love of God, looking for the mercy of our Lord" (Jude 21). In addition, we must "Be merciful to those who doubt; save others by snatching them from the fire" (Jude 22, 23 NIV). In true religious war, we fight by remaining in Christ, offering mercy to those weak in faith, and striving for the salvation of others.

KEY BIBLE TEXT: "As you therefore have received Christ Jesus the Lord, so walk in Him, rooted and built up in Him and established in the faith, as you have been taught, abounding in it with thanksgiving. Beware lest anyone cheat you through philosophy and empty deceit, according to the tradition of men, according to the basic principles of the world, and not according to Christ" (Colossians 2:6–8).

DAY 333 The Smell of Prayer

An Amazing Fact: *One of the three gifts offered to Jesus shortly after His birth was frankincense. It is a fragrant resin that grows in some of the world's harshest places—Oman, Yemen, and Somalia. The spindly trees themselves are actually disappointing to behold. They are lowly, twisted, thorny things with fat prickly branches spreading out into small crinkly leaves.*

Yet as soon as an incision is made into the silvery bark, brilliant drops of white resin ooze from the wound. These drops, known as luban, are left on the tree for two weeks to dry. Then the little pearls are gathered in the early morning. From Rome to India, frankincense was deemed one of the most prized substances in the civilized world. It was essential for a host of uses, ranging from religious to cosmetic to medicinal. Besides its lovely fragrance, frankincense is attributed with healing powers, which range from treatment of depression and irritability to ailments such as eczema.

The frankincense trade peaked in the Roman Empire in the first century. (Nero burned it by the ton at religious ceremonies.) To supply the copious need, this rare resin had to be carried overland via long and grueling journeys. Eventually, incense caravans grew in size to 3,000 camels in a single procession. Even today, satellite images reveal faint traces of these ancient caravan trails carved in the wilderness. The trade was so lucrative that Alexander the Great planned to invade Arabia in an effort to control and tax the roads, a plan thwarted only by his death.

For religious purposes, many great civilizations in the ancient world believed that prayers could only be carried to heaven in the smoke of sacred incense. It was also used in the sanctuary service to depict prayers rising before the God of Israel.

One of the most beautiful prayers in Scripture is found in Daniel 9:3–19. Read through this passage and make it your own prayer to the Lord. Let it rise like incense up to heaven, a sweet savor before God.

KEY BIBLE TEXT: "And the smoke of the incense, with the prayers of the saints, ascended before God from the angel's hand" (Revelation 8:4).

Wandering Planets

An Amazing Fact: *A rogue planet is a planetary object that has been moved from its system and is no longer bound by the gravitational forces of a star. Some astronomers actually believe there might be twice as many Jupiter-sized rogue planets as there are stars.*

The concept and understanding of planets have developed throughout history and have expanded to include worlds not only in our solar system, but also in hundreds of other solar systems. Trying to define what a "planet" is has led to much scientific controversy.

The five classical planets visible to the naked eye have been known since ancient times. They have had a large impact on mythology, religious cosmology, and ancient astronomy. Thousands of years ago astronomers noticed how certain lights moved across the sky in relation to the other stars. Ancient Greeks called these lights "wandering stars." The Greek word plan toi means "wanderers," from which today's word "planet" was derived.

In the short New Testament book of Jude, the writer warns of false teachers who were leading Christians astray. They might have preached about freedom and grace, but their lives showed that they didn't really believe in Jesus Christ. They were immoral and destructive. Jude describes them like this: "They are clouds without water, carried about by the winds; late autumn trees without fruit, twice dead, pulled up by the roots; raging waves of the sea, foaming up their own shame; wandering stars for whom is reserved the blackness of darkness forever" (Jude 12, 13).

Perhaps the writer of Jude understood astronomy better than his fellow astronomers back then. Maybe his description of wandering stars (rogue planets) actually captures well these planetary objects not tied to an orbit around a star. We too can find ourselves as wandering stars when we try to exist in our own spheres of orbit. We would find more meaning and purpose in life if we allowed ourselves to be pulled in by the Spirit into an orbiting relationship with the Son of Righteousness.

KEY BIBLE TEXT: "Now to Him who is able to keep you from stumbling, and to present you faultless before the presence of His glory with exceeding joy" (Jude 24).

DAY 335 A Gift Without Price

An Amazing Fact: *"Inventions have long since reached their limit, and I see no hope for future developments" (Julius Sextus Frontinus, A.D. 10). "Computers in the future may weigh no more than 1.5 tons" (Popular Mechanics, 1949). "I think there is a world market for maybe five computers" (Thomas Watson, IBM, 1943). "The world potential market for copying machines is 5,000 at most" (IBM to Xerox, 1959).*

Reading these obviously faulty predictions makes us smile—computers weigh in at 1.5 tons? There's an iPhone available that weighs 4.8 ounces and can be used in many ways as a mini-computer. Technology has developed quickly and brilliantly so that developers of the past would not even comprehend the capabilities, software, and accessories today. Software and accessories? Cables and docks? Headsets? What are those?

What about the Bible? Is God's Word more trustworthy than the rash statements above? Let's talk about Jesus. Sometime before 500 B.C., the prophet Daniel proclaimed that Israel's long-awaited Messiah would begin His public ministry 483 years after the issuing of a decree to restore and rebuild Jerusalem (Daniel 9:25, 26). He also predicted that the Messiah would be killed prior to a second destruction of Jerusalem. These prophecies were perfectly fulfilled in the life and death of Jesus.

Around A.D. 30, Jesus told His disciples they would be persecuted and hated because they followed Him. They, and millions of Christians after them, were grossly mistreated or lost their lives for serving the Lord.

Jesus said, "I go to prepare a place for you. And if I go ... I will come again" (John 14:1–3). Jesus is coming! He said it; you can believe it. He *will* make an end of all of the woes of this sin-weary world. "'Behold, I make all things new.' ... These words are true and faithful" (Revelation 21:5).

There's a perfect place reserved for you. It's free. And you can know that it is true.

KEY BIBLE TEXT: "He who is coming will come and will not tarry" (Hebrews 10:37).

Eternal Buildings

An Amazing Fact: *As one of the world's oldest structures at 4,600 years, the Great Pyramid of Giza in Egypt is the sole survivor of the seven wonders of the ancient world. It is believed that a slave force of about 25,000 men and women built the colossal structure. It took 20 years to build, using approximately 2.3 million blocks with an average weight of 2.5 metric tons. The largest block weighs as much as 15 metric tons.*

The pyramid currently stands at more than 450 feet high, but at one time stood as high as 480 feet—50 stories! It was the tallest manmade structure for more than 43 centuries—surpassed only in the 19th century.

In addition, the interior stones fit so well together that even a business card won't fit between them. It's engineering prowess was so advanced that even current technology can't duplicate the structure. The pyramid's core was constructed mostly of soft limestone, but the outer layer of the pyramid was crafted in a beautifully bright, protective layer of polished stone that made the structure durable against the elements. The casing stones, 144,000 in all, were so brilliant that when sunlight reflected off them, they could be seen from the mountains of Israel hundreds of miles away.

These outer "casing stones" are missing today because of a 13th century earthquake, which loosened them. Arabic looters, recognizing this great quarry of precut stones, carted these off to finish construction of palaces and mosques.

The great pyramid represents man's best attempt to build an eternal dwelling on Earth, but even the pyramids are slowly crumbling. In contrast, Jesus promises to build eternal dwellings for His children in which we can abide forever.

KEY BIBLE TEXT: "In my Father's house are many mansions; if it were not so, I would have told you. I go to prepare a place for you" (John 14:2).

DAY 337 No Orphans

An Amazing Fact: *George Washington Carver was born to slave parents in Diamond Grove, Missouri. He was rescued from Confederate kidnappers as an infant.*

Carver is perhaps the nation's best-known African-American scientist. In the period between 1890 and 1910, the cotton crop had been devastated by the boll weevil. Carver advised farmers to cultivate peanuts, and before long, he developed more than 300 different peanut-based products—everything from milk to printer's ink.

At Tuskegee, Carver developed a crop rotation method that alternated nitrate-producing legumes—such as peanuts and peas—with cotton, which depletes soil of its nutrients. Following Carver's lead, southern farmers soon began planting peanuts one year and cotton the next. While many of the peanuts were used to feed livestock, large surpluses quickly developed. When he discovered that the sweet potato and the pecan also enriched depleted soils, Carver found almost 20 uses for these crops, including synthetic rubber and material for paving highways.

George Washington Carver was not left as an orphan. His slave owners loved him so much that they adopted him when his mother was carried away by kidnappers one dark night when he was a baby. They cared for him as their own. Carver grew up to be one of the greatest turn-of-the-century scientists in American history.

We live on a planet torn by war and sin. Jesus promised His disciples, before the crucifixion, "I will not leave you orphans; I will come to you" (John 14:18). Carver longed to see his mother again, but that was not to be. We too have a longing to see our heavenly Father. We can be thankful that this longing will be fulfilled.

KEY BIBLE TEXT: "Pure and undefiled religion before God and the Father is this: to visit orphans and widows in their trouble, and to keep oneself unspotted from the world" (James 1:27).

The Gentle Power of Rain

DAY 338

An Amazing Fact: *A little cumulus cloud weighs about the same as 100 elephants, and a thunderstorm cloud can weigh as much as 200,000 elephants!*

Did you know that within one second, approximately 16 million tons of water evaporate? And contrary to popular belief, as raindrops fall, they are not in the shape of a "teardrop." As the size of the raindrop increases, they change from a spherical shape to a flat-bottomed disk shape, similar to a hamburger bun. Eventually, they can actually take the shape of a parachute before they split apart into two smaller droplets.

In awe of the Creator's marvelous physical laws of nature, Job observes that He "binds up the water in His thick clouds, Yet the clouds are not broken under it" (Job 26:8). Job knew that if this amount of water were carried in a sack common in his day, it would be ripped apart.

Imagine the effect if rain fell as if from a giant tub in the heavens. Because of their size and the way droplets are formed, however, raindrops can only reach a maximum of 22 miles per hour before they split into lighter drops. So when the rain falls, instead of destroying vegetation, it is evenly distributed in small droplets to refresh the grass, plants, and trees.

In the beautiful song of Moses, recorded in Deuteronomy 32, he illustrates the tenderness with which God instructs and teaches His precious people. "Let my teaching drop as the rain, My speech distill as the dew, As raindrops on the tender herb, And as showers on the grass" (v. 2). God knows that we are as tender grass (Isaiah 40:7). In His merciful dealings with us, He doesn't send all His teaching to us at once. We would be overwhelmed! He knows just the right amount of instruction we can handle. Let's just be sure that we are there to receive it every morning.

KEY BIBLE TEXT: "The Lord God has given Me the tongue of the learned, that I should know how to speak a word in season to him who is weary. He awakens Me morning by morning, He awakens My ear to hear as the learned" (Isaiah 50:4).

DAY 339 Pure Wine

An Amazing Fact: *In 1869, Dr. Thomas Bramwell Welch, a physician and dentist by profession, successfully pasteurized Concord grape juice to produce an "unfermented sacramental wine" for fellow parishioners at his church in Vineland, New Jersey.*

He was inspired to do this after a visitor became drunk and unruly following a communion service in which fermented wine was used. Since antiquity, there have been several methods of preserving wine from fermenting, but they always sacrificed much in the way of taste. Dr. Welch's process preserved both. Today, Welch's Grape Juice is an international food company.

Alcohol consumption is a national problem in America. It destroys people's ability to think clearly and act properly. Tests show that after drinking three bottles of beer, there is an average of 13 percent net memory loss. After taking only small quantities of alcohol, trained typists were tested and their errors increased 40 percent. Only one ounce of alcohol increases the time required to make a decision by nearly 10 percent, hinders muscular reaction by 17 percent, and increases errors due to lack of attention by 35 to 60 percent.

Using the illustration of grapes, Jesus said, "I am the true vine, and My Father is the vinedresser. Every branch in Me that does not bear fruit He takes away; and every branch that bears fruit He prunes, that it may bear more fruit" (John 15:1, 2). When we do not abide in Christ, the fruit that we bear is permeated with sin. Like fermented grape juice, the results of a life without Jesus are impure, broken, and impaired. Unless we are connected to Christ, we will not bear good fruit. Unless we abide in Jesus, we will be cut off.

Spend time with the Lord every day. Press the Word against your heart. Talk to God in prayer. And let the pure spiritual "wine" flow, unfermented by sin, out of your life to bless others.

KEY BIBLE TEXT: "Thus says the Lord: 'As the new wine is found in the cluster, And one says, "Do not destroy it, For a blessing is in it," So will I do for my servants' sake, That I may not destroy them all'" (Isaiah 65:8).

Persevere

DAY 340

An Amazing Fact: *After being drafted, Desmond Doss' refusal to bear arms gave his commanders fits, and his fellow soldiers often used the meek misfit as a punching bag. He believed his Christian faith forbade the taking of lives and promoted their saving. He always kept his Bible close by but refused to carry a weapon at his own peril. Yet as an infantry medic during World War II, Doss did as much as any great warrior to save the lives of his fellow men.*

During a bloody assault in Okinawa in April 1945, private first-class Doss exhibited magnificent fortitude and unflinching bravery in the face of deadly conditions. He retrieved 75 wounded men off a rocky cliff while under constant enemy fire. Doss believed this feat was made possible only by the guiding and protective hand of God. Doss received many wounds during that battle, but he always tended to others before himself.

His reputation as a soldier propelled his name as a symbol for outstanding faith. While seriously wounded after jumping on a grenade to protect his fellow men, Doss dragged himself through the battlefield to treat wounded soldiers until he was rescued. Doss later discovered he'd lost his Bible during the conflict. However, the respect of his fellow soldiers had grown so profound that they searched the battlefield until they found the beloved Book of the private they had all once mocked.

For his heroic efforts and bravery, Doss received this country's highest military honor. On Columbus Day in 1945, President Truman placed the Congressional Medal of Honor around Doss' neck and said, "This is a greater honor for me than being president." Doss is the only conscientious objector ever to receive the award.

Christ, in the same way, honors the church of Philadelphia. "I know your works. See, I have set before you an open door, and no one can shut it; for you have a little strength, have kept My word, and have not denied My name" (Revelation 3:8). And, "Because you have kept My command to persevere, I also will keep you from the hour of trial" (v. 10). Praise God for protection to those who persevere in His name.

KEY BIBLE TEXT: "And not only that, but we also glory in tribulations, knowing that tribulation produces perseverance" (Romans 5:3).

DAY 341 An Open Door

An Amazing Fact: *Number 10 Downing Street is one of the most famous doors in the world. It attracts millions of visitors every year. One woman and 52 men have passed through the grand doors of Number 10 Downing Street as British Prime Minister. Sometimes they were met by violent riots, passionate protests, and even a few celebrities. One interesting fact about this door is that it can only be opened from the inside.*

Another world-famous door is the Florence Baptistery in Florence, Italy. It took Lorenzo Ghiberti and two colleagues 27 years to produce the design that included 10 panels depicting scenes from the Old Testament. They are crafted from gilded bronze. Ghiberti's use of the "principle of perspective" led Michelangelo to refer to these doors as fit to be the "Gates of Paradise."

An ancient door famous among archaeologists is the Ishtar Gate from Babylon. Around 600 B.C. Nebuchadnezzar built this powerful blue-glazed brick gate. He emblazoned on the door the image of the dragon of Marduk. Also featured are golden lions and bulls. The gate is almost 50 feet high and 33 feet wide.

An interesting door in Rome is called the Holy Door of St. Peter's Basilica, or the "Door of the Great Pardon," which is sealed with a brick wall. Every 25 years the pope strikes the brick with a silver hammer and symbolically opens it. It remains open for the entire year. At the end of the year the brick wall is rebuilt. The Holy Door is meant to represent Jesus, as the gate to heaven and salvation.

The Bible describes Jesus standing before a door and knocking. "Behold, I stand at the door and knock. If anyone hears My voice and opens the door, I will come in to him and dine with him, and he with Me" (Revelation 3:20). Like 10 Downing Street, this door opens only from the inside. It is the door of your heart. You don't have to wait 25 years for someone to open it. You can do so right now.

KEY BIBLE TEXT: "See, I have set before you an open door, and no one can shut it" (Revelation 3:8).

Surprise Attack

DAY 342

An Amazing Fact: *On December 7, 1941, the Japanese attacked Pearl Harbor. The number of Americans who died was 2,388, the number wounded was 1,178, and the number of ships sunk or damaged was 21.*

Each year Americans commemorate Pearl Harbor Day in memory of the thousands who were injured or killed when the Japanese made their surprise attack on the American naval base in Hawaii. It was a major turning point in World War II. Though the number who remember that day becomes fewer over the years, many can still hear President Franklin D. Roosevelt's famous address, in which he says December 7, 1941, will be "a date which will live in infamy." Is it still remembered? About 4,000 people visit Pearl Harbor each day, and 1.5 million visit the USS *Arizona* memorial each year.

The attack lasted only 110 minutes, from 7:55 AM until 9:45 AM. Plans for the assault had been in the works for almost one year. Its code name was "Operation Hawaii" and was later changed to "Operation Z." The Japanese chose to attack on Sunday morning because they believed the Americans would be less alert and more relaxed. When the Japanese commander Mitsuo Fuchida called out "Tora! Tora! Tora! [Tiger! Tiger! Tiger!]" when flying over Pearl Harbor, it was a message to the entire Japanese Navy that they had caught the Americans totally by surprise.

The language of Joel when describing the "Day of the Lord" sounds familiar to those who watched the attack on Pearl Harbor. It is a grim comparison. "Blow the trumpet in Zion, And sound an alarm in My holy mountain! Let all the inhabitants of the land tremble; For the day of the Lord is coming, For it is at hand: A day of darkness and gloominess, A day of clouds and thick darkness. ... A people come, great and strong. ... A fire devours before them, And behind them a flame burns" (Joel 2:1–3).

What a great and dreadful day that will be! For those who give their lives to Christ, however, it will not come as a surprise attack.

KEY BIBLE TEXT: "But the day of the Lord will come as a thief in the night" (2 Peter 3:10).

DAY 343 Secret Codes

An Amazing Fact: *During the Pacific battles of World War II, the Japanese eavesdropped on U.S. Marine communications and managed to decipher the coded messages easily. In fact, Japanese cryptographers succeeded in breaking every U.S. code nearly as fast as it was developed. But there was one code they could never break.*

The idea originated with Philip Johnston, an engineer and World War I veteran, who knew of the military's need for an unbreakable code. He had been raised on a Navajo Reservation where his father had been a missionary. Navajo was virtually an unwritten language in 1942, with no alphabet or symbols, and was spoken only on the Navajo lands of the American Southwest.

Confident that few people in the world understood the complex syntax and tonal qualities of Navajo, Johnston suggested that the army use the language as the basis for code. After staging an impressive demonstration in which several Navajo friends transmitted English into Navajo and back to English, the Marines authorized an official program to develop and implement the code.

Twenty-nine Navajos fluent in their native tongue and English (some only 15-years-old) constructed and mastered the code, which they used to transmit crucial information in battles. More were trained later. Historians believe that the Navajo Code Talkers played a fundamental role in the U.S. victory in the Pacific.

A crisis in heaven once developed when no one could be found to open and look at a scroll. "'Who is worthy to open the scroll and to loose its seals?' And no one in heaven or on the earth or under the earth was able to open the scroll, or to look at it" (Revelation 5:1, 2).

"But one of the elders said to me, 'Do not weep. Behold, the Lion of the tribe of Judah, the Root of David, has prevailed to open the scroll and to loose its seven seals'" (v. 5). Here was a message that needed to go to the world and nobody could "break the code" ... except Christ. Jesus could reveal the message because He gave His life to save the world. That, in fact, *is* the message!

KEY BIBLE TEXT: "Therefore let it be known to you that the salvation of God has been sent to the Gentiles, and they will hear it!" (Acts 28:28).

Your Personal Guide

An Amazing Fact: *As far back as the 15th century, the Venetian Republic hired and paid local mountaineers to accompany mapmakers through the Dolimites mountain range in an effort to trace the Austrian-Venetian border. Later, in 1865, Austria officially authorized the discipline of Alpine Guide. These first explorers were often accompanied by local mountain-goat hunters, traditionally the true experts of the steep and dangerous mountain routes, and together can be considered the forefathers of the modern mountain guide.*

Mountain guides are trained and experienced mountaineers. They are professionals with a passion for the mountains. These experts have skills in climbing, hiking, and skiing. They have practical knowledge about rocks, avalanches, weather, navigation, snow, and health. Their main goal is your safety when climbing.

Certification for most guides is through the International Federation of Mountain Guides Associations. It requires a vigorous examination of three main areas: rock climbing, alpine climbing, and mountaineering skiing. It can take up to seven years to complete certification requirements. Other qualities that mountain guides can provide clients include a good knowledge of the route, weather, and snow and glacier conditions. They are prepared for emergencies and have equipment and knowledge to care for you and evacuate you from danger. Some have access to limited-use locations for hikers who want to explore new places.

On our journey to heaven, we will meet great difficulties. We are assured of trials and have been warned of an enemy who wants to pull us off course, attack us, or simply confuse our sense of direction. But we can be thankful for a promise made by Jesus to His disciples before returning to heaven. "However, when He, the Spirit of truth, has come, He will guide you into all truth; for He will not speak on His own authority, but whatever He hears He will speak; and He will tell you things to come" (John 16:13). We can have peace knowing that God has sent each of us a personal guide in Jesus.

KEY BIBLE TEXT: "Yea, though I walk through the valley of the shadow of death, I will fear no evil; For Your are with me" (Psalm 23:4).

DAY 345 Never Hungry

An Amazing Fact: *When Napoleon's armies invaded Europe, his general soon realized that an "army marches on its stomach" and that foraging for food was wasting time. But when the armies tried to carry their food with them, it spoiled. So in 1795, the French government offered a prize of 12,000 francs to any Frenchman who could find a way to preserve food. It wasn't until 1809 that a French confectioner named Nicholas Appert claimed the money.*

After almost 15 years of experimenting, Appert placed peas and carrots into wine bottles, cooked them at a high temperature, and then sealed the glass with a cork. The food remained edible after standing many days, and thus was discovered the basic principle of modern canning. Food preservation techniques have become so sophisticated that perishables can be preserved and remain edible for centuries!

Appert has been called the "father of canning" because of his invention of airtight food preservation. Later in 1810 a British inventor and merchant, Peter Durand, patented his own method of preserving food in a tin can. However, mass-producing canned food did not happen until the 20th century because of the difficulty of opening the cans with a hammer and chisel. Not until someone invented a can opener did it really take off!

Do you know what the most perishable food in history is? "And Moses said, 'Let no one leave any of it till morning.' Notwithstanding, they did not heed Moses. But some of them left part of it until morning, and it bred worms and stank. And Moses was angry with them. So they gathered it every morning, every man according to his need. And when the sun became hot, it melted" (Exodus 16:19–21).

We can be certain of one thing about food. Someday we will never have to worry about it spoiling. There will be plenty for us to enjoy in heaven. "They shall neither hunger anymore nor thirst anymore" (Revelation 7:16). God will supply our daily bread.

KEY BIBLE TEXT: "For He satisfies the longing soul, And fills the hungry soul with goodness" (Psalm 107:9).

From Sea to Sea

DAY 346

An Amazing Fact: *Born in the Chinese province of Yunnan in 1371, Ma Sanpao (Cheng Ho) was captured and sent to serve in the army under Chu Ti in 1382. There he helped Chu Ti become Emperor Yonglo of the Ming Dynasty. To reward his work, Ma was made Grand Imperial Eunuch—and his name was changed to Zheng He.*

Yonglo chose Zheng to head a series of naval expeditions to ports all over the Indian Ocean. Zheng had diplomatic, scientific, and commercial goals while traveling farther than any other admiral in history. He visited more than 35 countries, utilizing more than 100 ships and nearly 28,000 men in his Grand Fleet. The largest vessels were 444-foot treasure ships!

The fleet visited southern Asia in the first voyage, and by the seventh and last voyage, Zheng had been to east Africa, the Persian Gulf, Egypt, and Ceylon (Sri Lanka). Almost 30 countries sent envoys back to China to give homage to the emperor, and each nation welcomed Zheng and traded for Chinese goods.

Zheng's voyages not only established Chinese trade routes throughout Asia and Africa, but also established China as the dominant world power. China was far more technologically advanced than any other culture, and no European force could have successfully challenged its authority.

Emperor Yonglo died in 1424, ending all naval expeditions until 1431. Between two and five years after Yonglo's death, Cheng Ho himself died during a trip home from India, ending the seventh and final voyage of the Grand Fleet. China eventually banned all naval expeditions indefinitely. Future emperors practiced strict isolationism and burned all records of Cheng Ho's voyages. Chinese influence in the world ended, which opened the door for the rise of European superpowers.

The successful travels of Cheng Ho stand in contrast to a search that will take place on the day of the Lord. Someday people will seek God's Word but will not find it. "They shall wander from sea to sea, And from north to east; They shall run to and fro, seeking the word of the Lord, But shall not find it" (Amos 8:12). Are you searching for God's Word today?

KEY BIBLE TEXT: "And the word of the Lord was rare in those days; there was no widespread revelation" (1 Samuel 3:1).

DAY 347 Born Again!

An Amazing Fact: *Tucked inside the microscopic nucleus of every cell in our bodies is a six-foot long strand of protein molecules, called DNA. The information contained within makes it possible for each parent to contribute one-and-a-half billion bits of genetic information to each of their offspring!*

The DNA itself resembles a long, narrow, spiral ladder of pliable material. Before a cell is able to divide, the DNA must be "duplicated" so that each cell will have an original copy of the genetic code. As replication begins, an enzyme unwinds the spiral DNA ladder. Next, a protein molecule holds the two strands apart while another enzyme rapidly "transcribes" genetic code to RNA molecules. The code is then "proofread" and instantly corrected if an error is found. All of this happens in a matter of seconds! Finally, the RNA molecules exit the nucleus to begin communicating the genetic code to new cells.

As the RNA molecule takes critical information from the DNA and communicates it to the body, so Christ took the message of His Father's love from the "nucleus" of heaven and communicated it to our planet. "For I have given to them the words which You have given Me; and they have received them, and have known surely that I came forth from You; and they have believed that You sent Me" (John 17:8).

And now it is Christ's desire that we do the work of the RNA! "As You sent Me into the world, I also have sent them into the world" (John 17:18).

While we cannot help what genetic heritage we have been given from our parents, we can accept God's offer to be our Father and choose to be "born again." Let us bring joy to the Father's heart today, replicating the peace of heaven, by letting Christ transcribe the genetic code of heaven into our hearts!

KEY BIBLE TEXT: "O righteous Father! The world has not known You, but I have known You; and these have known that You sent Me. And I have declared to them Your name, and will declare it, that the love with which You loved Me may be in them, and I in them" (John 17:25, 26).

Warning Cry

An Amazing Fact: *At midnight, March 12, 1928, one of the worst catastrophes in Californian history occurred: The St. Francis Dam broke. Twelve billion gallons of water washed down the San Francisquito Canyon, killing hundreds in its path.*

The official body count was 450 dead, but the actual number was substantially higher, since San Francisquito Canyon was home to hundreds of transient farm workers who were never counted. This would likely have brought the death toll to higher than the famous 1906 San Francisco quake.

The dam broke just under two years after its completion. More than 900 buildings and $13 million in property were destroyed in the resulting flood. But the greatest tragedy of this disaster was that no one needed to perish!

There was ample warning time on the morning it broke. A worker at the dam saw water leaking through the dam wall. He warned his boss, William Mulholland, about this danger. After looking at the dam, Mulholland, who also designed the structure, decided that there was no cause for concern. But that night, the dam broke, sending a wall of water as high as 140 feet down the canyon through Saugus, Fillmore, Santa Paula, and finally the Pacific Ocean. It traveled 54 miles in 5.5 hours, destroying everything in its path.

Another disaster loomed over the city of Nineveh. God called Jonah to warn the people, but the reluctant prophet ran the other direction. Through some unusual turn of events, Jonah finally carried out his duty and saved a large city of people who might have perished.

We also have been given a message of warning to give to the world. It is found in Revelation 14. Will we ignore the warning signs? Will we run like Jonah or respond like Mulholland saying, "There is no cause for concern"? Let us be sober and responsible and do our part to warn our friends of impending disaster.

KEY BIBLE TEXT: "Then I saw another angel flying in the midst of heaven, having the everlasting gospel to preach to those who dwell on the earth... saying... 'Fear God and give glory to Him, for the hour of His judgment has come'" (Revelation 14:6, 7).

DAY 349 Taking Measure

An Amazing Fact: *The canal across the Isthmus of Panama in Central America is one of the greatest engineering marvels of the past 1,000 years. In 1513, Vasco de Balboa's discovery of the Pacific coast of Panama soon had merchants and empire-builders dreaming of a shortcut that would enable ships to sail westward from the Atlantic to the Pacific without making the grueling, 12,000-mile journey around the tip of South America.*

Over the next 200 years, visionaries ranging from Benjamin Franklin to Simon Bolivar advocated the digging of a channel. The Panama Canal was finally completed by the United States under Teddy Roosevelt from 1904 to 1914. At that time, it was the largest and most complex project of its kind ever undertaken, employing tens of thousands of workers and costing $350 million. The 50-mile canal handles a large volume of the world's shipping.

The canal consists of artificially created lakes, channels, and a series of locks, or water-filled chambers, that raise and lower ships 85 feet through the mountainous terrain of central Panama. Battleships of the world's navies are built to squeeze through the small 80-year old locks. The canal's 12 locks, three sets of double locks at each end, have the same dimensions: 110-feet wide by 1,000-feet long, with gates at each end. Because of the "S" shape of the Isthmus of Panama, a ship sailing through the canal will actually travel west to east to go east to west.

Creating the Panama Canal required sophisticated measurements that were limited at the turn of the century. John the Revelator was asked in vision to take measurements, not of a canal, but of "the temple of God, the altar, and those who worship there" (Revelation 11:1). Why would John be asked to conduct these measurements? Like in Ezekiel's vision, the restoration of God's work was marked by taking careful measure. Have you measured your own heart to see where you stand with Him?

KEY BIBLE TEXT: "Search me, O God, and know my heart; Try me and know my anxieties; And see if there is any wicked way in me, And lead me in the way everlasting" (Psalm 139:23, 24).

No More War!

DAY 350

An Amazing Fact: *At midnight, March 12, 1928, one of the worst catastrophes in Californian history occurred: The St. Francis Dam broke. Twelve billion gallons of water washed down the San Francisquito Canyon, killing hundreds in its path.*

On one cold September day in 1944, a prisoner of war (POW) hunched over a recently arrived Red Cross package and ravenously ate its remaining food. Then from the dim light of the window, he saw the special Monopoly game he had been briefed on when he was deployed. His hands shook as he opened the game.

To help prisoners escape, the British military requested that the makers of the game add a few "secret goodies" that could then be airdropped by the Red Cross into POW camps. Hidden ingeniously inside the little dog-playing piece was a magnetic compass. Breaking open a little wooden red hotel, the soldier found a tiny silk map of his region, detailing the location of his POW camp and where he could expect to find help. Tucked under the fake money were real French, German, and Italian currencies! It was what he needed to make the escape!

Each of us is trapped in the POW camp of "sin," but all heaven is working on our behalf to set us free! Someday soon, sin and wars will cease. Isaiah speaks eloquently of this time in chapter 14: "And it shall come to pass in the day that the Lord shall give thee rest from thy sorrow, and from thy fear, and from the hard bondage wherein thou wast made to serve. That thou shalt take up this proverb against the king of Babylon, and say, 'How hath the oppressor ceased! The golden city ceased! ... The whole earth is at rest, and is quiet'" (vs. 3, 4, 7).

KEY BIBLE TEXT: "Nation shall not lift up sword against nation, Neither shall they learn war anymore" (Micah 4:3 KJV).

DAY 351 Rivers of Oil

An Amazing Fact: *Since it first open in 1977, the Trans Alaska Pipeline System (TAPS) has moved 16 billion barrels of oil from the North Slope of Alaska to the northern most ice-free port in Valdez, Alaska.*

TAPS, also called "Alyeska Pipeline" or simply "The Pipeline," travels more than 800 miles over extremely cold and difficult terrain. Special construction techniques were invented to deal with issues like permafrost. Crude oil travels through 11 pump stations over the world's largest pipeline system. The actual pipe is 48 inches in diameter and begins in Prudhoe Bay, where oil was discovered in 1968. Environmental, legal, and political debates prevented immediate work on the project, but the oil crisis of the early 1970s changed all that.

It cost $8 billion to build TAPS. More than half of the pipe is above ground. It crosses about 800 streams and rivers and is actually built in a zigzag pattern to accommodate expansion and contraction. Around 88,000 barrels of oil go through the pipeline an hour. It takes four-and-a-half days for oil to travel the entire length. Workers are stationed all along the pipeline to oversee its function. Over 20,000 tankers have moved oil out of Valdez since the pipeline opened. This river of oil boosted the economy of Alaska and created several "boom" towns, especially during construction.

Micah, the Old Testament prophet who was a contemporary of Isaiah, was a creative writer. He asked God's people, "With what shall I come before the Lord, And bow myself before the High God? Shall I come before Him with burnt offerings, With calves a year old? Will the Lord be pleased with thousands of rams, Ten thousand rivers of oil?" (Micah 6:6, 7). Would all the oil from TAPS make God happy? Obviously not.

Think about Micah's response to his rhetorical question as you walk through your day. "He has shown you, O man, what is good; And what does the Lord require of you But to do justly, To love mercy, And to walk humbly with your God" (v. 8).

KEY BIBLE TEXT: "But go and learn what this means: 'I desire mercy and not sacrifice.' For I did not come to call the righteous, but sinners, to repentance" (Matthew 9:13).

Babylon Is Fallen

DAY 352

An Amazing Fact: *Ancient Babylon reached its greatest glory during the reign of King Nebuchadnezzar (604–562 B.C.) and was probably the largest city of antiquity. Babylon was an immense square, totaling 15 miles on each side, with Marduk's temple and the Tower of Babylon at its center. It was divided into two equal parts by the Euphrates running under the walls, which also served to irrigate and air condition the entire metropolis.*

Babylon had 25 avenues, 150 feet wide, which ran across the city from north to south. The same number of roads crossed them at right angles from east to west, making a total of 676 great blocks, each nearly three-quarter square miles. Nebuchadnezzar also built massive fortifications with thick walls that measured from 67 feet at the base to 54 feet at the top; four chariots could race side by side on the top of the walls.

Not only was ancient Babylon big, it was beautiful! The public buildings were faced with bright glazed bricks in different colors. The outer walls of the city were yellow, the gates blue, the palaces rose-red, and the temples white. All this, plus the famous hanging gardens, gave this metropolis a splendor that was unequaled by any other earthly city.

Yet God prophesied that ancient Babylon would be destroyed and never be rebuilt. (See Revelation 18:8.). A special message is also given about Babylon in Revelation 14. "And another [second] angel followed, saying, 'Babylon is fallen, is fallen, that great city, because she has made all nations drink of the wine of the wrath of her fornication'" (Revelation 14:8).

Babylon represents an organization that proclaims to be on God's side but is actually just the opposite. It's beauty and luxury fool people into thinking there must be truth found here. But it is a counterfeit of the real gospel of faith. This symbolic city stands behind all that opposes God throughout all human history.

Don't be fooled by what looks good on the outside. Truth that changes the heart is found deep in God's Word.

KEY BIBLE TEXT: "And I heard another voice from heaven saying, 'Come out of her, my people, lest you share in her sins, and lest you receive of her plagues'" (Revelation 18:4).

DAY 353 Waiting for the Master

An Amazing Fact: *For nine years after his master's death, a dog named Hachiko daily watched for his master's return at the train station where he had last seen him. Precisely when the train was due, the faithful dog would arrive. Disappointed each time, he never ceased watching until the day he died.*

It was a wintry day in Japan when Professor Ueno brought home a three-month-old Akita puppy named Hachiko. Every morning Hachiko would follow the professor to the train station, and every afternoon, just before 3:00, he would return to eagerly greet his master as he returned from work.

The dog was only a year-and-a-half old when, one afternoon, he did not see his master among the passengers leaving the train. Professor Ueno had suffered a fatal cerebral hemorrhage that day while giving a lecture. Disappointed, Hachiko returned again the next day, precisely at the time he had come to expect his master's return. Day after day, the poor dog faithfully returned to the train station, watching for his beloved master. Time would not erode Hachiko's loyalty and hope that he would again see his master's face.

Our Master has instructed us to watch and be ready for His return. Are we watching with the earnestness and faith of Hachiko? Or does time weaken our certainty in Jesus' soon return? Unlike Hachiko, who waited in vain, we have the promise, "The vision is yet for an appointed time, but at the end it shall speak, and not lie: though it tarry, wait for it; because it will surely come, it will not tarry" (Habakkuk 2:3). With this assurance, let us increase our diligence to watch, pray, and work in this fast-closing window of time before Jesus ceases His intercession for mankind.

KEY BIBLE TEXT: "But if that servant says in his heart, 'My master is delaying his coming,' and begins to beat the ... servants, and to eat and drink and be drunk, the master ... will come on a day when he is not looking for him, ... and will cut him in two and appoint him his portion with the unbelievers" (Luke 12:45, 46).

Fool's Gold

An Amazing Fact: *Gold coinage is composed of 90 parts gold to 10 parts silver. But counterfeit gold, or "fools gold," is made of iron pyrite, which is a mineral composed of iron sulfide. The mineral is brass yellow or opaque and has a metallic luster. The resemblance of pyrite to gold caused many prospectors to mistake it for gold. However, it is easily distinguished by its unusual brittleness.*

Iron pyrite was used in ancient Rome to create sparks when struck with steel. In the 16th and 17th centuries, it was used as a source of ignition in firearms. The name "pyrite" comes from the Greek word "pur," which means "fire." Some pyrite has a brass color and has been nicknamed "brass," "brazzle," or "Brazil."

Zephaniah, an Old Testament prophet, warned the people of Judah in the days of Josiah that the great day of the Lord would come upon them. They said, "The Lord will not do good, Nor will He do evil" (Zephaniah1:12). But the prophet answered, "Neither their silver nor their gold Shall be able to deliver them In the day of the Lord's wrath; But the whole land shall be devoured By the fire of His jealousy" (v. 18).

The prophet's message was not intended to lead them to despair but to wake them up and call them to repentance. They carried around with them a belief that "nothing is going to happen, don't worry, this too shall pass." Like fool's gold in their pockets, they assumed they were secure in their false riches. But the destruction of Jerusalem came like the flood and swept everyone away.

Today we also can be fooled in spiritual truth. Millions of people are toting around heavy bags bulging with fool's gold. They rejoice that they have discovered that which will make them rich, but though it sparkles on the outside it will be discovered useless at the bank of heaven. Make sure you have the real thing!

KEY BIBLE TEXT: "For it is by grace you have been saved, through faith—and this not from yourselves, it is the gift of God" (Ephesians 2:8).

DAY 355 Out of Place

An Amazing Fact: *The Catacombs of Paris are some of the more macabre tourist attractions in Paris. They reopened to the public after a $400,000 facelift and contain the bones of six million Parisians. Curious tourists descend via a narrow spiral staircase into the underground passages, where pile upon pile of shin bones lie in neat rows punctuated by a pattern of skulls. The gruesome attraction draws 160,000 visitors a year.*

The tunnels were originally stone mines but later became underground burial chambers when the cemeteries of Paris became overcrowded in the 18th century. Bones were dug up and stored underground.

Some 190 miles of passageways wind their way under the capital city, creating a network of tunnels twice as long as those of the Paris underground metro system. Only one mile of catacombs is open to the public. An intercom system was added to ensure visitors do not get lost, which should spare anyone else the fate of a hospital worker who decided to explore the tunnels alone during the French Revolution. His skeleton was found 11 years later!

Superstitious visitors are often unnerved by the thought that spirits of the dead will haunt them for gawking at their remains. On the other hand, Nestor Valence, who worked in the subterranean warren for eight years rearranging bones that fell out of place, says he had grown used to the grisly nature of his job. "Touching bones doesn't bother me anymore," he says. "When you start, it's a bit weird, but it becomes part of the routine."

A visit to Jesus' tomb by Mary Magdalene surprised her, not because she was afraid of a dead body, but because her Lord was not there! Christ had risen from the dead. "Then she ran and came to Simon Peter, and to the other disciple, whom Jesus loved, and said to them, 'They have taken away the Lord out of the tomb, and we do not know where they have laid Him'" (John 20:2).

Christ had not moved as a dead person. His bones hadn't "fallen out of place," needing to be rearranged. Jesus was alive! Praise God, for it means our salvation is secure in Christ's hands.

KEY BIBLE TEXT: "For as yet they did not know the Scripture, that He must rise again from the dead" (John 20:9).

God's Treasury

An Amazing Fact: *A single snowstorm can drop 40 million tons of snow and carry the energy equivalent to 120 atom bombs!*

On March 11, 1888, a light rain began to fall on New York City. As the rain increased in intensity, temperatures began to plummet. Gradually the torrential rains changed to heavy snow, and shortly after midnight, the historic storm known as the "Great White Hurricane" had begun in earnest.

For a day and a half, the blizzard raged with sustained winds of more than 45 miles per hour. Houses disappeared under drifting mountains of snow that towered 50 feet high. Smothered under the merciless drifts, New York City went into survival mode. In a desperate attempt to keep passenger trains moving, crews were organized to patrol the tracks with brooms and pails of salt water. But even as they worked, the salt water froze in their pails. When the storm at last abated, it left a trail of destruction that took months to recover from.

In the book of Job, God asks many questions designed to make His faithful servant consider His Sovereignty. When trials follow one after another, it can be easy to lose sight of God's power and ability to sustain us as we attempt to go into survival mode without Him. But let us remember that the God who has snow and hail at His command has many other means to relieve us as well!

KEY BIBLE TEXT: "Have you entered the treasury of snow, or have you seen the treasury of hail?" (Job 38:22).

DAY 357 Word Wonders

An Amazing Fact: *Scientists say that sound waves set in motion by our voices go on an endless journey through space. If we had the power to stand on some distant planet long years afterward, with instruments delicate enough, we might be able to find those sounds again and recreate the words we spoke here on Earth.*

What is sound? Technically it is a mechanical wave that is an oscillation of pressure transmitted through either liquid, solid, or gas. It is made up of different frequencies within the range of hearing. And, of course, it needs to be loud enough to be heard by the organs of hearing. That range for humans is between 20Hz to 20,000Hz. Dogs can hear things above the human's upper range but are deaf to sounds below 40Hz.

Repeated studies show that the ear is superior to the eye and people remember more from words they hear than words they see. In fact, the mind is able to understand a spoken word in 140 milliseconds, while it takes 180 milliseconds to understand the printed word! Why? Psychologists believe this 40-millisecond delay occurs while the brain translates the visual data into aural sounds it can understand.

The Old Testament book of Haggai, the second smallest book in that testament, was a call to God's people who returned from Babylonian captivity to rebuild the temple. It is interesting that the most repeated phrase in this entire book is, "Thus says the Lord." More than 25 times in only two chapters, Haggai makes it abundantly clear that his message comes from God. Haggai brings the "word" of the Lord to the people with emphasis. He speaks with divine authority on behalf of God.

Do you speak God's words? Do you say things that you would like to resound throughout all eternity? It's something to stop talking about and wrap your mind around!

KEY BIBLE TEXT: "All flesh is as grass, And all the glory of man as the flower of the grass. The grass withers, And its flower falls away, But the word of the Lord endures forever" (1 Peter 1:24, 25).

Big Eyes, Small Brain

DAY 358

An Amazing Fact: *Ostriches once flourished throughout Africa; the majority now live in protected reserves on the continent's east coast. Male African ostriches grow as high as nine feet tall and can weigh a hefty 345 pounds—making them the tallest and heaviest of all living birds.*

Ostriches live in family groups consisting of one male and several hens. During breeding season, each hen lays between two and 11 creamy white eggs in a communal nest, which is a hollowed-out crater in the ground about 10 feet across. Eventually, these nests can contain up to 50 eggs each, but only about 20 can be successfully incubated. The eggs of the ostrich are the largest of any bird, measuring from six to eight inches long and weighing between two and four pounds. (The record is over five pounds!) An ostrich egg has the volume of about 24 chicken eggs, and though the shell is only 1.5 millimeters thick, it can hold the weight of a grown man.

They are not the smartest birds, yet the notion that they bury their heads in the sand is actually a myth. Sadly, these tallest, fastest, and biggest of birds also cannot fly, so they are easily farmed throughout the world for meat, feathers, and leather.

God teaches Job that He is Creator over all things, including the ostrich. The description given is all too accurate: "The wings of the ostrich wave proudly, But are her wings and pinions like the kindly stork's?" (Job 39:13). God decided that the ostrich would not fly and would lay her eggs on the ground. He also decided just how smart to make this bird: "Because God deprived her of wisdom, And did not endow her with understanding" (v. 17).

Interestingly, the Bible also teaches us that the greatest of the angels had his wings clipped because his eyes were too big. So let's be sure to remain humble with all the talents that God has given us.

KEY BIBLE TEXT: "Because your heart is lifted up, And you say, 'I am a god, I sit in the seat of gods, In the midst of the seas,' Yet you are a man, and not a god" (Ezekiel 28:2).

DAY 359 A Love That Will Not Let You Go

An Amazing Fact: *After her six little ducklings were swept into a storm drain in the United Kingdom, a mother mallard waddled two miles tracking her baby's chirps from manhole to manhole.*

Trapped in a dark tunnel in the city's underground sewer system and floating at the mercy of the current, the tiny ducklings' only hope was in their mother. Hearing their distressed chirps emanating from somewhere under the ground, the dedicated mother followed their cries. Her heroic journey led her across a busy intersection, countless roads, a metro train line, a housing estate, and two school playing fields. When her chicks suddenly came to a halt in a housing development, she waddled to a stop over a manhole cover. And there, for the next four hours, the faithful mother remained.

Peter Elliott first noticed the little duck at 6:00 AM when he left his home to go for a run. Surprised that she had not moved when he returned, he went over to see if she was injured. Seeing nothing wrong, he went to breakfast, only to see her still sitting there when he finished. It was only later, when his daughter took his two-year-old grandson to see the mallard, that they heard the ducklings' little voices beneath the manhole cover.

Mr. Elliot quickly gathered some tools and, along with a neighbor, managed to remove the heavy cover. Peering down they saw six little ducklings paddling around in the drain. With a small fishing net, they lifted each little duck to safety and then released the reunited family in a nearby lake.

Just like that faithful mother duck, our heavenly Father will never forsake us. Though we might stray, His heart of love goes after us still. He is always there, seeking for every opportunity to be reunited with us. Even when His chosen people had broken His heart by their wayward course, He pleaded, "Turn now from your evil ways and your evil deeds" (Zechariah 1:4). The sad record is that "they did not hear nor heed." So today, for His sake, "if you will hear His voice, Do not harden your hearts" (Hebrews 4:7). You are precious in His sight.

KEY BIBLE TEXT: "He who touches you touches the apple of His eye" (Zechariah 2:8).

Fallen by the Sword

DAY 360

An Amazing Fact: *From the Latin gladius, which means "sword," gladiators were professional fighters who performed spectacles of armed combat in the amphitheaters of ancient Rome. The practice of armed slaves fighting to the death originated in central Italy and lasted for more than 700 years.*

The first gladiator exhibition in Rome was in 264 B.C., when three pairs of gladiators fought as part of a funeral celebration. By 174 B.C., 37 pairs were participating. On one occasion, Julius Caesar ordered large-scale exhibitions with 300 pairs of combatants! But the largest contest of gladiators was ordered by the emperor Trajan as part of a victory celebration in A.D. 107. It included 5,000 pairs of fighters! It appears that as the years went by, each generation of leaders wanted something more horrific, violent, and perverted to keep the masses entertained.

Gladiators were typically male slaves, condemned criminals, prisoners of war, and sometimes Christians. Forced to become swordsmen, they were trained in schools called *ludi*, and special measures were taken to discipline them and prevent suicides. Occasionally, freedmen and Roman citizens entered the arena, as did the insane Emperor Commodus. The escaped gladiator Spartacus avenged his captivity by leading an army of slaves in an insurrection that terrorized southern Italy from 73 to 71 B.C.

Sir Edward Gibbon wrote in his classic *The History of the Decline and Fall of the Roman Empire* that the mad craze for pleasure and sports is one of the five reasons the empire fell. Is it possible that the world today is following the same yearning for carnal entertainment that lead to the fall of Rome?

Revelation tells us Babylon fell. It says the beast and the false prophet are to be cast alive into the lake of fire burning with brimstone, "And the rest were killed with the sword which proceeded from the mouth of Him who sat on the horse" (Revelation 19:21).

On this day in which many remember the birth of Christ, let us remember Herod's horrific murder of innocent children by the sword. The enemies of God's people who killed with the sword will someday fall by the sword.

KEY BIBLE TEXT: "But Jesus said to him, 'Put your sword in its place, for all who take the sword will perish by the sword'" (Matthew 26:52).

DAY 361 More Than a Placebo

An Amazing Fact: *A placebo is a harmless pill or solution made from a neutral substance, such as sugar or starch, which is used to avoid bias when testing new drugs. But in some tests, patients have experienced dramatic results from these placebos based simply on their belief that the pill will help them.*

Doctors have administered placebos to patients who are thought to have incurable illnesses to induce the so-called placebo effect: a temporary or even permanent improvement of the patient's condition corresponding to their faith in the doctor or medicine. In 1955, a study by Dr. Henry Knowles Beecher reports that 35 percent of patients had their conditions improved by receiving placebos.

Little is understood of how this works, but one theory is that the patient's faith in a cure might be related to the release of brain chemicals that help promote healing. Perhaps this is one reason why Jesus always said to those He healed, "Your faith has made you whole."

Modern medicine is returning to the conclusion that a person's faith has a great deal to do with their rate of recovery. In fact, a 2001 *Reader's Digest* reported on a nationwide study that found those who attend religious services more than once a week have a seven-year longer life expectancy than those who never attend. The Bible also teaches that a person's eternal life expectancy is directly connected with their faith.

Thomas struggled with faith. He said, "Unless I see in His hands the print of the nails, and put my finger into the print of the nails, and put my hand into His side, I will not believe" (John 20:25). Fortunately for Thomas, Jesus revealed Himself and he believed. But notice Christ's words, "Thomas, because you have seen Me, you have believed. Blessed are those who have not seen and yet have believed" (v. 29).

John's Gospel intends to bolster the faith of people who have not physically seen Jesus. Until we get to, we can exercise our faith in the risen Lord as we read Scripture, pray, and hear His voice speak to our hearts. Faith will change us; Christ is more than a placebo.

KEY BIBLE TEXT: "These are written that you may believe that Jesus is the Christ, the Son of God, and that believing you may have life in His name" (John 20:31).

No More Sea

An Amazing Fact: *Although its average temperature is 39 degrees Fahrenheit, the top 10 feet of the ocean holds as much heat as our entire atmosphere.*

Many unusual things also happen on the ocean floor. Chimneys spew sulfuric acid, and underwater volcanoes shoot out mud and methane. Water at 650 degrees Fahrenheit—hot enough to melt lead—bubbles up from underwater hot springs. Despite the scalding temperatures, however, these springs boast a profusion of life, from giant clams to 10-foot tall tubeworms.

The ocean also houses some astounding topography. At more than 40,000 miles long, the Mid-Oceanic Ridge is the longest continuous mountain chain known to exist in the universe. This chain runs through the middle of the Atlantic Ocean and into the Indian and Pacific and has peaks higher than those in the Alps. The ocean's deepest point, known as the Challenger Deep, plummets to a depth of 6.86 miles. If Mount Everest was submerged in this trench, more than a mile of water would still cover it. Under such a volume of water, the pressure is a crushing eight tons per square inch—equivalent to one person trying to hold 50 jumbo jets!

As John surveyed the glories of the New Earth, he noticed something unique: "Now I saw a new heaven and a new earth, for the first heaven and the first earth had passed away. Also there was no more sea" (Revelation 21:1).

Considering how much of the Earth's surface is covered in water, it is not surprising that many associate the sea with separation. It divides friends and is often a barrier between us and those we love. Many people have stood on the shore and looked across those restless waves thinking with longing of someone far away. But in the Earth made new, there will be no more restless, murmuring waves and no more separation from those we love.

KEY BIBLE TEXT: "Who shall separate us from the love of Christ?" (Romans 8:35).

DAY 363 Messengers on Horse

An Amazing Fact: *The Pony Express transported mail 1,900 miles from St. Joseph, Missouri, to Sacramento, California, in only 10 days! Forty men, each riding 50 miles a day, dashed along the trail on 500 of the best horses the West could provide. Even though the express route was extremely hazardous, only one mail delivery is known to have been lost.*

The Express is credited with helping to keep California in the Union by providing rapid communication between the two coasts. News of Abraham Lincoln's election in 1860 and the outbreak of Civil War reached California via the Pony Express.

Stringent rules were followed to conserve weight. Clothing was light, saddles were small and thin, and no weapons were carried. Even the horses wore light shoes or none at all! Yet despite all the rigorous weight precautions, each rider carried a full-sized Bible! It was presented when a rider joined the unit, and he took it with him on his routes.

Horses have been important in many cultures for centuries in battle, transportation, and communication. In Zechariah's prophecy of the day of the Lord, the horses of the enemies will be struck blind (Zechariah 12:4) and are later said to receive a plague (14:15). Yet in that final day when God will reign forever, it says, "'HOLINESS TO THE LORD' shall be engraved on the bells of the horses" (14:20).

God loves horses, and someday even these creatures will proclaim (by their apparel) that the Lord is righteous and holy. Like the Pony Express, perhaps you will be one of the joyful riders on a horse through the streets of the New Jerusalem proclaiming this wonderful message.

KEY BIBLE TEXT: "'You shall be filled at My table With horses and riders, With mighty men And with all the men of war,' says the Lord GOD" (Ezekiel 39:20).

The Reef of Heaven

An Amazing Fact: *Eight degrees north of the equator in Micronesia, on the remote island of Pohnpei, can be found the haunting ruins of Nan Madol—known also as the Machu Pichu of the Pacific. On this jungle-clad island surrounded by beautiful coral reefs rests a lost city made of bizarre stone "logs."*

The ruins of this forgotten civilization are one of archaeology's best-kept secrets and greatest mysteries. Nan Madol, which means "reef of heaven," was abandoned centuries ago. The ruins cover nearly 150 acres in shallow tidal waters bordering the reef-protected jungle, and a labyrinth of stonewalled canals crisscrosses 92 small manmade islands.

Its major buildings are constructed of giant stone logs that are 18 feet long and several feet in diameter. These logs are made of volcanic basalt crystal and weigh up to two-and-a-half tons. They are stacked like cordwood to form walls up to 50 feet high and 18 feet thick.

The main structures resemble the ceremonial squares constructed by the Mayans and Aztecs. It would have required a large organized workforce and sophisticated culture to create this "Venice of the Pacific," but this race of builders has vanished. The reasons for its construction, how the massive stone were transported, or why it was abandoned are all unknown. Even the natives now presently living on Pohnpei are equally mystified by Nan Madol.

In the book of Revelation, John describes a civilization that will last forever. A holy city will come down from heaven to the Earth and will be inhabited by God's people for eternity. Immense and beautiful stones will be used in its construction. But one thing will be missing. Unlike Nan Madol, which had a temple, John says, "But I saw no temple in it, for the Lord God Almighty and the Lamb are its temple" (Revelation 21:22).

Will you choose to be part of this civilization?

KEY BIBLE TEXT: "But there shall by no means enter it anything that defiles, or causes an abomination or a lie, but only those who are written in the Lamb's Book of Life" (Revelation 21:27).

DAY 365 Our Steadfast Father

An Amazing Fact: *On April 29, 1903, the quiet mining town of Frank in Alberta, Canada, was jolted into worldwide publicity when the side of the mountain under whose shadow it lay gave way, resulting in the largest landslide in North American history. Native Indians, who called it the "mountain that walks," had always avoided the legendary mountain.*

It was 6:00 in the evening on April 28, and John Thornley had just bid the last customer in his shop goodnight. His sister, Ellen, stood in the kitchen finishing up the dishes. It was her last night in Frank before returning to her home in a nearby town. On a sudden impulse, John talked Ellen into spending her last night in a nearby hotel. Ellen packed her bags, and the two walked the short distance to Frank Hotel, where they both took rooms for the night. This strategic relocation, seemingly on a whim, was to save their lives.

At 4:10 the next morning, a loud crack resounded through the still night air as a huge rock far up on Turtle Mountain broke loose and plunged down the mountainside. The boulder was quickly followed by another ... and still another. The ground in the town below trembled as a 2,100- by 3,000- by 500-foot thick wedge of mountain broke away and thundered into the valley below. The slide spread out in a deadly fan, covering part of the town, including John's empty cabin shop.

When the tremors hit, Ellen Thornley was catapulted out of bed and dumped on the other side of the room. The terrible quaking lasted for more than a minute and then died to stillness. It was not until the first streaks of dawn lit the exposed heart of Turtle Mountain that the stunned survivors beheld the extent of the tragedy.

What a comfort it is, in a world of constant change, to hear the words of our steadfast heavenly Father: "I am the LORD, I do not change" (Malachi 3:6). Even though the dearest things to our hearts might be removed, He has said His love and kindness will never depart from us.

KEY BIBLE TEXT: "For the mountains shall depart and the hills be removed, but My kindness shall not depart from you" (Isaiah 54:10).

Sudden Destruction

An Amazing Fact: *In 80 B.C. Pompeii became a Roman colony; later it was used as a favorite resort for wealthy Romans. It reached a population of about 20,000 at the beginning of the Christian era.*

The city was severely damaged by an earthquake in A.D. 63 and then was completely demolished 14 years later by the famous eruption of the volcano Vesuvius. The blast and resulting carnage completely overwhelmed the towns of Pompeii and Herculaneum. For more than 1,500 years, Pompeii lay undisturbed beneath heaps of ashes and cinders. Not until 1748 were excavations undertaken.

Amazingly, the showers of wet ashes and cinders that accompanied the eruption formed a hermetic seal about the town, preserving many public structures, temples, theaters, baths, shops, and private dwellings. In addition, remnants of some of the 2,000 victims of the disaster were found in the ruins, including several gladiators who had been placed in chains to prevent them from escaping or committing suicide.

Ironically, the legion of soldiers most responsible for the sacking of Jerusalem and desecrating the Jewish temple were supposedly vacationing in Pompeii when it was destroyed. Another sad fact uncovered in many artifacts was the immorality of this city that came to sudden destruction.

The Bible ends with a message of destruction to those who would change the words of God's book. It adds, "He who testifies to these things says, 'Surely I am coming quickly'" (Revelation 22:20). For those who have given their lives to the Lamb of God, that is good news. For those who choose to worship and serve the beast of Revelation, it is a fearful message of warning about a destruction that will come down upon them more ferociously than the showers of ash on Pompeii.

As the end of another year comes to pass, might you consider where you will be when Christ comes again?

KEY BIBLE TEXT: "For when they say 'Peace and safety!' then sudden destruction comes upon them, as labor pains upon a pregnant woman. And they shall not escape" (1 Thessalonians 5:3).

Old Testament

Psalms

Proverbs

Song of Solomon

Isaiah

Matthew

Mark

NOTES

NOTES